The Dynamics of Turkish Foreign Policy

Ozan Örmeci

The Dynamics of Turkish Foreign Policy: Key Concepts and Strategic Approaches

PETER LANG
Berlin · Bruxelles · Chennai · Lausanne · New York · Oxford

Bibliographic information published by the Deutsche Nationalbibliothek
The Deutsche Nationalbibliothek lists this publication in the Deutsche Nationalbibliografie; detailed bibliographic data is available online at http://dnb.d-nb.de.

Library of Congress Control Number: 2025033850

ISBN 978-3-631-93687-0 (Print)
ISBN 978-3-631-93688-7 (E-PDF)
ISBN 978-3-631-93689-4 (E-PUB)
DOI 10.3726/b22845

Published by Peter Lang GmbH, Berlin (Germany)

info@peterlang.com

This publication has been peer reviewed.

www.peterlang.com

Table of Contents

List of Figures

List of Tables

Author

Dr. Ozan Örmeci is a Full Professor of Political Science at Uskudar University. He received his PhD from Bilkent University in 2011 with a dissertation on the famous Turkish social democrat politician and former Foreign Minister İsmail Cem. Over the years, he has held academic positions at Uşak University, Girne American University (North Cyprus/TRNC), Beykent University, Istanbul Gedik University, Istanbul Kent University, and Istanbul Aydın University. He was promoted to Full Professor in August 2024. He is currently affiliated with Üsküdar University in Istanbul. Prof. Dr. Örmeci has authored and edited numerous scholarly books and volumes on Turkish Foreign Policy, international relations, and comparative politics. Key titles include *Turkish Foreign Policy in the New Millennium* (Peter Lang, 2015), *Historical Examinations and Current Issues in Turkish-American Relations* (Peter Lang, 2020), *Turkish-French Relations* (Springer, 2022), *Turkish-American Relations in the 21st Century* (Lexington Books, 2024), and *Türkiye-Britain Relations* (Lexington Books, 2024). He also writes on global powers such as the United States, Russia, China, and the EU. In addition to his academic work, he serves as the General Coordinator of the International Political Academy

(UPA) and is the editor of the *UPA Strategic Affairs* academic journal. He publishes in both Turkish and English and is fluent in French and English.

Website: <http://www.ozanormeci.com.tr>
Email: <ozanormeci@gmail.com> mailto:/ <ozan.ormeci@uskudar.edu.tr>
X (Twitter): <https://x.com/#!/ozanormeci>
Facebook: <https://www.facebook.com/officialozanormeci>
Blog: <http://ydemokrat.blogspot.com>
LinkedIn: <http://tr.linkedin.com/in/ozanormeci>
Academia: <https://uskudar.academia.edu/OzanOrmeci>
Amazon.com: <https://www.amazon.com/-/e/B073PZ1KSY>
Goodreads: <https://www.goodreads.com/author/show/7245759.Ozan_Ormeci>
Kaynakça: <http://kaynakca.info/kisi/95857/ozan-ormeci>
Google Scholar: <https://scholar.google.com/citations?user=HSpF-ykAAAAJ&hl>
ResearchGate: <https://www.researchgate.net/profile/Ozan_Oermeci>
Scopus: <https://www.scopus.com/authid/detail.uri?authorId=39262224900>
Web of Science: <https://www.webofscience.com/wos/author/record/11905550>
ORCID: <https://orcid.org/0000-0001-8850-6089>
DergiPark: <https://dergipark.org.tr/en/pub/@ozan_ormeci>
Instagram: <https://www.instagram.com/ozanormeci/>
YouTube: <https://www.youtube.com/@ozanormeci>

Foreword

As a Political Scientist, my interest and familiarity with Turkish Foreign Policy literature began with my research on the esteemed statesman and thinker İsmail Cem (1940–2007), whom I determined as my thesis topic during my doctorate studies at Bilkent University. Cem, who was essentially a left-leaning journalist and intellectual, eventually entered active politics and led Turkish Foreign Policy as Minister of Foreign Affairs for many years. In this context, while studying his ideas and life, I naturally began to research Turkish Foreign Policy and adopt him as a role model.

After I started academic life and actively teaching, I realised that foreign policy in Türkiye was directed by state elites without knowing and teaching international law norms and completely focused on domestic politics, and I realised that I needed to do more serious work on this issue. I realised that although Türkiye is a very important state that observes and protects the balances in the international system, it may not be right on every issue and that the system can produce decisions against us on some issues. In this context, I have produced international and national academic books and articles on many different areas regarding Turkish Foreign Policy (Turkish-American relations, Türkiye-France relations, Türkiye-Britain relations, Türkiye-Germany relations, Türkiye-Russia relations, Türkiye-EU relations, Türkiye-China relations, Türkiye-Azerbaijan relations, Türkiye-TRNC relations, Türkiye's energy policy, Türkiye's soft power, Türkiye's defence strategy, etc.). The work I have done on the International Politics Academy/UPA (<politikaakademisi.org>) website with my valuable young colleagues and students has also made quite an impact and continues to do so. My academic publications and internet-based studies have attracted considerable attention over time and have sometimes been criticised. In fact, my aim was to keep these issues on the agenda, to raise the awareness of the Turkish public and people, and to provide a source for future discussions. Looking back, I see that I have already managed to create a considerable academic literature, and I think that this will develop further in the coming years.

At this point, I would like to share some of my findings with you. First of all, Türkiye, as a very young state founded just a century ago after the collapse of the Ottoman Empire, has been generally successful in its foreign policy to date. Ankara, which achieved serious successes such as the Treaty of Lausanne, the Montreux Straits Convention, and the annexation of Hatay to the homeland during the single-party period, has managed to advance in many areas such as membership in Western (Council of Europe and NATO) and international (primarily the United Nations) institutions, creating a respected and serious image, socioeconomic development, industrial and technological advancement, and military power in the following years. Türkiye also achieved a military success in the 1974 Cyprus Peace Operation and its almost five-decade-old fight against terrorism (mainly ASALA and PKK) and became the most powerful state in its region – together with Russia, Israel, and Iran. Today, Türkiye, as a young state, founded a century ago, is a real giant in its region and one of the rare actors without whom the game cannot be set up.

However, it is not always easy to maintain the balance between membership in Western institutions and Türkiye's national interests. As a superpower that demands unconditional obedience, the United States (US) is not always supportive of Türkiye's own initiatives/initiatives and can often be a hindrance. The European Union (EU), on the other hand, lacks the capacity to transform Türkiye and is reluctant to do so due to Türkiye's big size and prejudices and fears of millions of Muslim Turks in Europe. Another problematic issue is the capacity. Türkiye does not yet have the full socioeconomic power, technology, and human (social) capital necessary to achieve its ambitious goals. This was best demonstrated by the Syria adventure undertaken during the Arab Spring and was an important lesson for all of us although in the end Ankara was able to topple the Assad regime. Considering that regional studies, think-tanks, and the defence industry are still newly formed in Türkiye, this situation is very natural. Another serious problem is that Türkiye is deprived of the legal basis to defend some of its just causes (the Cyprus Conflict, etc.) within the United Nations (UN) order in the international system. Although these factors sometimes push Türkiye to act outside the rules and the system, it is always necessary to be within the '*game*'.

Türkiye, due to its structural conditions, is not a superpower successor like Russia, which is rich in energy and can stand on its own, or an autarkic state like North Korea, which can stand completely closed to the outside world. Similarly, Türkiye does not have the extraordinary population advantage of India with a population of 1.4 billion and China with a population of 1.3 billion. Türkiye is not yet a giant industrial and technological country like the United States, Britain, France, Germany, or China. In that sense, Türkiye is a state that develops with trade and can only stand as long as it produces. Therefore, while it is understandable for Türkiye to show that it can occasionally step outside the system and to demand certain privileges/exemptions from the system and key actors in this context, remaining completely outside the system is not a situation that will be in Ankara's favour. As a state that is deprived of energy, has economic problems, and has never fully managed to democratise, Türkiye can be more successful and prosperous to the extent that it is in line with Western and international institutions and other states. For example, to put it concretely, even if the view that lies in everyone's heart regarding the Cyprus Conflict is the independence of the Turkish Republic of Northern Cyprus (TRNC), its recognition by other states, and even its unification with Türkiye, this situation cannot happen unless the international system is changed. Moreover, this could bring Türkiye's political and economic relations with Western countries to the breaking point and drag the country into great economic destruction and internal turmoil. However, if Türkiye's grand strategy is to be in this direction, a new foreign policy and industrial strategy focused on the Turkic States, the Islamic world, Russia, China, and the global south countries should be adopted without delay. That is because Türkiye has some dependencies that shape its foreign policy. To put it simply, these can be summarised as dependency on Russia, Azerbaijan, and Iran in energy, European countries and the EU in economics/trade, and the United States in military technology and geopolitics.

In this book, I have included the summaries of some very important works that evaluate these issues and the general line of Turkish Foreign Policy, as well as some recent articles I have written on these issues. If these views cannot be placed within a theoretical framework, this is due to the slippery and pragmatic structure of foreign policy and politics. In other words, to be specific, Türkiye, which naturally refers to international law and UN resolutions in the Karabakh War or Ukraine, prefers to ignore them in the Cyprus issue. As can be understood, like all states, Türkiye is a realistic state that fundamentally wants to protect its own national interests and regime. For this reason, the foreign policy of any state can never be fully explained consistently and holistically with a single paradigm. In fact, the state that established the current international order, the United States, was not coincidentally the country that dealt the greatest blow to this system due to its interests in the 2003 Iraq War. In this context, the lack of theoretical consistency in all the articles in the book is not due to me, but to the nature of states.

Finally, as I try to enjoy my professorship these days with my family, I hope that this book will be a work that will inform readers, direct people to think, and orientate state elites to make future projections and plans. Moreover, since this is a book written for educational purposes, I do wish that this book would help students and researchers to make further studies after reading this work. I should also mention that the book consists of two main parts. In the first part, 'Theoretical and Strategic Approaches to Turkish Foreign Policy', I tried to explain and summarise theoretical and strategic approaches to Türkiye's foreign policy by citing important scholars and experts including Oral Sander, William Hale, Baskın Oran, Onur Öymen, İsmail Cem, and Ahmet Davutoğlu. This will give the necessary background information to the readers to understand subsequent discussions. In the second part, 'Contemporary Issues and Discussions', I shared my articles and analyses about contemporary Turkish politics and foreign policy on various matters including Turkish-Greek relations, Turkish-American relations, Türkiye's performance in the United Nations Security Council as a temporary member, Türkiye-European Union relations, Ankara's multi-dimensional foreign policy inclination that has become more apparent in recent years, Türkiye's potential BRICS+ membership, Türkiye-Syria relations, Turkish-Israeli relations, and Turkish-Spanish relations. Again, in addition to my views, I cited important scholars and experts such as John Mearsheimer, George Friedman, Çağrı Erhan, Cihat Yaycı, etc.

Last word, I would like to dedicate the book to my beloved aunt Uğur Durmuş who passed away a few months ago … I hope this book will keep her memory alive.

Prof. Dr Ozan ÖRMECİ
10.07.2025, Kartal-Istanbul

PART I

Theoretical and Strategic Approaches to Turkish Foreign Policy

Some Principles of Turkish Foreign Policy According to Oral Sander

Professor Oral Sander (1949–1995) was a distinguished Turkish academic who contributed a lot to the development of International Relations studies in Türkiye. Sander wrote important books on European Political History and Turkish Foreign Policy. In one of his books, *Türkiye'nin Dış Politikası* (*Türkiye's Foreign Policy*), Sander made critical comments on the basic principles and characteristics of Turkish Foreign Policy.

According to Sander, Turkish Foreign Policy has a very fundamental and stable characteristic and principle since the foundation of modern Türkiye: Western orientation. Although during the early Republican era Türkiye had to be more careful about the newly emerging superpower Soviet Union in its close geography and thus, chose to follow a more neutral foreign policy, in fact, modernisation reforms sought by Türkiye's founder Mustafa Kemal Atatürk aimed to Westernise Turkish society and make Türkiye closer to its Western allies. Following the disagreements with Stalin's Russia after the Second World War, Türkiye's Western orientation became stronger and more obvious. Stalin's territorial demands and threats also created a comfortable ground for Ankara's ambitious adventure for Western integration. Thus, Türkiye became a member of the Council of Europe and NATO after the Second World War. In that sense, Türkiye is a unique country having a permanent Western orientation although its rich history, Islamic background, and some social/cultural characteristics make it also an Oriental (Islamic) country.

Mustafa Kemal Atatürk was a wise statesman who knew the young republic was not strong enough to pursue an independent foreign policy and that is why, he acted more as a neutral country between the West and Soviet Russia.

His philosophy of '*Peace at home, peace abroad*' (*Yurtta sulh, cihanda sulh*) was not haphazard and he knew that Türkiye, as a young and weak country at those years, had to be very careful in its foreign policy in one of the most troubled regions of the world. This philosophy adopted by the Turkish state was not temporary as well; Türkiye has always preferred social and economic progress rather than territorial expansionism in its foreign policy. In fact, this ideal matched with the democratic ideals embraced by major European states after the great destruction of the Second World War via European integration project. Türkiye's geopolitical position also makes this country a European state; Türkiye is a bridge between Asia and Europe, and some parts of its territory are situated in the European continent. Anatolian peninsula has always been the starting point of Europe as well as where it ends. In that sense, Türkiye has also an Oriental (Islamic) dimension, which makes this country a model for the rest of the Muslim world.

Turkish Foreign Policy had some advantages and disadvantages during the Cold War. Neighbouring a giant communist state and a super military power like Soviet Russia (USSR) caused the supremacy of high politics in Türkiye and posed great risks to the country's democratic system. But on the other hand, this situation provided a unique and more important security role to Türkiye in the eyes of its European and American partners due to Moscow's communist expansionism. Thus, Türkiye has often been classified as a 'central state' by many geopolitics experts and International Relations scholars.

Türkiye's Western orientation can be analysed on three dimensions; (1) Turkish-American (US) relations, (2) Türkiye-NATO relations, and (3) Türkiye-Europe relations. According to Sander, Turkish-American relations mattered most during the Cold War compared to two others. In Sander's view, Turkish-American relations are solid and based on mutual interests. Two countries share a common vision in terms of providing peace and stability in world affairs after the Second World War via United Nations system. Both of these countries objected to Soviet expansionism during the Cold War and developed common strategies towards Middle East. However, since the United States was an international player and superpower contrary to Türkiye, a regional actor, two countries had sometimes conflicts of interests in their bilateral relations. However, certain things are stable in Turkish-American relations: (a) Türkiye has always been and will always be an important country for the United States because of its geopolitical location, (b) American military aid has always been and will always be very important for Türkiye due to security threats in the Middle East and risks caused by Russia. In Sander's view, these two characteristics are stable in Turkish-American relations.

Türkiye's geopolitical location in one of the most troubled regions of the world, make security-oriented politics in the country a necessity. That is why; Sander claims that ultra-optimistic policy initiatives or ideals will never work in terms of Turkish Foreign Policy. According to Sander, these orientations should be assessed as unchangeable principles and characteristics of Turkish Foreign Policy.

William Hale's Views on Turkish Foreign Policy

Introduction

Prof. William Mathew Hale (1940–) is a prominent academic who has become an important authority in Türkiye and the world with his writings on Middle East politics, Turkish politics, and Turkish foreign policy and lectures at the School of Oriental and African Studies (SOAS), University of London. Hale is one of the most cited scholars in the world in the field of Turkish politics and previously taught at Boğaziçi University and Sabancı University in Türkiye. Hale's famous book on Turkish Foreign Policy, originally titled *Turkish Foreign Policy 1774–2000* in English and published by Routledge Publications in 2000, was first translated into Turkish by Petek Demir in 2003 and published by Mozaik Publications under the title *Türk Dış Politikası 1774–2000*. This article will summarise and evaluate Hale's book, which is considered a classic in the field of Turkish Foreign Policy.

Foreign Relations of the Late Ottoman Empire, 1774–1918

The first chapter of the 414-page book consisting of ten chapters is titled 'Foreign Relations of the Late Ottoman Empire, 1774–1918'. According to Hale, the problems faced by the Ottoman Empire in the nineteenth century were both internal and external. The Ottoman Empire, which ruled a vast area from Hungary to Crimea and from Tunisia to the Persian Gulf, did not have the power to control such a vast state and protect it from external enemies. Moreover, the state, which was on an equal footing with the European states in terms of military, technological, economic, and administrative aspects in the sixteenth century, started to fall far behind its European rivals in all areas from the eighteenth century onwards. Indeed, in 1912, the Austrian ambassador to İstanbul, Count Johann Von Pallacini, argued to his government that '*Türkiye was not a state in the sense that Europe understood it, neither in the past nor in the present.*' Indeed, the Ottoman Empire was basically no more than a 'tax state'. In this context, the Empire could actually be seen as a state composed of local provinces. Even though the central authority was strengthened and a new state structure was established with the Tanzimat period, state authority could not be established in remote regions and moreover, foreigners and non-Muslims were privileged in İstanbul and the big cities due to capitulations. Nevertheless, the pluralistic nature of the Empire was quite evident in these years; for example, in the 1880s, foreigners constituted 15 per cent of the population in İstanbul. In addition, Christians constituted one-third of the population, which was estimated at 26 million in an 1844 census; the remaining two-thirds were Muslim subjects. As non-Muslim subjects rebelled, gained independence or emigrated abroad, the proportion of Muslims increased rapidly. As a matter of fact, the proportion of Muslims in the total population, which was estimated at 18.5 million in 1914, rose to 81 per cent. In terms of the proportion of Turks, the proportion of ethnic Turks is thought to have been around 45–50 per cent in the last quarter of the nineteenth century.

The Ottoman system had some unique characteristics. The subjects were given wide autonomy, also due to the weakness of the central authority. Each nation could preserve its own religion and language and was not forced to convert or learn the language. Christians and Jews may be seen as 'second class' citizens because they were not conscripted into the army and paid taxes, but in fact they were also granted extensive rights within their own nations, such as the right to elect religious leaders and heads of nations and to be subject to their own laws. This system worked quite well during the founding and rising period of the Empire, but from the nineteenth century onwards, the idea of ethnic nationalism began to spread to all the peoples of the Empire, starting with the Greeks and Serbs, and shattered the old system. In the late nineteenth century, the population that remained loyal to the state was almost exclusively Muslim. The Ottoman Empire panicked in the face of non-Muslim uprisings and imposed harsh measures; the massacre of

Chios in 1822, the Bulgarian horror of 1876, and the Armenian deportation of 1915 are the most important examples of this. However, such practices further accelerated the disintegration of the Empire and completely destroyed the favourable view of the European states towards the Ottoman Empire. Moreover, in reaction to such practices, the Turkish-Muslim population in the Balkans was massacred. Indeed, the massacres and forced migration of the Muslim population in the Balkans later played an important role in the rise of Turkish nationalism and led to a deep sense of injustice in Anatolia. In this way, Mustafa Kemal Atatürk and his friends were able to find a population that could fight valiantly during the Greek invasion (1919–1922).

In the last few centuries of the Empire, the main goal of Ottoman statesmen was to ensure the continuity of the state and prevent its collapse. Many reforms and foreign policy moves were, in fact, driven solely by these motives. In this context, strengthening the army was one of the main objectives. However, the dependence on imported weapons, the economic bottleneck and the lack of modern transportation made it difficult to make a breakthrough in this field. Technological backwardness forced the Ottoman Empire to be dependent on the West. The capitulations exaggerated the unequal relations even more. Another aim of the reforms and foreign policy moves was to strengthen the central authority. In fact, this was the main objective of the Tanzimat and Islahat processes. In addition to all these efforts, the main goal of diplomacy was to keep the state afloat. Indeed, diplomacy was the most important factor that ensured the survival of the Ottoman Empire in its final periods. The reign of 'Sultan Rouge' Abdulhamid II is a clear example in this respect. During these years, Ottoman statesmen tried to survive by balancing the European states (Britain, France, Austria, Germany) and Russia against each other. From these years onwards, Europe's main concern was the Eastern Question, that is, the disintegration of the Ottoman Empire. Therefore, the Ottoman Empire supported these countries against each other and tried to gain advantages for itself by creating competition among them. However, according to Hale, in order to conduct a serious scientific research, we have very little data on the foreign policy perceptions of the Ottoman Empire until these years. One could even say that the only sources of this information are the attitudes of the Ottoman governments in the face of developing events and the writings of European diplomats. Moreover, the Empire's foreign policy began to acquire a permanent character only in the late eighteenth century.

Until these years, even though ambassadors and observers were sent abroad from time to time, no permanent missions were established. In the period 1793–1796, this gap was rapidly closed with the establishment of representative offices in London, Vienna, Berlin, Paris, and later in other capitals. Apart from their diplomatic duties, these officials also tried to inform the Ottoman governments about the technological developments in the Western world. As a matter of fact, the Ottoman Empire, which did not even have a Ministry of Foreign Affairs at the beginning, first established a Chamber of Translation in the nineteenth century, and finally established the Ministry of Foreign Affairs in 1835 by elevating the office of '*Reîsü'l-küttâb*' to the level of a Ministry.

According to Professor William Hale, there were three major dangers that the Ottoman Empire faced in its final period. The first is the nationalist movements in the Balkans, which developed as a result of Russian-backed Panslavism policies. Secondly, Russia's policy of reaching the warm seas (Mediterranean), by excluding the Ottoman Empire, directly threatened the territorial integrity of the Empire. The third was the imperialist plans of France and Britain for the Middle East region under Ottoman control where Arabs lived. In the face of these problems, the Ottoman Empire saw Austrian-Hungarian Empire against Russia in the Balkans, Britain against Russia in the Straits and the Mediterranean, and Britain and France against each other in the Middle East and tried to exploit the differences of opinion between these countries. Therefore, the Ottoman Empire was largely trying to implement a 'balance of power' policy during these years. Another option was to abandon the balance of power policy and firmly side with one or more powers. This was not a desirable/preferred alternative as it would have antagonised other powers. However, the forced alliance with Germany in the First World War made this second option a reality and ultimately led the Ottoman Empire to destruction. However, it was not an easy process for the Ottoman Empire to give up its balance of power policy and side with one power. During these periods, Russia was always seen as the main enemy, both because of its territorial claims against the Ottoman Empire and because it provoked Ottoman subjects as the protector of Orthodox peoples. Moreover, almost all of the wars were fought against Russia and heavy defeats were suffered. Therefore, the Ottomans had the idea of forming the strongest alliance against Russia with Britain, France, Austria-Hungary, and Germany becoming sometimes allies and sometimes enemies. Although Britain seemed to be a very good ally in many respects, it was a country that had its own imperial plans for the Middle East and against the Ottomans. Moreover, the British Army's strength was mostly in naval forces, whereas what the Ottomans needed against the Russian threat was an ally with strength on land. France, on the other hand, was in a difficult situation due to its internal turmoil after the French Revolution of 1789 and did not appear to be a strong partner against Russia. Napoleon's attack on Egypt in 1798 would also sour Ottoman-French relations. Therefore, Germany (Prussia), the new rising power of Europe as of the beginning of the twentieth century, started to become an ideal partner for the Ottomans due to the strength of its land army and its search for a partner to balance against the Anglo-French superiority. In other words, the alliance with Germany before the First World War was not based on an exaggerated admiration for Germany, but rather on very reasonable geopolitical and military grounds.

After the nineteenth century, which witnessed many important events, wars, and treaties, the Ottoman Empire was forced to disintegrate with the First World War. This was perhaps the maximum postponement of an inevitable end. The Ottoman Empire, which was technologically, economically, and militarily much weaker than its rivals, actually survived longer than expected thanks to the balance of power policy in the nineteenth century. Turkish statesmen, on the other hand, learned important lessons from the collapse of the Ottoman Empire. First of all, they were overly anxious to clarify their borders with other countries and to settle Muslim Turkish populations in the border regions as a buffer. This was a consequence of the destruction and betrayal by non-Muslims. Secondly, the new state also had strong nationalist reflexes and anti-Western rhetoric. The reason for this is directly related to the process that led the Ottoman Empire to its destruction. In the case of any other nation, this could have led to a xenophobic, racist, and/or fundamentalist regime. But the Turks, considered by some to be the 'gentlemen of the East', became an anti-imperialist country modelled on the West, thanks to the great modernist leadership of Mustafa Kemal Atatürk. In this context, although Islam also served as cement for society, it was relegated to the background in the new state, and the elements that held society backward were polished down through secularisation reforms. At this point, the collapse of Islamism with the Arab revolts in the First World

War also played an important role. However, this problem is still not fully resolved in Turkish political life and foreign policy, and its effects are still visible today in society and politics through the secularist-Islamist conflict. Another element is related to prudence. The frustration of Enver Pasha's adventures, who wanted to establish a great Turanian (Turkic) Empire, and the disintegration of the Ottoman Empire, may be added to Hale's views here as a source of the emergence of a balanced and cautious mood among Turkish statesmen.

Resistance, Establishment and Diplomacy, 1918–1939

The second part, 'Resistance, Establishment and Diplomacy, 1918–1939', examines the foreign policy pursued by Mustafa Kemal Atatürk and his friends during the War of Independence and the single-party rule of the Republican People's Party (CHP). The period 1919–1923 is one of the most critical periods in Turkish history. During these years, for the first time in many centuries, Turks faced the danger of being stateless and expelled from Anatolia. As a matter of fact, with the Armistice of Mudros (Mondros) and the (Peace) Treaty of Sevres signed after the First World War, the Ottoman Empire was almost completely liquidated. From this date onwards, the period of 'National Struggle' (*Milli Mücadele*) began for the Turks. This period can be roughly divided into two. The first period, between June 1919 and March 1920, was the period in which the military-political structure was established, and the aim was to win over those sympathetic to the National Struggle in Anatolia from the Sultanate government in İstanbul, without having direct problems with the Entente powers. During this period, it was even claimed that Mustafa Kemal Atatürk wanted to overthrow the imperial government and take control himself. However, when the Entente forces, fearing the fusion of the Turkish resistance and the Bolshevik Revolution, occupied İstanbul in March 1920 and rounded up the nationalists, the second period of the National Struggle necessarily began with a harsher and more warlike struggle.

The War of Independence is undoubtedly an important achievement. However, the conditions were actually much better than the rhetoric of the 'seven powers' presented in official history. For the British, French, and Italians, despite occupying Anatolia, never really intended to fight the Turks.

In this sense, the Turks basically only had to deal with Greece. There were even politicians in these countries, such as Winston Churchill, who advocated supporting the Turks against the Russians. Therefore, Mustafa Kemal and his friends, having identified this situation well and seeing that their chances of success were high, embarked on this path and succeeded and were able to form a strong army against the invading Greek Army by improving their weapons and financial situation with the support of Soviet Russia (Bolsheviks). The Russians, who somewhat naively believed that Anatolia could be taken over by Bolshevik sympathisers, started to give Mustafa Kemal greater support after the failure of Mustafa Suphi, a Moscow-sent communist. In fact, the Treaty of Moscow and the Turkish-Russian friendship during these years, according to Bülent Gökay, was more like a business deal. What the Russians wanted was for Western imperialism not to win in Anatolia. In the end, after defeating the Greeks in the field with the help of arms and financial support from Russia, the '*Kuvâ-yi Milliye*' forces achieved a remarkable success in diplomacy at the Lausanne Conference and established the new Republic of Türkiye. For the Turks, Lausanne did not solve many problems such as the Straits (Bosphorus), Mosul, Aegean, and Hatay. But the most important issues, such as the '*Misak-ı Milli*' (National Oath), were largely accepted and political equality with other countries – with the abolition of capitulations – was also achieved. In this sense, Lausanne was an important success.

After Lausanne, the Republic of Türkiye prioritised modernisation and development. Atatürk made many important revolutions with unprecedented speed and depth, creating a new nation from scratch. During the single-party era, Türkiye moved forward in many ways. The main goal during these years was to reach the level of contemporary civilisation. Security and peace at home and abroad were other important considerations. Russia was not a serious military or political threat to Ankara during this period, as it had been in turmoil after the Bolshevik Revolution and had established friendly relations with Türkiye. Therefore, without the threat of Russia, development could become a priority agenda item. Relations with Greece were also improved and population exchanges were carried out through population exchanges. Joining the League of Nations in 1932, Türkiye gave up Mosul but achieved what it wanted in a short period of time through successful diplomacy on the Straits with the Montreux Straits Convention and again on Hatay. The main threat to Türkiye in the 1930s was fascist Italy. Therefore, Türkiye tried to provide security and stability by establishing the Balkan Pact with Greece, Romania, and Yugoslavia in 1934. In 1937, the Saadabad Pact was established with Iraq, Iran, and Afghanistan to ensure the security of the eastern borders. During this period, Atatürk's reforms and foreign policies were largely successful. There are also various legends about Atatürk's farsightedness. For example, it is reported that he made accurate predictions about the Second World War in a meeting with the American General Douglas MacArthur in 1932. Although there is no transcript of this meeting, Atatürk's concerns about Italy and Germany are clear, and they proved to be correct. However, due to the priority of development and lack of capital, the army could not be renewed during these years and remained quite weak militarily. In this context, security was ensured through pacts and bilateral security agreements (the most important of which was the agreement with Britain and France in 1939, shortly after Atatürk's death) and relations with Soviet Russia were kept at the best level. Indeed, one of the most important figures of this period was Tevfik Rüştü Aras, a good Moscow friend. These were not accidental, but well-thought-out and successful moves.

World War II and Türkiye

The third part of the book titled 'The Second World War and Türkiye' examines the foreign policy pursued by President İsmet İnönü and other important Turkish statesmen during the Second World War, which corresponded to a very important period in Turkish Foreign Policy. Türkiye pursued a very interesting foreign policy during the Second World War and tried not to take sides in the war until the last moment. Although various agreements were signed with Britain and France in 1939 and with other states in the following years, despite great pressure, Türkiye did not actively participate in the war and emerged from the war – in the end – stronger. During this period, İsmet İnönü, who was the 'National Chief' (*Milli Şef*), took control of foreign policy under his own auspices as he did in every field. He even pacified the Chief of General Staff, Fevzi Çakmak, whom he saw as a rival, and eventually dismissed him by retiring him on the pretext of age. İnönü's foreign policy was based on a single principle: caution. İnönü was a true master of buying time and always succeeded very well in stalling his opponents in diplomacy. He avoided daring foreign policy initiatives and was always cautious. Although there were some people who sympathised with Germany, Britain (England), France, Russia, and the United States around him, he adopted a stance that was above them and not openly taking sides. In these years, İnönü's Ministers of Foreign Affairs were senior figures such as Şükrü Saraçoğlu and Numan Menemencioğlu. These people were also his close friends. In these years, depending on the strength and influence of the winds blowing from the outside, Türkiye occasionally wobbled, but managed not to be anyone's primary target and emerged from the war with a victory.

From 1934 onwards, more than half of the Turkish Army's troops were shifted to Eastern Thrace. The reason for this was that the threat of an Italian or Nazi attack from the Balkans was now clear. When a trilateral alliance with Britain and France was formed in 1939, it became clear that Türkiye would enter the war if the Allied forces attacked the Balkans or if war broke out with Italy in the Mediterranean. In fact, President İnönü thought that similar to the First World War, the French could hold off the Germans for a long time thanks to the Maginot Line and Türkiye would not need to enter the war. However, when the Nazis surprised İnönü and took control of the whole of Europe in a very short time, alarm bells started ringing for Türkiye. As a matter of fact, there were many times during the war when Türkiye had to enter the war. Italy's entry into the war and the German invasion of Romania are examples of such situations. However, the Turks tried to explain their decision not to enter the war by saying that they had signed a tripartite agreement with France and Britain and that this agreement was invalid because France had withdrawn from the war after being captured by the Nazis. However, in the background, Türkiye's main concern was that France would fall in a very short time, leaving Türkiye alone against the Germans and Italians. In addition, the fact that the newly established cities were completely defenceless against air attacks was also an effective factor in Türkiye's decision to avoid war. Amazement at the success of the German '*blitzkrieg*' (lightning war) methods also encouraged the Turks to avoid war as much as possible. During these years, Germany also realised the importance of Türkiye and made various moves through its ambassador in Ankara, Franz Von Papen, to prevent the Turks from siding with the British. The trade network developed with Germany during this period, especially the chromium trade, was an important factor in Germany's favourable view of Türkiye and saved Türkiye from a possible Nazi invasion. The British, on the other hand, although they encouraged Türkiye to enter the war and even put direct pressure on Ankara later on, did not spoil the relations, calculating that they might lose this country to Germany if they put more pressure. As a matter of fact, Churchill even found it reasonable that Türkiye did not enter the war by not complying with the tripartite alliance agreement, but on the other hand, he continued to put pressure on Ankara to enter the war.

Relations with Russia were also tried to be good during this period; however, Stalin's insistence on the Straits was kept at a distance and the seeds of the conflicts with Russia after the war were sown. Stalin's demands were also effective in Germany's attack on Russia and partially sided the Turks with Germany against the Russians. However, the German advance in the Balkans was also a threat to Türkiye. Indeed, the Germans soon offered the Turks a comprehensive alliance agreement, implying that Türkiye could be captured in a matter of weeks if it refused. This proposal came from both Von Papen and Foreign Minister Joachim Von Ribbentrop. According to the allegations, Şükrü Saraçoğlu, under great pressure, was forced to accept the offer, but the Turks did not honour this agreement either. But in 1941, the two countries signed a 10-year friendship and non-aggression pact. In the preamble of this agreement, the phrase 'subject to the existing agreements of each party' was included, referring to the 1939 agreement with the British. With this agreement, Türkiye became a de facto neutral state. It is no coincidence that historians and International Relations experts label Turkish Foreign Policy in this era as 'active neutrality'.

In these years, Türkiye, whose diplomacy could be likened to 'tightrope walking', breathed a sigh of relief when Germany attacked Russia (Operation Barbarossa). When the Nazis shifted their large armies to Russia, the risk of invasion of Türkiye disappeared. However, this situation still did not comfort the Turks. Because a German victory would expose Türkiye to the Nazi threat, while a Soviet victory would suddenly make the Russians a great power. For this reason, Türkiye tried as much as possible to prolong the war and not to have a winner. In the words of Ottavio De Peppo, the Italian ambassador in Ankara, '*the Turkish ideal was that the last German soldier should fall on the last Russian corpse.*' But the Turks had no influence or power to ensure this. Therefore, the only thing Inönü could do was to buy time and avoid commitments. But the Germans also made some generous offers during these years to win Türkiye over to their side. It is even known that Von Papen offered Türkiye to gain territories in the Caucasus where the Turkish-Muslim population lived. Moreover, a pro-German Pan-Turkist group – consisting of Nuri Pasha, brother of Enver Pasha, and Zeki Doğan, a famous Pan-Turkist professor – even made an unofficial visit to Berlin during these years. Such initiatives and pro-German articles in the Turkish press were actually part of İnönü's grand plan, the sole purpose of which was to prevent a Nazi invasion of Türkiye. Moreover, the chromium trade with Germany was becoming a great strategic advantage. If Türkiye, which produced 16 per cent of the world's chromium in those years, had not continued to trade with Germany, the German Army could have thrown in the towel much earlier. However, Türkiye continued to trade chrome with the Germans despite objections from Britain. Domestically, with fascist practices like the Wealth Tax (*Varlık Vergisi*), wealth was taken from non-Muslims, who were seen as potential suspects in the new state, and transferred to Muslims. This practice, in which those who refused to pay taxes were sent to concentration camps, was racist and unbecoming of the new Turkish state. However, when compared to the murderous concentration camps in Europe, it was still more innocent. Indeed, Faik Ökte, the bookkeeper in charge of the tax in İstanbul at the time, would later self-criticise that '*this outrageous tax was the result of the racism that still prevailed in war-weary Europe*.' Even if the tax was beneficial in the short term, in the long term it seriously damaged Türkiye's reputation.

With the entry of Japan and the United States into the war, new fronts opened in Asia-Pacific, and Türkiye began to approach the Allies towards the end of the war. Despite this, war was not declared until the last moment and remained neutral. However, as time went by, pressure on the Turks to enter the war intensified. Britain and Churchill in particular were extremely insistent on Türkiye entering the war and came as far as Adana. During this period, Germany, which was closely following Türkiye's moves through its agent's nicknamed 'Cicero', was still active in Ankara. When it began to be understood that the Germans would lose the war, Türkiye's attitude also began to change. For example, the Wealth Tax was quickly abolished, and a legal war was declared against the Turkist-Turanist cause and extreme nationalists with German sympathies. As a result, commercial and diplomatic relations with Germany were also cut off as of 1944. In the final weeks of the war, war would even be declared on Germany for show. However, in these years, the main threat to Türkiye was not defeated Germany but the victorious Soviet

Russia and its ruthless leader Stalin. Indeed, soon after, Stalin, who used the Turks' refusal to fight against the Nazis as a trump card, suggested to Selim Sarper, Türkiye's ambassador to Moscow, that changes be made to the Turkish-Soviet Friendship Treaty, which had been renewed every year since 1925. Against Stalin, who had his eyes on the Straits, Türkiye would rapidly shift towards the axis of the United States and its allies in the following years.

According to Prof. William Hale, the policy Türkiye followed in World War II is a great example of success. Türkiye, which got through this period without firing a single weapon and not being targeted by a single bullet, quickly grew stronger while all other states experienced great destruction and lost their populations. Moreover, there was no loss of territory, and the effectiveness of diplomacy was increased. According to Hale, Türkiye actually always remained close to its allies (Britain, France, the United States) throughout the war. All other moves made due to the desire to avoid going to war were strategic and tactical. During this period, İnönü and his friends used one power against another, took maximum advantage of Türkiye's strategic position and were ultimately successful. However, some racist practices such as the Wealth Tax and the economic difficulties experienced during these years prevented the emergence of a picture of total success. Türkiye's policy of neutrality during these years is correct according to Hale; because if Türkiye entered the war against the Germans, it would be occupied by the Nazis like Greece and might later be subject to Soviet occupation, and if it entered the war on the German side, it would again face Soviet occupation.

The Cold War and Türkiye: The Initial Phase, 1945–1963

The fourth section titled 'The Cold War and Türkiye: The Initial Phase, 1945–1963' draws attention to the transformation that Turkish Foreign Policy experienced during the early phase of the Cold War. While a new bipolar order was being established under the leadership of the United States (US) and Soviet Russia (USSR) after the war, it was inevitable that Türkiye would approach the United States and the Western world in the face of Stalin's revisionist demands (a Soviet base in the Straits, the right of passage for Russian warships, the return of Kars and Ardahan to Russia). This is a historical development whose effects will also be seen in domestic politics. In fact, Stalin's move was probably aimed at gaining certain advantages in his favour rather than creating an excuse to actually invade Türkiye. However, the Turks, who feared a possible invasion when they saw that Soviet soldiers had begun to gather in Bulgaria, never forgave Stalin for this action. Although the alliance agreement signed with the British in 1939 continued, the British, who emerged from the war weak, had no power to protect Türkiye against the Soviets. Therefore, US support became a necessity rather than a choice for Türkiye during this period. The United States, which initially acted more moderately towards Russia and even suggested holding an international conference on the passage of warships of states bordering the Black Sea through the Straits, eventually came to believe that Russia wanted to occupy the Straits, as stated in an unsent letter by Secretary of State James F. Byrnes, and gave more support to Türkiye. For this reason, in 1946, the battleship USS Missouri anchored in İstanbul to bring the body of Turkish Ambassador Mehmet Münir Ertegün, thus demonstrating US support for Türkiye. From that date on, Türkiye rejected the Soviets' requests for new talks on the Straits. The situation became clearer with the Truman Doctrine and the Marshall Plan; the United States was beginning to provide military, economic, and political support to Allied countries against the Soviet threat. Türkiye, along with Greece, would also receive a partial share of this support. In parallel with these developments, Türkiye also became a member of the Organisation for European Economic Co-operation (OEEC, later OECD) during this period. The establishment of NATO and Türkiye's inclusion in this alliance clarified the situation.

During the rapprochement process with the United States, there were also significant changes in domestic politics, and in the multi-party system that followed the single-party system, the liberal and Western Democrat Party (DP) led by the Adnan Menderes-Celal Bayar duo came to power. The DP sent troops to the Korean War and ensured Türkiye's inclusion in NATO. These developments were experienced with the approval of İnönü, who had moved from the presidency to the leadership of the opposition party. Türkiye being pushed into the Western alliance actually caused various criticisms in Russia. For example, it is known that Nikita Khrushchev told Lavrenti Beriya (Beria) that Stalin had scared Türkiye into the arms of the Americans. From that date on, Türkiye became a neighbouring Russia and an 'aircraft carrier' that would never sink for the Western powers and gained great importance in terms of military and strategy. Although relations with Russia softened for a while after Stalin passed away in 1953, no change was seen in Türkiye's strategic preferences. Türkiye's stance on this issue would begin to change after 1963, when it became apparent with the Cyprus issue that NATO and the United States were reducing their support for their national interests. During this period, Russia openly declared that it did not claim any rights over Turkish territory. However, the Straits issue was still unclear, and Türkiye did not seem to be greatly affected by this declaration. However, with the economic aid received from Moscow in the late 1950s and Menderes' planned visit to Russia, it was thought that there might be a break in Turkish Foreign Policy in terms of Westernism (Atlanticism) for the first time. However, the Menderes government was overthrown by the coup of 27 May 1960 before it could make this important transformation. During this period, Khrushchev made an important opening and requested that the Cemal Gürsel administration in Türkiye be neutral rather than pro-Russian. In fact, a major economic aid offer would even come to Türkiye in the coming days. However, the Gürsel and İnönü governments did not respond to these offers and maintained the current balance. Because a difficult process had begun, and NATO and US bases had begun to be established all over Türkiye. There were even some nuclear weapons on Turkish soil. Turkish troops also began to serve abroad within NATO. The 1950s, until their final months, were actually Türkiye's 'golden years' or 'honeymoon period' within the Western alliance.

During this period, Türkiye also rapidly developed economic and political relations with Israel, which it recognised in 1949. The Israelis were very keen to develop relations with the Turks due to the Arab threat. The Baghdad Pact, or CENTO as it was later known, was another important issue in Turkish Foreign Policy during this period. This pact, established between Türkiye, Iran, Iraq, Pakistan, and the United Kingdom (Britain) to prevent the Soviet Union from gaining influence in the Middle East, emerged with the support of the United States. In 1958, Türkiye allowed the use of Incirlik Air Base to support the United States in its intervention in Lebanon. Even during this period, Israeli Prime Minister David Ben-Gurion visited Türkiye and a secret 'Peripheral Pact' was established between Israel, Türkiye, Iran, and Ethiopia (Abyssinia). During these years, Türkiye would also have to confront the Cyprus issue. With the rise of nationalist movements aimed at uniting Greece and Cyprus and the British losing control of the island in 1960, the Cyprus Conflict would deepen and become one of Türkiye's main foreign policy issues in the 1960s. The 1960 Republic of Cyprus, established with the London and Zurich Agreements, designated Türkiye, the United Kingdom (Britain), and Greece as the three guarantor countries and established a 7–3 balance between the Greeks and the Turks. This situation can be seen as a success when you consider that Türkiye had no previous rights over the island. However, interestingly, the transfer of control over the island from the British to the Turks and the Greeks brought conflicts, not peace, and further deepened this problem. The Cuban Missile Crisis of these years and its effects on Türkiye are also a subject of research in itself. This incident showed Türkiye that while the US alliance was advantageous in some respects; it could also be extremely risky in some cases. The placement of Jupiter missiles in Türkiye, which the Menderes government accepted with the agreement signed in 1959, led to Türkiye becoming a target for Russia during the Cuba-US crisis. The Jupiter missiles, which were later replaced with Polaris submarine ballistic missiles and removed from Türkiye, became an important element in the Khrushchev-Kennedy bargaining, and it seems that Kennedy, who responded to Khrushchev's first letter, which did not include this issue, did not accept this (removal of the Jupiter missiles from Türkiye).

When we look at the developments in the first phase of the Cold War between 1946 and 1963, William Hale, who thought that it was necessary for Türkiye to join the Western bloc during this period, also points out that there was not enough desire in the country on this issue. It should also be noted that joining the alliance brought three major risks to Türkiye. The first is the risk that the United States would turn Türkiye into a 'satellite state'. The second is the possibility that Türkiye could become a nuclear target in the event of a deepening US-USSR conflict. The third is the risk that Türkiye's national interests would not always coincide with the interests of the alliance (NATO). Indeed, this situation would be clearly seen and experienced in the Cyprus issue from 1963 onwards. According to Hale, two fundamental criticisms can be made about Turkish diplomacy during this period. The first is that Türkiye never tried to establish closer relations with Khrushchev, who initiated the de-Stalinization process after Stalin. There were also some misunderstandings in Menderes' Middle East policy. For example, the aggressive stance towards Syria and some policies that were completely pro-Israeli and pro-Western could have led to Türkiye becoming a target for the Soviets and their allies.

The Cold War and Türkiye: Global Changes and Regional Conflicts, 1964–1990

The fifth chapter, 'The Cold War and Türkiye, Global Changes and Regional Conflicts, 1964–1990', attempts to explain the transformations in Turkish Foreign Policy during the second phase of the Cold War, which lasted until its end in 1990. During these years, some important changes occurred as a result of some developments in the first phase of the Cold War. During these years, the fact that NATO viewed Turkish territory as an area that could be sacrificed in the event of a possible war with the Soviets increased the fears and concerns of the Turks. The Cyprus Conflict would also become a serious point of disagreement between Türkiye and its Western allies from these years onwards. Foreign policy developments would also seriously affect Turkish domestic policy during this period. Consequently, Türkiye would enter an extremely unstable and difficult period and experience a military memorandum (12 March 1971) and eventually a major military coup (12 September 1980). According to Hale, during leftist CHP chair Bülent Ecevit's second term as Prime Minister (1978–1979), the Republic of Türkiye almost came to the point of collapse.

The Cyprus issue deserves a special parenthesis here. With the withdrawal of the Turkish Cypriots from the parliament in 1963, Türkiye's concerns about Cyprus began to increase. The fact that the United States viewed this issue as a minor element of the Cold War and did not take a position in favour of Türkiye, considering Greece as well, caused great damage to Turkish-American relations. The crisis, which reached its peak with the infamous Johnson Letter in 1964, led Türkiye to a multi-dimensional search in its foreign policy. This letter stated that if Türkiye intervened in Cyprus, it would not be protected against the Soviets by its NATO allies and that Türkiye would not even be able to use NATO weapons. İsmet İnönü, who became Prime Minister again through the coalition governments after 27 May, gave his famous response after this incident, '*If necessary, a new world will be established and Türkiye will take its place in this world*.' Following this incident, a group of leftist circles led by the Turkish Workers' Party (TİP) began to make propaganda for Türkiye's withdrawal from NATO and were extremely effective. With the influence of this leftist opposition, politicians such as Süleyman Demirel and Bülent Ecevit, who later became Prime Ministers, and their Foreign Ministers (İhsan Sabri Çağlayangil, Turan Güneş, and

Gündüz Ökçün) always gave importance to multi-dimensional foreign policy and never fully trusted the United States again. In fact, some of Ecevit's advisers, such as Prof. Haluk Ülman, took the matter even further and began to advocate withdrawal from NATO as a rational policy. Starting from this period, the aid and investments that the Soviets provided to Türkiye on the path to industrialisation were also influential in this attitude. The balanced attitude of the Soviets between the Greeks and Turks on the Cyprus issue also pleased Ankara. Therefore, Moscow was able to establish seriously warm relations with Ankara, although it was still not on a par with Washington during these years.

In 1974, Türkiye intervened on the island using its guarantor right with the Cyprus Peace Operation. This happened during the strange coalition government of the pro-secular CHP, which had shifted to a socialist line under the leadership of Ecevit, and the Islamist MSP, led by Prof. Necmettin Erbakan. This situation was made possible when the junta in Greece organised a coup in Cyprus and overthrew Makarios and replaced him with fascist EOKA members. The EOKA members, who put the Akritas Plan into action to destroy the Turks, practically forced Türkiye to intervene. The United States, on the other hand, was busy with the Arab-Israeli talks and the Watergate Scandal, where Henry Kissinger was involved. Although the United States and the United Kingdom (UK) opposed the intervention, they did not make much effort to prevent it. This intervention prevented a possible major massacre and genocide in Cyprus and also led to the collapse of the junta government in Greece. Turkish-Greek relations had become quite tense during these years, not only due to Cyprus but also due to the Aegean Problem. A landing in Cyprus would cause Greece to have great concerns about the Aegean Islands and to rapidly arm itself. The 1974 Cyprus crisis would also negatively affect Turkish-American relations. Thanks to the Greek lobby, the United States made a decision to block military aid and sales to Türkiye during this period, triggering a breakthrough in the Turkish defence industry. Although the embargo was lifted within a few years, the conflict with the United States was reflected in Türkiye as economic difficulties. Under the influence of this embargo, Ecevit adopted a thoroughly Third Worldist (Non-Aligned Movement type) rhetoric in the second half of the 1970s and even began to advocate leaving NATO. In contrast, he did not make any active efforts in this direction and kept this issue on the table as a bargaining chip. For this reason, the process of breaking away from the West in the 1970s remained partial, temporary, and hesitant, and never turned into a serious and official anti-Western policy.

From the 1980s onwards, there was a rapid return to the Western alliance. The 12 September 1980 military coup and the subsequent Turgut Özal governments were the most important stages of this process. The attitude of the United States, which lost a very important ally with the 1979 Iranian Islamic Revolution, was also effective in this process. Indeed, the United States did not strain relations with Türkiye much during these years and preferred to remain silent in the face of the excesses of the 12 September regime. The US attitude also changed in this period regarding Cyprus and embargoes. Türkiye also remembered the Soviet threat as a result of the Soviet intervention in Afghanistan and the pro-Russian atmosphere of the 1970s quickly dissipated. The Özal period was also a period of rapid liberalisation similar to the Ronald Reagan and Margaret Thatcher periods. The transition to a free market economy, privatisations, and integration into the world economy began during this period. From these years onwards, the Armenian deportation of 1915 also began to become a problem in US-Türkiye relations. ASALA terrorism, on the other hand, ensured the securitisation of the issue and strengthened Türkiye's hand. However, during this process, Türkiye had to lose many valuable diplomats. The establishment of the Turkish Republic of Northern Cyprus (TRNC) in 1983, but its non-recognition by any state other than Türkiye, was another important development during this period. The risk of war with Greece was reduced thanks to its return to NATO in 1980, but the problems continued, especially in Cyprus. The stance of the junta leader and 7th President of the Republic Kenan Evren on this issue is open to debate. According to some, Türkiye lost a major trump card by not preventing Greece's return to NATO. The oppression of Turks in Bulgaria and the policies of forced migration were also important issues during this period and increased nationalist reactions within the country.

When Türkiye's Middle East policy is examined during this period, it is seen that there is greater interest and success compared to previous periods. Participation in the Organisation of Islamic Cooperation (then-called Organisation of the Islamic Conference) and increasing economic, political, and cultural relations with Arab countries were carried out in a balanced manner without damaging relations with Israel and the Western world. In the 1980s, Türkiye, understanding the importance of Jewish (Israel) lobby support in the United States, tried to establish closer relations with Israel again. With pressure from Türkiye, the Palestine Liberation Organisation (PLO) began to accept Israel's existence and the two-state solution. However, even during this period, relations with all Arab countries could not be developed. For example, problems with Syria continued and good relations could not be established. Issues such as Hatay, the support given by the Syrian state to the PKK, and control of the Euphrates and Tigris continued to be the main difficulties in Türkiye-Syria relations. Türkiye began to remember its tightrope walking again during the Iran-Iraq War that took place during these years. Another important domestic and foreign issue was PKK terrorism and Kurdish separatism (secessionism) that started with the Eruh raid in 1983. During these years, Türkiye became a country where very bloody terrorist incidents began to occur.

Relations with Europe have always been an important dimension of Turkish Foreign Policy. The Ankara Agreement signed in 1963 was an important step towards joining the European Economic Community (EEC). This step was also supported by the Additional Protocol Agreement in 1970. While the Islamists and socialist Ecevit supporters looked coldly upon the EEC, the Demirel supporters and those on the centre-left supported the European integration project. The 1980 military coup and the human rights violations that followed caused a rift between Europe and Türkiye. Indeed, the first reaction to the coup came from the Council of Europe, which Türkiye had joined in 1950. During the Özal era, relations improved partially with the return to civilian supremacy and democracy, and even an official application for EEC membership, which was rejected, was made. Greece's entry into the EEC would be a development that would put Türkiye in a difficult position in the long term. It is unclear what would have happened if Ecevit had not opposed the EEC by saying '*we are the market, you are the partners*' during these years. As a result, it can be said that the most successful area in foreign policy during this period was the Middle East. Because the support received from Arab countries began to provide Türkiye with a political advantage and generally economic advantages regarding the Cyprus issue. Moreover, this was achieved without damaging relations with Israel in an interesting way. This is a success of the Demirel governments in particular. On the other hand, the

Ecevit governments, apart from a concrete action such as the Cyprus Peace Operation, did not achieve any major success economically and politically.

Turkish Foreign Policy After the Cold War: Strategic Options and the Domestic Situation

The sixth chapter, 'Turkish Foreign Policy After the Cold War: Strategic Options and the Domestic Situation', examines the early 1990s, when many new opportunities arose for Turkish Foreign Policy after the end of the Cold War, but these opportunities were not very well utilised. The end of the Cold War brought about a very serious transformation for Türkiye. Because during the Cold War, Ankara's most important characteristic for the Western world was that it was a neighbour of Russia and a pro-Western country. The collapse of the Soviets and the emergence of new states, many of which were of Turkish and Muslim origin, created an uncertain situation similar to the 1920s. However, this time, Türkiye, which was very weak in the 1920s, was now much stronger and larger. Its traditional rivals, as in the case of Greece, no longer posed as great a threat as before. Only the newly established Russian Federation was a stronger state than Türkiye with its great military power and political influence. In such an environment, Türkiye could have considered leaving NATO and the Western alliance. But that did not happen; because, as İnönü stated years ago, Türkiye believed that this alliance was beneficial to it. Indeed, NATO and the United States were quick to find new tasks suitable for Türkiye in this new period. In addition, after the Cold War, it would have been possible for Türkiye to join the Customs Union of the EEC, which had become the European Union, and to start negotiations for membership with the EU. However, the 1990s would be even more difficult than the 1980s in terms of PKK terrorism and the Kurdish Question.

With the end of the Cold War, many experts initially thought that Türkiye's importance and role had diminished. There was even talk that NATO could be dissolved; because the Soviet Union, which was the purpose of its existence, had collapsed and the danger of the spread of communism had been eliminated. Indeed, on paper, Türkiye's importance to the West seemed to have diminished; it was no longer a buffer against Russia, it was not an EU member and had serious problems with EU members such as

Greece, and moreover, it did not have very high marks on its report card regarding human rights, especially the Kurdish Question. However, it soon became clear that Türkiye was a very important country in the fight against terrorism, regional stability in the Balkans, the Caucasus and the Middle East, and the preservation of global peace. In addition, in Özal's final years, with the collapse of the Soviets, Turkist and Islamist dreams began to revive. Özal's mention of the Turkic world '*From the Adriatic to the Great Wall of China*' in particular created great excitement in right-wing circles, but not much progress could be made in this regard. Türkiye's role in the US's Middle East policies also began to increase during this period. Türkiye's stance in the Gulf War and the Iraq War directly affected the US's success. It did not seem that Türkiye's importance in terms of Israel's security and stability would decrease. During these years, Turkish academics and intellectuals were trying to develop a strategy to establish relations with both the West and the East. For example, Ziya Öniş was one of the first people to make important observations on this issue and thought that this situation was in line with Türkiye's cultural heritage.

However, the collapse of communism also had serious negative repercussions on Türkiye's domestic politics. The disappearance of the Soviets and communism as a balancing element made the Islamist right-wing mentality very strong in Türkiye and disrupted the balance of secular practices. While the left gradually diminished starting from these years, the decline of the centre-right and the rise of the Islamist far-right began on the right. The failure of the centre-left and centre-right coalition governments established in these years to find solutions to economic problems and terrorism paved the way for Islamist politics, which were considered extreme in Türkiye, and brought the Islamists to power for the first time in the mid-1990s. In the 2000s, the Islamists would completely dominate Türkiye. Young centre-right leaders, who were highly hoped for such as Tansu Çiller and Mesut Yılmaz, could not replace charismatic figures such as Özal and Demirel in these years and virtually gave way to the Islamists. The fact that centre-right governments became synonymous with corruption was also a major problem and increased the popular support of Islamists who talked about a 'just order' and 'clean politics'. The biggest problem was the economic crises. Unemployment and inflation were breaking the back of the centre pillar starting from the Özal era and increasing support for radical movements. But Ecevit did the impossible once again in the late 1990s and formed the last left-wing government through a three-party coalition. The capture of PKK leader Abdullah Öcalan during the minority government and his return to Türkiye brought Ecevit, who had been steadily rising since the 1980s with his newly founded Democratic Left Party (DSP), to power with a great leap forward. However, after the disastrous 2001 economic crisis, the uninterrupted period of Islamist rule in Türkiye with the AK Parti (Justice and Development Party) began and this process continues today. The 28 February Process, which was a step back from the brink of an actual coup during these years, is also an important event that has gone down in history. The merger of the SHP and the CHP, the replacement of Alparslan Türkeş in the MHP by Devlet Bahçeli, and the Kurds forming a party and starting a civil political struggle are also the most important innovations of this period. Unsolved murders thought to be related to the PKK, Hezbollah, the mafia, and other criminal groups are also among the most widely discussed topics of this period. The reflections of the struggle with the PKK, which almost turned into a small civil war, were economic burden, political instability and social unrest, and led to the collapse of central politics.

The 1990s were a period in which the multi-dimensional process that began in the 1960s in Turkish Foreign Policy continued. The experience of Süleyman Demirel, who became President after Özal's death, from his time as Prime Minister was also effective in this. In addition, business circles and civil society organisations became more powerful in these years and began to influence politics and foreign policy. While large and secular capital groups such as TÜSİAD pressed for integration with the West, Islamist civil society organisations and capital groups began to create public opinion for closer relations between Türkiye and the Islamic World. Anti-Israel sentiment began to gain serious support on the right wing starting in this period. From these years on, economic rationality began to play a more important role in Turkish Foreign Policy. Many new steps were taken in foreign policy and the regions where it was active were increased with factors such as expanding trade volume and opening up to the world. In addition, energy policies and Türkiye's need for natural gas and oil would also become an important foreign policy element from this period onwards and would make Türkiye dependent on Russia and other Eurasian countries. The Baku-Tbilisi-Ceyhan Pipeline project is one of the most important initiatives of this period. İsmail Cem, who served as Minister of Foreign Affairs between 1997 and 2002, was one of the people who, together with Süleyman Demirel, guided the multi-dimensional foreign policy process.

Türkiye and the West After the Cold War

The seventh section titled 'Türkiye and the West after the Cold War' is an important section examining Türkiye's relations with the West after the Cold War. With the EU becoming a separate political structure from 1992, Türkiye's relations with the West began to differ from a single holistic approach. Three different dynamics emerged: relations with the United States, relations with NATO, and relations with the EU. Furthermore, relations with the EU did not mean one-to-one relations with European countries. As a result, relations with the West had become much more complex. The importance of relations with the United States had not diminished; because both countries supported the Western-oriented development of countries in the former Soviet geography. However, disagreements could occur in Middle East policies. For example, serious disagreements could occasionally occur between the United States and Türkiye on issues such as the territorial integrity of Iraq, a major military intervention there, and the Kurdish Question. The roles played by the United States in the crises in Bosnia-Herzegovina and Kosovo pleased Türkiye and brought the two countries closer together during this period. Türkiye had opened the Incirlik Air Base to the United States in the Gulf War and helped but had not directly entered the war. Although many American bases were closed after the Cold War, Incirlik Air Base always maintained its importance and became one of Türkiye's most important advantages for the United States. Özal was also a very good partner for the United States with his pro-American policies and his knowledge of regional policies. After Özal, the United States had difficulty finding another politician in Türkiye who could get along so well with him. However, Özal's first pro-American revisionist position in the Middle East after the Baghdad Pact did not please everyone in the country or abroad. The increase in anti-Americanism in the Turkish Armed Forces was an innovation of this period. The disagreements experienced especially regarding the Kurdish Question and civilianisation had interestingly started to direct the Turkish Pashas towards Eurasianist alternatives starting from this period. The Armenian Question allegations started to become a serious problem in relations with the United States and later in relations with the EU from these years onwards. The frequent use of the term 'genocide' greatly disturbed the Turkish state and public opinion and had an extremely negative impact on relations.

Relations with the EU and with European countries in general also progressed on problematic ground in the 1990s. With the influence of Greece's internal lobbying, the EU began to take a position against Türkiye on almost all controversial issues. Apart from traditional issues such as the Aegean Question and the Cyprus Question, the quality of democracy and human rights violations in Türkiye, the Kurdish Question, and the Armenian Question were now serious problems in relations. However, the inclusion in the Customs Union and becoming a candidate country for the EU in 1999 were very important developments that made us forget all these failures and managed to turn the general picture from a negative to a positive. In addition, the trade shares of Türkiye and European countries increased rapidly during this period and European companies settled in Türkiye and Turkish companies in Europe. Increasing Islamism was seriously damaging bilateral relations on cultural and political grounds. In response to this, Islamophobic and anti-Turkish sentiment in Europe also began to become a serious problem from those years onwards and disrupted Europe's internal stability (and even began to threaten the existence of the EU at the point we have reached today). The fact that no progress was made on the Kurdish Question after the capture of PKK leader Öcalan is also a great example of failure in this period. However, Türkiye could have taken serious steps in domestic politics to solve the problem with rational policies during this process; thus, it could have placed its relations with the EU on a better footing.

Türkiye's Regional Policies After the Cold War: (1) Greece, Cyprus, the Balkans and the Caucasus

The eighth chapter of the book titled 'Türkiye's Regional Policies after the Cold War: (1) Greece, Cyprus, the Balkans and the Caucasus' examines Türkiye's foreign policies in terms of regional issues. Interestingly, Turkish-Greek relations have not experienced any major changes since the end of the Cold War. Although the rapprochement process in 1999 brought the two countries closer for a while and relations are at a better level today than in the past, the end of the Cold War had a limited effect on these transformations. Factors such as the EU's transformative power and Türkiye's good use of the terror card have been influential in this process. Despite all efforts, there has been no change in the Cyprus Conflict. The war, which was stopped by the Cyprus Peace Operation, continues today with diplomatic struggle. The 2004 Annan Plan named after then-UN Secretary-General Kofi Annan – is a historical event that took place during this period and has greatly strengthened Türkiye's hand in the international arena. The fact that Türkiye and the Turkish Cypriots, who are seen as occupiers, supported the Annan Plan and the solution, while the victimised Greece and the Greeks opposed it, showed the whole world that Türkiye may be right on this issue. In addition, the idea of a two-community and two-region federal solution has been generally accepted all over the world, and the isolations against the Turkish Cypriots have been lifted – albeit partially. However, despite all these positive developments, the Cyprus Conflict continues to challenge Türkiye in terms of international law. According to many experts in international law, the Turkish military is an 'occupier' on the island. According to them, due to the principle of territorial integrity, it is out of the question for the Turkish Cypriots to establish a state by exercising a separate right to self-determination. Indeed, Türkiye did not recognise the Nagorno-Karabakh Republic for the same reason and defended the territorial integrity of Azerbaijan, which it sees as a brother country. However, the steps taken by the Iraqi Kurds towards the autonomy and independence they have achieved, some autonomous region practices in Europe, and the independence of Kosovo supported by the United States are current developments that contradict this. As a result, according to Hale, it is very difficult for Türkiye to become an EU member without resolving this issue. Because the EU is openly protecting its own member Greece and the Greek Cypriots who represent the entire island. Moreover, some of the promises made to Türkiye and the Turkish Cypriots during the Annan Plan period were not kept by the European states and the EU. However, since Türkiye's EU membership has generally fallen off the agenda and has become a very difficult possibility, time will determine where this issue will evolve.

From the Balkan perspective, it can be said that Türkiye's influence in this region has been steadily increasing after the Cold War. Economically, politically, and culturally, Türkiye is now much stronger in this region compared to the Cold War. The silence of Europe regarding the massacres and genocides committed against Muslim Bosnians and Kosovars in this region has increased Türkiye's influence and has also caused nationalist and Islamist reactions in the Turkish domestic public opinion. The United States, on the other hand, has pursued human rights and pro-democracy policies during the Bill Clinton era and has created great sympathy in the Islamic World and Türkiye by not being anti-Muslim. In parallel with the increase in Türkiye's influence, the Muslim Turkish population in the Balkans has also become more influential. For example, Bulgarian Turks have many political formations and the 'Movement for Rights and Freedoms' (*Dviženie za Prava i Svobodi*) has even come to power several times.

When we look at the Caucasus and Russia geography, Türkiye is now much stronger in this area compared to the Cold War. The establishment of Azerbaijan and its development of close relations with Türkiye is an important development in itself. The increasing economic relations with Russia and the mutual economic dependency that has been created also show that fears of occupation will no longer easily become reality as in the past. On the other hand, the fact that this dependency is against Türkiye – due to the energy factor – is a serious source of problems for Türkiye. In addition, Russia's occasionally harsh policies towards Muslims, as in the case of Chechnya, occasionally strains the relations between the two countries. The latest example of this was the confrontation between the two countries in Syria in the 2010s. In addition, Russia's open support for Armenia, which occupied Azerbaijani lands, is another problem and creates a negative situation where the two countries will never be political allies despite the increasing economic relations. Türkiye's most important partners in this region are Azerbaijan, whose population is predominantly Shiite Muslim, and Georgia, whose population is predominantly Orthodox Christian. This situation is also proof that Türkiye does not pursue Islamist or sectarian (Sunni) policies in this region. The Armenia-Azerbaijan conflict still prevents Türkiye from fully establishing stability and order in this region and leaves Armenia out of the game in the context of major projects.

Türkiye's Regional Policies After the Cold War: (2) Central Asia and the Middle East

The ninth chapter of the book titled 'Türkiye's regional policies After the Cold War: (2) Central Asia and the Middle East' is the chapter in which William Hale examines the Central Asia and Middle East dimensions of Turkish Foreign Policy. The Turkic Republics established in Central Asia after the collapse of the Soviets could have been a very big factor in terms of Türkiye's ability to grow stronger in this region. However, unlike the Azeris and Turkish Cypriots, the fact that the Turkish spoken by the people of this region is quite different from the Turkish spoken in Türkiye and Russia's 'big brother' position in this region has prevented Türkiye from making a big step. In addition, China has recently become another country that has been as influential in this region as Russia. In addition, although some American statesmen such as George Bush and James Baker spoke of the 'Turkish model' as an example for these countries in the early 1990s, the United States does not base its policies towards this region on Turkishness or Türkiye. Therefore, Enver Pasha's dreams of Turan must be limited to political, economic, and cultural relations with Azerbaijan, Cyprus, and the Turkmens in Iraq and Syria for the time being. However, the close relations of leaders such as Nursultan Nazarbayev and Turkmenbashi with Süleyman Demirel and their emphasis on Türkiye could be seen as promising for the future. However, it seems that the phrase 'one nation, two states' will remain limited to Azerbaijan for many years to come. The schools established in these countries, which were affiliated with the Gülen community and which Türkiye greatly supported until the 15 July 2016 coup attempt last year, are drawing criticism and are being closed by the states on the grounds that they spread American sympathies and educate Islamist youth.

It is also necessary to re-examine relations with Israel and Middle East policy in light of current conditions. As a result of the increasing Islamist policies since the mid-1990s, Türkiye has lost its neutral position in the Israeli-Arab conflict and has begun to be seen as an Islamist country close to the Arabs. In contrast, even the Islamists have not considered completely disrupting relations with Israel – until the recent Mavi Marmara Crisis – or rather; they have not dared to do so. In fact, during extraordinary periods such as 28 February, Türkiye-Israel co-operation has been further deepened.

Türkiye's relations with Arab countries – especially the Gulf countries – are also developing regularly and economic and political relations are rapidly increasing. However, an important problem for Türkiye in the Middle East is the situation of the Kurds. Western policies and Türkiye's policies on this issue do not fully coincide. A current example can be given as the different perspectives of the United States and Türkiye on the PYD/YPG. When it comes to relations with Syria, the bilateral relations developed with the Adana Agreement have been disrupted again due to the Syrian civil war and it is not yet known where they will evolve. As for Iran, there have never been very good or very bad relations. Economic and cultural relations between the two countries were developing rapidly for a while; thanks to the nuclear agreement signed between the P5+1 and Iran, the political crisis and the risk of a major war seem to have been eliminated, and this situation is a relief for Türkiye.

Results and Possibilities

The tenth and final chapter of the book, titled 'Results and Possibilities', is an important section where Professor William Hale evaluates the results of the book and discusses the possibilities for the future. When Hale's book is examined in its entirety, the following situation is clearly seen: Türkiye's influence in world politics has increased/is increasing steadily throughout the history of the Republic. Türkiye's economic power and military capacity are also developing steadily. However, it is not easy to predict the future. According to Hale, China may become a great power in the future of the world and establish dominance in East Asia. Turkish businessmen may also increase their economic relations by making new investments in China over time. However, according to the author; this situation will never reach a point where it can replace Türkiye's relations with the United States. According to the author, relations with the United States and NATO will continue despite the problems and there will be no rupture. EU membership does not seem easy.

This study, which was written after years of effort after creating a rich bibliography, is, in my opinion, one of the most important works ever written in this field. The fact that Hale is not a Turk and makes evaluations far from emotional sensitivities, in my opinion, further increases the credibility and objectivity of the book. For this reason, this book should be in all libraries.

'Unarmed Warfare: Diplomacy As an Art of Struggle' by Onur Öymen

Introduction

Dr Onur Öymen (1940–) is a well-known Turkish diplomat and politician. Öymen, who completed his primary, secondary, and high school education at Galatasaray High School, later graduated from the Faculty of Political Sciences in Ankara. Öymen, who also completed his doctorate at the same faculty, had his doctorate thesis on 'Technological Development and Defense Policy'. Öymen, who represented the Republic of Türkiye in foreign countries for a long time as a diplomat, later entered politics. Öymen, who was a deputy for İstanbul in the 22nd term and Bursa in the 23rd term of the Grand National Assembly of Türkiye, also served as the Deputy Chairman of the Republican People's Party (CHP) from 5 November 2003 to 23 May 2010 – during the term of Deniz Baykal. Öymen, who viewed foreign policy and politics in line with the principles of Realism and more as a power struggle between nation-states, was involved in various political polemics in this direction during his time as a politician. In addition to his political identity, Öymen is also a prolific writer. Öymen's third book, *Unarmed War: Diplomacy as an Art of Struggle* (*Silahsız Savaş: Bir Mücadele Sanatı Olarak Diplomasi*), which was first published in 2011, is a very informative and useful work in which the author combines his Foreign Affairs experiences with his academic knowledge. This article will summarise this book, which was published by Remzi Kitabevi and has been printed many times.

The Real Face of Diplomacy

Hans Morgenthau, an important academic, defined diplomacy as '*the peaceful protection of national interests*'. According to another definition, diplomacy is '*the art of conducting international relations by peaceful means and tools*'. According to Hüner Tuncer, diplomacy is '*the continuation of relations between states through negotiations*'. According to Ernest Satow, diplomacy is '*the use of intelligence by peaceful means in relations between governments*'. According to Hedley Bull, diplomacy is '*the peaceful continuation of international relations by official officials*'. This definition is extremely inadequate today because diplomacy has become too important and widespread to be left only to state officials and diplomats.

The tools of diplomacy are persuasion, compromise, and the threat of using force. According to Hans Morgenthau, diplomacy has failed when war breaks out. Because the problem could not be resolved by peaceful means and war could break out. Diplomacy is not only practiced against foreign countries. Diplomatic activities are also carried out against different groups within the country. Therefore, diplomacy is carried out in two dimensions, domestically and internationally, and these two dimensions sometimes interact with each other. A famous saying by British Prime Minister Lord Palmerston reveals the dirty side of diplomacy; '*Britain has no permanent friends or enemies, it has unchanging interests.*' Diplomacy allows countries to protect these interests outside of military means.

Today, it is not enough for states to be strong militarily in order to survive; they must also be diplomatically advanced. The golden rule of diplomacy is to be determined in essence but gentle in style. In order to achieve the desired result, both 'struggle' must be made and 'compromise' must be sought in order to avoid further damage. Diplomacy, in its narrow sense, is practiced by career diplomats (career officers) working in Foreign Ministries. In addition, politicians and special representatives assigned by them also serve as diplomats. In a broader sense, it can even be claimed that all citizens perform diplomatic duties in order to represent their countries.

The word diploma meant 'to double' in ancient Greek and was used for official documents and papers folded in half. As relations between countries developed, clerks who prepared and kept these documents emerged and these people served as the first diplomats. The first person to use the concept of diplomacy in the sense of the art of conducting international relations was Edmund Burke in 1796. The transition from temporary diplomacy to permanent diplomacy first began in the Italian states of the fifteenth century. It then spread rapidly in European countries and the understanding that each country should have representatives in other countries developed. As the idea of nationalism increased, diplomacy naturally developed. The legal status of diplomats was determined in the Congress of Vienna in 1815.

Diplomats are state officials responsible for carrying out the foreign policy determined by governments. Therefore, failures in foreign policy are primarily the responsibility of governments. Diplomats are obliged to take the most beneficial steps for their countries in line with the main lines determined by governments. Diplomats have privileges based on the Vienna Convention of 1961. The duties of diplomats can be summarised as (1) representing their country, (2) protecting the interests of their state and citizens, (3) negotiating on behalf of their state in the countries to which they are assigned, (4) conveying information about the countries they serve to their own countries, and (5) developing friendly relations between their own country and the countries they serve. During negotiations, diplomats are expected to be creative and take tough and soft positions when necessary.

The first permanent representations in the Ottoman Empire were opened in the 1790s during the reign of Selim III. However, permanent representations of foreign states had existed in the Ottoman Empire since the sixteenth century. The Ministry of Foreign Affairs was established in 1835 under the name of '*Hariciye Nezareti*'. The Republic of Türkiye has continued the diplomatic tradition it inherited from the Ottoman Empire by supporting it with the ideals of national honour, equality, and independence. The Republic of Türkiye, which had thirty-nine foreign representations in 1924, currently has 257 foreign representations. According to Öymen, diplomacy does not only deal with daily events and problems but also prepares solution proposals according to the possibilities that may arise in the future. A policy followed or a decision taken today may have a positive or negative effect many years from now. As the French say, '*governing is being able to see the future.*'

When diplomacy is examined in terms of this ability to see the future, it becomes clear that the US President Woodrow Wilson was extremely unsuccessful. Wilson thought that peace and stability could be achieved in the world after World War I, but the world was at a level that it had never seen before.

Towards a New World Order

The Second World War, which could not be prevented despite the British 'appeasement policy', quickly dragged the world into a great disaster. At first, the Germans were gaining great superiority over their opponents on every front. However, in time, due to reasons such as the United States entering the war after being subjected to the Japanese attack on Pearl Harbour and the Nazis being bogged down by the Soviets, the Allies gained the upper hand. Efforts to shape the future of the world began when Roosevelt, Stalin, and Churchill met in Tehran on 28 November 1943, while the war was still ongoing. The British saw the Soviets as a great threat even then. However, the US President Franklin Delano Roosevelt believed that something could come from Germany again in the future as a threat and did not view the USSR negatively; he thought that the United States and Britain (United Kingdom), together with the Soviets and China, could be the protectors of the 'new world order'. Churchill foresaw the Soviet threat at that time and realised that communism would also create instability in Western regimes. However, Britain was no longer as powerful as it used to be, and the United States and the USSR were at the forefront of the scene. Roosevelt, who was sympathetic to socialism and implemented economic policies close to statism (New Deal), perceived Stalin as a friend, unaware of the cruelty and massacres he was committing in his country.

In this environment, intense pressure was exerted to bring Türkiye into the war. The first effort was Churchill's letter to İsmet Pasha dated 31 January 1941. The letter suggested that British planes and anti-aircraft guns be brought into Türkiye to stop Germany's advance. Since this would mean entering the war, İsmet Pasha rejected the proposal on 11 February. However, the British were insistent. On 26 February 1941, British Foreign Minister Anthony Eden came to Ankara. Eden wanted Türkiye to declare war on Germany if Germany attacked Greece. Türkiye also responded negatively to this proposal, stating that they would only resist the Germans if they were attacked. Hitler also wrote a letter to İsmet Pasha on 4 March 1941, promising that Germany would not attack Türkiye. The British and Russians, who also wanted to bring Türkiye into the war, later agreed on a proposal from Stalin. Accordingly, the Turks would be given the Dodecanese (Twelve) Islands, some parts of Bulgaria, and Northern Syria in return for entering the war. Türkiye found this generous proposal suspicious and rejected it, thinking that rights could be claimed from the Straits in the future. A similar proposal came from the Germans at a later date. German Ambassador Franz Von Papen, who visited Foreign Minister Numan Menemencioğlu on 23 September 1943, implicitly offered Türkiye the Dodecanese Islands. Ankara found this situation suspicious as well and did not want to enter the war. Indeed, there were other plans and goals hidden behind these proposals, and Menemencioğlu and other experienced Turkish statesmen could easily sense them. However, the British efforts were endless. On 30 January 1943, Churchill came to Adana and met with İsmet Pasha. He wanted to bring Türkiye into the war and open the Turkish bases in Thrace to the British. This permission was not granted, but the British still provided some small military aid to Türkiye in order to modernise the Turkish Army. In a meeting held in Moscow between 18 October and 1 November 1943, with the participation of the United States, British, and Russian Foreign Ministers, Hull, Eden, and Molotov, it was jointly requested that Türkiye enter the war. In November, Eden and Menemencioğlu met in Cairo. The Turks were unwilling to enter the war because they did not trust Stalin. In addition, the British had only provided a small portion of the military aid they had promised up until that day. Türkiye, which had just come out of the War of Independence and had a small population, did not want its cities to be destroyed by entering a war with Germany. For this reason, the offer was rejected despite insistence. On 4 December 1943, Roosevelt, Churchill, and İnönü met in Cairo. Churchill reiterated his demand that Turkish air bases be opened to the British. İsmet Pasha accepted this proposal in principle; however, he stipulated that the Turkish Army be equipped with modern weapons and that British aircraft would reinforce Turkish aircraft in protecting the airspace. In the end, despite Churchill's threats after the war, no agreement was reached, and Türkiye was saved from entering the war.

İsmet Pasha's resolute attitude during this period had protected Türkiye from a war. Indeed, the Soviets' ambitions towards Türkiye soon became apparent. After World War II, the Soviets rapidly increased their power and, in Churchill's words, *'an iron curtain was drawn over the east of Europe.'* Moreover, Stalin demanded bases in the Straits and some lands in the east from Türkiye. The Soviets' desire to change the Montreux Treaty had already become apparent before the war had even begun, and Türkiye was already aware of this. Another reason for not wanting to go to war with the Allies was the possibility that Soviet soldiers could enter Türkiye while repelling the Germans. 19 March 1945 was the day when Turkish-Soviet relations seriously deteriorated and the Cold War began. On this date, Soviet Foreign Minister Molotov invited Selim Sarper, the Turkish ambassador to Moscow, to his office and stated that they wanted to terminate the 1925 Treaty of Friendship and Neutrality signed by Atatürk and Lenin. These developments also disturbed the United States. When Roosevelt died, the United States also became concerned about Stalin's ambitions. When the Turkish Ambassador Mehmet Münir Ertegün passed away in 1946, the United States sent him to Türkiye with the famous battleship Missouri. This was a gesture towards Türkiye and a message to the Soviets. The Cold War had now begun with all its might.

The Truman Doctrine was announced in 1947, and financial support was provided to many countries for their development in line with the Marshall Plan. Türkiye and Greece were also included in the plan, but they did not receive serious aid like Germany and Japan. The North Atlantic Treaty Organisation (NATO) was established in 1949 and Türkiye became a NATO member country by sending troops to the Korean War in 1952. Türkiye had now become a country that had chosen the West in the Cold War. The Cold War would have very serious economic and political costs for Türkiye. For example, in the Cuban Missile Crisis of 1963, the presence of US missiles in Türkiye in exchange for the nuclear missiles placed in Cuba by the USSR made Türkiye a target for the Soviets. America occasionally took initiatives that would put Türkiye's security at risk. This situation, which cooled relations, was further confirmed when Türkiye wanted to intervene against the massacres committed by the Greeks against the Turks in Cyprus in 1964. The new US President Lyndon Johnson clearly stated in a letter (Johnson Letter) that Türkiye could not use NATO weapons in an intervention on the island and that NATO would not support this country if the USSR attacked. A significant cooling period had begun in bilateral relations and Türkiye would now begin to pursue a multi-dimensional foreign policy.

Türkiye, despite everything, took its place within the NATO order. Despite participating in the Non-Aligned Movement meetings, Türkiye acted more like a NATO spokesperson here and was therefore perceived negatively. Türkiye's failure to recognise Algeria's independence and siding with France during this period completely destroyed its reputation within the Non-Aligned Movement. However, the independence fighters in Algeria took Atatürk and the Turkish Revolution as their role models. The Cold War also had other negative effects on Türkiye's domestic politics, such as two military coups, a military memorandum, serious internal polarisation and terrorism.

Diplomacy and Power Politics

When we look at the history of international relations, we see that there is often a close connection between a country's foreign policy and the power it possesses. The countries that are most influential in world politics are always among the most powerful countries in the world. Indeed, diplomacy and armed forces are considered the two most important tools for protecting the sovereignty and independence of states and defending their national interests. Defence capability is one of the most important elements that constitute national power even today. The power that deters other countries is the armed forces of that country. For this reason, the use of the threat of using armed forces in foreign policy, that is, power politics and (the use of hard power), is an important element of foreign policy.

A state's convincing demonstration that it will not hesitate to resort to force in cases where its national security interests necessitate it, is often effective in foreign policy. Of course, for this, that country must have sufficient power and the will to use force. Although war is the point where diplomacy ends, the threat of war is still a field of diplomacy. According to thinkers such as Carl von Clausewitz, even war is a continuation of diplomacy with other tools. For this reason, in powerful states, there is a strong harmony between diplomacy and the armed forces. Even today, despite the increasing democratic consciousness and tendencies, high military expenditures show how serious the struggle between states is and how possible war is.

Although power politics seems to be fundamentally related to military power, it should not be understood only in this way. In order to become an effective actor in international politics, economic and political power is also necessary in addition to military power. This is the basis of states' economic competition and search for new markets today. In fact, the structure of domestic policy and the integrity of domestic policy also affect the power in foreign policy. The founder of our Republic, Mustafa Kemal Atatürk, expressed the effect of domestic policy on foreign policy as follows; '*Foreign policy is closely related to the internal structure of a society. Because foreign policies that are not based on the internal structure are always defeated. The stronger and more solid the internal structure of a society is, the stronger and more durable its foreign policy will be.*' According to 2001 data, Türkiye has the second largest army among NATO member countries after the United States This is also an important advantage for Türkiye in foreign policy. However, this needs to be supported by economic and political power.

The methods of putting pressure on foreign states, which we call pressure methods, are as old as the history of states. Throughout history, powerful states have tried to influence weaker countries by putting pressure on them in order to expand their spheres of influence. The last two centuries of the Ottoman Empire are quite an example in this respect. For this reason, the new Republic of Türkiye, which was established in place of the Ottoman Empire, built its foreign policy on the principles of independence and reciprocity, remembering these bad experiences.

Pressure Methods

Economic Pressures: The first and most commonly preferred pressure methods in international relations are economic pressures. States often use international trade relations as a tool to achieve certain political and economic interests, to encourage the development and strengthening of friendly countries, and to prevent those they see as enemies or rivals. Therefore, it would be correct to talk about 'carrot and stick policies' in foreign policy. In this sense, major states can economically encourage other states (carrots) to pull them to the line they want, or if this does not work, they can impose various economic sanctions (sticks) to punish them. Therefore, achieving economic power is also a very important factor in terms of foreign policy. There are types such as restrictions, quotas, and anti-dumping.

International Sanctions: Sanctions can also be imposed on countries that pose a threat to the international order under the umbrella of the United Nations. Article 41 of the UN Charter is related to this. Article 42 regulates the military intervention to be made in the event that these sanctions are insufficient. However, the United Nations Military Force, which the UN Charter foresees to be established, has not yet been established, except for temporary missions. Therefore, the application of Article 41 is quite common. One recent sanction decision was made in 2010, citing the nuclear programme that Iran carries out, which threatens world peace. Türkiye voted 'no' together with Brazil as a non-permanent member of the UN Security Council. In the vote where Lebanon abstained, twelve members voted 'yes' and the sanctions decision was made (the UN has five permanent and ten temporary Security Council members).

Bilateral Sanctions: Sanctions can also be imposed at a bilateral level. Large states may want to bring smaller states that oppose them into line by imposing embargoes. The United States is a country that has imposed sanctions over 120 times to date.

Dependency: One of the conditions for pursuing an independent foreign policy is not to be overly dependent on a single country in foreign economic and commercial relations. It will become impossible for countries that are overly dependent on a country to act independently of that country. Today, Mexico, Canada, Japan, and Israel are highly dependent on the United States. Similarly, Belarus is highly dependent on Russia, Hungary, Poland, Austria, Slovakia, France, and Greece are highly dependent on Germany, and Germany and Morocco are highly dependent on France. This is measured by the share in imports. Türkiye also has serious dependencies in terms of natural gas, oil and weapons technology. Our dependence on Russia, Iran, and Azerbaijan in the field of natural gas, and the United States in the defence industry is at a remarkable level. Foreign debts are also an important element of foreign dependency.

Diplomacy and Human Rights

Today, human rights constitute one of the most important agenda items not only for countries but also for international relations. States and civil society organisations prepare reports on this issue, evaluate and criticise the laws and practices of countries in this area. Democratic countries no longer consider human rights violations as internal problems. Member countries of the Council of Europe accept the judicial review of the Court of Human Rights on this issue. Some politicians, such as former US President Bill Clinton, go even further on this issue and say that they have the right to intervene in human rights violations all over the world. Organisations such as the Council of Europe and the European Union even list compliance with human rights as a condition of membership. The Copenhagen Criteria are actually related to these fundamental values and criteria on human rights and minority rights. The US Department of State publishes reports on the extent to which countries in the world comply with human rights every year. The United Nations Human Rights Commission also has studies on this issue. The issue of human rights, which has become so important in international relations, should therefore be examined thoroughly. First of all, we should start with the development of the concept of human rights after World War II.

Throughout history, war had been a natural element of international relations. Throughout history, millions of people had lost their lives in wars and conflicts, and this had been seen as an extension and necessity of human nature. However, after the indescribable suffering experienced during and before World War II (the interwar period), the idea that a serious breakthrough in human rights had to be made began to prevail in the Western world, and concrete initiatives were started to be taken in this regard. The massacres before and during World War II were largely caused by racist and extreme nationalist (chauvinist) thinking. Racism also provided a legitimate basis for colonial and imperialist activities in the past. Racist thinking, nourished by Social Darwinism, had a great impact on the genocide (Holocaust) crimes committed against the Jews, especially in Nazi Germany, and the lack of public reaction. For this reason, great importance was given to human rights since the establishment of the United Nations, and since the Nuremberg Trials, where Nazi war criminals were put on trial; it was aimed to develop international law on this issue. With the collapse of the apartheid regime in South Africa, which was founded on racist principles, racism gradually became more marginal over the years. According to Bernard Lewis, the

Ottoman Empire and Türkiye, unlike many European countries, had a relatively clean record on human rights.

Following the establishment of the United Nations and the adoption of various international conventions in the field of human rights, human rights became part of international law. The five countries that signed the Western European Union Treaty in Brussels on 17 March 1948, clearly stated their commitment to human rights. Based on these ideas, shortly after the Brussels Treaty, preparatory work began for the Council of Europe, based on the principle of respect for human rights and fundamental freedoms among European countries, and this organisation, which had no equivalent before, was founded in Strasbourg in May 1949. Within the framework of this organisation, a European Parliamentary Assembly was also established for the first time. The European Convention on Human Rights was signed in Rome on 4 November 1950. The Human Rights Commission and the Court of Human Rights were established. On 1 November 1998, these two organisations were merged and continued their work under the name of the European Court of Human Rights. It was not only wars and conflicts that threatened human life. Perhaps the greatest threat to people's right to life was the threat of hunger. According to a study conducted by the United Nations Children's Fund (UNICEF), even today, 1,000 children die every hour due to easily preventable diseases and hunger. However, Article 25 of the Universal Declaration of Human Rights states that people have certain basic rights to be protected from hunger and diseases. For this reason, many agreements have been made in this area. Since social problems in Europe were intense in the years following the war, certain norms and rules were determined for social rights with the European Social Law signed in Turin in 1961. This was called the 'European Social Charter'. Although states were not obliged to comply with all of these conditions, social rights developed rapidly in Europe thanks to the fact that some of the conditions were mandatory. In 1996, a new European Social Charter was signed in Strasbourg, and the mandatory articles were expanded.

The International Covenant on Economic, Social and Cultural Rights, signed within the framework of the United Nations, is a very important text that regulates economic and social rights at a universal level. This agreement, which is considered one of the most fundamental documents in the field of human rights, was opened for signature in 1966, but many states were in no hurry to sign the agreement. Similarly, Türkiye only signed this agreement in 2000. In addition, some countries that signed the agreement have placed certain reservations next to their signatures. For example, France and United Kingdom say that if there is a conflict between the right to self-determination mentioned in this agreement and the provisions of the UN Charter regulating the same issue, they will apply the UN Charter, not this agreement. Belgium also defends the view that the rule that states that there can be no discrimination based on national origin, in the reservation it placed in the same agreement, does not mean that states will grant equal rights to citizens and foreigners.

Diplomacy and the Press

Especially since the mid-twentieth century, public opinion has become increasingly influential in foreign relations, and states have often acted in accordance with public opinion. Some thinkers, such as Walter Lippmann, argue that involving public opinion in politics and foreign policy is risky, because public opinion is always in favour of radical solutions. The events before World War II confirm Lippmann. However, it is also possible to find examples to the contrary. Foreign policy issues, which were previously conducted behind closed doors, are now openly discussed in public. When politicians make decisions that are disturbing to foreign countries, they often explain this under pressure from the press and the public. Today, the press has become an important element of foreign policy (public diplomacy).

The extent of the relationship between the press and statesmen is also important. Journalists must, on the one hand, abide by the rule of impartiality required by their profession, and on the other hand, maintain the relationships with statesmen required by their profession. Being able to receive interviews from important statesmen is important for a journalist's professional success. It is known that such statements are often made to members of the press who write positive articles and remain within reasonable limits in their criticisms. In short, statesmen need the press, and the press needs statesmen in order to be successful in their fields. For this reason, the press is now considered a part of the work of the government and parliament in many countries. In some cases, hiding news from the press and not accepting the press's requests for interviews on certain issues can prevent the publication of undesirable news for a while. America's press policy during the Vietnam War is a typical example of this. The fact that journalists sometimes work together with the government, especially on foreign policy issues, has led to the press being called the 'fourth arm of the government' or even the 'shadow government'. The prevailing opinion in America is that the press plays an effective role in implementing and explaining foreign policy to the public rather than forming it. Indeed, it is seen that the press strongly supports the basic policy preferences of governments, at least in the early stages. The great support of the press in the US Cold War policies is an example of this.

Trying to influence the press in line with certain ideas and tendencies is not a new phenomenon. During the British colonial rule in America, the government had a great deal of control over the press. Since then, influencing and even controlling the press and therefore the people has been the main goal of governments and different political actors. A free press is one of the most important elements of democratic life. In fact, Thomas Jefferson believed in the importance of a free press in democratic life to the extent that he said, '*If I had to choose, I would choose a free press over a democratic government.*' The most important characteristics of authoritarian regimes are the pressures on the free press, the frequent arrests of journalists, and the state's intervention in the publishing policies of newspapers. In our country, especially the last years of the Democratic Party government, the periods of military intervention, and the policies towards the press in the recent period have been subject to serious criticism. It is seen that even in democratic regimes, the press can resort to self-censorship practices in some important events. However, journalism is a universal profession rather than a national profession and has international responsibilities. For this reason, a journalist may need to report a news story even if it is against his own country.

Today, the press also provides an environment for the propaganda and psychological warfare activities of states. The First and Second World Wars are important in terms of showing how dangerous and ruthless propaganda can be. The Nazis, through the Ministry of Propaganda they established (Joseph Goebbels), carried out an incredibly successful but also ruthless and unrealistic propaganda war during the Second World War. The propaganda activities of the British against the Ottomans during the First World War are also a subject of study in themselves. The *Blue Book*, written by Arnold Toynbee during this period, is actually a great propaganda book that still serves as a source for Armenian theses today.

The Diplomatic War of Lausanne

Lausanne has gone down in history as a very important peace treaty. However, the diplomatic struggles that took place until this conclusion were in many ways no different from a war. First of all, it seemed certain that a new war would break out if the negotiations failed. All parties participating in the conference constantly felt this. Everyone understood that the Turks would not hesitate to risk a new war if their fundamental interests were not respected. On the other hand, if their sovereignty, independence, and territorial integrity were respected and they were treated as an equal state, they were ready to show flexibility on some issues in order to reach an honourable peace. The road to the Lausanne Conference passed through the Armistice of Mudros and the Treaty of Sevres signed during and after World War I. However, it was impossible for the Turks to accept a very heavy treaty like Sevres; in fact, a resistance movement began in Anatolia under the leadership of Atatürk in a short time. Türkiye, which fought against the Greeks in the war, also knew the British power behind them. At the Mudanya Armistice Conference that started on 3 October 1922, these forces behind the Greek Army were at the table in front of the Turkish delegation headed by İsmet Pasha. Despite the traditional condescending efforts of the British, İsmet Pasha, as the representative of a victorious army and nation, wanted all Greek forces to leave the region up to the Maritsa border and never backed down. As a result, when Atatürk conveyed to the conference the threat that the army would march to İstanbul, the allies backed down; Thrace was evacuated by the Greeks and Turkish forces took control of the region instead. After the conference, the French representative Bouillon sent the following message to Atatürk; '*My friend, this is your day of victory.*' The success of Atatürk and the Turks also led to the fall of the Lloyd George government in Britain, which was hostile to the Turks, and Türkiye, which used armed force (hard power) as an element during the Mudanya Armistice period, won a great victory in the political arena.

Now it was Lausanne's turn. However, the struggle intensified even before the conference began. The Allied countries invited both the Ankara government and the İstanbul government, which had lost all influence, to the Lausanne Conference. The Ankara government reacted strongly to this. It was announced that they would not attend if the İstanbul government attended the conference. During this period, Atatürk developed an ingenious solution and separated the Sultanate and the Caliphate. Thus, on 1 November 1922, he abolished the Sultanate and rendered the İstanbul government powerless. Atatürk sent İsmet Pasha, who had a very stubborn personality and whom he trusted very much, to Lausanne. Rıza Nur and Hasan Saka were also delegates in the delegation. Before Lausanne, İsmet Pasha went to Paris and met with the French Prime Minister Raymond Poincaré. The French were positive about the independence of the Turks and their control of Anatolia, but they did not want the capitulations to be lifted. İsmet Pasha, on the other hand, stated that this issue was as important as the others. The Lausanne Peace negotiations began in this environment. According to Atatürk, this conference, where issues that were not 3–4 years old but centuries old were discussed, really experienced very tough struggles. In Lausanne, one of the parties was Britain, France, Italy, Japan, Greece, Romania, and the Serb-Croat-Slovenian state, while the other was Türkiye. The USSR and Bulgaria were also invited to the work on the Straits upon Türkiye's suggestion. The United States was an observer. Türkiye would struggle with all these states on its own. The composition of the delegations was high, unprecedented in similar conferences. France was represented by Prime Minister Poincaré, Italy by Prime Minister Mussolini, and Britain (England) by Foreign Minister Lord Curzon. The agenda consisted of vital issues for Türkiye, the determination of borders, Ottoman debts, judicial, financial, economic and cultural capitulations, minorities, the Straits issue, and the Greek war compensation.

The conference started on 20 November 1922. The discussions at the conference started in the opening speech. It was planned that the President of Switzerland would make a speech at the opening and that Lord Curzon would respond to him. İsmet Pasha opposed this and said, '*If he speaks, I will speak too.*' In the end, İsmet Pasha's request was accepted and İnönü gave a speech describing the sufferings of the Turkish nation. From the first day of the conference, Lord Curzon was trying to crush the Turks by taking his allies with him. İsmet Pasha, on the other hand, reacted strongly to this in line with the instructions he received from Atatürk. The topics discussed at the conference and the discussions that took place there can be summarised as follows: Drawing of borders, the Straits issue, the minorities issue, and the abolition of capitulations.

Drawing of borders: Regarding the Thrace borders, which had been largely resolved with the Mudanya Armistice, Türkiye wanted the Meriç River to be accepted as the border and advocated that a plebiscite be held in Western Thrace and that the people themselves should decide on the future of the administration. The Turks knew that the Turkish-Muslim population was predominant in Western Thrace. In fact, the Unionists (the CUP) had even established an independent Turkish Republic there in the past. Venizelos, on the other hand, was not in favour of a plebiscite. The British were also against the plebiscite. As a result, the Turkish-Greek land border became the line extending from the point where the Greek-Bulgarian border meets, following the Arda and Meriç rivers, to the Aegean Sea. Karaağaç and its surroundings were left to Türkiye, despite being west of the Meriç. Regarding the Aegean Islands, Gökçeada, Bozcaada, and Tavşan islands were left to Türkiye. The islands within three miles of the Turkish coast also remained in Türkiye. The Turkish-Syrian border was determined according to the Ankara Treaty signed with France on 20 October 1921. Hatay remained outside the Turkish border; however, the expression in the Ankara Treaty was preserved so that it would be given a special administration. Cyprus was left to Britain. The Turkish-Bulgarian border was determined according to the 1913 Turkish-Bulgarian Peace Treaty. The Mosul issue was left unresolved for now. The Turkish-Iranian border was also shaped according to the Kasr-ı Şirin Treaty of 1639.

The Straits Issue: At Türkiye's request, the USSR and Bulgaria also participated in negotiations on this issue. The military and political security of the Straits was very important for Türkiye. Lord Curzon wanted the Straits to be demilitarised and placed under the control of the League of Nations. The Russian representative, Georgiy Chicherin, suggested that the Straits be closed to warships from countries other than Türkiye. The British proposal was that the Straits should be open to warships in peacetime. The disarmament of the Aegean Islands was also important for the security of the Straits.

Finally, the principle of freedom of passage and transportation through the Straits was included in the agreement. A Straits Commission was established under the presidency of a Turkish representative. Permission was granted to merchant ships in peacetime. If Türkiye was neutral in wartime, warships could still pass through the Straits. If Türkiye was a party in wartime, Türkiye would also have the right to prevent passage through the Straits. The final solution to the Straits issue was the 1936 Montreux Convention. The Straits were completely under Turkish sovereignty.

The issue of minorities: The allies brought the issue of minorities to the agenda of the conference as a fait accompli. Türkiye's stance on this issue was clear; the rights of minorities in Türkiye would be protected within the framework of the general principles in the agreements recently signed by the Turkish government in Europe. However, for this, the rights of Turkish minorities in neighbouring countries should also be protected in the same way. Türkiye wanted to act in accordance with the principle of 'reciprocity' on this issue as well. A sovereign and equal state should do this. At the conference, İsmet Pasha stated that no element of the Muslim population would be considered a minority. In this sense, the Kurds were accepted as the primary element of the state. The Armenians used the issue of minorities to advocate that a region or even an autonomous state be allocated to them in Türkiye. The British also supported them. However, these were not accepted, and only non-Muslims were considered minorities and had the same minority rights as in Europe. The Patriarchate was another important issue. The Turkish delegation allowed the Patriarchate to remain in Türkiye in return for not having a universal (ecumenical) title and being a Turkish religious institution. In addition, a decision was made on the Turkish-Greek exchange.

The abolition of capitulations: One of the most difficult topics in Lausanne was the capitulations. The allies were very insistent on this issue. Türkiye, on the other hand, was in clear opposition and considered the abolition of capitulations as a condition for becoming an equal state. As a result, as a result of Türkiye's insistence, the capitulations were completely abolished, and the West was finally forced to accept the Turkish state embodied in the person of İsmet Pasha and its demands for equality.

War reparations: The Allied Powers gave up the war reparations they had requested due to World War I. Only Greece gave the Karaağaç region as war reparations.

Ottoman debts: Ottoman debts were shared among the states that separated from the Ottoman Empire. It was decided that the portion that fell to Türkiye would be paid in French francs in instalments. Thus, the Ottoman Public Debt (*Düyûn-ı Umûmiye*) institution became history. Türkiye was able to pay these debts in full only at the end of the 1950s. Other countries, on the other hand, did not pay these debts. As a result, Türkiye achieved great success at the Lausanne Conference. It had its borders accepted by the allies in accordance with the National Pact to a large extent, gained an equal state status by abolishing the capitulations, and largely got what it wanted regarding the minority. Türkiye could not fully get what it wanted in the Mosul issue, and after the Sheikh Said Rebellion in 1925, this region was definitely given up. With the Montreux Convention, the incomplete victory of Lausanne in the Straits was later achieved, and the new Republic of Türkiye secured itself.

According to Dr Onur Öymen, İsmet Pasha's struggle strategy and attitudes in Lausanne should be an example for all Turkish diplomats. British Deputy Delegate William Tyrell expressed his admiration for İsmet Pasha as follows: '*We have known two types of Turks until now; old Turks and Young Turks. Old Turks are dead, and Young Turks are no longer around. Today, we see a third type of Turk who is different from both of them, and that is İsmet Pasha. His personality and behaviors greatly affected the conference, and it was understood that he was a great personality. It is with these Turks that we want to make peace.*' The 143-article Lausanne Peace Treaty and the fifteen agreements, protocols, and declarations related to it were signed on 24 July 1923. Türkiye, which had been defeated in World War I, had emerged from Lausanne with a result that only a victorious state could achieve. The Treaty was ratified by the Turkish Grand National Assembly on 23 August 1923. Foreign state forces withdrew from Türkiye. Atatürk describes the Treaty of Lausanne as follows; '*Lausanne is a work that declares that a great assassination attempt against the Turkish nation, prepared for centuries and thought to have been completed with the Treaty of Sevres, has failed. It is an unprecedented political victory in Ottoman history.*' The US Ambassador Joseph Grew, who attended the conference as an observer, also thought that İsmet Pasha had won a great victory in Lausanne. According to him, what opened the door to victory for İsmet Pasha was his being ready to go to war at any moment and the Europeans not wanting to fight. According to British Prime Minister Lloyd George, '*Lausanne was the most humiliating treaty that Britain had ever signed.*'

Hatay's Accession to the Homeland

With the Ankara Treaty signed between the Government of the Turkish Grand National Assembly and the Government of France on 20 October 1921, İskenderun and Antakya, which were within the borders of the National Pact, remained outside the borders of Türkiye (within the borders of Syria under French mandate). However, the Ankara Treaty separated the Hatay region, which included İskenderun and Antakya, from Syria and recognised a special form of administration for the region. Accordingly; the people of Sanjak (İskenderun) would remain loyal to Turkish culture and they would be provided with convenience for the preservation of their national culture. In addition, Turkish currency would be valid there. In accordance with the provisions of the Treaty, a special administration was established in the Hatay region on 8 August 1922. When France lifted the mandate administration over Syria and Lebanon in 1936 and accepted to grant independence to these two countries, Türkiye also began working to have Hatay join the homeland. When France withdrew from Syria, İskenderun and Antakya came under Syrian administration. This new situation began to cause concern in Türkiye. Atatürk was determined to annex İskenderun and Antakya to the homeland. The Turkish government sent a note to the League of Nations on 6 October 1936, and to France on 9 October 1936, requesting that the independence granted to Syria and Lebanon be granted to İskenderun and Antakya as well. However, France did not accept Türkiye's request and suggested that the issue be referred to the League of Nations. Türkiye accepted this offer.

After this, the League of Nations took over the issue. Negotiations were held between France and Türkiye through the League. The two countries reached an agreement in Geneva on 29 May 1937. An agreement was signed to jointly guarantee Hatay's territorial integrity, and the League of Nations accepted the constitution prepared for Hatay. However, France was creating obstacles to implementing the constitution, as there had been a difference of opinion on the electoral system. Finally, an agreement was reached on the election system, and it was decided that the elections would be held on 15 July 1938. During this time, the danger of war in Europe was becoming increasingly evident. In the face of Germany's annexation of Austria in March 1938, France needed a strong Türkiye in the Middle East against Germany and Italy. The importance of the Straits also increased due to the increasing crises and disagreements in Europe. For this reason, France, which had to approach Türkiye, changed its stance on the Hatay issue and developments showed a direction in favour of Türkiye. After the Friendship Treaty was signed between Türkiye and France on 4 July 1938, the solution to the Hatay issue became easier.

As a result of the elections held after the Turkish-French rapprochement, the Hatay Turkish State Assembly held its first meeting on 2 September 1938 and accepted the name Hatay Republic for the independent state. Tayfur Sökmen was elected as the President and Abdurrahman Melek as the Prime Minister. The establishment of the independent Hatay Republic was not enough, because Hatay administrators and people wanted to join Türkiye. However, with the agreement of 29 May 1937, Hatay was under the joint guarantee of Türkiye and France. For this reason, the desire of the people of Hatay to join the homeland became a problem between the two states again. However, the events that took place in Europe starting from March 1939 led to dangerous developments that would lead to World War II, and this brought France closer to Türkiye. Therefore, France had to accept the demands of Türkiye and the people of Hatay. With an agreement made between the two states on 23 June 1939, France accepted the annexation of Hatay to Türkiye. With the unanimous decision of the Hatay Turkish State Assembly on 29 June 1939, Hatay joined the borders of the Republic of Türkiye (30 June 1939). The annexation of Hatay to Türkiye was the last major success of Atatürk in foreign policy.

Hatay, which was outside the borders of our country contrary to the National Oath, was annexed to the borders of Türkiye in accordance with the principles of the National Oath. Atatürk, who made great efforts for Hatay's independence and incorporation into Türkiye, devoted his time to solving this problem and struggled in the last months of his life without even considering his health. As a result of his ingenious policy, the Hatay issue was resolved in favour of Türkiye. Thus, the Türkiye-Syria border took its current form.

Fight for Peace in Cyprus

The island of Cyprus has been the centre of attention throughout history due to its important strategic location in the Eastern Mediterranean. History records that the island was first invaded by the Egyptians in 1450 BC. Later, the empires that dominated the Eastern Mediterranean also took Cyprus under their rule. The Romans invaded the island in 58 BC. After 450 years of Roman rule, the island passed to the Byzantines and remained under Byzantine rule until 1191. At that time, the English King Richard I conquered Cyprus and gave the administration to the Lusignan (Dynasty), which also ruled Jerusalem at the time. In 1489, the island came under Venetian control. In 1571, the Ottomans conquered Cyprus and maintained their absolute sovereignty on the island until 1878. In the early years of the Ottoman period, approximately 30,000 people migrated from Anatolia to Cyprus. The ancestors of the Turkish Cypriots are these Anatolian immigrants.

A brief summary of the long history of Cyprus can be made like this. The island has always been at the forefront with its strategic dimension. So much so that in the nineteenth century, the Jewish leader Theodor Herzl, who was looking for a homeland for the Jews, at one point thought of Cyprus as a Jewish State and even held various meetings with the British on this subject. The Cyprus Conflict first emerged simultaneously with the rebellion launched in Greece against the Ottomans in 1821. The Greek rebels obtained volunteers, money, and weapons from the Greeks of the island through the Archbishop of Cyprus. The Ottoman Governor Küçük Mehmet Pasha immediately suppressed these activities. A large number of weapons were seized, and the rebels were punished. Some of the leaders were exiled from the island. These exiles gathered in Rome and published a declaration on 6 December 1821, demanding '*enosis*', that is, the unification of the island with Greece. They also called on the Christian world to support these demands. However, the Ottoman administration suppressed these rebellions. The Ottoman Empire, which was defeated by the Russian Empire in the 1877–1878 Ottoman-Russian War, or the War of 93, in order not to make too many concessions against the Russians, rented the island to the British in return for an annual rent of $500,000 and support for the Ottomans. According to the agreement; Ottoman ownership in Cyprus would continue, but the administration would completely pass to the United Kingdom. The United Kingdom governed the island with high-ranking administrators called 'Commissars'. From this period on, the Greeks would always demand '*enosis*' from the British, and the Turks would fight against these demands. In the First World War that began in 1914, when the Ottomans entered the war on the side of Germany against the United Kingdom, the United Kingdom annexed Cyprus and appointed a governor to the island. According to Article 21 of the Treaty of Lausanne signed in 1923, the annexation of the island to the United Kingdom was recognised. In 1925, the island was declared a 'Cyprus Crown Colony' and the first consul of the Republic of Türkiye was appointed to the island.

In order to understand the current problem in Cyprus, it is necessary to know this history well. If you pay attention, the two major communities on the island, the Turks and the Greeks, lived together for 300 years but could not integrate. In other words, a single nation did not form in Cyprus. By 1974, according to official statistics, the number of families formed by Turkish-Greek marriages on the island did not exceed five. The Greeks' *enosis* rebellion began in 1931; as a result of the Greeks' uprising against the British administration, the British policy became harsher. The Turkish community declared that it was against '*enosis*'. In 1943, the Cyprus Island Turkish Minority Institution (KATAK) was established. However, finding the activities of KATAK inadequate, Fazıl Küçük left KATAK and founded the Cyprus National Turkish People's Party (KMTHP) on 23 April 1944. When the tendency towards the liquidation of colonies became widespread after World War II, Makarios III was elected as the leader of the Greek Orthodox Cypriots on 18 October 1950. In 1954, the Greek government applied to the United Nations for the right of nations to self-determination to be applied to Cyprus. This request, which Türkiye opposed, was rejected by the United Nations. The organisation called EOKA, founded by fanatic Greek nationalists who supported '*enosis*', began its activities on the island on 1 April 1955. Türkiye accepted to be a party to the problem for the first time and was represented at the meeting attended by the United Kingdom and Greece in London on 29 August. The Turkish Resistance Organisation (TMT) was founded on 15 November 1957. According to the MacMillan Plan, which came to the agenda in 1958, it was decided that Cyprus would remain within the British Commonwealth of Nations but would also have ties with Türkiye and Greece.

Following the London and Zurich Agreements of 1959, the Republic of Cyprus was established in 1960, and both communities were given sufficient representation in every institution according to their population. However, the President of the Republic of Cyprus, Makarios III, presented his constitutional amendment proposals consisting of thirteen articles on 30 November 1963. These included the unchangeable articles of the constitution, the elimination of the veto right of the Turkish Cypriot Vice President, the elimination of the principle of separate majorities in the House of Representatives and the adoption of decisions by simple majority, and the elimination of separate municipalities. US President John F. Kennedy suggested that Makarios abandon this, and Türkiye announced that it would not accept the amendments. Upon the rejection of the Turkish Cypriots, the Greek Cypriots launched an island-wide attack on the Turkish Cypriots on 21 December 1963. When Türkiye wanted to intervene in the island, it came across US President Lyndon Johnson's infamous Johnson Letter and understood that NATO and the United States had left it alone on this issue. Although the conflicts stopped for a while, the intention of the Greeks did not change. According to the Akritas Plan published in the *Patris* newspaper on 21 April 1966, the Turkish people would be destroyed, and the island would eventually be annexed to Greece. In 1967, the Greek attacks started again. 15,000 soldiers of the Greek Army were unofficially settled on the island. When the meeting held between the Prime Ministers of Türkiye and Greece to stop the policy of intimidation against the Turks did not yield any results, Türkiye announced that it would intervene militarily on the island. The Turkish Grand National Assembly authorised the government to intervene. Turkish planes began flying over Cyprus. The navy and landing forces took action. When the withdrawal of Greek troops was ensured through the mediation of the United States, Türkiye stopped the operation. When the Greek soldiers withdrew from three Turkish villages, they left twenty-four dead behind. Rauf Denktaş, who had been in Türkiye since 1964, secretly went to the island during this period. Denktaş was arrested by the Greeks but was extradited upon the objection of Türkiye and the United States.

After the EOKA-B led by Nikos Sampson launched a massacre of Turks on the island following the fascist coup against Makarios, the Bülent Ecevit government launched a military intervention on the island in 1974. With this operation, called the Cyprus Peace Operation, the regions where Turks lived in the north of the island were secured and the Turkish Federated State of Cyprus (KTFD) was established in 1975. On 15 November 1983, the assembly of the Turkish Federated State of Cyprus exercised its right to self-determination and declared the Turkish Republic of Northern Cyprus (KKTC-TRNC) with a unanimous decision. The founding President Rauf Denktaş read the declaration of the establishment of the TRNC. The establishment of the

Turkish Republic of Northern Cyprus drew the reaction of the Republic of Cyprus, Greece, and many other states, as well as the United Nations Security Council. The Security Council condemned the independence decision with a decision taken on 18 November. On 13 May 1984, the Security Council defined the declaration of the Turkish Republic of Northern Cyprus as a separatist movement with its resolution numbered 550. Since the Cyprus Conflict entered the world's agenda, many activities have been carried out with the aim of uniting the island, especially the work within the United Nations. However, no results have been obtained from these yet. One of these, the 2004 Annan Plan referendum, was not realised with the 'no' of the Greek Cypriots, despite the acceptance of the Turkish Cypriots. On 1 May 2004, the Greek Cypriot Administration of Southern Cyprus entered the European Union under the name of the Republic of Cyprus and representing the entire island.

According to Onur Öymen, the Cyprus case of the Republic of Türkiye is a just cause and derives its legitimacy from international agreements. The fact that the 1974 intervention was carried out against a fascist junta is also a positive feature for Türkiye. However, Türkiye cannot explain its just cause to the West because it remains outside the EU.

Kardak Crisis

The Kardak (Imia) Crisis is a crisis that broke out in January 1996 when a Turkish-flagged ship ran aground on the Kardak Rocks between Greece and Türkiye, resulting in disagreements between Turkish and Greek rescue teams, and brought the two countries to the brink of war. The crisis developed as follows; The Turkish ship named Figen Akat ran aground on the Kardak Rocks in the Aegean Sea on 25 December 1995. After this incident, Greece claimed that the shipwreck occurred in its territorial waters. Türkiye, on the other hand, stated that the islands in question belonged to it. After a while, the Greek Army landed soldiers on the islet in the east and erected the Greek flag there. Thereupon, the naval forces of the two countries began to deploy around the island. The Turkish Prime Minister of the time, Tansu Çiller, stated that the Turkish Armed Forces were ready for war by saying, '*That flag will come down, that soldier will go*' and requested that soldiers be landed on the island on the night of 30 January 1996. Turkish SAT and SAS commandos passed through the Greek Navy surrounding Eastern Kardak and landed on the second island (West Kardak) right next to it with a night operation and planted the Turkish flag. Later, with a phone call from US President Bill Clinton and the efforts of American delegate Richard Holbrooke and NATO Secretary-General Javier Solana, tensions were reduced, and the pre-crisis situation was restored.

During the Kardak Crisis, the Turkish state achieved significant diplomatic success with its determined stance. All the important political actors of the period, especially Prime Minister Tansu Çiller and Minister of Foreign Affairs Deniz Baykal, had a share in this success. After being quite tense during this period, Turkish-Greek relations were restored to peaceful ground after 1999 thanks to the İsmail Cem-Yorgo Papandreou duo.

Conclusion

In conclusion, Dr Onur Öymen's book *Unarmed Warfare: Diplomacy as an Art of Struggle* (*Silahsız Savaş: Bir Mücadele Sanatı Olarak Diplomasi*) is a very useful and instructive work that should be taught to students in this field.

İsmail Cem's 'Turkey in the New Century'

İsmail Cem (1940–2007) was a famous Turkish social democrat politician, journalist, and writer who also served as the Foreign Minister of Türkiye between the years 1997 and 2002. His book *Türkiye in the New Century* is a collection of Cem's speeches, interviews, comments, and memoirs about his tenure in office as the Foreign Minister. The book has certain aspects of an autobiography but also carries the qualities of an academic international relations book since Cem from the first-hand knows important details about Türkiye's foreign policy. The book is published from Rustem Publishing Company in 2000, but Cem revised the book every year and added new chapters.

In the book, Cem offers a new approach to Turkish Foreign Policy by criticising certain aspects of classical Turkish politics and diplomacy. Cem believes that Turkish Foreign Policy had been alienated from its cultural roots and historical past, and it must be replaced with a new understanding which was based on the awareness of Türkiye's rich identity and historical assets coming from the Ottoman State (Empire). He assumed that the end of Cold War, the phenomena of globalisation and the development in technology created many new opportunities in the foreign policy. He wanted Türkiye to be confident of herself, not ashamed of its past and bold and peace-seeking at the same time for the future. He criticised Turkish politicians' habitude of perceiving foreign policy in the form of idealistic prescriptions such as friendly countries or hostile countries and offered a more flexible and rational approach to problems. Cem defined foreign policy as '*a mathematical equation of a country's interests*'. He tried to create a convenient environment to be more flexible and active in foreign policy. Cem was not afraid to consider diversities in the country as richness and tried to overcome the forced alternatives. By forced alternatives he meant the concepts often presented as contradictions such as Islam-secularism or West-East. He thought that these dichotomies are exaggerated considering their relevance in both Türkiye's domestic and foreign politics. He defined Türkiye as both European (Western) and Asian (Eastern).

Cem, in the next chapters tried to explain his views and analyses on Turkish-American, Turkish-EU, Turkish-Eurasia, and Turkish-Middle East relations and offered a new rational and multi-dimensional approach to these relations in order to increase Türkiye's benefit. Especially he focused on Türkiye's full accession to EU and energy agreements made with Eurasian countries such as Baku-Tbilisi-Ceyhan Pipeline project. In his view, Türkiye should develop a rational and peace-seeking multi-dimensional relationship style with all important organisations and countries based on protecting and developing Türkiye's profit. Becoming totally engaged in EU or United States would be a big mistake in Cem's view. He later concentrated on international war against terrorism and the ways through which Türkiye could solve its own terrorism problem. The last parts of the book are separated to Turkish-Greece and Turkish-EU relations. Cem points out that with a liberal understanding in international politics, Türkiye could never be successful and would always give concessions to EU. He offers a more rational and interest-based approach to EU relations and claims that if this happens EU would approach Türkiye in a different manner. Cem also labelled AK Parti officials and diplomats as inexperienced and incompetent in foreign policy in the early 2000s.

İsmail Cem's *Türkiye in the New Century* is really a valuable book that points out the late reconstruction of Turkish Foreign Policy after the end of the Cold War during his tenure in office. Cem, who died a few years ago, will always be remembered with his contribution to Turkish Foreign Policy and his important books.

'Strategic Depth' by Ahmet Davutoğlu

Introduction

Prof. Ahmet Davutoğlu (1959–) is an influential Professor of Political Science and International Relations who has held very high-level positions in Türkiye, such as the Prime Ministry (2014–2016) and the Ministry of Foreign Affairs (2009–2014). Although much has been written about Davutoğlu in the Turkish media to date, and his ideology and strategic vision for Türkiye's future have been simplified and labelled with adjectives such as 'Islamist' or 'Neo-Ottomanist', comprehensive studies on his most important work, *Strategic Depth* (*Stratejik Derinlik*), which has been translated into many foreign languages, are extremely limited in number. In this article, I will summarise Davutoğlu's important work, which was first published in 2001 by Küre Publications and has gone through many editions to date, in general terms, and then evaluate it with a critical eye.

General Information About the Book

In the 'Preface' section of the 584-page book, which consists of three parts and twelve chapters, excluding the 'Introduction' and 'Conclusion' sections, Prof. Ahmet Davutoğlu, in summary, states that Türkiye is a country that is rapidly transforming after the Cold War, and therefore determines that determining Türkiye's strategic position – within this dynamic process – is a difficult task.

Summary of the Book

Introduction: In the 'Introduction' section of the book, Davutoğlu includes some methodological information and findings regarding International Relations studies. According to the author; in Social Science studies, which have five different dimensions such as (1) description (description), (2) explanation, (3) understanding, (4) meaning, and (5) orientation, evaluations should be made within a certain process, and strategic results should be reached only by establishing a logical connection between changes and transformations. Davutoğlu explains this situation, which he likens to the 'law of motion' in physics, with the example of the dissolution of the Soviet Union. According to the author, the dissolution of the Soviet Union, which was still considered a superpower in the late 1980s, in the early 1990s was due to the lack of such process analyses. Therefore, in strategic evaluations, processes and trends should be examined/researched as much as the current situation (picture). This inevitably necessitates an interdisciplinary approach.

In line with this approach, Davutoğlu explains in his book that he will not evaluate Türkiye as an ordinary nation-state founded in the early twentieth century; therefore, he will try to evaluate the power elements left from previous periods of the Republic of Türkiye, the successor of the Ottoman Empire, and the socio-cultural and socio-psychological effects of having governed these regions for a long time. Davutoğlu also emphasises that it is very difficult to make theoretical and strategic evaluations about Türkiye, due to the dynamic nature of the international system as well as Türkiye's. In fact, according to him, the reason why the analyses made about Türkiye reach very different points is that the dynamism of the international system outside and Türkiye's own dynamism inside sometimes force the country and intellectuals to change their shells and develop different reactions towards this. Davutoğlu thinks that in such situations, people and intellectuals can react in three different ways. The first is to adopt a static approach that limits internal dynamism, as societies and their intellectuals who do not trust their own dynamism do, and to try to reduce the effects of change originating from external dynamism. The counterpart of this approach in foreign policy today is isolationism, that is, introversion and a defensive state reflex. The second is the approach of leaving oneself to the flow of international dynamism without being able to accurately determine the power elements of one's own dynamism. This can be considered as an expression of a passive foreign policy approach in which globalising liberalism is absolutely adopted. The third approach, which Davutoğlu prefers, is to transform the elements of national dynamism into power elements within the elements of global dynamism. This can be formulated as a foreign policy attitude that is globalising but protects the power elements of the state and its national interests, as applied by major states today. According to the author, while the first approach suffers from self-confidence, the second approach lacks identity, these deficiencies are not seen in the third approach with the contribution of the History and Geography branches. In this way, the power elements are determined in advance and appropriate strategies are developed on how to develop them within global dynamism.

Part One: Conceptual and Historical Framework

Davutoğlu named the first section of the first part of the book titled 'Conceptual and Historical Framework' as 'Power Parameters and Strategic Planning'. In this section, the author first explains how to formulate the concept of 'power'. In this formula, fixed data (SV) constitute History (t), Geography (c), Population (n), and Culture (k), while potential data (PV) constitutes Economic Capacity (ek), Technological Capacity (tk), and Military Capacity (ak). Other elements to be added to this equation are Strategic Mentality (SZ), Strategic Planning (SP), and Political Will (Sİ). Therefore, we come across a 'power' formula as follows: G = (t + c + n + k) + (ek + tk + ak) x (SZ x SP x Sİ). The author then tries to detail these elements. In this context, according to the author, fixed data (History, Geography, Population, and Culture) cover elements that a country cannot change by its own will in the short and medium term. Such elements can only undergo comprehensive transformations in long-term processes with the change of the borders and systems of states. However, in the short and medium term, it is possible for the position of these elements within the specific weight of a state to increase or decrease. Potential data covers areas where states can make a difference with short- and medium-term planning and successful implementations, such as Economic Capacity, Technological Capacity, and Military Capacity. Apart from these two main elements, Davutoğlu also evaluates the concepts of Strategic Mentality, Strategic Planning, and Political Will as separate parameters and adds them to his equation. Strategic Mentality covers the consciousness that is the common product of the historical accumulation that contains a society's own cultural, psychological, religious and social value world, and the geographical life area where this accumulation is formed and reflected. Strategic Planning, on the other hand, is making a plan for the future within a rational structure with the potential data that is the content of the Strategic Mentality determined by fixed data. However, Political Will is also necessary to coordinate all these elements and manage them in harmony like a maestro. Even if all other data are suitable, it is not possible for a state to realise its strategic plans in the absence of Political Will.

In the second section titled 'Inadequacy of Strategic Theory and Its Results', the author analyses the deficiencies and inconsistencies resulting from the inadequacy of theory in the Turkish Foreign Policy making process. In this context, the first problem that the well-known author and statesman focus on is the institutional and structural background. Davutoğlu is of the opinion that all institutions, including the Ministry of Foreign Affairs of the Republic of Türkiye, are not sufficient in these matters. Davutoğlu particularly points out the resource and infrastructure deficiencies in this regard. Emphasising that there are similar problems in the General Staff, universities, think-tanks, the National Security Council, and other institutions, which are other important elements of the foreign policy making process, the academic emphasises that political parties can become functional in this process if they prepare consistent and comprehensive foreign policy proposals suitable for themselves and bring them to the TBMM and discuss them (this is a work written during the period when the parliamentary system was implemented). Davutoğlu also defends the view that Turkish academics have been inadequate in producing grand theories to date. The author, who emphasises that there are few successful examples in the world on this subject, mentions names such as Alfred Thayer Mahan, Nicholas J. Spykman, Karl Haushofer, Halford Mackinder, Samuel Huntington, Henry Kissinger, Zbigniew Brzezinski, and Francis Fukuyama as important theorists. Another important issue in terms of Turkish Foreign Policy is that the Ottoman Empire was struggling to preserve its own internal integrity in the nineteenth century, when other major states were developing imperial reflexes, and therefore its historical background was inadequate in this area. According to Davutoğlu, this situation led to the formation of a tradition in which defensive reflexes were dominant in Ottoman-Turkish Foreign Policy. In addition, the adoption of the 'absolute abandonment' strategy regarding the lost territories and the failure to put different power elements into play are also important deficiencies according to the author. In this context, the well-known author, academic, and statesman brings up political elements such as the abandonment of territories seen in imperial states, leaving a political elite close to them, using cultural characteristics (language, religion, etc.) and creating tactical manoeuvre areas by creating conflicts of interest between great powers. In this context, the author is of the opinion that the Ottoman Empire and later the Republic of Türkiye have not been able to make good use of the power elements originating from the past, especially in the Balkans, the Caucasus (Caucasus), and the Middle East. At this point, Davutoğlu brings up for discussion the concept of 'The Divided Self' by R. D. Laing, which has an important place in the field of psychology, and by adapting this theory, which deals with the alienation of a person from their own body and the subsequent creation of a false self, to social life, he concludes that societies should not alienate themselves from their own historical/local elements.

In the third and final section titled 'Historical Heritage and Türkiye's International Position', Davutoğlu attempts to analyse the international position of the Ottoman Empire and the Republic of Türkiye in a historical perspective. According to the author, the Ottoman Empire is the political structure of the only civilisation basin that has established direct dominance over Europe. This dominance accelerated the liquidation of Europe's feudal structure and forced European states to open up to the world by sea in order to find new trade routes. In addition, as in the period of Suleiman the Magnificent, the Ottoman Empire also evaluated intra-European political conflicts in its own diplomatic strategy. The Ottoman Empire was in a front position in the relationship between two different civilisation basins. This situation directly affected the Ottoman Empire and its political elite psychologically and politically. The Ottoman Empire, which lost territory in Europe for the first time with the Treaty of Karlowitz in 1699, now abandoned its strategy of advancing into Europe and turned to the strategy of regaining the lost lands and protecting its existing lands. For this reason, from this date onwards, the Ottoman Empire began to evaluate intra-European political conflicts more in the context of survival. With the Treaty of Küçük Kaynarca in 1774, the issue of minorities was also politicised and caused European states and Russia to gain power within the Ottoman Empire. The Crimean War of 1853–1856 was a manifestation of the policy that the Ottoman Empire implemented to maintain its balance of power policy among the great powers. During the reign of Abdulhamid II, this policy was supported by the politicisation of Muslim elements and the creation of a 'hinterland' based on Muslims with the ideologies of Islamism and Ottomanism. During the period of the Union and Progress (CUP), efforts were made to create a different hinterland with the policies of Turkism, and in addition, Islamism and Ottomanism continued to be used as a tactical tool against imperialist states. Approaching Germany, which was believed to be invincible, in order to weaken the British colonial system was also one of the most important policies of this period. However, major mistakes were made in strategic planning during this period; these also had tragic consequences (the events during the Armenian deportation, the Sarıkamış Disaster, etc.). In the Republican period, after the loss of a great empire, and under the pressure of international conditions, the reflexive defensive impulse approach became dominant in foreign policy, as it was in the last period of the Ottoman Empire. During this period, when Islamism and Turkism were held captive by Bolshevism, a strategy of building and defending a nation-state based on the National Oath borders was adopted. In addition, the view of being a part of the rising Western civilisation, rather than being opposed to it, was adopted. This approach, embodied in Atatürk's words '*Peace at home, peace in the world*', is the product of a defensive Realist paradigm. During this period, a defensive approach was adopted against Western imperialism, and the understanding of protecting and developing what was in place became the general paradigm. However, according to Davutoğlu, even during this period, the relations developed with powers such as Iran, Afghanistan, and Russia are important in terms of understanding Atatürk's vision of the future. In addition, during this period, a rejection of the Ottoman period was made, and a reform process was initiated towards becoming a Western nation-state. In this context, according to the author, Türkiye pursued a strategy of becoming a regional power under the security umbrella of the West during this period. In fact, becoming a member of NATO in the 1950s (1952) proves a more advanced stage of this strategy. In this way, it was aimed to protect Türkiye from the communist and Soviet Russian threats. Despite this, the problems experienced with Greece, which was under the same security umbrella

(Aegean Problems and increasingly the Cyprus Conflict), kept Türkiye's relations with the West away from absolute harmony. Especially after the Johnson Letter (1964), the trust in the West and the United States in Turkish Foreign Policy decreased relatively and the East and Russia began to be rediscovered. In addition, due to the loneliness experienced on the United Nations platform regarding the Cyprus Conflict, the negative aspects of the politics compatible with the West were understood and in order to develop relations with third-world countries and especially Islamic countries, it became one of the founding members of the Organisation of the Islamic Conference. After the Cold War, while Türkiye had not yet completely escaped the influence of the Cold War era politics, it suddenly found itself in the middle of global and regional scale growth. Davutoğlu, who evaluates the states in the world in four categories – superpowers, major states, regional powers, and minor states – states that during the Cold War, Türkiye preferred to be under the dominance of the United States, one of the two superpowers, as a regional power. When Türkiye had problems with the United States, the superpower (for example, the Cyprus Conflict), it was generally partially punished (1975–1978 arms embargo). Davutoğlu, who later began to examine Türkiye's political culture, first points out the tension between the society and the state due to the radical revolutionary transformation processes in the Ottoman-Turkish political culture as an important problem. The author emphasises that the political representatives of the Western culture, which Türkiye joined with the Ottoman modernisation and later the Republican revolution, have constantly shown a reflex of political exclusion – despite Türkiye's sacrifices – and thinks that European states have occasionally realised their mistakes, such as after the 1997 Luxembourg Summit and during the 1999 Helsinki Summit, but that this approach has generally continued until today. Ultimately, according to the author, the humiliation of a state that was the centre and leader of an important civilisation (Islam and Turkish-Islamic civilisation) in the past in the face of representatives of the Western culture it has been trying to integrate with in the last few centuries is one of the most important reasons for tension in society. The second important problem is that, in the process of integrating into Europe, Türkiye began to become alienated from its immediate geocultural environment in the Balkans, Caucasus, and Middle East. Although this did not create a serious problem during the Cold War, as a result of the development of relations with these regions from the 1990s onwards, Türkiye began to remember its power here again. At this point, Davutoğlu lists the four main trends that have been influential in Turkish Foreign Policy after the Cold War as follows: Neo-Ottomanism, Islamism, Radical Westernism, and Neo-Nationalism. Starting from the Turgut Özal era, the Neo-Ottomanism trend began to be influential in Türkiye. The main reasons for this are the effort to create a superordinate identity against the increasing micro-nationalisms (Kurdish and Turkish ethnic nationalisms) in domestic politics, the need for a new ideology in an environment where the state needed to be restructured, and the effort to create a new political culture and identity that would blend traditional and modern values. Islamism, which was first effective during the reign of Sultan Abdulhamid II, started to rise again due to the developments in line with the Clash of Civilizations thesis after the Cold War. With traumatic events such as the Bosnian events (Sbrenica Massacre), this movement started to find a response in society and became popular. Indeed, the period in which these events took place (1990s) corresponds to the years when the Islamist movement (Welfare Party) in Türkiye also started to rise rapidly and even came to power. Radical Westernism has always been effective in the Ottoman Empire and Türkiye since the Tanzimat period and was again adopted at the highest level – by the state – after the 28 February 1997 process. However, the reactions created by the close relations with the United States and Israel among the public and the attitude based on double standards towards Türkiye during the EU membership process made it very difficult for the Radical Westernist movement to be politically successful in the country; indeed, except for extraordinary periods (military coups and interim regime periods), the parties representing this movement have not been able to achieve great political success. New Nationalism, on the other hand, is a movement that came to the fore due to the social anger created by the PKK terrorism and the Turkic world that Türkiye virtually rediscovered after the Cold War. The success of the MHP after the capture of PKK leader Abdullah Öcalan in the 1999 elections was an important sign that this movement could develop. According to Davutoğlu, Türkiye in the 2000s was a period when Türkiye began to better understand its 'bridge' position within all these ideological contradictions/alternatives. While being a part of different cultural families (Western, Islamic, Turkic world, etc.) leads some societies to identity crisis, for Türkiye this has been a source of wealth and power. Politically, a design that is suitable for this multicultural structure of Türkiye is required rather than belonging to a single movement and ideology.

Part Two: Theoretical Framework: Gradual Strategy and Basin Policies

The second part of the book titled 'Theoretical Framework: Gradual Strategy and Basin Policies' is divided into four different sections by Prof. Ahmet Davutoğlu. In the first section titled 'Geopolitical Theories: Post-Cold War Period and Türkiye', the author first explains the perception of time-space and the impact of geography on the formation of civilisations with reference to Fernand Braudel's words '*Maps tell the true story*.' In this context, according to the author, the emergence of Islamic civilisation was also affected by geographical conditions. Similarly, mercantilism, which reflects the pre-capitalist period in the Western world, should be evaluated as a product of new conditions that emerged directly due to geographical discoveries. Therefore, geopolitical theories should be created by taking geographical conditions into consideration. According to the author, geopolitical theories are also produced by states to realise their own strategic goals and provide political legitimacy for the expansionist policies of states in the past. For example, the theory of '*lebensraum*' (living space) developed by Friedrich Ratzel, inspired by Charles Darwin, was later used by Western imperialist states as a justification for their own expansionist policies. Ratzel, who saw the state as a living organism, wrote that states, like every organism, needed to be nourished and that this nourishment could only be achieved through the annexation of new lands. According to him, states that were helpless in the fight for nourishment were doomed to perish. Ratzel and his follower Rudolf Kjellén prepared the theoretical groundwork for the land, sea and air geopolitics that would later be developed with their writings. In this context, the first important theory on land geopolitics was developed by Halford Mackinder. Mackinder divided geography into three areas: the heartland, the inner belt and the outer belt. According to the land domination theory, first of all, an axis area protected against threats from the sea should be taken under control. The most suitable region for these conditions is Eurasia. Karl Haushofer also evaluated geopolitics as a branch of science that encompassed all human and natural sciences and tried to use the theory of '*lebensraum*' as a shield against Nazi expansionism. Nicholas J. Spykman, who thought that

Mackinder gave excessive importance to the 'heartland', that is, the axis area, claimed that the real potential area of dominance was in the 'rimland', that is, the border belt line consisting of Western Europe-Türkiye-Iraq-Pakistan-Afghanistan-India-China-Korea-Eastern Siberia.

Based on this view, Spykman advised the United States to follow a policy that would prevent another state from dominating this zone, thus becoming the leading theorist of American foreign policy that took shape after World War II with initiatives such as NATO-CENTO. The maritime geopolitics approach developed by the famous strategist Alfred Mahan (Alfred Thayer Mahan) was based on a dominance strategy that developed from the zones to the centre and from the seas to the lands. In this context, Mahan advised the American state to surround Russia and keep China under control. Mahan, who also advised the American administration during the Theodor Roosevelt era, suggested two basic strategic priorities: (1) fighting the war in seas far from the United States and (2) establishing a chain of alliances that would provide access to developments in Eurasia. Alexander P. De Seversky, who developed the theory of aerial geopolitics, divided the world into two zones of dominance, indicating the spheres of influence of the United States and Soviet Russia, in accordance with the conditions of the Cold War period. Seversky also wrote that the geopolitical air superiority to be achieved in the 'decision' region outside of these two areas would be decisive. Saul Cohen, who developed Spykman's 'rimland' theory, developed a new approach based on the contradiction and balance between 'trade-based naval power' and 'Eurasian continental power'. As these theories also indicate, geography is a fixed factor for a country. However, the diplomatic dimension of geopolitics determined by geography can change/be reinterpreted according to international balances of power. In this context, Türkiye is at the centre of transition regions. These are both advantages and risks if not used correctly for Turkish Foreign Policy. In this context, Davutoğlu evaluates Türkiye's geopolitics in three main regions:

1. Near Land Basin: Balkans-Middle East-Caucasus.
2. Near Ocean Basin: Black Sea-Adriatic-Eastern Mediterranean-Red Sea-Gulf-Caspian Sea.
3. Near Continental Basin: Europe-North Africa-South Asia-Central and East Asia.

In the second section titled 'Near Land Basin: Balkans-Middle East-Caucasus', Davutoğlu analyses Türkiye's immediate surroundings as the first element of Türkiye's geopolitics. The characteristic of these three regions is that they have direct land borders with Türkiye. These regions are evaluated by the author as Türkiye's natural spheres of influence, and it is argued that these regions should not be neglected due to the close relations developed with the Western alliance. According to Davutoğlu, having influence in these regions is also important in terms of Türkiye's ability to ensure its internal integrity. Among these three regions, the Balkan geography is of great importance in terms of the elimination of the Ottoman Empire from Europe at the beginning of the twentieth century. While the project of purging this geography of Turks and Muslims was pursued by Western countries at the beginning of the century, stability in the region could not be achieved after this period. According to Davutoğlu, Türkiye's fundamental power element in this region is the Muslim communities that are the remnants of the Ottoman Empire. Accordingly, while Bosnia and Herzegovina, which have a large Muslim population and Albania are pivot countries for Türkiye, Bulgaria, Greece, Macedonia, Kosovo, and Romania, which have a Turkish-Muslim population, are other important states in the region. According to the author, in order to be effective in this region, Türkiye must obtain the status of protector of the rights of the Muslim population and make it permanent. Because the recent Cyprus Peace Operation (1974) could only be carried out thanks to a regional right/guarantee/status. In order to obtain such a right/guarantee/status, Türkiye must follow an active Balkans policy. The security of the Balkans, as a nearby geography, is also important for Türkiye's internal and external security. When an evaluation is made in terms of the Caucasus or the Caucasus region, Davutoğlu points out 3 important levels: (1) international global changes and their effects on the region, (2) the political plane among the countries in the region, and (3) the intra-regional balances developing in line with the ethnic and religious conflicts of the region. When evaluated in the first level; after the Cold War, the period of only Russian influence in this region has ended and countries such as the United States, United Kingdom (Britain), Germany, and Japan have also started to have more or less influence on regional policies. When looked at from the second level; while the rapprochement between Russia and Armenia and Türkiye and Azerbaijan is remarkable, there are also developments in Iran-Armenia and Türkiye-Georgia relations. On the third level, the main conflicts are the Azeri-Armenian conflict in the region and the Russian-Chechen struggle in the North Caucasus. Of these conflicts, the Azeri-Armenian conflict is of particular interest to Türkiye. Indeed, according to the author, the fact that one-fifth of Azerbaijani territory was under Armenian occupation was a very important (even the most important) strategic loss for Türkiye. Because, according to the author, Azerbaijan is Türkiye's most important strategic partner in the region. In this context, Davutoğlu thinks that making Albania a regional power in the Balkans and Azerbaijan a regional power in the Caucasus will have positive results for Türkiye. The third region that inevitably affects Turkish Foreign Policy is the Middle East. Like other regions, the Middle East was forgotten in Türkiye due to financial inadequacies and international political dynamics during the early Republic and Cold War periods, and Türkiye's influence in these regions could not be sufficiently evaluated. This region, which remained under Ottoman rule for many years, later came to be directed by Western imperialism. In line with the 'Eastern Question' approach, countries such as Britain, France, and Russia reduced the Ottoman influence in the region, and the order they tried to establish after the Ottomans were eliminated from the region was also not stable. During the Cold War, Russia's strategy of reaching the warm seas and the US containment strategy were effective in the region. Accordingly, new developments such as (1) ideological and geocultural polarisation in the region, (2) oil-centred geoeconomic structuring, (3) geopolitical divisions in line with global conflicts, and (4) increasing intra-regional cultural and political conflict areas emerged after the establishment of Israel. In addition, after the Islamic Revolution in Iran (1979) and the Gulf War, the region began to become a region where Samıel Huntington's 'Clash of Civilizations' thesis was put into practice.

In the third section titled 'Nearby Sea Basin: Black Sea, Eastern Mediterranean, Gulf, Caspian Sea', the author Prof. Ahmet Davutoğlu first criticises Türkiye's failure to develop a long-term and coordinated sea and waterways strategy. However, since it is a peninsula, according to the author, Türkiye's sea and waterways strategy is critical. Because a country on the Anatolia-Balkan axis can only ensure its security in this way. Indeed, the basis of the Ottoman Empire's past success was its dominance over the Aegean, Mediterranean and Black Sea. In fact, the decline of the Ottoman Empire was a situation that developed in parallel with the decrease in its influence over these seas. The burning of the Ottoman fleet by the Russians, French, and British in Navarino in 1827 was a turning point in this sense. The Ottoman Empire's alliance with Germany, a land-based military power like itself, in World War I was also insufficient in terms of complementarity. Because countries like France and Britain, which were against the Ottoman Empire, were maritime empires. Although a gain was made in this regard with the Montreux Straits Convention during the Republic period, the great weakness in naval power and dominance continued for a long time. The loss of the Dodecanese (Twelve) Islands to Greece was a very unfortunate development in this respect. Today, while the Straits are an important strategic advantage for Türkiye against Russia, the Aegean Islands are also an important strategic trump card for Greece against Türkiye. During the Cold War, in the competition between Soviet Russia, a typical land-based state, and the United States, which developed a sea-centred strategy, Türkiye had to become an ally of the United States due to the threatening demands coming from the Soviets. According to the author, the two great and critical mistakes of the Soviet Union during the Cold War were first, pushing Türkiye completely to the opposite bloc due to the threats regarding the Straits, and second, the invasion of Afghanistan. Due to these mistakes, the Soviet Empire collapsed in the early 1990s. Türkiye, on the other hand, was able to develop very limited strategies for the near-sea basin within the framework of the moulds drawn for it by the West during the Cold War and had to integrate/adapt itself to the strategies drawn on the US-NATO axis. Although it is important that certain sensitivity was formed on the Cyprus issue during these periods, a comprehensive strategy for the Eastern Mediterranean could not be developed. After the Cold War, Türkiye caught a suitable conjuncture to develop its policies and strategies for the near-sea basin. To begin with the Black Sea; since Türkiye is surrounded by countries in the communist bloc such as the USSR, Romania, and Bulgaria, it initially experienced a '*psychology of being surrounded*'. For this reason, the share of the Black Sea and Danube waterway in Türkiye's trade (6 per cent in exports, 7 per cent in imports) and maritime transportation (1 per cent) remained very limited. Although the longest coastline is on the Black Sea, the use of the Black Sea was also inadequate in terms of loading and unloading capacity. After the Cold War, the communist ties between the three countries in the region dissolved; moreover, new actors such as Ukraine and Georgia emerged. Therefore, a suitable conjuncture was created for Türkiye; thanks to this, Türkiye-Georgia and Türkiye-Ukraine relations also began to develop. According to Davutoğlu, the establishment of the Black Sea Economic Cooperation Organisation (BSEC) is also an important and positive development. In this context, Davutoğlu proposes a comprehensive strategy that integrates military and economic interests in the region to Ankara in the new period. As a concrete element of this strategy, he suggests connecting the Constanta-Trabzon line with the Dnieper, Dniester, Volga, and Don rivers. Another suggestion is to provide the economic routes and trade network in this region through Türkiye in the vast geography between East Asia and Central Europe. Later, the author evaluates the Straits from a geopolitical perspective and states that the Bosphorus and Dardanelles Straits, which separate Asia and Europe and connect the Black Sea to the Mediterranean, are one of the most important passages in the world – perhaps the first – along with the Suez Canal, Bab al-Mandeb Strait, Hormuz Strait, Gibraltar Strait, Malacca Strait, Sunda and Lombok Passages (Lombok Strait), and Panama Canal. The reason for this is that such passages play a key role in global trade and raw material flow, geoeconomic transfer lines, intercontinental interaction zones and global and regional security strategies. Historical data also confirms this. Indeed, the rise of the Ottoman Empire and its transformation into an Empire were made possible by the conquest of İstanbul and the control of the Straits. The granting of free passage to Russian merchant ships through the Treaty of Küçük Kaynarca in 1774 indicates the beginning of a new era. In 1798, the Russians obtained the same right for their warships – with the Treaty of İstanbul. In this context, according to Davutoğlu, the restoration of sovereignty over the Straits with the Treaty of Montreux during the Republic period is a considerable achievement and this treaty was also a very important and historical step in terms of eliminating the weaknesses of the Treaty of Lausanne. Thanks to this, Russian pressure on the Straits was reduced; however, with Stalin's demands, the Straits soon became a problem in Turkish-Russian relations again. According to the author, Türkiye should constantly strive to increase its control and authority in the Straits. In addition, the fact that Türkiye's most important economic centres, such as İstanbul and the Marmara Region, are located here makes the Straits even more important in terms of security. Therefore, the Straits are Türkiye's most important strategic element. The Aegean and Cyprus, which form the Eastern Mediterranean basin, are another important area. According to the author, it is not possible for a Türkiye that is isolated from the Aegean and surrounded by the Greek Cypriot administration to be effective in the Eastern Mediterranean. In particular, the fact that the Aegean Islands are under the control of Greece is a great disadvantage for Türkiye. If the 12-mile territorial waters concept is accepted, Türkiye will no longer be able to access the Aegean Sea. Even if the 6-mile territorial waters concept is accepted, Greece will control 35 per cent of the Aegean and Türkiye will only control 8.8 per cent. Therefore, according to the author, Türkiye should not make any more concessions to Greece in the Aegean. Similarly, according to Davutoğlu, Cyprus is a vital issue for Türkiye. In this sense, two important factors play a role for Türkiye. The first is the issue of ensuring the security of the Turkish Cypriots, who are a Turkish and Muslim community. The second is the great geopolitical importance of Cyprus. Therefore, according to the author, even if there is not a single Turk or Muslim in Cyprus, Cyprus should still be important in terms of Turkish Foreign Policy. Similarly, the Persian Gulf and the Indian Basin and the Caspian Basin should be evaluated as other important near-sea basin regions of Turkish Foreign Policy.

In the fourth and final section titled 'Near Continental Basin: Europe, North Africa, South Asia, Central and East Asia', the academic examines Turkish Foreign Policy and Turkish geopolitics in the context of near continental basins and the examples of Europe, North Africa, South Asia and, Central and East Asia. Türkiye is a country with extremely diversified natural geography conditions that can establish multiple continental connections at the same time and is in direct contact with many sea and waterway basins. For example, the Balkans connection makes Türkiye a direct Eastern European country, while the Middle East connection makes it a Western Asian country. Türkiye, which can intervene in the waterways of Eastern Europe and the Eurasian steppes via the Caucasus, can also be included in the balances of the Caspian and Central Asia via the Caucasus, and Southwest Asia and North Africa via the Eastern Mediterranean. The special location of the Straits also adds strength to Türkiye in this context. The straits constitute the nodal point of the passageways in the north-south and east-west directions of the Eurasian mainland. Starting from the European continent; Türkiye is a direct and natural part of Europe. In this context, the author thinks that it is wrong to reduce Türkiye-Europe relations to Türkiye-European Union (EU) relations. Europe, which achieved its unity after the Cold War, is still one of the most important regions for Türkiye today. The author evaluates Türkiye's position within the European continental basin under five headings. First of all, Türkiye is both a Balkan and an Eastern European country with its connection to Eastern Thrace. Secondly, due to its connection to the Black Sea, Türkiye falls within the parameters of north-eastern steppe Europe. Thirdly, due to its Aegean and Eastern Mediterranean coasts, Türkiye should also be evaluated as a Southern European country. Fourthly, thanks to the political and economic ties it established during the Cold War, Türkiye also carries the identity of a Western European country. Fifthly and finally, Türkiye has a special and indispensable position within the continental connections of Europe with Asia in the east-west direction and with Africa in the north-south direction. When evaluated in the context of Asia, Türkiye is again a very important country; However, the geopolitical and geocultural importance of Asia for Türkiye has not been sufficiently examined to date. However, Asia is the centre of the 'Great Game' between the United States, Russia, and other great powers. The fact that Türkiye has been a Western-oriented country since the Ottoman Tanzimat period has been a factor in the failure to sufficiently recognise the importance of Asia. However, a renewed interest in this region has been noticed in the post-Cold War period. The African continent is one of the most neglected elements of Turkish Foreign Policy. However, the Ottoman Empire was also an African country. During the Republican period, the anti-imperialist and anti-colonialist character of the War of Independence created sympathy for Türkiye in Africa and inspired many political movements in this continent. However, during the Cold War period, Türkiye's ties with this continent almost came to a breaking point. Interestingly, Türkiye's position within the Western bloc against Soviet threats left Türkiye on the side of Western-centred colonialist politics, which contradicts its own historical stance. However, since the conditions of the Cold War have disappeared today, suitable conditions have emerged for Türkiye to review and re-establish its Africa policy. The Atlantic, Steppes, North Africa, and Western Asia, which the author lists as intercontinental interaction zones, are other regions that should be evaluated in Turkish geopolitical thought.

Part Three: Application Areas: Strategic Tools and Regional Policies

The author named the third and final part of the book 'Application Areas: Strategic Tools and Regional Policies'. This part is divided into five different sections. In the first section titled 'Türkiye's Strategic Connections and Foreign Policy Tools', the author takes stock of Türkiye's foreign policy alliances and platforms that it can use to turn geopolitical elements into an advantage in foreign policy. While Türkiye's NATO and OIC memberships and the close relations it developed with the EU were important gains as a remnant of the Cold War period, new platforms such as the ECO, BSEC, D-8, and Turkic world Summits were added to these structures after the Cold War period. If we start with NATO, which can be considered the most important of these; first of all, it is necessary to analyse how NATO, which was established against the expansion of the USSR and communism, entered a transformation process after the collapse of the Soviet Union. This transformation, which started with the 1991 Rome Summit, continued with the Kosovo Operation. Relations with NATO are also important in the context of Türkiye-US relations, Türkiye-EU relations, and Eurasia policy and Türkiye-Russia relations. To be more specific; according to Davutoğlu, Türkiye, as a neighbour of Russia, which was a NATO member in the 2000s but not a member of the EU, will be affected by all these parameters in the context of its relations with NATO and will have the capacity to affect all these parameters. According to the author, NATO's expansion towards Eastern Europe may have two different effects on Türkiye. In the first approach, this situation may contribute to the development of Türkiye's relations with Eastern European countries and the increase of Türkiye's regional power. The second possibility is that Türkiye will lose value in terms of NATO and the United States due to the entry of these countries into NATO and their closeness to Russia. Another important organisation is the Organisation for Security and Co-operation in Europe. This organisation, which emerged in the 1970s (1975 Helsinki Summit) after the resistance of the United States and NATO was broken, was also beneficial in terms of opening up room for manoeuvre in foreign policy for Türkiye, which had problems with the United States regarding the Cyprus Conflict after the Johnson Letter. The Soviet Union also provided a similar benefit at that time. The OSCE, which became an important organisation with a permanent secretariat with the 1994 Budapest

Summit, also affects Türkiye in terms of domestic political parameters in terms of its importance to issues such as democracy and human rights. The third important organisation, the OIC (Organisation of Islamic Cooperation), seems to gain even more importance in the twenty-first century. The reason for this is that the religion of Islam and Muslim identity have started to become a reality and subject from the interior of Europe to Far East and the new period of its influence is not limited to the Middle East and North Africa. According to the author, this situation provides Türkiye with some advantages for a more successful and aggressive foreign policy. Because the Islamic identity and religion are the only power that can resist the Russian/ Slavic influence in the Eurasian region. The fact that Muslim societies could not be completely assimilated during the Cold War period shows the power of the Islamic religion and culture. In addition, Islam has become the second largest religion in many countries in the Western world. For this reason, the Islamic identity that Muslim communities adopt as a requirement of their religion can be perceived as a challenge by Western states. The orientation towards the OIC and the Islamic world in Turkish Foreign Policy has been brought to the agenda as a reaction during the period of conflicts with the United States and the EU. However, in this new period, Türkiye should adopt an understanding based on self-confidence in its relations with both the West and the East and should continuously develop its relations in a way that is appropriate for its 'bridge' role. In this context, another important international organisation is the Economic Cooperation Organisation (ECO). The Black Sea Economic Cooperation Organisation (BSEC) will also be more important in the new period. D-8 is also a very unique foreign policy initiative of Türkiye that is not often brought to the agenda in international politics. Finally, new organisations targeting the Turkic world may also provide gains for Turkish Foreign Policy in the post-Cold War period.

In the second section titled 'Strategic Transformation and the Balkans', the author examines the transformation in the Balkans. The Balkans were affected by the characteristics of the bipolar system during the Cold War. When this period ended, the complex ethnic structure and problems of the region became the main issue of regional politics. After the dissolution of Yugoslavia, according to the author, Serbia turned to Russia-centred policies, while Bulgaria and Romania adopted a more independent foreign policy.

In this new period, Greece turned to the policy of controlling Albania and Macedonia together with Serbia. Slovenia, and Croatia, on the other hand, entered the sphere of influence of Italy and Germany and entered the path of becoming a Western European state. In addition, despite the Dayton Agreement, stability and order have not yet been fully established in Bosnia and Herzegovina. Another important and historical event that changed the dynamics in the region, apart from the Bosnian War, is the Kosovo Operation. The two main elements of Türkiye's policy in the region are the Bosnians and Albanians. These two peoples, who have been able to preserve their Islamic-Ottoman culture, should also be at the forefront of Türkiye's regional policy. According to the author, Türkiye's permanent influence in the region can only be achieved in this way. However, Türkiye must definitely pay attention to regional balances when forming this policy. The two basic instruments that Türkiye can use in its Balkan policy are (1) NATO membership and NATO policies – which the author calls a systemic tool, (2) Organisation of Islamic Cooperation (OIC) membership and policies – which the author defines as an alternative tool.

In the third section titled 'Middle East: The Key to Economic-Political and Strategic Balances', the author examines Türkiye's Middle East policies. The fundamental difference between the Middle East and other geographical regions is some geocultural characteristics brought about by its historical depth. At this point, Davutoğlu particularly draws attention to the issue of Jerusalem and emphasises that this historical city is the common centre of three major religions. In this context, the presence and influence of Israel in the region is also a very important dynamic. Lebanon, the only state based on Christian sovereignty, is another important state that the author refers to at this point. The emergence of micro-nationalisms and tribal/clan identities along with national identities during the process of establishing a nation-state in the region has further complicated regional dynamics. The most important geoeconomic factor in the region is undoubtedly oil resources and their impact on politics. Another important factor is water resources and their sharing. Davutoğlu then explains in detail the regional policies and goals of the United States and Israel. Later, the academic, who evaluated Türkiye's regional policies, thinks that Türkiye should be able to keep up with the pulse of the Arab world and establish close relations with Arab states and societies.

The aim of such a policy should not be ideological-religious sensitivities, but to establish a successful foreign policy. Getting rid of generalist and reductionist approaches towards Arab societies would also be a very important and useful approach at this point, according to the author. The author also highlights relations with Iran as an important and necessary element at this point. Davutoğlu, who then focuses on Türkiye-Israel relations, emphasises that Türkiye's position in the Western camp on a global scale has led to the development of its relations with Israel, and that on a regional scale, Israel has established close co-operation with Türkiye within the context of its strategy to develop close relations with non-Arab elements (external environment strategy or periphery pact). Israel has also implemented a policy of provoking conflicts between Arabs in order to prevent Arab unity. Despite its close relations with Türkiye, Israel is trying to develop close relations in different areas with countries such as the Greek Cypriot Administration of Southern Cyprus and Greece, a point Davutoğlu draws attention to. Another important dynamic in the region is the Kurdish factor. The author analyses all these dynamics in detail in his book.

In the fourth chapter titled 'Central Asia Policy in the Eurasian Power Equation' and the fifth chapter titled 'European Union: Analysis of a Multidimensional and Multi-Level Relationship', he similarly examines the policies of Eurasia/Central Asia and the European Union. In these chapters, he explains Türkiye's power elements and historical developments along with regional dynamics.

Conclusion

In the 'Conclusion' section of the book, Prof. Ahmet Davutoğlu states that Türkiye has significant regional power potential in terms of the parameters he examined and summarises some of the results he reached in his research. In this context, Davutoğlu rejects both approaches that consider Türkiye as a 'pivotal state' and a 'torn country' after the Cold War. In addition, according to the author, due to its geographical conditions and geopolitical position, Türkiye is a state that can only grow and become stronger by globalising. According to the author, the fact that Türkiye is not an ordinary nation-state as a remnant of an Empire is also an important advantage at this point. Because

Davutoğlu sees Türkiye's opening up to the outside world as inevitable; however, he says that there are discussions on what mentality, institutions, tools and what kind of psychology this will be done with. The author also thinks that in order not to be passive in history, it is necessary to dominate time and space and that Türkiye has all the potential to achieve this.

Evaluation of the Book

If we are to evaluate the book with a critical eye; it should be noted that this work, written by Prof. Ahmet Davutoğlu in the early 2000s, before he was yet engaged in active politics, is a pioneering book in terms of introducing the geopolitics school to Turkish Foreign Policy. Geopolitics, which is still in its infancy in our country, is a very comprehensive multidisciplinary branch of science that has developed in the United States, Russia, and some European countries within the common cluster of all Social Sciences and Humanities disciplines such as History and Geography. Although geopolitics is the most important science that directs the long-term grand strategies of states and their security units, the number of books and studies written in this field in Türkiye is extremely limited. Therefore, Davutoğlu's work deserves praise primarily as one of the first studies in this field. However, a criticism that can be made about the book is that Davutoğlu's analysis is mostly limited to Türkiye's power elements, since geopolitics is a field that encompasses all states and all their elements by its nature. However, in order to understand the attitudes of the states that are neighbours to Türkiye and have close relations with Türkiye, their geopolitical elements should also be evaluated in such works. In particular, the Russian Federation, a large state neighbouring Türkiye, and its geopolitical characteristics and approaches should be evaluated at the forefront of factors that can directly affect Türkiye in such a work. Mr Davutoğlu's approach on this issue has also emerged as a problem in Türkiye's Syria policy, and after Russia's intervention in Syria in 2015, Türkiye's Syria policy has faced a negative picture. Another deficiency is that Türkiye's internal elements (natural resources, underground resources, climate and vegetation characteristics, and areas where economic activities are concentrated, etc.) have not been sufficiently evaluated in this work. Again, the fact that maps and visual materials are not included in the book has made it difficult to understand the geopolitical theories and ideas discussed in the work. Therefore, after serving for years at various levels of government, it would be appropriate to say that if Mr Davutoğlu were to write a new edition of this book in the coming years, it would be much more comprehensive and better. Finally, it should be emphasised that the author of this book, Prof. Ahmet Davutoğlu, is a very important scientist, a serious intellectual, and an important statesman who is definitely distant from radical ideologies.

Theoretical Framework of Turkish Foreign Policy and the Concept of 'OBD' According to Baskin Oran

Prof. Baskın Oran (1945–) is an intellectual and an experienced social scientist who worked as a faculty member for many years in the Department of International Relations of the Faculty of Political Sciences of Ankara University, known as Mülkiye for short. Oran, with his line that differed greatly from the official view on the Armenian issue and the definition of Turkishness, went through difficult times politically from time to time and made an unlucky attempt at a political career by failing to be elected by a narrow margin from the 2nd district of İstanbul in the 2007 general elections, where he ran as an independent candidate. One of Baskın Oran's most important contributions to science in Türkiye was his 3-volume work *Turkish Foreign Policy* (*Türk Dış Politikası*), which he edited. This article will summarise the section titled 'Theoretical Framework of Turkish Foreign Policy' in the first volume of this 3-volume book.

According to Prof. Baskın Oran; Despite the sharp ruptures and transformations experienced in many areas during the transition from the Ottoman Empire to the Republic of Türkiye, some issues in Turkish Foreign Policy have been institutionalised and have formed a strong tradition that has continued to this day without breaking.

The first of these is the 'Cultural Dimension'. According to Oran, Türkiye, the successor of the Ottoman Empire, has multifaceted connections and cultures. These can be roughly classified as Asia, the Middle East/Islam, and the West.

Asia: Türkiye, whose lands are mostly located in the Asian continent, still bears traces of its Asian local culture despite all modernisation/Westernisation efforts, and the effects of this can be seen in foreign policy. From the strong desire for leadership that directs politics and the tendency to eliminate rivals, to the dominance of kebabs and pide, which are seen in the culinary culture and bear traces of nomadic societies, and to reactions such as tension and resentment, which are sociological events, it is not that difficult to find the 'Eastern' influence in Turkish society and the state system. The effects of this situation can be seen even in foreign policy; behavioural patterns such as occasionally withdrawing from the table and acting out of anger have even spread to Türkiye's state administration.

Islam/Middle East: Since 98 per cent of the population in Türkiye is Muslim and Türkiye is located right next to the Middle East, the Middle East/Islamic influence in Türkiye is undeniable. Therefore, oppression of Muslim peoples causes great reactions in Turkish society and creates a negative view towards Russia, which has historically conquered the Muslim geography. In addition, despite the internalisation of the Muslim identity, Turks have a clear idea that they are not Arabs, and the people do not consider their country as a Middle Eastern state.

West: Although only 3 per cent of Türkiye's land is located in Europe, the European/Western influence in Türkiye is very intense. Türkiye, along with Israel, is the most democratic and secular state in the Middle East. In terms of secular practices, Türkiye was seen as the country that implemented the strictest regulations until recently. The Republican revolution carried out by Atatürk radically modernised Türkiye and Turkish society on the basis of the Ottoman Westernisation legacy. For this reason, a dual cultural structure emerged in Türkiye – especially felt more intensely by the elite and the ordinary people. Another important issue is that, while the secular/elite segments of Türkiye, in particular, consider themselves Western, the Western world does not see Türkiye as Western. The hesitations and syntheses between Western and Eastern (Islamic) cultures also make Türkiye a unique country.

The second important element that forms the theoretical framework of Turkish Foreign Policy is the 'Historical Dimension'. Although the Republic of Türkiye was founded by destroying the Ottoman Empire, it has actually continued many elements specific to this state. The Ottoman Empire is undoubtedly a European state. The vast majority of Ottoman Viziers – until the Stagnation Period – were of Rumelian, i.e. European origin. Especially in the period immediately after the conquest of İstanbul, Grand Viziers of

Anatolian origin are rarely seen; for example, seven of the nine Grand Viziers of Suleiman the Magnificent were of Christian origin. The Ottoman Empire has been an inseparable part of the European balance of power system for centuries. Moreover, although the sharia order seems to have been dominant in the Ottoman Empire, in fact the worldly authority of the Sultan was more important in the system. Although the conformity of the Sultan's decrees to sharia was determined by a fatwa issued by the Sheikh al-Islam, the head of the religion; however, this highest-ranking cleric was a civil servant appointed and brought by the Sultan and therefore could be dismissed. Moreover, non-Muslims constituted a large segment of the society. It is possible to see many elements in Turkish Foreign Policy that are the continuation of the relations and traditions that were institutionalised during the Ottoman period. The most obvious example of this is that religion is under state control through the Presidency of Religious Affairs (the concept of secularism). A large part of the foreign relations established with other countries were also shaped by Ottoman accumulation. According to Oran, the most important difference between the two states is that the task given to Ottoman diplomacy was to maintain a multi-national and multi-religious/sectarian empire, while the task given to Turkish diplomacy was to maintain the nation-state.

The third important element that constitutes the theoretical framework of Turkish Foreign Policy is the 'Strategic Dimension'. It would be correct to examine this dimension in three contexts: Geographic Factor, Regional Security Circles, and World Power Axes.

Geographic Factor: This factor has many positive and negative effects on Türkiye. Due to its geopolitical and geostrategic location, Türkiye is located between the West and the East and is in the middle of many important geographies (Balkans, Caucasus, Middle East, North Africa, Black Sea). This location gives Türkiye a very special position. In fact, this situation is used as an advantage in terms of energy policies and transportation projects today. However, the fact that this region is established on the East-West migration line and is an unstable geography also becomes a source of great risks for Türkiye. It is not a coincidence that Türkiye is one of the countries where terrorist incidents occur most frequently and hosts the largest immigrant population in the world. Türkiye's neighbours are also an inseparable part of its geography and are the source of many problems for Türkiye. Iran, Iraq, Syria, Armenia, Greece, Bulgaria, and even Cyprus and Russia, which are neighbours by sea, are neighbours with whom Türkiye has had more or less problems. Azerbaijan (due to Nakhchivan) and Georgia, as well as Romania and Ukraine, which are neighbours by sea, are the only neighbours with whom Türkiye has had almost no problem-free relations to date. Regardless of who is at fault, Türkiye's serious problems with many of its neighbours have led Türkiye to seek different alliances in the past. The threat of Soviet Russia, which was especially prevalent during the Cold War, still partially continues today despite the collapse of communism due to Russia's expansionist policies. Türkiye's most important geographical feature is that it has control of the Straits. The Straits are a region that is extremely difficult to defend and is very important not only for Türkiye's security but also for international security. For this reason, the 1st Army is positioned here and the situation in the Straits has caused serious crises between Türkiye and Russia in the past.

Regional Security Circles: Türkiye is located in a geography where many different security circles intersect. Therefore, it is naturally quite difficult to create a holistic approach in foreign policy in this difficult geography. As Oral Sander emphasises, Türkiye, which acts as a pivot between these security circles, has experienced/is experiencing great difficulties in the past and today in harmonising them with each other. There are five perspectives on this issue. The European perspective requires Türkiye to be in the Western military bloc (NATO) and therefore to take a position against Russia and its neighbouring threats to the east. However, due to the deep political and economic relations that developed with Russia after the Cold War, Türkiye can sometimes find itself in difficult situations. A similar situation is actually valid for relations with the European Union (EU). This union, which we are trying to become a full member of, is a political structure that contradicts Türkiye's current position in domestic and foreign policy in many ways. The second perspective, the Balkan perspective, is also very important for Türkiye. Because the Balkans are Türkiye's gateway to Europe. In order to reach out to people like the Bosnians here, it is most important for Türkiye not to be at odds with Greece and Bulgaria at the same time. The third perspective, the Mediterranean perspective, is an area dominated by Turkish-Greek relations. The tensions with Greece over the Aegean Islands and Cyprus have weakened Türkiye's position in the Western world and made EU membership more difficult. In contrast, Türkiye must also protect its national interests in this issue, which is very important in terms of security and maritime trade. The fourth perspective, the Middle East perspective, necessitates a very difficult foreign policy – which can be likened to an acrobatic act – for Türkiye, which wants to both be involved in developments and not be swept away by the vortex of developments in this most difficult geography of the world. This geography, which is one of the main sources of terrorism in the world, also poses great difficulties for Türkiye due to the struggles of a stateless people like the Kurds, with a very large population, towards statehood. Türkiye still does not approach the concept of a Kurdish state favourably according to its official documents. The fifth and final perspective is the Caucasus perspective. This geography, where Russia is the dominant power and is extremely important for Türkiye and Europe in terms of energy policies, requires Türkiye to follow a multi-dimensional foreign policy due to the balance of power.

World Power Axes: The term 'bridge' used for Türkiye is true in many ways. Türkiye is truly a bridge country in both the East-West and North-South axes. Although Türkiye has made its political and strategic choice in favour of the Western world, it has turned to a multi-dimensional foreign policy since the 1960s due to political and economic interests and conflicts with the West and has tried to diversify its relations by remaining allies with the West. Membership in the Organisation of Islamic Cooperation (OIC) is a concrete indicator of this. Likewise, the developing economic relations with Russia are a good example of this.

The fourth issue that provides a theoretical framework for Turkish Foreign Policy is the 'Internal Structural Dimension'. From a general-historical perspective; some elements that have been filtered through different civilisations in Anatolia still affect the Turkish people and foreign policy to a certain extent today. For example, it is possible to find Byzantine traces in many Ottoman-Turkish political traditions. It should also be noted that the direction of the Turks has always been the West for hundreds of years and there have been migrations towards the West. Elements such as the Sunni-Shiite differences in Anatolia and the negative view of the Turkmens in the Ottoman system are also among the issues listed by Baskın Oran. In addition, the situation of non-Muslims in the Ottoman Empire and the political influence of European states on the Ottoman Empire through these groups are also historical elements of the internal structural dimension and have had a serious impact on the formation of the diplomacy of the Republic. From a specific-current perspective; the situation of the Kurds and their opposition to the official ideology of the Republic of Türkiye have become a very critical and challenging issue for Türkiye in domestic and foreign policy over the years. Especially since the 1980s, the Kurdish opposition (Kurdish Question), which has become a terror problem, has forced Türkiye to take different attitudes in foreign policy. From an ideological perspective, the development model determined by Türkiye, which was founded as a poor and underdeveloped country, has also closely affected its foreign policy. Following the statist policies preferred in the early years of the Republic, Türkiye has rapidly adopted the capitalist development model and taken steps in this direction. This has brought Türkiye closer to the capitalist United States and Western Europe rather than communist Russia.

Following this theoretical framework, Baskın Oran sets out to examine and analyse Turkish Foreign Policy in the light of the concept of medium-sized state (OBD-*orta büyüklükte devlet*). According to Oran, OBD countries, which are positioned somewhere between large and small states, are states whose effects on the international system are generally marginal but can seriously affect regional politics (especially their small neighbours) and, more importantly, can withstand pressures from large states to some extent and can occasionally enter into bargaining with them. In the Middle East, Israel, Iran, Türkiye, and to some extent Egypt can be given as examples of OBD countries. When OBDs are exposed to threats from major powers, they can resort to two options: playing to the balance of power between major powers or taking the wing of one of the major powers. Entering into the balance of power game with major powers is not an easy task; because this issue, which İsmet İnönü describes as '*getting into bed with a bear*', can put pressure on OBD countries due to changing balances of power and differences in capacity. However, the second option is not always guaranteed to succeed either; because major powers can also force the countries, they take under their wing to take steps in line with their own national and regional interests. In a very strictly bipolar system (for example, the Cold War), it becomes almost impossible for OBDs to choose the first option. Because, according to the view referred to as the 'Aron Paradigm' by Raymond Aron, developing policies independent of the blocs in such cases is much riskier.

The OBD countries have some characteristic features in terms of economy and military geostrategy. For an OBD country, the economy must be developed to some extent. Continuous crisis or a closed economy prevents becoming an OBD. A certain amount of developed military and geostrategic power is also a must for OBD countries. However, it should be noted that there are certain conditions for OBDs to use their military power. If an OBD country expands territory in a geostrategic region of the world that is not approved by the effective power or hegemonic power in that region, it can get into serious trouble. For example, since Türkiye annexed Hatay in 1939 with the approval of the 'regional power' France, it does not face a serious problem in this regard today. However, when Türkiye, even though it is in accordance with its guarantor rights on the island and international law, invades Cyprus without the approval of the hegemonic power, the United States, and more importantly, still maintains military units there, it can cause great headaches in diplomacy. Today, Türkiye's military operations in Syria and the position it will take on the Kurdish Question must be carefully constructed and implemented around the concept of the OBD. Because OBDs do not have the luxury of being imaginary; however, it is also unnecessary to meet every demand from major powers. Realistic and measured steps that comply with international law and prioritise national interests can bring great success to OBD countries in foreign policy.

Prof. Baskın Oran's 3-volume book *Turkish Foreign Policy* (*Türk Dış Politikası*) is an extremely useful and comprehensive resource that can be taught in university courses. It is also an undeniable fact that Oran can maintain his impartiality on the issues he deals with and can speak/write scientifically and objectively without resorting to bombastic literature due to his oppositional personality and anti-nationalist worldview.

Seven Stages of Turkish Foreign Policy

There is no denying that Turkish is one of the most important countries in the world due to its key geopolitical positioning between Asia and Europe and its unique identity composed of both Eastern (Muslim population, problems of democracy, patriarchal culture, etc.) and Western (secularism, modern market economy, highly developed infrastructure) characteristics. In that sense, Türkiye has a great potential in contributing to the global trends in politics and economy with its decisions. Turkish Foreign Policy is the most important arena where Turkish state's decisions can be observed most clearly. In this piece, I am going to categorise seven different stages of Turkish Foreign Policy by looking at the different periods during the republican history so far (1923–).

1. **Isolationism:** Similar to all other countries, Türkiye can also adhere to isolationism in its foreign policy from time to time due to domestic necessities. For instance, after the proclamation the Republic in 1923 and the signing of the Lausanne Treaty, due to the existence of a heavy agenda (revolutions and reforms in every aspects of life) in domestic politics, Türkiye's founding leader and first President of the Republic Mustafa Kemal Atatürk (1923–1938) implemented a more isolationist foreign policy in the first decade of the republic throughout the 1920s. Türkiye made its transition into a secular state in 1928 when the Article II of the 1924 constitution stating the '*Official religion of the state is Islam*' was removed from the constitution. Moreover, Atatürk tried to eradicate the monarchical and theocratic model of governance by

his republican and secular reforms. He even changed the alphabet into Latin in order to closen Turkish culture with that of Western (European) countries. So, during the 1920s, the foreign policy of the country was more oriented towards domestic politics and in favour of status quo in terms of relations with the West and the USSR. After the military coups in 1960 and 1980 also, Türkiye – for a while – implemented isolationism as its main foreign policy inclination due to the priority of domestic political issues.

2. **Regional Pacts Model:** Regional Pacts model was implemented by Türkiye in the 1930s, the second half of the Atatürk era. During this period, Türkiye first established the Balkan Pact or the Balkan Entente in 1934 together with Greece, Romania, and Yugoslavia. Balkan Pact was a treaty of solidarity and mutual understanding against the irredentist claims of Bulgaria and Italy to secure each country's territorial integrity. Second important step of this policy was to introduce the Saadabad Pact via signing the Saadabad Treaty in 1937. Saadabad Pact was a non-aggression pact signed by Türkiye, Iran, Iraq, and Afghanistan on 8 July 1937 and lasted for 5 years. With this Treaty, Türkiye tried to secure its eastern borders as well. So, in a world open to new wars and aggressions, Türkiye wanted to secure itself by establishing friendly relations with its neighbours and countries in its near abroad. In the meantime, by Montreux Treaty (1936), Türkiye gained full control over the Straits.
3. **Neutrality:** Throughout the Second World War (1939–1945), Türkiye's second President of the Republic İsmet İnönü (İsmet Pasha) (1938–1950) implemented the policy of 'active neutrality'. The neutrality policy was based on Türkiye's continuing relations with both the Allies and Axis powers including the Nazi Germany. So, in order to secure its territories from a possible Nazi invasion, Türkiye continued to make chrome trade with Germany and did not engage in the war although it had previously signed the Anglo-French-Turkish Treaty in 1939. This policy was based on complete Realist interpretation of world politics and aimed at securing Turkish people as well as newly built Turkish cities by staying out of the war at all costs. Some observers of Turkish Foreign Policy resemble this policy to Türkiye's current attitude towards Russia and claim that Türkiye tries to get the best

possible for its people and its national interests during the Russian invasion of Ukraine.

4. **Transatlanticism:** After Stalin's unacceptable demands following the Second World War, a new era of Transatlanticism began in Turkish Foreign Policy with the 'Missouri Event', which symbolises the new pro-American diplomatic inclination of Ankara. Türkiye, in this new era of bipolarism, in order to survive against the giant USSR, began to look for a seat in the Western bloc and eventually became a member of NATO together with Greece in 1952. Ankara's new superpower ally (that is the United States) helped Türkiye in economic and military issues and Türkiye benefited from the Marshall Plan. Thus, the first phase of Cold War (1945–1963) was kind of a 'honeymoon' between Washington and Ankara as two allies were almost in perfect harmony in their foreign policy preferences. Transatlanticism was revived during Bill Clinton and Barack Obama periods, but both ended again with the failure of two sides in agreeing on many issues including the Kurdish Question, Turkish democracy, etc.
5. **Multi-Dimensional Foreign Policy:** Honeymoon period with Washington ended with the emergence of problems between two countries. First of all, Türkiye realised that it could be treated as a pawn by Washington in events such as the Cuban Missile Crisis (1962). So, Kennedy administration secretly withdrew Jupiter missiles from Türkiye in exchange to USSR decision not to implant nuclear weapons into Cuba following the American blockade. In addition, Ankara became very angry when President Lyndon Johnson wrote a disrespectful letter to then-Turkish Prime Minister İsmet İnönü and warned him not to interfere into Cyprus politics although Türkiye was a guarantor state. So, as a reaction, between 1963 and 1980 (until the military take-over), Ankara began to implement a new strategy of multi-dimensionalism with developing economic relations with the USSR, becoming a member of the Organisation of Islamic Conference (today's Islamic Cooperation Organisation), and attending to Non-Aligned Movement's Foreign Ministers Conference.
6. **Europeanisation:** After the Helsinki Summit of 1999, Türkiye was given candidacy for full membership to the European Union (EU). In fact, accession talks began in 2005 during the early years of the AK Parti

(Justice and Development Party) and then-Prime Minister Recep Tayyip Erdoğan. During this period, Türkiye tried to pursue a pro-European foreign policy by not accepting the 1 March memorandum in 2003 to join the American invasion of Iraq, supported the Annan Plan – proposed settlement plan by the then-UN Secretary-General Kofi Annan – in Cyprus in 2004, legislated new laws for becoming harmonious with Brussels, and intensified its political, economic, and cultural relations with all EU countries. Europeanisation helped Türkiye to embrace and adopt a more Idealist foreign policy first time in its history. However, as Türkiye's EU membership hopes faded in the 2010s, Türkiye began to search for a new foreign policy.

7. **Eurasianism:** Starting from the 1990s, many Turkish soldiers, statesmen, and intellectuals began to dislike and openly criticise American foreign policy choices such as supporting Kurdish and Islamist groups under the name of democratisation and commenced to look for membership into an alternative bloc. Although it began as a marginal choice, Eurasianism transformed into a reasonable option in the 2020s with Türkiye's transformation into a different and authoritarian regime as well as its endless political disagreements and problems with both Washington and Brussels. The contemporary Turkish Eurasianism has important pillars such as the use of the Organisation of Turkic States as leverage to increase Turkish influence in Eurasia, using developing relations with Russia and China to be an important actor in the region as well as to become a dialogue partner of the Shanghai Cooperation Organisation (SCO) and a potential full member to BRICS+. So, as the global economy shifts towards Asia, Turkish Eurasianism gains more power day by day.

These are seven main foreign policy tendencies in Türkiye. Of course, as a large and important country, Türkiye always makes use of many of them at the same time. However, one inclination often dominates over the others. Nowadays, it seems like Türkiye tries to implement a multi-dimensional foreign policy with more Eurasianist accents and a kind of neutrality for Russian-Ukraine War.

PART II

Contemporary Issues and Discussions

John Mearsheimer's Views on Turkish Foreign Policy

American Professor of Political Science and former co-chair of the Centre for International Security Policy at the University of Chicago, John Mearsheimer, whose views I frequently seek in my articles for the Academy of International Politics (UPA), gave a conference titled 'Turkish Foreign Policy: A Realist's Assessment' to the employees of the Ministry of Foreign Affairs of the Republic of Türkiye on 4 October 2012, in İstanbul, upon the invitation of the Centre for Strategic Studies – SAM. This article will summarise the views Mearsheimer expressed at this conference.

Mearsheimer begins his remarks by reminding that he is not an expert on Türkiye but adds that he is interested in Middle Eastern politics and that he has always followed Türkiye closely, as Türkiye is an important country in the region. Stating that this 'outsider' identity can sometimes turn into an advantage for analysts, Mearsheimer reminds us that the person who wrote one of the most important books about the United States was the French historian and traveller Alexis de Tocqueville. Stating that he is a Realist thinker, Mearsheimer reminds the audience that he makes his analyses in this direction. Stating that he thinks that many Turks, especially those working in the Foreign Ministry and security bureaucracy, are inclined to this school due to the geography in which Türkiye is located, Mearsheimer reveals that what he has to say in this context will not be shocking. Also stating that it is difficult to defend Realism in the United States due to liberal indoctrination, Mearsheimer says that he sees Türkiye as closer to him in this sense.

According to Professor Mearsheimer, who began to explain his theory after this introduction, every state in the international system has two basic goals: 1) To increase/maximise their relative power due to their distrust of neighbouring states and the inadequacy of international institutions, and 2) To have a smart foreign policy and grand strategy in the face of threats. In this context, Mearsheimer thinks that being a 'regional hegemon' is the best option for states, as he always says. Stating that the United States, which he sees as the only country in the world that truly fits the regional hegemon model, has the luxury of making mistakes in foreign policy due to its enormous power, Mearsheimer claims that Türkiye, on the other hand, does not have such a luxury and therefore must always have a 'smart' foreign policy.

Following this theoretical background, Mearsheimer began to explain Türkiye's situation according to the 'balance of power' model. According to Mearsheimer, Türkiye is in an 'excellent' position in the Middle East. At this point, Mearsheimer emphasises two basic criteria while praising Türkiye: population and wealth. Reminding that these two characteristics make the United States strong, Mearsheimer says that there is no country in the region other than the Russian Federation that can compete with Türkiye and emphasises that the difference between Russia and Türkiye is much smaller compared to the Cold War (Soviet Union). Stating that Greece, which was once considered an equal status actor to Türkiye when determining US policies towards the region, is now far behind Türkiye, Mearsheimer states that Russia is also gradually losing power compared to Türkiye due to its decreasing population. In the Middle East, Mearsheimer says that Türkiye's only rival is the Islamic Republic of Iran, and he thinks that Iran is at a disadvantage against Türkiye due to its low birth rates (Türkiye: 2.1 babies per woman, Iran: 1.8 babies per woman). Stating that Türkiye is also far ahead of Iran economically, Mearsheimer thinks that Türkiye is the greatest power in the Middle East, but that it is still not easy to become a regional hegemon like the United States. Reminding that Türkiye is the intersection of three important regions, Europe, Asia, and the Middle East, Mearsheimer adds that these three regions are regions worth fighting for the United States.

According to Mearsheimer, Türkiye, which is located in such a difficult and important geography, is exposed to certain problems and threats. A significant portion of these problems stem from the geography itself, while others develop due to difficult processes such as the Arab Spring. Emphasising that Türkiye's 'zero problems with neighbours' (*komşularla sıfır sorun*) policy, which worked very well until recently, can no longer continue, Mearsheimer says that this is not due to Türkiye and that Türkiye cannot prevent this. The American Professor also states that it is not always possible to solve problems in international politics, and that decision makers are generally forced to choose the least bad option.

Moving on to the subject of threat perceptions towards Türkiye, Mearsheimer claims that Greece and Russia do not pose a serious threat to Türkiye today and that the main problems stem from the Middle East. According to Mearsheimer, the countries that pose the main threat to Türkiye are Syria, Iran, and Iraq, which are its neighbours. Stating that the deteriorating relations with Israel are also a problem for Türkiye, Mearsheimer draws attention to the fact that the alliance with the United States has brought many problems as well as many benefits to Türkiye and the necessity of carefully managing bilateral relations with the United States.

Following these basic findings, Mearsheimer states that there are four main sources of threat to Türkiye and explains them. Adding that one of the most basic problems for Türkiye is the Kurdish separatist PKK terrorist organisation and regulating relations with the Kurds, John Mearsheimer claims that the second most important problem is the sectarian (Sunni-Shia) competition that will deepen in the Middle East in the coming years. He states that the third most important problem is the nuclear proliferation and that the Iranian nuclear programme is the most critical issue in this regard. According to Mearsheimer, the fourth most important problem is the risk of Türkiye being dragged into war in Syria and other geographies in the coming years. Stating that he thinks Türkiye could come to this point, especially in Syria, Mearsheimer says that this step could be very risky. Reminding that the Syrian crisis is also related to Iran, Iraq, and Russia, Mearsheimer states that despite Türkiye's calls for reforms to the Bashar Assad administration, the rebellion in Syria quickly turned into a civil war and says that the idea of getting rid of Assad is dominant on the US and Türkiye sides. Stating that he foresees that this will be difficult due to the support of Iran, Iraq, and Russia, Mearsheimer also draws attention to the formation of an anti-Türkiye Shiite bloc in the region. Stating that he thinks it would be risky for Türkiye to send ground forces to Syria, Mearsheimer adds that this will also have a very negative impact on Türkiye-Iran relations. Drawing attention to the fact that Türkiye mostly acts together with the United States and anti-Assad Sunni powers in terms of regional policies, Mearsheimer says that Iran will be a very critical country in this sense. Thinking that failure to reach an agreement on Iran's nuclear programme could lead to a major war in the region, Mearsheimer claims that Türkiye-Israel relations will not easily improve due to the Palestinian Question and the Mavi Marmara crisis.

If we are to make a general assessment of Mearsheimer's views, it is necessary to start with the determination that the views have lost their relevance in some respects since they were stated in 2012. However, Mearsheimer's views are coherent and are clearly based on Realism's premises in terms of International Relations Theory.

According to George Friedman, Türkiye in 2050

American strategist and geopolitics expert George Friedman (1949-) has made a name for himself in recent years with the private intelligence and think-tank Stratfor, which he founded in Austin, Texas in 1996 (he left the organisation's presidency to Dave Sikora in 2015 and now works solely as an analyst) and has published various publications containing predictions about the future of world politics. The most important of these publications is Friedman's book *The Next 100 Years: A Forecast for the 21st Century*, published in 2009. In this 253-page book, Friedman attracted attention with his ambitious predictions about the future of world politics and different countries in the world in the twenty-first century, and in 2015 his work was translated into Turkish by Pegasus Publishing House under the title *Gelecek Yüz Yıl*. The most striking feature of this book for readers who are citizens of Türkiye, and the Republic of Türkiye is undoubtedly the projection made on what kind of country Türkiye will be in its region in 2050.

Friedman first determines Türkiye's current situation and states that the region's most modern and largest economy is in a very important geopolitical position between Europe, the Middle East, and Russia. According to Friedman, who develops strategies for the benefit of this country by focusing on the United States, Türkiye does not have a stance that is contrary to American interests and therefore can never be perceived as a threat by this great country. Therefore, with its developing economy, it is possible that Türkiye will emerge as the most important power centre in the region in the near future.

Following this introduction, Friedman begins historical evaluations, and according to Friedman, Türkiye, which was a huge empire (the Ottoman Empire) when it entered World War I just 100 years ago, has been an important world power that has managed to dominate the Mediterranean, the Middle East, North Africa, Europe, and the Caucasus for centuries. The Turkish state, which was forced to shrink with the collapse of the Empire and the proclamation of the Republic, has created a modern and secular society under the control of the army in its new system and has managed to become the most advanced economy in the region despite the rising Islamist movement in recent years.

Figure 1: Türkiye's sphere of influence map in 2050 according to George Friedman

The most striking and controversial part of Friedman's analysis of Türkiye is the map he published about the sphere of influence that this country will reach in 2050. The most important point that needs to be emphasised about the new map of Türkiye that has caused controversy is that it is not a political map reflecting Türkiye's geographical expansion, as stated by some Turkish press and publication organs, but a map that determines its sphere of influence. In other words, the author thinks that rather than expanding Türkiye's territory, it will become the most powerful actor economically, politically, and culturally in the geographies/countries specified in the map. When the map is examined, it is seen that Türkiye will be influential in a region in North Africa that includes Egypt and Libya and extends to Tunisia in 2050. The geography where Türkiye will make the most progress and become politically, economically and culturally dominant is the Middle East. According to Friedman, Türkiye will turn the entire Arabian Peninsula, Syria and Iraq, into a basin of influence in 2050. All countries except Israel and the Islamic Republic of Iran will remain under Türkiye's political influence and will accept this. In the Balkans, according to the author, only Bosnia and Herzegovina and Albania will remain countries where Türkiye is influential. In the Caucasus, Azerbaijan, Georgia, Armenia, the southeastern part of Russia, Crimea, Kazakhstan, and the western parts of Turkmenistan are considered to be in Türkiye's sphere of influence in 2050.

This map can be criticised from many perspectives. First of all, it should be remembered that this map and the book and vision in general were developed by Friedman in the early 2000s. This period was a period when the Justice and Development Party (AK Parti) government in Türkiye (2002-) implemented comprehensive reforms for harmonisation/full membership with the European Union, managed to melt Islamism and secularism in one pot, and prevented extreme movements. During these years, great sympathy was formed in the world public opinion towards Türkiye, and a problem-free period was experienced in Turkish Foreign Policy. However, this period rapidly deteriorated starting from 2009; Turkish Foreign Policy has faced some difficulties during the Arab Spring, and domestically, the reformist and secular democratic qualities of the AK Parti have been overshadowed by the strengthening authoritarianism and Islamist tendencies. For this reason, Türkiye's 'model country' identity has begun to be jeopardised, and especially

President Recep Tayyip Erdoğan has been subject to harsh criticism in the foreign press.

Apart from these, Türkiye's performance in North Africa has declined with the emergence of radical Islamist groups during the Arab Spring and the re-emergence of the secular authoritarian model with General Sisi in Egypt; Türkiye's ties with Egypt and Libya have rapidly weakened. It seems difficult for Türkiye to regain its influence in these regions – at least in the short term. But of course, many things can change by 2050.

While Friedman's predictions seem reasonable in the context of the Middle East due to President Erdoğan's popularity in the Arab world, dissenting voices regarding Türkiye's political leadership are also extremely strong in the Arab world. Again, the fact that the United States and the United Kingdom are very influential in the Gulf region is an obstacle to Türkiye becoming a dominant actor. The political tension and even partial war with Syria also negatively affect Türkiye, albeit in a smaller part of the Arab world. For this reason, it seems that Türkiye's sphere of influence will remain limited to the Sunni Arab world for now. The future of the Kurds in this region and Türkiye's relations with the Kurds are also important mysteries.

While the author exaggerates Türkiye's power in North Africa and the Middle East (since he sees the power of Islamism as the only factor), I believe he understates Türkiye's power in the Balkans. Because, in addition to Bosnia-Herzegovina and Albania, which are shown in the map as part of its sphere of influence, Türkiye is already very active in Kosovo and Macedonia. Apart from these, Türkiye also has the potential to gain more economic power over countries such as Serbia and Greece.

The assessment in the context of the Caucasus is also open to discussion. Türkiye attempted a normalisation process with Armenia immediately after the publication of this book; however, this process failed due to Armenia's attitudes and, moreover, caused Türkiye to face the risk of losing Azerbaijan. The author's observations on Azerbaijan and Georgia are quite reasonable and appropriate, considering the recent energy and transportation projects. However, normalisation with Armenia might not be possible in the near future. This country will most likely always remain under Russian control despite its pro-Western tendency. As is known, Crimea joined Russia in 2014 and Türkiye's influence there was suddenly eliminated. Therefore, it is very difficult for Türkiye to establish a presence against Russia in the east and southeast of Crimea and Ukraine. As for the Caspian region, although the Caspian is historically a Turkish lake, it is a geography where power struggles are mostly between Iran and Russia and the countries in the region. The most powerful actor in the region is Russia, and in countries such as Turkmenistan, Kazakhstan, and Azerbaijan, Russia's power is no less than Türkiye's. In this context, while it seems likely that Azerbaijan will become closer to Türkiye in the medium and long term, I do not think it is possible for Kazakhstan and Turkmenistan to break away from Russia. Therefore, Türkiye's sphere of influence in the Caucasus will be limited to Azerbaijan and Georgia. However, in the event of the collapse of the Islamic Republic of Iran, Türkiye and Azerbaijan's influence in this region may increase even more, of course thanks to the millions of Turks in South Azerbaijan.

Ultimately, Friedman's projection of Türkiye in 2050 that he discusses in his book is open to discussion in many respects. Since the author wrote this book at a time when the moderate Islamist AK Parti government in Türkiye was very successful, I think he made optimistic predictions in the book in many respects. However, Türkiye has been going through a difficult period in political and economic terms in the last few years. On the other hand, the fact that the author is not sufficiently aware of Türkiye's power in the Balkans is, in my opinion, a mistake he made because he considered Türkiye's historical legacy from the Ottoman Empire solely in the context of Islamism. Nevertheless, it would be beneficial for those working in this field to read and analyse Friedman's book carefully.

Türkiye in CIA World Factbook Data

Introduction

The Central Intelligence Agency (CIA) has been publishing an almanac (annual) called the *World Factbook* since 1981, sharing its current statistical data on all countries and international organisations in the world with the American and international public. One of the countries covered in this study is undoubtedly Türkiye. Türkiye is evaluated in the geographical category of 'Middle East' in this study. The last update on Türkiye was made on 3 December 2024. This article will summarise the CIA World Factbook Türkiye data.

Türkiye in CIA World Factbook Data

Introduction Section

The first paragraph of the 'Introduction' section of the CIA World Factbook Türkiye page states that the Republic of Türkiye was founded in 1923 by Mustafa Kemal Atatürk, who later took the surname 'Father of the Turks' and was a great national hero in the country, from the ruins of the Ottoman Empire. It is stated that Türkiye undertook radical social, economic, legal, and political reforms during the Atatürk era, and that the country was governed by a single-party regime until 1950. It is noted that in 1950, a peaceful transition to a multi-party regime was made with the election victory of the Democrat Party. It is stated that many political parties have been established in the country since that period, and that the civilian regime was interrupted by military coups in 1960, 1971, and 1980. It is emphasised that after all these coups, power was transferred to civilians again in a short time, and it is stated that in 1997, the Islamic government was removed from office without a coup in the process called the 'post-modern coup', and that there was an unsuccessful coup attempt in 2016.

In the second paragraph of the 'Introduction' section, it is emphasised that Türkiye carried out a military intervention in Cyprus in 1974 in order to prevent the island from being connected to Greece, and that the TRNC was established there, and that since then, Türkiye has acted solely as the 'patron state' of this state. It is also stated that a separatist movement called the PKK (Kurdistan Workers' Party) emerged in Türkiye as of 1984 and that the United States considered this movement a terrorist organisation, and that 40,000 citizens have lost their lives due to PKK terrorism since then. It is also noted that a negotiation process was initiated between the Republic of Türkiye and the PKK in 2013, and that a period of conflict resumed in 2015. In addition, it is recalled that Türkiye became a member of the United Nations in 1945 and NATO in 1952, and that the membership process to the European Economic Community was initiated with the Ankara Agreement in 1963. It is also emphasised that Türkiye began full membership negotiations with the European Union in 2005, and that the reforms made during this process contributed to the country's rapid development; however, these reforms have slowed down in recent years.

In the third and final paragraph of the 'Introduction' section, it is recalled that major terrorist attacks were carried out in Türkiye in 2015 and 2016, and that more than 240 people died and more than 2,000 were injured during the failed coup on 15 July 2016. It is said that the people took to the streets to prevent the coup, while the government blamed Fethullah Gülen's religious and social structure called 'Hizmet' for this coup attempt. It is written that the government purged more than 130,000 people from the state after the coup attempt, and that a 'state of emergency' was in effect in the country between July 2016 and July 2018. Finally, it is noted that Türkiye switched to the presidential system with the referendum held on 16 April 2017, and it is emphasised that the first presidential and parliamentary elections were held with the new system in 2018.

Geography Section

In the 'Geography' section, it is first stated that Türkiye is located between Southeastern Europe and Southwestern Asia and is surrounded by the Black Sea, Bulgaria, Georgia, the Aegean Sea, the Mediterranean, Greece and Syria. After giving Türkiye's geographical coordinates, it is written that the country's land area is 783,562 square kilometres and that Türkiye is the 38th largest country in the world. In this sense, it is emphasised that Türkiye is slightly larger than the state of Texas. It is also emphasised that the country has a border of 2,816 kilometres, while the borders are; Syria 899 kilometres (km), Iran 534 km, Iraq 367 km, Armenia 311 km, Georgia 273 km, Bulgaria 223 km, Greece 192 km and Azerbaijan 17 km. The country's coastline is stated as 7,200 km, while Türkiye claims a 6-mile maritime jurisdiction in the Aegean Sea and a 12-mile exclusive economic zone in the Mediterranean and Black Seas.

Türkiye's climate is stated as temperate and hot, with mild summers and rainy winters. It is emphasised that the climate in the inner regions is harsher. The average elevation in the country is calculated as 1,132 metres, while the highest point is Mount Ararat (5,137 metres) and the lowest point is the Mediterranean (0 metres). The country's natural resources are; coal, iron, copper, chrome, antimony, mercury, gold, barite, borate, celestite (strontium), emery, feldspar, magnesite, marble, perlite, pumice, natural sulfur, clay, arable lands and electrical power produced from water. It is stated that 49.7 per cent of the country's land is agricultural land, 14.9 per cent is forest land and the remaining 35.4 per cent is claimed to be other areas.

It is stated that approximately 20 per cent of the country's population lives in İstanbul and the Bosphorus region, while it is written that the capital Ankara and its surroundings are developing, and that there is also environmental development around the coasts of the Aegean region and the Euphrates and Tigris rivers in the southeast. It is emphasised that the biggest natural disaster risk in the country is earthquakes, and it is stated that earthquakes are frequently experienced in a wide area from the Marmara Sea to Lake Van, especially in the northern regions. It is also written that volcanic activity has occurred in the past in mountainous regions such as Ağrı, Nemrut, and Tendürek Mountains, but that there has been no development in this regard since the nineteenth century. It is also written that there are current problems such as water pollution, air pollution, deforestation, erosion, oil spills in Bosphorus sea traffic, and the protection of biodiversity. Additionally, while Türkiye's Straits region is stated as the most strategic location, it is also stated that 3 per cent of the country's territory is located on the European continent.

Society Section

The total population of the country is stated as 84.1 million in the 'Society' section. In this sense, Türkiye is the 18th most populous country in the world. While it is stated that the citizens in the country are called 'Turks', ethnically 70–75 per cent of the population is ethnic Turkish (Turkish), 19 per cent is Kurdish and 6–11 per cent is other ethnic groups. It is stated that the only official language is Turkish, while Kurdish and other ethnic minority languages are also spoken in the country. The largest age groups in the country are listed as follows; 0–14 (21.7 per cent), 15–64 (68.6 per cent), and 65 years and older (9.6 per cent). The average age of the country is calculated as thirty-four. It is stated that the population growth rate in the country is surprisingly only 0.61 per cent and ranks 139th in the world in this field. In addition, when considered as a group of 1,000 people; it is written that the number of births is 13.8 (122nd in the world) and the number of deaths is 6.1 (151st in the world). The urbanisation level in the country is measured as 77.5 per cent and an urbanisation rate of 1.11 per cent is mentioned. The largest cities in the country are İstanbul (15,848,000), Ankara (5,397,000), İzmir (3,088,000), Bursa (2,086,000), Adana (1,836,000), Gaziantep (1,805,000).

In addition, the average age of motherhood in the country is calculated as 26.6, while the maternal mortality rate at birth is stated as 17 per 100,000 people (130th in the world). The child mortality rate is stated as 18.4 per 1,000 people, emphasising that it is 83rd in the world in this area. While the average life expectancy is calculated as 76.7, it is noteworthy that women have a life expectancy of 5 years longer than men. While it is stated that the health expenditures in the country remain at 4.6 per cent, it is calculated that there is an average of 2.9 hospital beds per 1,000 people. It is also stated that there is a 32.1 per cent obesity (overweight people) rate in the country, and that it is 17th in the world in this regard, while the rate of children under the age of five suffering from developmental disorders is stated as 1.5 per cent.

In addition, the education expenditures in the country are calculated as 3.4 per cent, and it is stated that it is 145th in the world. While the literacy rate is given as 96.7 per cent, it is noteworthy that this rate is 5 per cent higher for men. It is stated that the average expectation of education in the country is 19 years for men and 18 years for women. In addition, the unemployment rate in the country is calculated as 9.41 per cent. It is also stated that youth unemployment is around 17.6 per cent which ranks Türkiye at 79th rank in the world.

State/Government Section

In the 'State/Government' section, first of all, it is stated that the official name of the country is the Republic of Türkiye. In addition, it is written that the capital of the country, which is governed by a presidential system, is Ankara, that the country is governed by eighty-one provinces or cities, and that this date is celebrated every year as 'Republic Day' since it was founded on 29 October 1923. It is stated that the 1982 constitution is in force in the country, and that the legal system is influenced by European legal systems, especially Swiss law. It is stated that citizenship cannot be obtained by birth in the country, that one of the parents must be Turkish for citizenship, that dual citizenship is possible with government permission, and that citizenship requires living in the country for at least 5 years. It is also stated that the voting age in the country is 18.

In terms of the executive power, President Recep Tayyip Erdoğan is mentioned, and that Erdoğan is both the head of state and government. It is reminded that the cabinet is formed by the President's appointment, the President is elected for 5 years, and in the last election in 2023, Recep Tayyip Erdoğan defeated Kemal Kılıçdaroğlu with 52.2 per cent to 47.8 per cent of the vote.

In terms of legislative power, it is stated that the TBMM (TGNA) is the country's law-making parliament, consists of 600 seats, and the deputies are elected for 5 years. It is stated that in the last parliamentary election, the People's Alliance (*Cumhur İttifakı*) formed by the AK Parti, MHP (Nationalist Action Party), YRP (New Welfare Party), and BBP (Great Unity Party) won the election with 49.9 per cent of the vote (AK Parti 35.6 per cent, MHP 10.1 per cent, YRP 2.8 per cent, and BBP 1 per cent), while it is emphasised that the AK Parti won 268 seats and the MHP fifty seats. It is stated that the

Nation Alliance formed by the CHP, İYİ Parti and Saadet Party received 33.9 per cent of the votes in the same election (CHP 24.3 per cent and İYİ Parti 9.7 per cent), while it is reminded that the CHP won 169 seats and the İYİ Parti forty-three seats. It is also stated that the pro-Kurdish YSGP (now DEM Parti) won sixty-one seats in this election and that there are 480 men and 119 women in the parliament; therefore, the rate of women deputies is limited to 19.9 per cent.

In terms of judicial power; it is stated that the Constitutional Court is the highest judicial authority in the country, that the Constitutional Court consists of one President, 2 Vice Presidents, and twelve judges, and that the Courts of Appeal, which are divided into civil and criminal courts, and the Council of State, where 390 judges serve and has fifteen branches, are another important court. It is also emphasised that three of the Constitutional Court members are elected by the TBMM and twelve by the President, judges serve for 12 years, retire at the age of 65, and the Chief Justice and Vice Presidents are elected for 4 years.

It is stated that there are many legal political parties in the country, are listed by name. These are; Democracy and Progress Party or DEVA, Democrat Party or DP, Democratic Regions Party or DBP, Felicity Party (Saadet Partisi) or SP, Free Cause Party or HÜDAPAR, Future Party (Gelecek Partisi) or GP, Good Party or İYİ Parti, Great Unity Party or BBP, Justice and Development Party or AK Parti, Labour and Freedom Alliance (electoral alliance includes YSGP/HDP-now DEM Parti and TİP-Turkish Labour Party), Nationalist Action Party or MHP, New Welfare Party or YRP, and the Republican People's Party or CHP.

It is also stated in this section that Türkiye is a member of many international institutions and organisations, and it is reminded that the country's Ambassador to Washington has been Sedat Önal since 2024. It is also stated that in addition to the Embassy in Washington, there are Turkish Consulates in Boston, Chicago, Houston, Los Angeles, Miami, New York, and San Francisco.

In the last section, the Turkish flag is defined in detail, national symbols are explained, and the 'Independence March', whose lyrics were written by Mehmet Akif Ersoy and whose composition was written by Zeki Üngör, is stated.

Economy Section

In the 'Economy' section, it is stated that Türkiye's economy is largely a free market economy, that it has developed through the industry and service sectors, while the agricultural economy is still an important source of employment at around 25 per cent. It is emphasised that the automotive, petrochemical and electronics industries have developed rapidly in recent years and have surpassed traditional sectors such as textiles and clothing in the economy, while it is stated that there have been uncertainties in the economy recently. It is also claimed in this section that the government has abandoned structural reforms in recent years, turned to more populist spending and credit methods and used economic mechanisms against political opponents, and it is implied that this harms the economy. While Türkiye's external dependence on oil and natural gas is also stated, it is emphasised that TANAP, developed in partnership between Türkiye and Azerbaijan, has a strategic structure in terms of supplying energy resources in the Caspian region to Europe.

It is reminded that Türkiye strengthened its economy in line with the IMF (International Monetary Fund) programme after the great economic crisis it experienced in 2001 and grew by an average of 6 per cent until 2008, while it draws attention to the fact that the state's influence on the economy was reduced with the aggressive privatisation policy implemented during this period. It is also stated in this section that the 2009 economic crisis was easily overcome in Türkiye, and that a tremendous growth rate of 9 per cent was achieved in 2010 and 2011. However, it is noted that the economy has been in decline since 2016, and the current account deficit, rising unemployment and inflation, and the rapid depreciation of the Turkish lira against international currencies such as the dollar, euro, and pound are highlighted as the most important economic problems.

While the country's economic size is stated as 1.108 trillion dollars (2023 data), it is stated that the situation is better in terms of purchasing power parity and that it ranks 12th in the world. It is also stated that 54 per cent of the country's gross national product is made up of the service sector, while the other 28.3 per cent is industry and 6.2 per cent is agriculture. The most important agricultural products are tobacco, cotton, grain, olive, sugar beet, hazelnut, legumes, citrus fruits, and animals. The most important industrial commodities are textile, food processing, automobile, electronics, mining, oil, construction, joinery, and paper. While the industrial growth rate is given as 2.34 per cent as of 2023, it is stated that it is 112th in the world in this field.

It is also emphasised that there are 35 million workers in the country and that it is 19th in the world in this field. The population below poverty line in the country is given as 14.4 per cent (2020 estimate). While the country's exports are given as 352.514 billion US dollars, Germany (8 per cent), the United States (8 per cent), Iraq (5 per cent), the United Kingdom (5 per cent), and Italy (5 per cent) are stated as important countries in this regard. The country's imports are given as 386.828 billion dollars, while Türkiye's most important import partners are the People's Republic of China (13 per cent), Germany (9 per cent), Russia (8 per cent), and the United States (5 per cent), and Italy (5 per cent). Additionally, Türkiye's external debt is stated as 133.882 billion dollars (2022 data).

Energy Section

Following the statistical data showing that the country can provide electrification services to all regions and citizens, this section first determines that 280,458 billion kilowatt-hours (kWh) of electricity was consumed in the country as of 2022. It is also stated in this section that a total of 3.71 billion kilowatt-hours (kWh) of electricity was exported, and 6.423 billion kilowatt-hours (kWh) of electricity was imported annually in Türkiye, and that 58.2 per cent of the electricity produced in the country was provided by hydrocarbon resources, 21.7 per cent by hydroelectric power plants, and around 20 per cent by renewable energy resources.

Communication Section

The number of fixed telephone lines in the country is stated as 11.198 million, while the number of mobile phones is given as 90.298 million (2022 data). It is stated that the telecommunications sector in the country is developing rapidly, 4G technology has been brought to 93 per cent of the country's population and 5G technology is being developed with the help of the Chinese company Huawei. It is also explained in this section that there are many private television channels and radio stations in the country other than the state television *TRT*, while the total number of national and local TV channels is given as 567 and the total number of radio stations is given as 1,007 (2019 data). There are 68.85 million internet subscribers in the country, equivalent to 81 per cent of the population, placing Türkiye 13th in the world in terms of the number of internet users.

Military and Security Department

While military expenditures in the country have been increasing steadily since 2015, they are at 2.1 per cent as of 2024. This is not a very high rate and ranks Türkiye 60th in the world. The defence mission undertaken by the Turkish Armed Forces (TSK) is carried out in accordance with the conscription system. The duration of military service is limited to 6–12 months; in addition, a 'paid military service' application has been recently developed. Women, the disabled, and those with health problems are excluded from this scope.

The AK Parti, which has been in power since 2002, has taken important steps towards establishing civilian dominance over the army. In this way, the TSK has withdrawn from the political arena but maintained its power in security and foreign policy issues. The TSK, a NATO member army, also serves in many NATO missions. There is also a NATO Land Forces Command in İzmir. In addition, Türkiye purchased the S-400 air defence system from Russia for $2.5 billion in 2019 and added it to its military inventory. The TSK has around 400,000 active personnel, of which around 300,000 are in the Land Forces and around 50,000 each in the Naval and Air Forces. There are also 150,000 Gendarmerie and 5,000 Coastal Forces personnel. While the TSK inventory also includes weapons and ammunition made in China, Russia and South Korea, the country's largest weapons provider is still the United States. Italy, South Korea and Spain are other major weapons providers. When we look at the country's soldiers serving abroad; It is estimated that 600 personnel (NATO) are on duty in Afghanistan, 250 in Bosnia and Herzegovina (EUFOR), 30,000 in Cyprus, 300 in Kosovo (NATO), 170 in Lebanon (UNIFIL), 200 in Qatar, 200 in Somalia and 15,000–20,000 in Syria. In addition, Turkish soldiers and 3,500 fighters from the Syrian civil war were deployed in Libya in 2020.

Transportation Department

In terms of air transportation; there are exactly 15 registered airline companies and 618 aircraft actively operating in the country, 115,595,495 people travel by plane annually as of 2018 and it ranks 46th in the world in this regard with a total of 115 airports. There are also 213 helicopter areas (heliports), 14,666 km of natural gas pipelines, and 3,293 km of oil pipelines in the country. Railway lines are 11,497 km long. The length of the highways is given as 68,526 km as of 2023. The length of the waterway is also stated as 1,200 km. There are also 1,170 maritime trade fleets in the country and it ranks 22nd in the world in this sense. Important ports are listed as follows; Haydarpaşa, İstanbul, İzmir, Mersin, Nemrut Limani Bay, and Samsun.

Terrorism Section

The most important terrorist organisations in the country are stated as the ISIS (Islamic State of Iraq and Syria), Islamic Movement of Uzbekistan (IMU), Islamic Revolutionary Guard Corps (IRGC)/Qods Force, Kurdistan Workers' Party (PKK), al-Qa'ida, and the Marxist-Leninist DHKP/C.

Transnational Issues Section

The foreign policy issues that Türkiye has problems with are listed in the transnational issues section. Türkiye, which has existing air, land and sea jurisdictions and border problems with Greece regarding the Aegean Sea and the Cyprus Conflict, has also not been able to improve its relations with the Kurds in Iraq. Türkiye, which also continues to have political problems with Armenia, has not been able to achieve results from the rapprochement it started with this country in 2009.

When looking at the refugee numbers, as of 2022 in Türkiye; It is thought that there are nearly 3,122,899 Syrian immigrants.

Türkiye, which has an important place in the world drug traffic as a transit area for Southwest Asian drugs to Europe and the United States, also hosts laboratories where morphine is converted into heroin, according to the CIA World Factbook. However, the government implements strict controls on opium production.

Conclusion

In conclusion, some interesting findings regarding the CIA World Factbook data can be listed as follows: Türkiye is evaluated as a country in the Middle East region in the CIA World Factbook. This may not be considered a very wrong approach when you consider that 97 per cent of the country's lands are beyond Europe. However, due to Türkiye's deep-rooted ties with Europe, there are also platforms where it is evaluated within the scope of Europe. The World Factbook claims that there is a 19–20 per cent ethnic Kurdish population in Türkiye. This may be considered a bit exaggerated when you consider that due to interracial marriages, the Turkish identity has been adopted by ethnic Kurds in new generations. The report states that Türkiye's population is 84 million. It is also understood that the population growth rate in Türkiye is not as high as it is thought. The report states that the population of İstanbul is almost 16 million. However, it is thought to be much higher. According to the report, the obesity problem in Türkiye has become so widespread that it is seen in one out of every three people today. The average age of Türkiye is thirty-four. This shows that it is a very young society. Over the years, Türkiye has become an 'urban' society that is urbanised by over 77 per cent. The literacy rate in Türkiye has exceeded 96 per cent. The average unemployment rate in the country is over 9 per cent. The report determined that the Turkish economy has been stagnant and even regressed in recent years. Türkiye's dependence on foreign energy is also stated in the report.

Türkiye's Temporary Membership of the UN Security Council (2009–2010)

Introduction

Türkiye, one of the fifty-one founding member states of the United Nations,[1] which had previously been a non-permanent member of the United Nations (UN) Security Council in 1951–1952, 1954–1955 and for a one-year half-term in 1961, which it shared with Poland[1], became a candidate from the Western European and Other States Group (WEOG) for the non-permanent membership of the Security Council for the 2009–2010 term at the 63rd UN General Assembly on 17 October 2008 and was elected in the first round with the votes of 151 of 192 states, well above the required two-thirds majority (128).[2] Although the non-permanent members of the UN Security Council (there are ten non-permanent members of the UN Security Council and they are elected for two years each) do not have veto power like the five permanent members (the United States, Russia, China, France, and the UK), being elected to this position can be considered as an important indicator for a state to show that it is on the right track in its foreign policy and that it has high support in the world. Moreover, a state, especially if it is a country like Türkiye, to which the members of the UN Security Council are not very favourable on controversial issues (e.g. the Cyprus Question), has the opportunity to better explain its arguments to the permanent members.

Between 29 August 2007 and 1 May 2009, during Ali Babacan's tenure as Foreign Minister, Recep Tayyip Erdoğan's tenure as Prime Minister, and Abdullah Gül's tenure as President of the Republic, this achievement is a very important event that needs to be examined carefully[3], considering the fact that Türkiye, which was a candidate again in the following periods, did not achieve this success.

In this article, I will first analyse how Türkiye was elected to the UN Security Council in 2008, then summarise the reactions to this success, and finally, I will touch upon the votes Türkiye participated in during the period of Türkiye's temporary membership in the UN Security Council (2009–2010). In an environment where Türkiye is gradually losing confidence in the United Nations order and adopting a reformist approach in line with the 'The world is Bigger than Five' discourse, I believe that analysing this period will be extremely necessary for Turkish Foreign Policy.

How Did Türkiye Succeed in 2008?

The Justice and Development Party (AK Parti), which came to power in Türkiye by a big surprise in 2002, has had strained relations with the Turkish establishment or establishment (especially the Turkish Armed Forces) from the first day of its rule, as it was founded by politicians with Islamist roots and raised in the National Outlook (View) tradition,[4] such as Recep Tayyip Erdoğan, Abdullah Gül, Bülent Arınç, and Abdüllatif Şener. Accordingly, the AK Parti skillfully used foreign policy – in its early years – both to secure itself against military tutelage and possible military coups and to consolidate its international legitimacy. Ankara adopted a strategy of opening up to the world and making the utmost effort to get along with everyone, based on concepts such as 'rhythmic diplomacy' and 'zero problems with neighbours' espoused by Prof. Ahmet Davutoğlu, who was a foreign policy adviser to Prime Minister Erdoğan and President Gül at the time. Based on Davutoğlu's concepts, Ankara adopted a strategy of opening up to the world and making the utmost effort to get along with everyone, indeed engaging in an unprecedented activism in foreign policy; the number of Turkish foreign missions opened in this period increased rapidly, and aid programmes to the least developed countries, especially African countries, helped them to support Türkiye in UN votes.[5]

Another successful strategy of Türkiye during this period was its attempt to assume the role of a neutral and fair mediator on many international issues (such as the US-Iran tension over the Iranian nuclear program, the Israeli-Palestinian conflict, Russia-Georgia relations, the Kashmir issue between India and Pakistan, etc.) and to become a rising diplomatic power capable of talking to everyone. Türkiye's role was so widely accepted at the time that even in the extremely tense Israel-Syria relations over the Golan Heights, both sides supported Türkiye's mediation.[6] In fact, Ankara, together with Brazil, even persuaded Iran to accept an international agreement limiting its nuclear program at the time, although the US later rejected it.[7] Moreover, Abdullah Gül (2003-2007) and Ali Babacan (2007-2009), who served as Foreign Ministers during those years, engaged in intensive talks with their counterparts from over 150 countries in line with the instructions of the Erdoğan government, which had set being elected as a temporary member of the UN Security Council for the 2006-2008 term as a strategic goal.[8] Türkiye's continued rapprochement with countries historically viewed as adversaries, such as Greece and Armenia, its assumption of significant responsibilities under the UN Peacekeeping Force in various regions and countries from Haiti to Lebanon, and its leadership alongside Spain in the Alliance of Civilizations initiative[9] have greatly contributed to Ankara's positive image and high prestige in foreign policy.[10]

Commenting on the outstanding efforts of the AK Parti government in this period, Prof. Berdal Aral, in an article he wrote in English for *Insight Turkey* magazine in 2009, highlighted six elements in this context. These are:[11]

1. AK Parti's foreign policy approach based on the leadership of Islamic civilisation, with a different scale and vision than the previous Republican governments,
2. AK Parti's ability to develop constructive relations with all states, rich and poor, West and East,
3. The AK Parti's positioning of Türkiye as a 'centre country' in foreign policy – as it was during the Ottoman Empire – and its willingness to take responsibility for international problems,
4. The AK Parti government, which wants to increase its prestige and influence in international politics, sees the temporary membership of the UN Security Council as useful for this purpose,

5. Ankara's belief that the UN and the UN Security Council can be functional in resolving problems between East-West and Islamic-Christian civilisations,
6. It wants to show the EU how important an international diplomatic power it is, as hopes for EU membership remain high.

Reactions After Success

Following Türkiye's election as a non-permanent member of the UN Security Council after 48 years, Ali Babacan, then Minister of Foreign Affairs, stated that this success was the result of Türkiye's intensive efforts for 5 years and praised the intensive activities of Abdullah Gül as Foreign Minister and President and Recep Tayyip Erdoğan as Prime Minister and their constant reminding of this issue in their contacts with their interlocutors.[12] Babacan answered the question '*What kind of Türkiye will we see in the UN Security Council?*' as follows: '*Türkiye will bring its own unique perspective to the Security Council. It will definitely bring its own independent foreign policy perspective, but one that is increasingly appreciated by the world. If we look at the problems that come before the Council; Africa, the Middle East and the Balkans are issues that Türkiye has already worked hard on and is familiar with. The fact that we have intensified our work on Africa in recent years will give us important advantages. Because we will be sitting there as a country that has started to understand Africa better. We had decided to open 15 new embassies in Africa, and that process continues. Currently, TİKA is active in 37 African countries. This process has given us very important qualities. On the occasion of the Security Council elections, Türkiye came into contact with numerous countries with which it had not been in contact until now. We have established diplomatic relations with many countries in the last 5 years. Türkiye's foreign policy horizon has become much wider. Undoubtedly, all these contacts will provide us with great gains during the Security Council mandate.*'[13] Ali Babacan also expressed support for the then-TRNC President Mehmet Ali Talat on the Cyprus Conflict and gave moderate messages on the solution of the problem.[14] Babacan also emphasised that they had initiated an opening process towards Armenia in order to ensure peace between Azerbaijan and Armenia and stated that they would strengthen their team to work at the UN Security Council in New York from now on.[15]

The then-President of the Republic, Abdullah Gül, thanked all those in office for Türkiye's success and underlined that they had acted with a foreign policy approach in line with Atatürk's motto '*Peace at home, peace in the world*' and that they had succeeded in creating love and respect among other states. Recep Tayyip Erdoğan, the Prime Minister of the time, expressed his satisfaction with the election result, saying that it was the crowning achievement of their success in foreign policy and that '*Türkiye's preference is an indication of the international community's trust in our country.*' [16] The then-Republican People's Party (CHP) Chairman Deniz Baykal and Deputy Chairman Onur Öymen also made statements congratulating the government on this result.[17] Although this result did not create much of an agenda in the domestic public opinion at the time due to intense political polemics, it went down in the history of Turkish Foreign Policy as an important achievement and a proud event. The vote also boosted the self-confidence of the AK Parti government in Türkiye and led to positive opinions in favour of a more active and aggressive approach in foreign policy.

Türkiye's Performance as a Temporary Member of the UN Security Council (2009–2010)

In this section, the important votes that Türkiye participated in after being elected as a non-permanent member of the UN Security Council for the 2009–2010 period will be analysed, allowing for political/diplomatic implications.

2009 Resolutions

On 8 January 2009, in the first vote (UN resolution 1860) in which Türkiye took part as a temporary member of the UN Security Council, fourteen member states (4 permanent members and temporary members such as Türkiye, Austria, Burkina Faso, Costa Rica, Croatia, Japan, Libya, Mexico, Uganda, Vietnam) voted in favour of the withdrawal of Israeli troops from the Gaza Strip and the declaration of a ceasefire, except for the United States, which did not participate in the vote.[18] In this way, Türkiye once again reaffirmed its pro-peace and diplomatic position on the Israeli-Palestinian Conflict in accordance with international law.

In the second vote No. 1861 on the extension of the mandate of the UN Mission in Central Africa and Chad (MINURCAT), in which Türkiye took part as a non-permanent member of the UN Security Council, all fifteen member states were present and Türkiye voted in favour.[19] In such matters related to the establishment or extension of the mandate of UN Missions, Türkiye has always supported the legitimacy of the UN and its missions during its two-year term as a non-permanent member of the Council. To give concrete examples; 1864 extension of the mandate of UN Mission in Nepal UNMIN[20], 1865 extension of the mandate of UN Mission in Côte d'Ivoire UNOCI[21], 1866 extension of the mandate of UN Observer Mission in Georgia UNOMIG[22], 1867 extension of the mandate of UN Mission in Timor-Leste UNMIT[23], This attitude of Türkiye can be seen in many other resolutions such as resolution 1868 on the extension of the mandate of the UN Mission in Afghanistan UNAMA[24], resolution 1870 on the extension of the mandate of the UN Mission in Sudan UNMIS[25], resolution 1871 on the extension of the mandate of the UN Referendum Mission in Western Sahara MINURSO[26], and resolution 1890 on the extension of the mandate of the Afghanistan Peacekeeping Force ISAF[27]. However, Ankara voted 'no' in resolutions 1873 and 1898 on the extension of the mandate of UNFICYP, the UN Peacekeeping Force in Cyprus, in contrast to the other 14 Council members.[28] This means that Türkiye has a different stance on the Cyprus Conflict than the international system.

On internationally contentious issues, Türkiye has tended to act in favour of preserving the liberal world order, often in concert with other Council member states. For example, in resolution 1874, Ankara, like fourteen other member states, voted in favour of preventing the Democratic People's Republic of Korea, commonly known as North Korea, from testing nuclear weapons.[29] Türkiye also voted in favour, along with all other countries, in session 1887 on nuclear non-proliferation.[30] In resolutions such as 1888 on sexual violence against women and the protection of children in armed conflict and 1894 on the protection of civilians in conflict,[31] Türkiye's position, like all other states, was in favour of the international liberal order and human rights.[32] Resolutions such as resolution 1897 on ending piracy activities in Somalia, which was agreed upon by all member states,[33] and resolution 1904 on continuing measures against the Taliban and Al-Qaeda[34] are also important in terms of showing Türkiye's line in line with the global liberal system.

2010 Decisions

In 2010, Türkiye almost exclusively voted 'yes' on the establishment or extension of the mandates of UN Missions. To give a few examples; UN Mission in Afghanistan UNAMA (1917)[35], UN Mission in Sudan UNMIS (1919)[36], UN Mission in Western Sahara Referendum Mission MINURSO (1920)[37], UN Mission in Nepal UNMIN (1921)[38], In resolutions 1937 on the extension of the mandate of the UN Mission in Lebanon, UNIFIL[39], 1944 on the extension of the mandate of the UN Mission in Haiti, MINUSTAH[40], and many others, Ankara voted in favour with all members. However, in 2010, as in 2009, Ankara voted against the extension of the mandate of the UN Mission in Cyprus, UNFICYP, in resolutions 1930 and 1953, and took a stance against the other 14 members of the Security Council.[41]

An interesting 2010 resolution (resolution 1929) concerns measures to address the Iranian nuclear programme. On this issue, Türkiye and Brazil voted 'no', unlike the other 12 member states. Lebanon did not participate in this vote.[42] In this way, Türkiye, together with Brazil and, in a sense, Lebanon, took a different stance than the liberal world order regarding Iran's uranium enrichment activities. This, of course, does not mean that Türkiye supports the Iranian nuclear programme. In fact, immediately after this vote, Türkiye, together with Brazil, signed the agreement restricting Iran's uranium enrichment and announced it to the international community. However, this issue, along with the refusal to support the extension of the mandate of the UN Mission in Cyprus, was the second major issue on which Türkiye was at odds with the international liberal order.

In resolution 1940 on lifting the oil and arms embargo on Sierra Leone[43], Ankara voted in favour in parallel with other states. Another important piece of evidence that Ankara acted in line with the international system was the 1957 resolution on the elimination of weapons of mass destruction.[44] In this way, it was observed that Türkiye generally acted in line with the other member states in the 2-year period.

Conclusion

In conclusion, an assessment of Türkiye's performance in the UN Security Council, which Ankara managed to be elected for the 2009–2010 term with a great diplomatic effort, shows that Türkiye's interests and stance do not fully coincide with the liberal international order on issues such as the Cyprus Conflict and the Iranian nuclear programme, and therefore draws a distinctive image, but on all other issues, it takes a stand in favour of the protection and continuation of the international liberal order pioneered by the UN.

Endnotes

1 Türkiye Cumhuriyeti Dışişleri Bakanlığı, "Türkiye'nin Birleşmiş Milletler, Güvenlik Konseyi Adaylığı", Date of Accession: 10.09.2020 from <http://www.mfa.gov.tr/turkiye_nin-birlesmis-milletler_-guvenlik-konseyi-adayligi.tr.mfa>.

2 *Cumhuriyet* (2008), "Türkiye, BMGK geçici üyesi oldu", 17.10.2008, Date of Accession: 10.09.2020 from <https://www.cumhuriyet.com.tr/amp/haber/turkiye-bmgk-gecici-uyesi-oldu-16350>.

3 For example, Türkiye, which received 109 votes in the first round of voting in October 2014 for the 2015–2016 term, received seventy-three votes in the second round, leaving it behind New Zealand, which was elected in the first round, and Spain, which was elected in the second round, and failed to be elected to the Security Council. See; *BBC Türkçe* (2014), "Türkiye BM Güvenlik Konseyi'ne giremedi", 17.10.2014, Date of Accession: 10.09.2020 from <https://www.bbc.com/turkce/haberler/2014/10/141016_turkiye_bm>.

4 The term used for the political tradition of Islamist political parties such as the National Order Party (MNP), National Salvation Party (MSP), and the Welfare Party (RP) led by Prof. Necmettin Erbakan.

5 Berdal Aral (2009), "Turkey in the UN Security Council: Its Election and Performance", *Insight Turkey*, Fall 2009, Vol. 11, no: 4, p. 153.

6 *Amerika'nın Sesi* (2008), "'Türkiye İsrail'le Suriye Arasında Arabulucu'", 24.04.2008, Date of Accession: 10.09.2020 from <https://www.amerikaninsesi.com/a/a-17-2008-04-24-voa1-88117882/866575.html>.

7 *BBC Türkçe* (2010), "İran, Türkiye ve Brezilya ile nükleer anlaşmayı imzaladı", 17.05.2010, Date of Accession: 10.09.2020 from <https://www.bbc.com/turkce/haberler/2010/05/100517_turkey_iran>.

8 Berdal Aral (2009), "Turkey in the UN Security Council: Its Election and Performance", *Insight Turkey*, Fall 2009, Vol. 11, no: 4, p. 153.

9 The Alliance of Civilizations is an important initiative launched in 2005 by Recep Tayyip Erdoğan, then-Prime Minister of Türkiye, and José Luis Rodríguez Zapatero, then-Prime Minister of Spain, and subsequently adopted by the Secretary-General of the United Nations (UN) as a UN initiative. In essence, this initiative envisaged dialogue and co-operation between Islamic and Christian civilisations based on tolerance, and in this context, Global Forums were organised under the leadership of Türkiye on behalf of the Islamic civilisation and Spain on behalf of the Christian civilisation, aiming to deliver moderate messages and discuss problems between civilisations. Following the Global Forums held in Madrid (2008), İstanbul (2009),

Rio (2010), Doha (2011), Vienna (2013), Bali (2014), and Baku (2016), the 8th Global Forum of the Alliance of Civilizations initiative was hosted by the UN Secretary-General at the UN Headquarters in New York on 19–20 November 2018. See; Türkiye Cumhuriyeti Dışişleri Bakanlığı, "Medeniyetler İttifakı Girişimi", Date of Accession: 10.09.2020 from <http://www.mfa.gov.tr/medeniyetler-ittifaki-girisimi.tr.mfa>.

10 Berdal Aral (2009), "Turkey in the UN Security Council: Its Election and Performance", *Insight Turkey*, Fall 2009, Vol. 11, no: 4, p. 154.

11 Ibid., pp. 154–155.

12 *CNNTürk* (2008), "Türkiye BM'de geçici üyeliğe seçildi", 18.10.2008, Date of Accession: 10.09.2020 from <https://www.cnnturk.com/2008/dunya/10/17/turkiye.bmde.gecici.uyelige.secildi/497124.0/index.html>.

13 Ibid.

14 *Cumhuriyet* (2008), "Türkiye, BMGK geçici üyesi oldu", 17.10.2008, Date of Accession: 10.09.2020 from <https://www.cumhuriyet.com.tr/amp/haber/turkiye-bmgk-gecici-uyesi-oldu-16350>.

15 *CNNTürk* (2008), "Türkiye BM'de geçici üyeliğe seçildi", 18.10.2008, Date of Accession: 10.09.2020 from <https://www.cnnturk.com/2008/dunya/10/17/turkiye.bmde.gecici.uyelige.secildi/497124.0/index.html>.

16 *Cumhuriyet* (2008), "Türkiye, BMGK geçici üyesi oldu", 17.10.2008, Date of Accession: 10.09.2020 from <https://www.cumhuriyet.com.tr/amp/haber/turkiye-bmgk-gecici-uyesi-oldu-16350>.

17 *CNNTürk* (2008), "Türkiye BM'de geçici üyeliğe seçildi", 18.10.2008, Date of Accession: 10.09.2020 from <https://www.cnnturk.com/2008/dunya/10/17/turkiye.bmde.gecici.uyelige.secildi/497124.0/index.html>.

18 See; <https://digitallibrary.un.org/record/645652?ln=en>.

19 See; <https://digitallibrary.un.org/record/647397?ln=en>.

20 See; <https://digitallibrary.un.org/record/647419?ln=en>.

21 See; <https://digitallibrary.un.org/record/647426?ln=en>.

22 See; <https://digitallibrary.un.org/record/649141?ln=en>.

23 See; <https://digitallibrary.un.org/record/649147?ln=en>.

24 See; <https://digitallibrary.un.org/record/650684?ln=en>.

25 See; <https://digitallibrary.un.org/record/653260?ln=en>.

26 See; <https://digitallibrary.un.org/record/653264?ln=en>.

27 See; <https://digitallibrary.un.org/record/667440?ln=en>.

28 See; <https://digitallibrary.un.org/record/656252?ln=en>; <https://digitallibrary.un.org/record/673479?ln=en.

29 See; <https://digitallibrary.un.org/record/659964?ln=en>.

30 See; <https://digitallibrary.un.org/record/667427?ln=en>.

31 See; <https://digitallibrary.un.org/record/671179?ln=en>.

32 See; <https://digitallibrary.un.org/record/667429?ln=en>.

33 See; <https://digitallibrary.un.org/record/672501?ln=en>.

34 See; <https://digitallibrary.un.org/record/673920?ln=en>.

35 See; <https://digitallibrary.un.org/record/685860?ln=en>.

36 See; <https://digitallibrary.un.org/record/685863?ln=en>.

37 See; <https://digitallibrary.un.org/record/685864?ln=en>.

38 See; <https://digitallibrary.un.org/record/685867?ln=en>.

39 See; <https://digitallibrary.un.org/record/689425?ln=en>.

40 See; <https://digitallibrary.un.org/record/692056?ln=en>.

41 See; <https://digitallibrary.un.org/record/685889?ln=en>; <https://digitallibrary.un.org/record/695094?ln=en.

42 See; <https://digitallibrary.un.org/record/685888?ln=en>.

43 See; <https://digitallibrary.un.org/record/690993?ln=en>.

44 See; <https://digitallibrary.un.org/record/695281?ln=en>.

Why Is the World Bigger Than Five?

Figure 2: Turkish President Recep Tayyip Erdoğan

Turkish President Recep Tayyip Erdoğan began to use the slogan '*The world is bigger than five*' (*Dünya beşten büyüktür*) in his international speeches in the last few years. The slogan was first used by President Erdoğan in 2013 and repeated many times in the subsequent years. Erdoğan used this phrase especially during his United Nations (UN) speeches in order to take support from other countries. Although Türkiye so far was unable to develop a concrete foreign policy based on this slogan and its implications, expectations and plans for reforming the United Nations (UN) could become more popular in the near future. In this piece, I will try to analyse why this slogan is crucially important and necessary for a better future.

United Nations was established after the Second World War in accordance with the post-war conditions. Accordingly, United States of America (U.S), Soviet Union (USSR), United Kingdom, France, and Taiwan became permanent members of the UN Security Council (they are called as P5 countries). However, UN was able to reform itself in time; for instance, in the early 1970s (1971), People's Republic of China replaced Taiwan in the Security Council. Moreover, Russian Federation succeeded Soviet Union after the dissolution of USSR in the early 1990s (1991). These two changes prove that UN could reform itself with reasonable arguments and consensus.

UN so far was unable to solve major political problems in the world including Israel-Palestine Conflict, Cyprus Dispute, Kashmir Conflict, and Nagorno-Karabakh Dispute. This was caused by P5 countries' political preferences and their indifference towards other countries and nations' sufferings. In many times, one country was able to block the UN Security Council to make a decision because of its national interests or historical rivalry towards another state. That is why, Turkish President's slogan in fact carries a very important and politically correct message: we cannot create a peaceful world when five countries have right to decide over the future of other 192–93 states.

I should admit that, as an academic it is very hard to explain to my students why millions of Muslims, Hindus, and Jews are not represented in the UN Security Council and only Christian nations, and China were given such privilege. That is why; Türkiye could actually turn this slogan into a macro reform project for the UN. In that case, it is much easier to abolish the UN Security Council and to transform UN General Assembly into a world parliament (as it was hoped by Immanuel Kant long decades ago) where all decisions could be taken by 2/3 majority in voting. If this happens, naturally, all countries will increase their diplomatic efforts and lobbying activities towards other countries. This will not only increase UN's legitimacy but also boost peace in global politics. Moreover, diplomacy and the study of International Relations will also develop during this process since all countries will try to improve their legitimacy and take more support from other countries by making academic studies and diplomatic activities.

For all these reasons, I think reforming the UN should be the top priority of all states in the twenty-first century. Otherwise, clashes of national interests and the structure of P5 will lead us towards new wars and conflicts in addition to existing ones in the following years. For many, this slogan and political ideal might be conceived too idealistic for the moment; but remember that just few decades ago male-female equality and racial equality were also unthinkable in many states. However, nowadays UN and all states work together in order to provide gender equality and prevention of racial discrimination. So, equality of states could also be a very reasonable argument in the near future in case Türkiye is politically supported by other countries. Especially Russia and China, two countries trying to become more influential in global politics could support the Turkish cause; because this might lead these two countries to take more support from developing countries (especially in Africa) and diminish criticism towards their domestic regimes.

Understanding Official Turkish Stance on the Question of Eastern Mediterranean Through Retired Rear Admiral Cihat Yayci's Book

Introduction

'Cyprus Dispute and the Eastern Mediterranean Question' is still considered as one of the most important topics in Turkish Foreign Policy. The issue needs a clarification since Türkiye officially supports peace talks and settlement negotiations between Turkish Cypriot and Greek Cypriot administrations, but at the same time continues to invest – both politically and economically – in the very existence and development of Turkish Republic of Northern Cyprus (TRNC), a state that was founded in 1983 and recognised until now only by Türkiye.

It is a fact that the Cyprus Dispute has evolved into a more complex political/diplomatic issue with the discovery of natural gas resources in the Eastern Mediterranean and Greek Cypriot administration's (officially named as the Republic of Cyprus or Cyprus Republic) success in bringing big energy companies from France (Total), Italy (ENI), South Korea (KOGAS), and the United States (Noble Energy, ExxonMobil) to this region as well as exclusive economic zone agreements made between Nicosia and some countries including Egypt, Greece, and Israel (negotiations are continuing with Lebanon and Syria as well). Türkiye responded to Greek Cypriot efforts by an exclusive economic zone agreement made with TRNC and a recent maritime jurisdiction zone agreement made with officially recognised Libyan government (represented by Prime Minister Fayez al-Sarraj). That is why, the issue still on the agenda as a hot topic although it is less spoken these days due to coronavirus disease.

In order to understand Türkiye's official position in terms of Cyprus Dispute and the Eastern Mediterranean Question, it is necessary to read and grasp Rear Admiral Cihat Yaycı's new book (2020, Kırmızı Kedi Yayınevi) entitled *Doğu Akdeniz Paylaşım Mücadelesi ve Türkiye (Eastern Mediterranean Allocation Struggle and Türkiye)*. Due to copyright issues, a short summary of this book covering the main ideas will be provided here in order to enlighten international (non-Turkish speaker) readers.

The Author

Rear Admiral Cihat Yaycı (1966–) is Turkish high-rank soldier who is known with his books on Turkish-Greek relations, Aegean Dispute, and Eastern Mediterranean Question. He has MA degree in Engineering Physics and Electronic Engineering from Naval Postgraduate School (NPS), California and PhD degree in International Relations from İstanbul University. Yaycı speaks English and Russian languages. As a natural consequence of his profession, Read Admiral Cihat Yaycı defends Turkish interests and puts forward a Turkish outlook while analysing these issues. Since he is an important soldier on active duty, it is very beneficial to understand the essence of Yaycı's views in order to interpret Turkish Armed Forces' official positioning in terms of Cyprus Dispute and Eastern Mediterranean Question.

The Brief Summary of the Book

According to author, the Eastern Mediterranean is very important for strategic reasons such as neighbouring the Middle Eastern region which contains more than half of world's oil reserves, big countries' military and logistic settlements within this region[1], being a very dynamic transit location in terms of international naval trade, and recently becoming a new potential energy centre with oil and gas discoveries made around Cyprus, Israel, and Egypt. The author claims that Eastern Mediterranean hydrocarbon resources could respond to Türkiye's natural gas need for 572 years or Europe's natural gas needs for 30 years. Moreover, it is worthy to note that there could be new discoveries made within this region in the near future. However, riparian states within this region so far could not agree on a partition plan to draw the lines of maritime jurisdiction zones as well as exclusive economic zones.

That is why, it is an urgent need to understand riparian states' diverging positions, the stance of international law on this matter and to work on how to create consensus in order to avoid a possible clash.

Cihat Yaycı analyses the issue first from the perspective of international law. As the author mentions), the 1982 United Nations Convention on the Law of the Sea (UNCLOS)[2] limits countries' exclusive economic zones to 200 nautical miles from the baselines from which the breadth of the territorial sea is measured (Article 57). In order to claim rights over a maritime zone, countries need to declare their own economic economic zones (*münhasır ekonomik bölge*/MEB in Turkish), draw detailed maps including the coordinates and submit a copy of these to the Secretary-General of the United Nations in accordance with the Article 75 of the UNCLOS. Moreover, Article 83 of the UNCLOS states that '*the delimitation of the continental shelf between States with opposite or adjacent coasts shall be effected by agreement on the basis of international law, as referred to in Article 38 of the Statute of the International Court of Justice, in order to achieve an equitable solution.*' However, there is no article in the UNCLOS that interdicts states to declare their exclusive economic zones unilaterally.

In relation to this issue, Yaycı criticises the Greek Cypriot administration's declared exclusive economic zones on the basis of the fact that they are violating the rights of Egypt, Israel, Türkiye, and Turkish Cypriots (TRNC). According to author, the problem between Ankara and Nicosia emerges due to clash taken place in the 7th parcel (Nicosia gave the rights of drilling in this parcel to Italian ENI and French Total) in addition to 2nd, 3rd, 8th, and 9th parcels which were licenced to Türkiye's TPAO by the TRNC government. As a legal and political argument, Yaycı puts forward two main ideas: (1) exclusive economic zone declared by Nicosia clashes with Ankara's plans (although Türkiye until now did not officially declare its official exclusive economic zone in the Eastern Mediterranean, Turkish media and retired Turkish soldiers frequently publishes[3] articles on this matter) on the 7th parcel, (2) Greek Cypriot administration acts as the only people on the island in declaring exclusive economic zone by ignoring the rights of Turkish Cypriots. Yaycı later proposes Turkish government to declare its exclusive economic zone with a detailed map and declare it to the world. The author also underlines that in order to guarantee peace and stability in the Eastern Mediterranean; all countries should act responsibly and make their steps by creating consensus with other states. In that sense, Yaycı criticises Eastern Mediterranean (EastMed) pipeline project initiated by Greece, Cyprus, and Israel.

Conclusion

Finally, in my opinion, Rear Admiral Cihat Yaycı's book is crucially important to understand Turkish security bureaucracy's look towards recent developments taking place in the Eastern Mediterranean. It is fact that Türkiye might have its own democratic problems, but as a country that makes more humanitarian help (aid) than any other country in the world in the last few years, Türkiye's voice deserves to be heard by Athens, Nicosia, and Jerusalem (Tel Aviv) in order to avoid a possible clash in the near future. The solution is not impossible; all we have to do is to bring all riparian states' delegates and experts together for an international conference to reach consensus and encourage them to act responsibly and give some concessions to protect peace and stability in the Mediterranean.

Endnotes

1 For instance, the United Kingdom has two military bases in Cyprus (Akrotiri and Dhekelia), the United States has a naval base in Crete, Russian Federation has a logistic base and naval facility in Tartus/Syria, and France has been recently given the right to use Andreas Papandreou Air Base in Paphos as well as Evangelos Florakis Naval Base near Zygi, between Limassol and Larnaca.

2 See; <https://www.un.org/depts/los/convention_agreements/texts/unclos/unclos_e.pdf>.

3 See; <https://www.aa.com.tr/en/africa/analysis-strategic-legal-aspects-of-turkey-libya-deal/1673079>.

Can Türkiye Join Brics+?

Introduction

Having been pointed out as one of the six key '*swing states*' of the twenty-first century – together with Brazil, India, Indonesia, Saudi Arabia, and South Africa – by Cliff Kupchan[1], Türkiye is an important regional power that contributes a lot to the shaping of the emerging multipolar world order. Being a full member of the building stone Western institutions including the Council of Europe since 1950 and NATO since 1952, Türkiye has also been in accession talks with the European Union (EU) since 2005. However, Turkish membership in the EU does not seem a realistic target recently due to the Cyprus Conflict in addition to various other problematic issues that distance Brussels and Ankara.

To diversify its search for multi-dimensionalism in foreign policy since the 1960s, Ankara also became a member of the Islamic Cooperation Organisation in 1969 (Organisation of Islamic Conference previously) and the Organisation of Turkic States in 2009. Moreover, to further diversify its strategic options, Türkiye recently became a dialogue partner in the Shanghai Cooperation Organisation (SCO) (2013) and the Association of Southeast Asian Nations (ASEAN) (2017) in addition to its strategic partner status in the African Union since 2008. Being also a full member of economic organisations such as the World Bank (WB), International Monetary Fund (IMF), IDB (Islamic Development Bank), Organisation for Economic Co-operation and Development (OECD), Economic Cooperation Organisation (ECO), Black Sea Economic Cooperation (BSEC), Economic Commission for Latin America and the Caribbean (ECLAC), Developing Eight Organisation for Economic Cooperation (D-8), and the Group of Twenty (G-20), there are now serious political discussions about Türkiye's possible membership to BRICS+.

In this article, I am going to analyse and discuss Türkiye's potential membership to BRICS+. But first, I am going to summarise the history of BRICS+ as well as its current status and powerful characteristics.

The History of BRICS+

BRICS is an abbreviation used for pointing out 5 countries that have been challenging the United States (US)-led Western hegemony in global affairs: Brazil, Russia, India, China, and South Africa. The informal grouping of these 5 countries in the early 2000s, later turned into an important intergovernmental organisation. The process started in 2006, when – at a time when the United States was a very unpopular international actor in the world due to the Iraq War – representatives of Brazil, Russia, India, and China held an informal meeting during the United Nations (UN) General Assembly.[2] It was Goldman Sachs economist Jim O'Neill who first coined the term in 2001 from an economic perspective in his study called 'Building Better Global Economic BRICs'[3], to describe these four countries that might dominate the global economy by 2050. In 2009, BRIC meetings turned into a legal intergovernmental organisation upon the wishes of these four states and the first official meeting took place in Ekaterinburg, Russia. In this first official meeting, following Russian President Vladimir Putin's infamous speech at the Munich Security Conference in 2007[4], BRIC pledged commitment to a multipolar world order and global non-interventionism and called for a new global reserve currency as an alternative to the US dollar.[5] In 2011, South Africa became the fifth member of the platform as the name BRIC turned into BRICS. BRICS' second meeting convened in Brasilia, Brazil, the third in Sanya, China, the fourth in New Delhi, India, the fifth in Durban, South Africa, the sixth in Fortaleza, Brazil, the seventh in Ufa, Russia, the eighth in Benaulim, India, the ninth in Xiamen, China, the tenth in Johannesburg, South Africa, the eleventh in Brasilia, Brazil, the twelfth in Saint Petersburg, Russia (as video conference due to COVID-19 pandemic), the thirteenth in New Delhi, India, the fourteenth in Beijing, China, and the last one, the fifteenth last year in Johannesburg, South Africa.[6]

Although BRICS made some steps for institutionalisation such as the inauguration of the BRICS-based New Development Bank (NDB)[7] and the BRICS Interbank Cooperation Mechanism[8], the organisation continues to be a political platform based on mutual understanding and the search for harmony among its member states and especially their leaders. So, the organisation still does not have a charter, it does not work with a fixed secretariat, nor does it have any funds to finance its activities.[9] In addition, there is no formal application process to join BRICS, rather, new members must be unanimously approved by existing ones.

However, in time, BRICS member states were able to develop a kind of shared values and common interests that underlie mutually beneficial co-operation and a shared vision for a better world. According to the 2023 Declaration announced at the 2023 BRICS Summit in South Africa, BRICS' guiding principles for membership are as follows:[10]

- The BRICS spirit of mutual respect and understanding, equality, solidarity, openness, inclusiveness, and consensus,
- The BRICS practice of full consultation and promoting concrete co-operation based on consensus,
- The BRICS vision of strengthening multilateralism, strengthening and reforming the multilateral system, and upholding international law,
- The BRICS objective of strengthening co-operation under the three pillars of political and security, economic and financial, and cultural and people-to-people co-operation,
- A resolve to maintain the identity, coherence, and consensus-based nature of BRICS by consolidation of co-operation and promoting institutional development,
- Acceptance of the purposes and principles enshrined in the Charter of the United Nations as an indispensable cornerstone of multilateralism and international law,
- Support for increased representation of, and a more significant role for, emerging and developing countries in the international system, including geographical balance,
- Support for a comprehensive reform of the United Nations, including its Security Council, to make it more democratic, representative, effective, and efficient, and to increase the representation of developing

countries in the Council's memberships so that it can adequately respond to prevailing global challenges and support the legitimate aspirations of emerging and developing countries from Africa, Asia and Latin America, including Brazil, India, and South Africa, to play a greater role in international affairs, in particular in the United Nations, including its Security Council,
- The commitment to the central role of the United Nations in an international system in which sovereign states cooperate to maintain peace and security, advance sustainable development, and ensure the promotion and protection of democracy, human rights, and fundamental freedoms for all.

Following these principles, at the 2023 BRICS Summit in Johannesburg, South Africa, BRICS+ members approved the membership of six states: Saudi Arabia, Iran, the United Arab Emirates (UAE), Egypt, Ethiopia, and Argentina. Among these states, Argentina withdrew its formal application under its new President Javier Milei and Saudi Arabia has not yet ratified its membership. So, among these 6 states, 4 of them became new members of the organisation, thus, BRICS+ reaching the number of nine member states by 2024. In 2025, Indonesia became the 10th member of BRICS+. With its new members approved, the organisation has been started to be called the BRICS+ by the international media[11], although so far, no official name change has been announced. Becoming a more important economic and diplomatic platform each year, so far, many countries applied for membership in BRICS+. According to South Africa's BRICS+ Ambassador, Mr Anil Sooklal, twenty-two countries formally applied for membership.[12] These potential member states include Algeria, Bahrain, Bangladesh, Belarus, Bolivia, Cuba, Kazakhstan, Kuwait, Nigeria, Pakistan, Palestine, Senegal, Thailand, Venezuela, and Vietnam. South African Foreign Minister Naledi Pandor on the other hand said that there is a huge worldwide interest in the BRICS+ group and she received many official letters from twelve different countries for their potential membership.[13] Among these willing states, Mexico, Tunisia, and Türkiye (Türkiye) are also stated by some journalists. In that sense, further growth of BRICS+ in the coming years is a strong possibility.

BRICS+ in Numbers

BRICS represented 42 % of the world's population (3.2 billion), 30 % of the world's total surface, 23 % of the total global GDP, and 18 % of total trade in the world.[14] According to IMF's 2020 data, BRICS already represents a much larger portion of the global economy compared to the G7. Accordingly, the share of BRICS in world GDP is 34 %, whereas the share of G7 countries in the world GDP is 29 %.[15] With five more important members included in 2024, BRICS' numbers in these categories are now even further increased. The most striking feature of the BRICS experience so far is the positive economic outcomes similar to the EU experience in the past. BRICS member states' economies since the 2000s have shown steady growth, making the organisation an attraction centre for new members. In that sense, the role of BRICS+ in the global economy will be even more dominating compared to G7 in the near future.

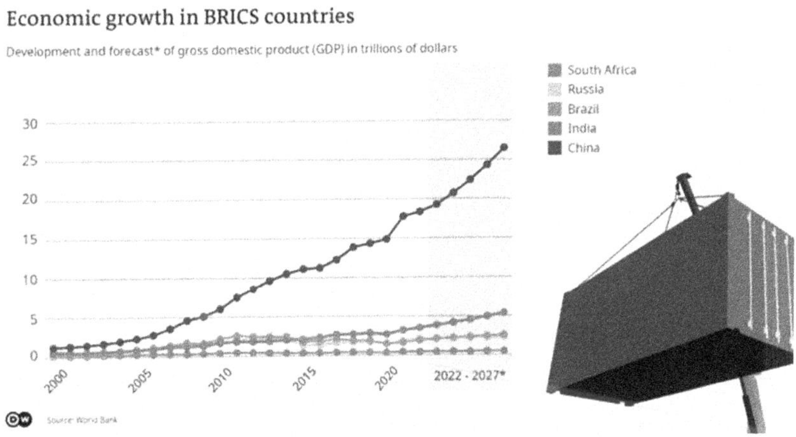

Figure 3: BRICS countries' economic performance[16]

Within the current 10-member BRICS+, six countries belong to the Asian continent, more specifically three or even four (including Egypt, which is in fact in the African continent) members are from the Middle East, whereas three members are situated in Africa, and Brazil is the only South American member. In that sense, BRICS+ could play an important role in the future for the solution of political crises in the Middle East as well as Asia due to its encouragement of increasing economic ties between states rather than military-based approaches. Moreover, with energy-producer countries included, BRICS+ could now also play an influential role in the energy market and contribute to the pricing of oil and gas. In addition, with countries having important geopolitical positioning such as Egypt controlling the Suez

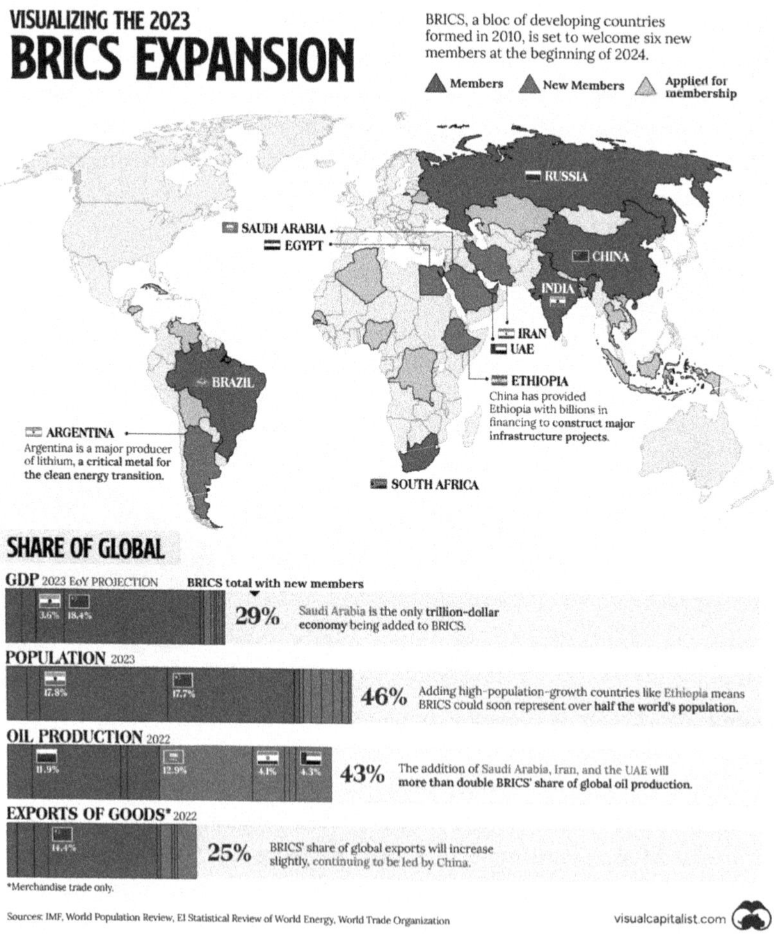

Figure 4: BRICS map[18]

Canal[17] and Iran controlling the Persian Gulf, BRICS+ geopolitically also has recently become a key player in world affairs both in geopolitics and in geoeconomics.

BRICS so far was instrumental in the development of economic relations between Russia and China and challenging the hegemonic status of the US dollar in global trade by encouraging the use of local currencies. For instance, by 2023, 80 % of trade between China and Russia is already conducted in ruble and the yuan.[19] In the coming years, BRICS will further pressure the use of local currencies in trade for its members, which would certainly weaken the hegemonic situation of the US dollar. However, it should be stated except for a critical stance against US interventionism and the hegemonic status of the American dollar, BRICS members do not have a strict political agenda, and they have a lot of differences among themselves in terms of ideological and political preferences. For instance, while China, and especially Russia and South Africa are more assertive and critical towards Western countries, Brazil and India are less anti-Western and want to keep their close ties with the United States and European countries.

Türkiye's Potential Membership: Why Not?

Türkiye's potential membership in BRICS+ is a widely discussed issue in the country in 2018. It should not be forgotten that Turkish President Recep Tayyip Erdoğan attended the BRICS Summit in 2018 and called for Turkish membership in the organisation.[20] In addition, Türkiye became a dialogue partner recently for the SCO although it had some military characteristics which might be in contradiction with Ankara's membership in NATO. President Erdoğan even talked about a full membership to SCO in 2022.[21] In that sense, BRICS+, not having a military feature, seems to be an ideal and less risky organisation for Türkiye's full membership compared to the SCO.

Demircan thinks that there are five good reasons for Türkiye to become a member of the BRICS: (1) It is a platform for developing countries like Türkiye, (2) Both sides defend multipolarity and justice in the world order, (3) It is the union of producer countries which seek for new markets similar to Türkiye, (4) It is an institution for colonised and oppressed nations and Türkiye never truly was an imperialist state like Western countries, (5) Both BRICS members and Türkiye have a young and dynamic population.[22] The man who invented the term, Jim O'Neill also thinks that Türkiye could be an ideal member of the BRICS expanded or BRICS+ due to its problematic relations with the US-centred world system.[23]

Chinese ambassador to Ankara, His Excellency Mr Liu Shaobin already announced in 2023 that his country endorses Turkish membership to BRICS+.[24] Chivvis, Coşkun, and Geaghan-Breiner on the other hand wrote that Türkiye's new and '*360-degree foreign policy*' is based on flexibility and strategic independence and Ankara does not consider its multi-dimensional diplomatic openings as a contradiction with its classical foreign policy.[25] Diriöz wrote that the EU's unfair treatment of Ankara during the full membership process also increased Ankara's search for strategic autonomy and appetite to become a member of BRICS.[26] Karataş also believes that Ankara's strategic stance is not pro or anti-West, but rather based on the '*Türkiye Century*' understanding, which represents a more independent-minded, assertive, and national interest-based foreign policy.[27] However, Karataş also adds that the Turkish political elite does not question the country's membership in NATO or give up on the EU membership process. That is why, he concludes that due to the risks of fully aligning with BRICS+, Türkiye for the moment will try to improve its economic and political relations with BRICS+ members and not seek membership.[28] But Victor Gao from the Centre for China and Globalization (CCG) thinks that there is no Quran-based holy restriction for Ankara to become a member of BRICS+, so Türkiye and Mexico could very well become members of this organisation shortly.[29]

From my perspective, BRICS+ membership would be an advantageous step in many ways. First of all, the global economy is shifting towards the East (Asia) and none of the countries in the world could do anything about this systemic change. In that sense, BRICS+ membership and close co-operation with strong Asian states such as China and Russia would not be an irrational decision for Ankara. Secondly, Türkiye is not treated equally and fairly in its relations with Washington (the United States) and Brussels (EU) recently. Although Ankara's accession to the EU was blocked by European countries and the freezing of the full membership process led to the deterioration of Türkiye's democratic progress, only Ankara was accused of this toxic relationship by the Western public and media. In my opinion, since relations involve a minimum of two sides, mistakes are reciprocal in diplomacy. In that sense, to fix its relations with the West, Türkiye's search for strategic autonomy and BRICS+ membership is a rational, wise, and pragmatic solution. Maybe thanks to its membership in BRICS+, Ankara could even finally reach a real chance to become a full member of the EU. Thirdly and lastly, Turkish membership to BRICS+ could trigger demands and efforts for a UN reform, which seems absolutely necessary to keep peace and stability in the world. President Erdoğan has been implementing that kind of foreign policy in the last few years with the motto of '*The World is Bigger Than Five*' to criticise the composition of the UN Security Council, which could not do anything to prevent genocides, massacres, and wars.

However, one should be aware of the risks of such a move as well. In that sense, the main risk would be the growing isolation of Ankara from and/or within Western institutions. But since Türkiye's cordial ties with the West will continue due to – still – undisputed NATO membership and BRICS+ does not carry any security/military features, the consequences of this move might not be that risky for Ankara. Secondly, trying to keep its political system within the boundaries of democracy and free market, Ankara, distancing itself from the West and getting closer to the East might create extra burdens and new problems in terms of governance and democracy. But considering the position of Brazil and India, two large democracies, Ankara might very well keep and even improve its democracy with BRICS+ membership. After all, BRICS+ does not intervene into the domestic politics of member countries and encourage states to cooperate with each other rather than competition.

Conclusion

To conclude, due to failures to provide a just and well-functioning world order, the United States and its allies are constantly losing power, and the world is progressing towards a new multipolarism. In such a system, countries having a wide range of trade networks, geopolitical advantages, and stable domestic political systems will be more influential. In that sense, Türkiye has great potential to become a regional power having a global appeal if it could further enrich its diplomatic ties with countries all around the world. Türkiye has a true potential to achieve this if it does not fall into Western traps as in the case of the Syrian civil war. In that sense, Türkiye's BRICS+ membership should be achieved as soon as possible so that Ankara will show its Western allies that it is very serious about this '*new deal*' in foreign policy. Türkiye's role in the BRICS on the other hand could be like Lula's Brazil, better integrated and having good relations with the West though not ignoring or underestimating but rather strengthening the power of the '*global south*'. Lastly, especially China's contribution to Türkiye's involvement in BRICS could be a great asset for both sides since Beijing needs strong regional partners to further develop and successfully implement its Belt and Road Initiative (BRI) project and Türkiye needs strong investors to develop its economy.

In the 2024 Kazan meeting of BRICS+, despite high expectations, Türkiye was not invited for full membership. Instead, Ankara was given the status of partner country, which did not satisfy the Turkish public and created anger towards the organisation. However, Türkiye's BRICS+ membership could be a geopolitical reality in the near future if especially Türkiye cannot fix its relations with its traditional Western allies.

Endnotes

[1] Cliff Kupchan (2023), "6 Swing States Will Decide the Future of Geopolitics", *Foreign Policy*, 06.06.2023, Date of Accession: 07.03.2024 from <https://foreignpolicy.com/2023/06/06/geopolitics-global-south-middle-powers-swing-states-india-brazil-Türkiye-indonesia-saudi-arabia-south-africa/>.

[2] Britannica.com, "BRICS", Date of Accession: 07.03.2024 from <https://www.britannica.com/topic/BRICS>.

[3] Jim O'Neill (2001), "Building Better Global Economic BRICs", Goldman Sachs, November 2001, Date of Accession: 07.03.2024 from <https://www.goldmansachs.com/intelligence/archive/building-better.html>.

[4] RussianPerspective, "Putin's famous Munich Speech 2007", Date of Accession: 07.03.2024 from <https://www.youtube.com/watch?v=hQ58Yv6kP44>.

[5] Britannica.com, "BRICS", Date of Accession: 07.03.2024 from <https://www.britannica.com/topic/BRICS>.

[6] Ozan Örmeci (2024), "BRICS'in Genişlemesi ABD Hegemonyasına Bir Meydan Okuma Mı?", Uluslararası Politika Akademisi, 05.01.2024, Date of Accession: 07.03.2024 from <https://politikaakademisi.org/2024/01/05/bricsin-genislemesi-abd-hegemonyasina-bir-meydan-okuma-mi/>.

[7] New Development Bank website, Date of Accession: 07.03.2024 from <https://www.ndb.int/>.

[8] BRICS Interbank Cooperation Mechanism website, Date of Accession: 07.02.2024 from <https://xn--90ab5f.xn--p1ai/en/international-multilateral-cooperation/the-brics-interbank-cooperation-mechanism/>.

9 Instituto de Pesquisa Econômica Aplicada (2014), "Learn about BRICS", Date of Accession: 07.03.2024 from <https://www.ipea.gov.br/forumbrics/en/learn-about-brics.html#:~:text=As%20a%20group%2C%20BRICS%20has,funds%20to%20finance%20its%20activities>.

10 BRICS 2023 (2023), "BRICS Membership Expansion: Guiding Principles, Standards, Criteria and Procedures", Date of Accession: 07.03.2024 from <https://brics2023.gov.za/wp-content/uploads/2023/11/BRICS-Membership-expansion-guiding-principles-criteria-and-standards-2023.pdf>.

11 José Antonio W. Cai (2023), "BRICS+: An alternative to the Western bloc?", Aceprensa, 28.10.2023, Date of Accession: 07.03.2024 from <https://www.aceprensa.com/english/brics-an-alternative-to-the-western-bloc/>.

12 Kate Bartlett (2023), "40 More Countries Want to Join BRICS, Says South Africa", *Voice of America*, 21.07.2023, Date of Accession: 07.03.2024 from <https://www.voanews.com/a/more-countries-want-to-join-brics-says-south-africa-/7190526.html>.

13 *WION* (2023), "South Africa's Foreign Minister Naledi Pandor sees India's G20 leadership as opportunity for Global South", 05.03.2023, Date of Accession: 07.03.2024 from <https://www.wionews.com/world/south-african-foreign-minister-naledi-pandor-sees-indias-g20-leadership-as-opportunity-for-global-south-568817>.

14 BRICS 2023 (2023), "Evolution of BRICS", Date of Accession: 07.03.2024 from <https://brics2023.gov.za/evolution-of-brics/>.

15 Necati Demircan (2023), "Is it possible to see Türkiye into BRICS?", *Modern Diplomacy*, 26.07.2023, Date of Accession: 07.03.2024 from <https://moderndiplomacy.eu/2023/07/26/is-it-possible-to-see-turkiye-into-brics/>.

16 Astrid Prange de Oliveira (2023), "A new world order? BRICS nations offer alternative to West", *DW*, 04.10.2023, Date of Accession: 07.03.2024 from <https://www.dw.com/en/a-new-world-order-brics-nations-offer-alternative-to-west/a-65124269>.

17 Emile Amin (2023), "BRICS Plus ve yeni dünya düzeninin temelleri", *Independent Türkçe*, 24.08.2023, Date of Accession: 07.03.2024 from <https://www.indyturk.com/node/656646/d%C3%BCnyadan-sesler/brics-plus-ve-yeni-d%C3%BCnya-d%C3%BCzeninin-temelleri>.

18 Marcus Lu (2023), "Visualizing the BRICS Expansion in 4 Charts", *Visual Capitalist*, 24.08.2023, Date of Accession: 07.03.2024 from <https://www.visualcapitalist.com/visualizing-the-brics-expansion-in-4-charts/>.

19 Necati Demircan (2023), "Is it possible to see Türkiye into BRICS?", *Modern Diplomacy*, 26.07.2023, Date of Accession: 07.03.2024 from <https://moderndiplomacy.eu/2023/07/26/is-it-possible-to-see-turkiye-into-brics/>.

20 *Turkish Minute* (2023), "[OPINION] Is Türkiye serious about joining BRICS?", 02.08.2023, Date of Accession: 07.03.2024 from <https://www.turkishminute.com/2023/08/02/opinion-is-Türkiye-serious-about-joining-brics/>.

21 Baris Balci & Selcan Hacaoglu (2022), "Türkiye Seeks to Be First NATO Member to Join China-Led SCO", *Bloomberg*, 17.09.2022, Date of Accession:

07.03.2024 from <https://www.bloomberg.com/news/articles/2022-09-17/Türkiye-seeks-china-led-bloc-membership-in-threat-to-nato-allies>.

[22] Necati Demircan (2023), "Is it possible to see Türkiye into BRICS?", *Modern Diplomacy*, 26.07.2023, Date of Accession: 07.03.2024 from <https://moderndiplomacy.eu/2023/07/26/is-it-possible-to-see-turkiye-into-brics/>.

[23] Gokhan Kurtaran (2023), "Türkiye obvious nation for expanded BRICS, says leading economist", *AA*, 12.05.2023, Date of Accession: 07.03.2024 from <https://www.aa.com.tr/en/turkiye/turkiye-obvious-nation-for-expanded-brics-says-leading-economist/2896122>.

[24] *Press Tv* (2023), "China announces desire for Türkiye to join BRICS", 02.09.2023, Date of Accession: 07.03.2024 from <https://www.presstv.ir/Detail/2023/09/02/710130/China-BRICS-Türkiye-membership-idea-envoy>.

[25] Christopher S. Chivvis & Alper Coşkun & Beatrix Geaghan-Breiner (2023), "Türkiye in the Emerging World Order", Carnegie Endowment for International Peace, 31.10.2023, Date of Accession: 07.03.2024 from <https://carnegieendowment.org/2023/10/31/t-rkiye-in-emerging-world-order-pub-90868>.

[26] Ali Oğuz Diriöz (2023), "What should be Türkiye's approach to BRICS?", *Daily Sabah*, 19.09.2023, Date of Accession: 07.03.2024 from <https://www.dailysabah.com/opinion/op-ed/what-should-be-turkiyes-approach-to-brics>.

[27] İbrahim Karataş (2023), "Should Türkiye Join BRICS?", *Politics Today*, 04.09.2023, Date of Accession: 07.03.2024 from <https://politicstoday.org/should-Türkiye-join-brics/>.

[28] Ibid.

[29] Burak Ünveren (2023), "Türkiye'nin BRICS'e katılamayacağı Kur'an'da yazmıyor", *DW Türkçe*, 10.12.2023, Date of Accession: 07.03.2024 from <https://www.dw.com/tr/t%C3%BCrkiyenin-bricse-kat%C4%B1lamayaca%C4%9F%C4%B1-kuranda-yazm%C4%B1yor/a-67682398>.

Are Greece and Türkiye Heading to a War?

Introduction

Turkish-Greek relations have always been tense and open to conflict and military escalation though there had been smooth times in the past. We should not forget that two countries are historical rivals to each other due to their nation-creation process. Thus, as Babacan points out, some labelled 'tension as ordinary and stability an exception' in Turkish-Greek relations.[1] However, after Türkiye's victory against invading Greek powers in 1923, two visionary statesmen Atatürk and Venizelos were able to establish friendly relations. Two countries were both acted as United States (US) allies against the expansionism of communism and Soviet Union during the Cold War. However, this did not prevent two countries to engage in a political/diplomatic clash in 1974 when Türkiye rightfully intervened into the island of Cyprus as a guarantor state following a military coup organised by Greek Cypriots aiming to annex the island to Greece (an idea known shortly as '*enosis*').

Starting from the late 1990s, as Türkiye began to make progress for becoming a full member of the European Union (EU), two countries improved their relations in every aspect. For instance, discovery talks (*istikşafi görüşmeler*) and High-Level Cooperation Council (Yüksek Düzeyli İş Birliği Konseyi-YDİK) meetings were initiated.[2] However, after the take-over of a new and assertive right-wing government in Greece in 2019 by Kyriakos Mitsotakis, two countries' relations were quickly deteriorated. Mitsotakis' take-over in Greece coincided with Türkiye's authoritarian transformation and created a reverse magnetisation in bilateral relations. Nowadays, experts in both countries even talk of a possibility of a war between two NATO allies.

In this paper, I am going to analyse Turkish-Greek relations in short for those who are not familiar with the topic. In order to do that, I will first take a glance at the history of Turkish-Greek relations. Secondly, I am going to analyse the rapprochement process between two countries that took place in the late 1990s and early 2000s during Türkiye's EU integration process. Thirdly, I will focus on seven major problems in Turkish-Greek relations, namely, the Cyprus Conflict, Greek support to terror-related groups, demilitarisation of the Aegean Islands, continental shelf dispute, territorial waters dispute, airspace and the Flight Information Regions (FIR) dispute, and the minorities issue in both countries. Lastly, I am going to focus on recent developments taking place in the Aegean and East Mediterranean in order to understand the current trends in bilateral as well as regional and global relations.

Turkish-Greek Relations: A Short History

After the Conquest of İstanbul in 1453, in 1460, with the seizure of the Morea, the Byzantine Empire was fully collapsed, and Greeks began to live as part of the Ottoman Empire. Greeks, similar to other non-Muslim groups, were subjected to '*millet system*' and considered as equal subjects of the Empire. Greek descendants were also given chance to rise within the Ottoman bureaucracy thanks to the '*devshirmeh system*'. In fact, many Ottoman Pashas had Greek origins. More importantly, two societies had gone through a process of acculturation due to long decades of living together. However, due to the failure of the Ottoman Empire to modernise and renew the system as a modern multi-ethnic empire as well as rising nationalist waves after the French Revolution of 1789, Greeks began to concentrate their efforts in establishing their independent state.

Almost four centuries later after Ottoman capture of Greek lands, in 1821, Greeks started their War of Independence (1821–1832) against Ottoman Turks, which resulted in the formation of independent Kingdom of Greece. The independence movement did not solve all problems as millions of Orthodox Christian Greeks continued to live under Ottoman rule in Anatolia. During the fall of the Ottoman State, Greece – with the aim of '*Megali Idea*'[3]– engaged in an imperial struggle together with

Britain, France, and Italy to capture Ottoman lands. However, Greek military campaign turned into the *'Asia Minor Catastrophe'* or *'Asia Minor Disaster'* as Turkish War of Independence (1919–1922) resulted in the formation of a modern Republic of Türkiye under the leadership of Mustafa Kemal Atatürk. Two countries made population exchanges in 1923–1924 and 1930 and tried to strengthen their nation-state. However, Turkish minority in Greece and Greek minority in Türkiye continued to exist. Although they were on the battlefront against each other, Mustafa Kemal Atatürk and his Greek counterpart Eleftherios Venizelos showed great skills in establishing peaceful relations between their countries following the Lausanne Peace Treaty. Venizelos even nominated Atatürk for Nobel Peace Prize in January 1934.[4] In addition, in 1934, both countries engaged together in the Balkan Pact with Yugoslavia and Romania. During the Second World War, Türkiye even helped Greek people during the great famine in Athens by forgetting the bad memories of the past. In 1947, with the Paris Peace Treaty, Dodecanese Islands were given to Greece by Italy, an event which complicated the bilateral relations in terms of the Aegean Dispute.

Figure 5: Venizelos and Atatürk[5]

During the Cold War, Türkiye and Greece both became earlier members (not founding members) of the Council of Europe in 1949 and 1950. Moreover, both countries became members of NATO in 1952. In addition, in 1953,

Greece, Türkiye, and Yugoslavia formed a new Balkan Pact for mutual defence against the Soviet Union. Thus, two countries were aligned as allies in the early Cold War period. However, starting from the 1950s, especially after the formation of the Republic of Cyprus in 1960, Turkish-Greek ethnic clashes in the island began to overshadow Türkiye-Greece relations as well. Attacks organised by ultra-nationalist Greek Cypriots (EOKA-B) towards Turkish Cypriots disturbed Türkiye whereas in Türkiye as well, events such as 6–7 September 1955 showed the dangerous consequences of ethnic nationalism towards non-Muslim minorities. Eventually, Turkish-Greek relations evolved into a conflictual relationship although two countries continued to keep their NATO membership.

After Türkiye's intervention into Cyprus in 1974 (Cyprus Peace Operation), Greece temporarily withdrew from NATO's military command. This could have been a great chance for Türkiye to direct Greece and other states to recognise the de facto state of Turkish Cypriots on the northern part of Cyprus. However, as the military rule in Türkiye allowed Greek return to NATO's military command for increasing its own legitimacy in the Western world, Turkish Republic of Northern Cyprus (1983) is so far recognised only by Türkiye. Moreover, Turkish military presence in the island became a matter of controversy due to several United Nations (UN) Security Council decisions. In addition, after the Cyprus Peace Operation, Greece began to openly support ASALA and afterwards PKK terrorism against Türkiye. Two countries signed the Bern Agreement on 11 November 1976 to prevent a potential crisis arising from the dispute related to the continental shelf issue in the Aegean Sea. In the meanwhile, Greek accession to EU in 1981 strengthened Athens' position against Ankara.

In 1987, two countries engaged in a serious political crisis in the Aegean[6], which was later solved upon the efforts of the United States and then-NATO Secretary-General Lord Carrington. The crisis emerged when Türkiye learned that Greece was starting to drill for oil in the Aegean Sea in the vicinity of Thasos (Taşoz), a Greek territory. In response, the Turkish survey ship Piri Reis was sent to the area with an escort of Turkish warships. Then-Greece Prime Minister Andreas Papandreou gave the orders to sink the ship if it was found in Greek waters. Then-Turkish Prime Minister Turgut Özal on the other hand said that '*If Greece interferes with our vessel in any way, and this is what Papandreou is saying, we will act in the same way against him. As a result, it could be cause for war.*' But he also added that '*We are waiting for the first move from them.*'[7] Eventually two sides were calmed down upon the diplomatic efforts of the United States and NATO.

Rapprochement in the Late 1990s and Early 2000s During Türkiye's EU Integration Process

Turkish-Greek rapprochement in the late 1990s took place after a very conflictual period. In 1996, two countries engaged in a military escalation due to the ownership dispute of small Aegean Islands (rocks) called '*Kardak Kayalıklari*' (Imia or Kardak Rocks). For sure, Kardak Crisis was part of a larger Aegean Dispute that also includes disputes over the continental shelf, the territorial waters, the airspace, the Flight Information Regions (FIR), and the demilitarisation of the Aegean Islands. In January 1996, two NATO allies – years after the 1987 Aegean Crisis – once again had tense times in their relationship. When a few Greek citizens put their flag on uninhabited Kardak or Imia, the issue became sensational in the Turkish media. Then, two countries sent their Special Forces to these rocks (islets) and came very close to a military conflict.[8] Later on, after a phone call from then-US President Bill Clinton and efforts of NATO's then-Secretary-General Javier Solana, tension got lower between two sides and the crisis ended without a military clash.

Furthermore, in 1997, Republic of Cyprus bought Russian-made S-300 air missile defence system (event known as Cypriot S-300 crisis), which led to harsh Turkish reaction. Eventually, upon Turkish reaction, in December 1998, Greek Cypriots had to hand over their S-300 system to Greece. Making the bilateral relations even worse, PKK leader Abdullah Öcalan was captured by Turkish Special Forces in Greek Embassy in Kenya. This was perceived as Athens' open political support provided to PKK, an internationally recognised terrorist organisation, by Ankara. At those days, Türkiye was also having domestic political problems due to the ongoing 28 February Process, during which the Turkish Armed Forces forced Islamist Necmetttin Erbakan's government to resign.

Figure 6: George Papandreou and İsmail Cem became architects of Turkish-Greek rapprochement in the late 1990s[9]

In this complicated picture, after successive earthquakes hit both countries in the summer of 1999, two countries' Foreign Ministers İsmail Cem and George Papandreou initiated the so-called 'earthquake diplomacy'[10] to provide help to their neighbours, which completely changed the public perception about the other side.[11] Also called by some as 'disaster diplomacy'[12], Cem and Papandreou picked up the historically hostile relationships initially starting with some confidence-building measures. In the coming days, with reciprocal visits, two statesmen opened the way for a rapid and positive change in the image of their countries. Moreover, Greece welcomed Türkiye's gaining of EU full membership candidacy status at the 1999 Helsinki Summit and stopped supporting terrorist groups against Ankara. Remembering these days, George Papandreou years after said: '*I decided that there was no meaning of being the Minister of Foreign Affairs if I do not dare to challenge our security rules. I was lucky; my counterpart in Türkiye was İsmail Cem. He was a charismatic and courageous politician. Our relationship was built on trust. İsmail and I, we tried to establish a new local cooperation rhetoric.*'[13] It should be added that the Clinton administration in the United States also helped the fixing of relations between Türkiye and Greece during this period.

As Turkish Foreign Ministry states, starting from 1999, thanks to the efforts of Cem and Papandreou, Turkish-Greek relations entered into a new period based on co-operation and dialogue.[14] Starting from this period, many people hoped that this could lead to a political solution in Cyprus as Türkiye will be gone through EU harmonisation process. However, Greek Cypriots blocked a political solution by rejecting the referendum of Annan Plan in 2004 although Turkish Cypriots voted in favour of the plan and Türkiye did not interfere. To summarise, Turkish-Greek rapprochement of the late 1990s was materialised on two main issues: (1) Greek support and encouragement for Turkish accession to EU, (2) Search for a political solution to the decades-old Cyprus Conflict.

Despite of the continuity of the Cyprus Conflict, two countries continued to improve their bilateral relations during the AK Parti (Justice and Development Party) rule as well. State visits became more frequent and new mechanisms were established. For instance, discovery talks were initiated between two sides. So far, sixty-one rounds of discovery talks were made, the last one organised in 2021.[15] Moreover, High-Level Cooperation Council meetings took place in order to improve political and economic relations. The first of these meetings took place in 2010 in Athens, second in 2013 in İstanbul, third in 2014 in Athens, and the fourth in 2016 in İzmir.[16] Thanks to these mechanisms, bilateral trade volume reached a record of 5.6 billion US dollars in 2014.[17] In 2020, due to negative effects of the Covid-19 pandemic, bilateral trade volume was only around 3.12 billion US dollars.[18] Moreover, in the 2010s, Aegean neighbours improved trade and Greece allowed Turkish citizens to visit its Eastern Aegean Islands visa-free.[19] These facts were concrete proofs of the continuing rapprochement process between two countries in the 2000s.

However, in time, as Türkiye lost its hopes and incentives for the EU membership, Turkish-Greek and Turkish-EU relations began to be shaped mainly by co-operation and sometimes confrontation vis-a-vis the refugee crisis. The Türkiye-EU refugee deal in 2016 downgraded the relations into transactionalism and EU membership perspective for Türkiye was weakened. European countries including France and the Republic of Cyprus that blocked Turkish accession to EU due to Cyprus Conflict also strengthened this trend. In addition, although the refugee deal was intended to realise the visa-free travel for Turks to EU countries, so far it is not materialised. In fact, since

Figure 7: President Erdoğan had several meetings with Greek Prime Minister Kyriakos Mitsotakis (2019–) and Alexis Tsipras (2015–2019)

2016, Türkiye's accession talks have stalled. Brussels since then has become increasingly critical of Türkiye's status of democracy and rule of law. In 2019, a European Parliament committee even voted in favour of the suspension of accession talks.[20] However, in the last few years, in order to create a positive agenda, issues such as the renewing the Customs Union and visa-free travel for Europe are also discussed between two sides.

Main Problems in Turkish-Greek Relations

Türkiye and Greece are not two haphazard countries; their history is full of antagonistic and conflictual themes and events. For instance, Turkish Independence War (1919–1922) and the Treaty of Lausanne (1923) were referred as events that are '*very painful for the Hellenism in Türkiye*' by the Greek Foreign Ministry[21], which shows the historical barriers between two states. So, fixing Turkish-Greek relations is not an easy task. However, we can categorise Turkish-Greek disagreements in seven subheadings in order to solve these problems or to find middle ground in these disputes:

I. **Cyprus Conflict and the Eastern Mediterranean Question:** Cyprus Conflict[22] is still the most important barrier in bilateral relations. Greece and Türkiye, together with the United Kingdom (UK), are three guarantor states of the Republic of Cyprus (1960). However, as Greek nationalists pursued a policy favouring the annexation of the island by Greece, Türkiye also began to support Turkish Cypriots as a guarantor state.

> Eventually, upon the military coup organised by EOKA-B members, Türkiye rightfully intervened militarily into the island. Türkiye then tried to create two separate zones in order to prevent further clashes between Turkish Cypriots and Greek Cypriots. However, although the first Turkish intervention was not criticised by other powers, the second intervention aiming to divide the island into two zones was not welcomed by the UN Security Council members. Accordingly, UN Security Council resolutions favoured Greek Cypriot position in terms of territorial integrity of the Republic of Cyprus.[23] Today, Greece, Greek Cypriots, and most of the EU member states approach to Turkish military presence in the island as '*Turkish invasion*'. Although Ankara never accepts such accusations and underline that there is a formal agreement between the TRNC government and Turkish government about the presence of military units, Turkish military presence is not welcomed by Western powers. Cyprus Conflict has also become a headache for Turkish accession to EU in the 2000s as Turkish failure to open its harbours to Greek Cypriot ships led to the suspension of eight chapters as well as the non-closure of all other chapters.

In recent years, Cyprus Conflict gained another dimension with the recent natural gas discoveries made around the island by Greek Cypriots and energy companies that were licenced by Nicosia. So, energy dimension could lead to a new type of co-operation between two communities of the island as well as Türkiye and Greece in case all sides act with the '*win-win*' mentality. Although Cyprus Conflict is in fact the biggest issue in bilateral relations, the problem is largely seen as a frozen conflict. However, the situation of seismic vessels sent to the disputed areas by Türkiye and Cyprus could still create military escalation between Türkiye and Cyprus as well as Türkiye and Greece. In the meantime, TRNC leadership's decision (TRNC President Ersin Tatar) not to carry on any further negotiations after the failure of Crans-Montana meeting in 2017 until the acceptance of sovereign equality of TRNC[24] might not be the best option for easing the tension.

Another problem related to Cyprus Conflict is the lack of an agreement between two parties about the maritime delimitation in the Eastern Mediterranean and Exclusive Economic Zones (EEZ) of small Greek islands in the region. One particular island is Meis, a small island very close to

Türkiye. Two countries have very opposing visions in relation to this issue as Greece defends 'Sevilla Map', whereas Türkiye defends 'Blue Homeland' (Mavi Vatan). International Court of Justice's decision of the case between Nicaragua and Columbia shows that the international law does not recognise or recognise with its limits the EEZ claims of the small islands.[25] Examples can be multiplied, as in the case of the various islands between Tunisia and Italy. In that sense, Greek claims in the Eastern Mediterranean seem maximalist and two countries should have a negotiation process to determine their EEZ zones.

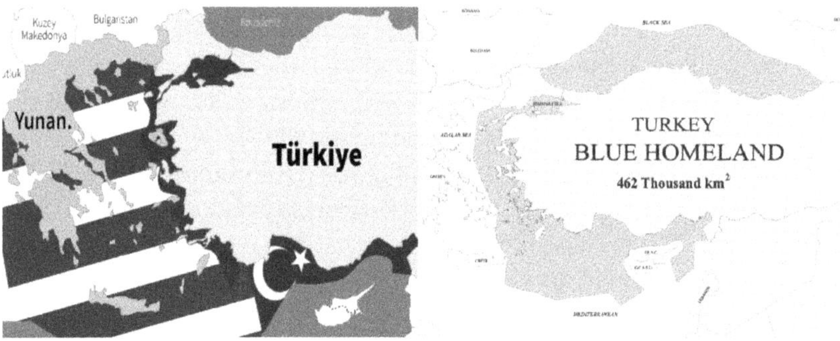

Figure 8: Two countries' opposing EEZ claims: Seville Map vs Blue Homeland

II. **Greek Support to Terror-Related Groups:** Greece in the past openly supported ASALA and PKK terrorists. Especially the Lavrion Camp became the centre of anti-Turkish activities. However, starting from Turkish-Greek rapprochement of 1999, Greece ceased its activities encouraging terrorist groups. However, Turkish media claims that in recent years Greece began to support groups that Türkiye considers terrorists once again. These groups primarily include PKK, DHKP-C, and FETÖ. Turkish media claims that Lavrion Camp is operational again and hosts PKK and DHKP-C terrorists.[26] Moreover, Turkish authorities claim that there are around 10,000 FETÖ members in Greece.[27] Although Greece formally condemned the coup attempt in Türkiye on 15 July 2016 and expressed its support to the democratically elected government[28], due to so-called human right issues, it continues to host FETÖ members. These issues create huge reactions against Greece in Türkiye especially among the security bureaucracy and nationalist circles. Greece on the other hand claims that Lavrion is basically a refugee camp.[29]

III. **Demilitarisation of the Aegean Islands:** Türkiye claims that, in accordance with the 1923 Lausanne Treaty and 1947 Paris Peace Treaty, Aegean Island that were previously agreed as demilitarised zones should stay as the same. According to Article 13 of the Lausanne Treaty, '*With a view to ensuring the maintenance of peace, the Greek Government undertakes to observe the following restrictions in the islands of Mytilene, Chios, Samos and Nikaria: (1) No naval base and no fortification will be established in the said islands; (2) Greek military aircraft will be forbidden to fly over the territory of the Anatolian coast. Reciprocally, the Turkish Government will forbid their military aircraft to fly over the said islands; (3) The Greek military forces in the said islands will be limited to the normal contingent called up for military service, which can be trained on the spot, as well as to a force of gendarmerie and police in proportion to the force of gendarmerie and police existing in the whole of the Greek territory.*'[30]

Moreover, Article 14 of the Paris Peace Treaty of 1947 states that '*1. Italy hereby cedes to Greece in full sovereignty the Dodecanese Islands indicated hereafter, namely Stampalia (Astropalia), Rhodes (Rhodos), Calki (Kharki), Scarpanto, Casos (Casso), Piscopis (Tilos), Misiros (Nisyros), Calimnos (Kalymnos), Leros, Patmos, Lipsos (Lipso), Simi (Symi), Cos (Kos), and Castellorizo, as well as the adjacent islands; 2. These islands shall be and shall remain demilitarized; 3. The procedure and the technical conditions governing the transfer of these islands to Greece will be determined by agreement between the of the United Kingdom and Greece and arrangements shall be made for the withdrawal of foreign troops not later than 90 days from the coming into force of the present Treaty.*'[31] These are clear proofs of Greek violation concerning the demilitarised status of these islands.

Unfortunately, Greece, starting from the 1960s began to remilitarise these islands.[32] This militarisation effort was accelerated after the Cyprus Peace Operation of 1974 and more recently with the US military settlement into Greece. Türkiye on the other hand, as a reaction to this, recently began to question the sovereignty of these islands. For instance, Turkish Foreign Minister Mevlüt Çavuşoğlu stated that the armament of these islands is a 'violation' and '*if this violation is not remedied, the sovereignty of the islands will be discussed.*'[33]

The demilitarisation of the Aegean Islands has become in the recent months the riskiest issue having a potential to bring two countries into a war or limited armed clash. The reason for this is Greek insistence on the rearmament of the islands as well as Türkiye's reaction to consider the sovereignty of these islands. Considering the fact that in both countries right-wing governments lose popularity due to different reasons (in case of Mitsotakis it is the wiretap scandal whereas in case of Erdoğan it is the economic failures of the government), 2022 and 2023 would be very dangerous years for keeping the peace in the region. Greece expert Professor Zuhal Mert Uzuner also believes that Mitsotakis' election as the new Greek Prime Minister accelerated the spoiling of bilateral relations since Mitsotakis and his party New Democracy (*Néa Dimokratía*) represents Greek nationalism.[34] International Relations scholar Professor Serhat Güvenç on the other hand underlines that none of these states will be likely to become the side that starts the war.[35] On the other hand, he also points out that Greek provocations in the last weeks could be part of a deliberate strategy to force Ankara to activate the S-400 air missile defence system in order to spoil Turkish-American relations completely.[36]

In addition to this problem, we should also state that there are also uninhabited small islets and rocks in the Aegean Sea whose ownerships are not determined yet between Türkiye and Greece. As in the case of Kardak, these small islands' ownership could turn into a political clash and even a military confrontation when there are no friendly relations and mutual trust between these states.

IV. **Continental Shelf Dispute:** Türkiye and Greece are two littoral states that have legitimate and legal rights and concerns about the Aegean Sea. There is no specific arrangement or previous agreement between the parties about delimitation of the continental shelf in the Aegean Sea. The UN Security Council, in its resolution 395, adopted in 25 August 1976, called upon Türkiye and Greece to do everything in their power to reduce tensions in the Aegean and asked them to resume direct negotiations over their differences and appealed to them to ensure that these negotiations result in mutually acceptable solutions.[37] The International Court of Justice in its ruling on 11 September 1976, determined the Aegean continental shelf beyond the territorial waters of the two littoral states as '*areas in dispute*' with respect to which both Türkiye and

Greece claim rights of exploration and exploitation.[38] Furthermore, the International Court of Justice, in a decision taken in 1982, stated that *'delimitation is to be effected by agreement in accordance with equitable principles and taking into account all relevant circumstances.'*[39] Subsequent to the International Court of Justice ruling and the Security Council resolution, Türkiye and Greece signed the 1976 Bern Agreement.[40]

V. **Territorial Waters Dispute:** According to Lausanne Treaty, the territorial waters of both countries were set as 3 miles.[41] However, both countries enjoy 6 miles of territorial waters in the Aegean for several decades. On the other hand, the clear boundaries between two states are not determined yet.[42] In the mid-1990s, ties were strained after Greece ratified the UN Convention on the Law of the Sea of 1982[43] -which Türkiye is not a part of it-, under which it claimed the right to extend its territorial waters in the Aegean from 6 to 12 nautical miles. Türkiye said it would view Greek exercise of this option as an act of war (*casus belli*) and Turkish Parliament (TBMM) ratified a specific law on this issue.[44] From Türkiye's perspective, since the Aegean is a common sea between Türkiye and Greece, the threat of extending Greek territorial waters beyond their present width of 6 miles (Greece extended her territorial waters from 3 miles to 6 miles in 1936, Türkiye followed suit in 1964[45]) will have negative implications for Turkish-Greek relations.[46] In short, any increase beyond 6 miles is totally unacceptable to Türkiye.

VI. **Airspace and the Flight Information Regions (FIR) Dispute:** The FIR arrangement on the Aegean airspace devised in 1952 within the framework of ICAO (International Civil Aviation Organisation), is a technical responsibility. Greece, however, is using it to further its claims of de facto sovereignty over the Aegean airspace by demanding flight plans from Turkish state aircraft and allegations of 'infringements of the Athens FIR'.[47] Moreover, Athens claims that it has a right to 10 miles 'national air space' over territorial waters of 6 miles that was perceived as an abuse by Ankara.

VII. **Minorities Issue:** Both countries approach to the minorities issue from the perspective of reciprocity. For instance, in case Greece increases pressure over Turkish minority in their territory, Türkiye would also do the same to Greek minority living in Türkiye. Türkiye put the election of Muftis by the Muslim Turkish minority in Western Thrace (Batı

Trakya) as a precondition for opening the Halki Seminary which was closed in 1971. Greece, in 1972 as a reaction, closed the Turkish school in Rhodes. Although Türkiye in recent years engaged in efforts to restore some cultural sites such as the Sumela Monastery, the situation of migrants still poses a problem in bilateral relations. Moreover, Türkiye took criticism from Greece and Western world upon the transformation of Hagia Sophia into a mosque in 2020.[48] The situation of Fener Greek Patriarchate is also relevant here as the historical church claims ecumenical rights although it does not have such authority under Turkish law according to the Lausanne Treaty.[49]

Recent Developments

Turkish-Greek bilateral relations have transformed into a risky relationship starting from the year 2020. The first crisis took place in relation to Kastellorizo Island or Meis in Turkish. On 21 July 2020, Türkiye announced plans to prospect for gas in disputed waters south of the Greek island of Kastellorizo, roughly 2 kilometres (1 mile) off the south coast of Türkiye. As a reaction, Greece put its naval forces on alert, sparking the full deployment of the Greek and Turkish fleets across the Aegean and Eastern Mediterranean seas.[50] Then, on 12 August 2020, one of the two Turkish warships escorting the Oruç Reis, a seismic research vessel, collided with a Greek frigate shadowing it. The bump so noticeably rattled Ankara and Athens that a half-day's silence ensued. The scare helped pull them back from the brink of a larger confrontation, but tensions simmered for weeks before the warships steamed back to port. Greek diplomacy and military settlements that create Turkish anger continued throughout the year 2020.[51]

In 2021, with the efforts of the EU and the restart of the discovery talks, tension was eased, and more cooperative relations were established between Athens and Ankara. However, the year 2022 was particularly problematic in terms of Turkish-Greek relations. Turkish authorities and media blamed Greece for its frequent hostile acts against Turkish jets. According to *Demirören News Agency*, Greece has committed 1,123 violations and harassment against Turkish airspace and territorial waters in the first eight months of this year.[52] Greece and Greek media on the other hand made the same accusation against Türkiye. Especially the activation of S-300 radar system based in Crete Island against Turkish jets conducting a NATO mission created anger among Turkish authorities and people. Turkish authorities claimed that on 23 August 2022, Turkish jets carrying out a reconnaissance mission over the Eastern Mediterranean and Aegean were put under the radar lock of the Greek owned S-300 air defence systems.[53] Although Türkiye submitted its complaint to NATO with alleged proofs[54] and former US Ambassador to Azerbaijan Matthew Bryza praised Türkiye's responsible behaviour[55], so far no statement condemning Greece came from NATO sources. Greece on the other hand blamed Türkiye for airspace violation and not informing about the flight plans beforehand. Turkish Defence Minister Hulusi Akar replied to Athens' version of the incidents, informing that all the flight plans have already been shared with all the NATO countries since early July.[56] Akar also added that '*Greek harassment of the Turkish jets by the S-300 air defense system over the Aegean is unacceptable*' and '*It's unfortunate that this bad neighboring country is continuing its harassment in different ways. Let me clarify once again: Our forces will never retreat when they are harassed*.'[57] In the coming days, Akar also warned Greece to keep peaceful relations with Türkiye instead of militarising attempts.[58]

Turkish President Recep Tayyip Erdoğan also warned Greece that it would pay a 'heavy price' if it continued to 'harass' Turkish planes over the Aegean and the Eastern Mediterranean.[59] Although Greek Prime Minister Mitsotakis recently said that he is open to a meeting with Erdoğan[60], the negative trend in relations that commenced after Mitsotakis' speech at the US Congress in May 2022[61] continues with a rapid pace. After this speech during which Mitsotakis accused Türkiye, Erdoğan said that '*he will not meet Mitsotakis once again*'[62]. Erdoğan warned Athens with the popular slogan of the 1960s related to the Cyprus events: 'We May Come Suddenly One Night' (*Bir Gece Ansızın Gelebiliriz*).[63] Erdoğan also did not refrain to remind Greeks their historic defeat 100 years ago; '*Hey Greece, take a look at history. If you go further, you will pay a heavy price. We have only one thing to tell Greece: Do not forget İzmir.*' he said.[64] Turkish Foreign Minister Mevlüt Çavuşoğlu also accused Greece of provocation.[65] Greek Foreign Minister Nikos Dendias on the other hand said that '*Greece "deconstructs Türkiye's unfounded claims" with arguments*' and '*We are facing an unprecedented escalation of Turkish provocations and at the same time an occasional escalation in the field, where the neo-Ottoman revisionism is projected upon.'*[66]

Figure 9: US Military Bases in Greece[67]

Greek provocations continued with the announcement of the opening of a Pontic Hellenism Genocide Monument in Kos Island (İstanköy), just 7 miles from Muğla's Bodrum district.[68] Moreover, on 10 September 2022, wo Greek coast guard boats opened fire on the Comoros-flagged Ro-Ro ship 'Anatolian', sailing in international waters off the Bozcaada district of Çanakkale.[69] The event was largely spoken in the Turkish media in the subsequent days and it was perceived as an act of aggression to provoke Türkiye. The official in charge of the Turkish ship attacked by Greek officers has said that '*Greeks threw rope at the ship's screw to stop them and then fired more than 30 times.*'[70] More recently, the deployment of US-made armoured military vehicles on two Aegean Islands (Lesbos and Samos) created further anger in Türkiye and Ankara protested Washington and Athens for violating the demilitarised status of these islands.[71] The event became known after Turkish drones were able to photograph the military vehicles during their deployment into these islands. Although Greek provocations were documented by Türkiye, EU continued to support its member state Greece. This led to a harsh reaction in Ankara towards Brussels as well.[72]

Greece, in recent years, showed a great diplomatic success in developing close security ties with the United States. For instance, with the ratification of the US-Greece Mutual Defense Cooperation Agreement (MDCA) in 2022, US military gained access to Georgula Barracks in Greece's central province of Volos, Litochoro Training Ground, and army barracks in the north-eastern port city of Alexandroupoli apart from the naval base in Souda Bay in Crete which the United States has operated since 1969.[73] The MDCA agreement was first signed between Washington and Athens in 1990 and was renewed every year. The new arrangement allows the government to review and renew the agreement in every five years and if none of the parties do not lodge an objection, the agreement is renewed automatically. Greek media reports that United States aims to transform the Alexandroupoli (Dedeağaç) Port, which it has used for the shipment of weapons and personnel to the Balkans and Europe in recent years, into a military naval base.[74] Although American officials underline that these bases are built for containing Russia, Turkish President Recep Tayyip Erdoğan does not believe in this pretext and claims that these bases' target is Türkiye.[75]

American support to Greece is crucial for Turkish-Greek relations since the United States still dominates the Western bloc and has the capacity to punish its allies with some instruments such as the CAATSA that is implemented against Ankara for purchasing S-400 system from Moscow. Moreover, in case there is a war between Athens and Ankara, the presence of American troops in Greece could become a discouraging factor for Türkiye. For instance, the US military presence in Alexandroupoli (Dedeağaç) region directly poses a barrier to possible Turkish land-based military operation. Kozan Erkan, a senior defence and security expert, concludes that US deployment in Greece intends to deter Türkiye from responding to a possible assault by Greece.[76] An attack by Türkiye on Greece could also lead to increasing scepticism and negative views about the presence of Ankara within NATO. At the same time, there are criticisms towards the Athenian government about the increasing American military presence in Greek soil and some even label Greece as a 'garrison state'. Greek opposition led by Alexis Tsipras (Syriza party) is also critical of the government's bold steps.

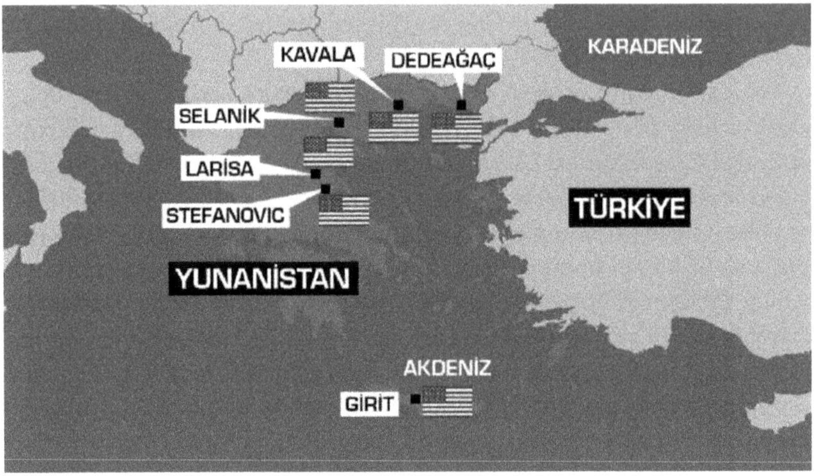

Figure 10: US Military Presence in Greece[77]

In addition, Greece has also signed a defence agreement with France in 2021. So-called the Franco-Greek Defence Agreement was signed between France and Greece on 27 September 2021 and it includes a mutual defence clause (Article 2) should either be attacked by a third country.[78] At the signing ceremony in Paris, French President Emmanuel Macron said the agreement is part of a deeper 'strategic partnership' between the two countries.[79] In that sense, against increasing Turkish discontent for the violation of Lausanne and Paris treaties, Athens plays the card of its defence co-operation with Washington and Paris to counterbalance potential Turkish offensive. It should not be forgotten that Greece recently purchased Rafale jets and frigates from France and tries to seal the deal for purchasing

F-35 fifth-generation warrior jets from the United States while Türkiye is removed from the F-35 programme and is not even allowed to acquire F-16 jets from Washington yet. In addition, Greece recently signed a recent historic defence agreement that is worth of 1.65 billion US dollars with Israel.[80] Greece has also established close ties with Israel together with the Republic of Cyprus in the Eastern Mediterranean. These developments show that Greece is increasing its military capacity especially in terms of aerial forces in addition to its diplomatic backings, while Türkiye is tried to be punished and weakened by Washington and Brussels after acquiring S-400 air missile defence system from Russia.

Rıfat Öncel from Turkish think-tank SETA claims that increasing Greek provocations are part of a larger strategy he called as the 'Athenian Trap' and Athens wants Türkiye to become the aggressor in order to take American, French, and European support.[81] He also adds that in order to overcome this trap, Türkiye should follow prudent diplomatic action and change its relations with the United States and France.[82] Retired Admiral Cihat Yaycı, as one of the creators of '*Mavi Vatan*' (Blue Homeland) doctrine (together with Ramazan Cem Gürdeniz) – also closely follows Turkish-Greek relations and warns Ankara of Western intention to kick Türkiye out of NATO and to include Cyprus and Israel instead.[83] Professor Mesut Hakkı Caşın on the other hand points out Greece as the aggressor side and threatens Greece that a war between two states would result in the catastrophe for Athens.[84]

Conclusion

Solving political problems between Türkiye and Greece is not impossible. However, both sides need to act reasonably and with a peaceful mentality. To analyse objectively, in relation to Aegean Dispute, Turkish Foreign Policy seems more in favour of status quo, whereas Greek foreign policy is more assertive, hawkish, and revisionist. That is why, for solving many of these problems related to the Aegean, Greek attitude should be changed. However, in case of Cyprus on the other hand, Türkiye and Turkish Cypriots should act more in conformity with the international law.

Finally, as retired Turkish diplomat Özdem Sanberk claims, although two nations have a lot in common, the political institutions in two countries could not solve their problems and the main reason for this is Greece's failure to recognise many problems.[85] Professor Hasan Ünal on the other hand advocates a new foreign policy for Türkiye as Türkiye's hope for EU membership has faded in recent years.[86] Ünal even claims that Russia and Azerbaijan could formally recognise TRNC in case Türkiye takes right steps.

Lastly, Ankara should be also aware of the fact that during the 1987 Aegean Crisis and 1996 Kardak Crisis it was mainly NATO and the United States that prevented a possible military clash between two sides but now Washington clearly supports Athens. Thus, Türkiye should be cautious to take its steps. The reason for this is that, in case of a war between Greece and Türkiye, United States could be involved militarily (French involvement is not expected) and more importantly, although Türkiye might prevail militarily as in the case of Cyprus intervention in 1974, this might not be enough to solve the problem diplomatically/politically.

Endnotes

1 Mehmet Babacan (2022), "Türkiye-Yunanistan Gerilimi: Yüksek Tansiyona Rasyonel Zeminde Çözüm Arayışları", Uluslararası Politika Akademisi, 19.09.2022, Date of Accession: 27.09.2022 from <http://politikaakademisi.org/2022/09/19/turkiye-yunanistan-gerilimi-yuksek-tansiyona-rasyonel-zeminde-cozum-arayislari/>.

2 Türkiye Cumhuriyeti Dışişleri Bakanlığı, "Türkiye-Yunanistan İlişkileri", Date of Accession: 27.09.2022 from <https://www.mfa.gov.tr/turkiye-yunanistan-siyasi-iliskileri.tr.mfa>.

3 The goal of reviving the Byzantine Empire.

4 Zafer Çakmak (2008), "The Nomination of Atatürk by Venizelos for the Nobel Peace Prize", *Erdem İnsan ve Toplum Bilimleri Dergisi*, No: 52, pp. 91–110.

5 Stelyo Berberakis (2020), "30 Ağustos Zafer Bayramı: Venizelos, Atatürk'ü Nobel Barış Ödülü'ne aday gösterirken ne demişti?", *BBC Türkçe*, 30.08.2020, Date of Accession: 26.09.2022 from <https://www.bbc.com/turkce/haberler-dunya-53964004>.

6 Alan Cowell (1987), "Greeks and Turks Ease Aegean Crisis", *The New York Times*, 29.03.1987, Date of Accession: 27.09.2022 from <https://www.nytimes.com/1987/03/29/world/greeks-and-turks-ease-aegean-crisis.html>.

7 Ibid.

8 Stavros Atlamazoglou (2022), "How the US defused a deadly showdown between 2 NATO allies' special-operations forces", *Business Insider*, 08.05.2022, Date of Accession: 27.09.2022 from <https://www.businessinsider.com/imia-kardak-island-dispute-between-greece-Türkiye-almost-sparked-war-2022-5>.

9 Faruk Bildirici – Medya Ombudsmanı (2020), "Nefret söylemi ve savaş çığırtkanlığı aldı başını gidiyor", 28.08.2020, Date of Accession: 26.09.2022 from <https://farukbildirici.com/nefret-soylemi-ve-savas-cigirtkanligi-aldi-basini-gidiyor/>.

10 Stephen Kinzer (1999), "Earthquakes Help Warm Greek-Turkish Relations", *The New York Times*, 13.09.1999, Date of Accession: 26.09.2022 from <https://www.nytimes.com/1999/09/13/world/earthquakes-help-warm-greek-turkish-relations.html>.

11 For details, see; Ozan Örmeci (2020), *A Turkish Social Democrat: İsmail Cem*, İstanbul: Libra Books.

12 N. Emel Ganapati & Ilan Kelman & Theodore Koukis (2010), "Analysing Greek-Turkish disaster related cooperation: A disaster diplomacy perspective", *Cooperation and Conflict*, Vol. 45, No: 2 (June 2010), pp. 162–185.

13 Fikriye Susam Uyar (2016), "'Cem-Papandreu Uluslararası Barış Ödülü' ilk sahiplerini buldu", *Anadolu Ajansı*, 16.04.2016, Date of Accession: 27.09.2022 from <https://www.aa.com.tr/tr/yasam/cem-papandreu-uluslararasi-baris-odulu-ilk-sahiplerini-buldu/556302>.

14 Türkiye Cumhuriyeti Dışişleri Bakanlığı, "Türkiye-Yunanistan İlişkileri", Date of Accession: 27.09.2022 from <https://www.mfa.gov.tr/turkiye-yunanistan-siyasi-iliskileri.tr.mfa>.

15 Behlül Çetinkaya & Mümin Altaş (2021), "Türkiye ve Yunanistan arasındaki istikşafi görüşmelerin 61. turu yapıldı", *Anadolu Ajansı*, 25.01.2021, Date of Accession: 27.09.2022 from <https://www.aa.com.tr/tr/turkiye/turkiye-ve-yunanistan-arasindaki-istiksafi-gorusmelerin-61-turu-yapildi/2122252>.

16 Türkiye Cumhuriyeti Dışişleri Bakanlığı, "Türkiye-Yunanistan İlişkileri", Date of Accession: 27.09.2022 from <https://www.mfa.gov.tr/turkiye-yunanistan-siyasi-iliskileri.tr.mfa>; Hellenic Republic Ministry of Foreign Affairs, "Türkiye", Date of Accession: 27.09.2022 from <https://www.mfa.gr/en/blog/greece-bilateral-relations/Türkiye/>.

17 Türkiye Cumhuriyeti Dışişleri Bakanlığı, "Türkiye-Yunanistan İlişkileri", Date of Accession: 27.09.2022 from <https://www.mfa.gov.tr/turkiye-yunanistan-siyasi-iliskileri.tr.mfa>

18 Ibid.

19 International Crisis Group (2021), "Türkiye-Greece: From Maritime Brinkmanship to Dialogue", Report no: 263, 31.05.2021, Date of Accession: 27.09.2022 from <https://www.crisisgroup.org/europe-central-asia/western-europemediterranean/263-Türkiye-greece-maritime-brinkmanship-dialogue>.

20 European Parliament (2019), "Parliament wants to suspend EU accession negotiations with Türkiye", 13.03.2019, Date of Accession: 27.09.2022 from <https://www.europarl.europa.eu/news/en/press-room/20190307IPR30746/parliament-wants-to-suspend-eu-accession-negotiations-with-Türkiye>.

21 Hellenic Republic Ministry of Foreign Affairs, "Türkiye", Date of Accession: 27.09.2022 from <https://www.mfa.gr/en/blog/greece-bilateral-relations/Türkiye/>.

22 For a research on the history of this problem, see; Örmeci, Ozan & Kısacık, Sina (2020), "Cutting the Gordian Knot: Turkish Foreign Policy Towards Cyprus During AK Parti Era (2002–2020)", *Studia i Analizy Nauk Polityce*, no: 1 (2020), pp. 21–64

[23] For instance, resolution no 353 mentioned about "*all States to respect the sovereignty, independence, and territorial integrity of Cyprus*". See; <http://unscr.com/en/resolutions/353>. In addition, resolution no 541 of 1983 underlined that the declaration of TRNC is "*incompatible with the 1960 Treaty of Guarantee*". See; <https://digitallibrary.un.org/record/58970?ln=en#record-files-collapse-header>.

[24] *Voice Kıbrıs Haber* (2022), "Tatar 'Negotiations will not start without acceptance of sovereign equality'", 16.09.2022, Date of Accession: 27.09.2022 from <https://voicekibrishaber.com/tatar-negotiations-will-not-start-without-acceptance-of-sovereign-equality/371864/>.

[25] See; <https://www.icj-cij.org/en/case/124>.

[26] *TRT Haber* (2022), "Yunanistan'da mülteci değil, terör kampı: Lavrion", 05.09.2022, Date of Accession: 27.09.2022 from <https://www.trthaber.com/haber/gundem/yunanistanda-multeci-degil-teror-kampi-lavrion-706532.html>.

[27] *Hürriyet Daily News* (2022), "Greece hosts some 10,000 FETÖ members: Official", 14.08.2022, Date of Accession: 27.09.2022 from <https://www.hurriyetdailynews.com/greece-hosts-some-10-000-feto-members-official-176115>.

[28] Hellenic Republic Ministry of Foreign Affairs, "Türkiye", Date of Accession: 27.09.2022 from <https://www.mfa.gr/en/blog/greece-bilateral-relations/Türkiye/>.

[29] *TRT Haber* (2022), "Yunan medyası, Lavrion Kampı'nda aklamaya çalıştığı PKK'nın varlığını ifşa etti", 06.09.2022, Date of Accession: 27.09.2022 from <https://www.trthaber.com/haber/dunya/yunan-medyasi-lavrion-kampinda-aklamaya-calistigi-pkknin-varligini-ifsa-etti-706729.html>.

[30] Republic of Türkiye Ministry of Foreign Affairs, "Lausanne Peace Treaty", Date of Accession: 27.09.2022 from <https://www.mfa.gov.tr/lausanne-peace-treaty-part-i_-political-clauses.en.mfa>.

[31] "Treaty: Treaty of Peace with Italy, signed at Paris, on 10 February 1947", Date of Accession: 27.09.2022 from <http://gis.nacse.org/tfdd/tfdddocs/135ENG.pdf>.

[32] Republic of Türkiye Ministry of Foreign Affairs, "Lausanne Peace Treaty", Date of Accession: 27.09.2022 from <https://www.mfa.gov.tr/lausanne-peace-treaty-part-i_-political-clauses.en.mfa>.

[33] Sedat Ergin (2022), "President Erdoğan's new rhetoric towards Greece", *Hürriyet Daily News*, 08.09.2022, Date of Accession: 27.09.2022 from <https://www.hurriyetdailynews.com/opinion/sedat-ergin/president-erdogans-new-rhetoric-towards-greece-176756>.

[34] *CNNTürk* (2022), "Miçotakis'in son açıklamaları Türk-Yunan ilişkilerini nasıl etkiler? Zuhal Mert Uzuner anlattı", 17.09.2022, Date of Accession: 27.09.2022 from <https://www.youtube.com/watch?v=c60kfAeCsWY>.

[35] Serhat Güvenç (2022), "Serhat Güvenç yazdı: Yunanistan'ın acelesi ne?", *Medyascope*, 04.09.2022, Date of Accession: 27.09.2022 from <https://medyascope.tv/2022/09/04/serhat-guvenc-yazdi-yunanistanin-acelesi-ne/>.

[36] Ibid.

[37] See; <https://digitallibrary.un.org/record/93723?ln=en>.

38 Republic of Türkiye Ministry of Foreign Affairs, "Background Note on Aegean Dispute", Date of Accession: 27.09.2022 from <https://www.mfa.gov.tr/background-note-on-aegean-dispute.en.mfa>.

39 Ibid.

40 These are ten principles of the agreement:

1. The two parties agree that the negotiations shall be frank, thoroughgoing and pursued in good faith, with a view to reaching an agreement based on their mutual consent with regard to the delimitation of the continental shelf as between themselves.
2. The two parties agree that these negotiations shall by their very nature be strictly confidential.
3. The two parties reserve their respective positions with regard to the delimitation of the continental shelf.
4. The two parties undertake not in any circumstances to make use of the provisions of this document, or such proposals as may be made by either side during these negotiations, outside the context of the negotiations themselves.
5. The two parties agree that there shall be no statements or leaks to the press on the contents of the negotiations, unless they decide otherwise by common accord.
6. The two parties undertake to refrain from any initiative or act concerning the Aegean continental shelf that might trouble the negotiations.
7. The two parties each undertake, so far as their bilateral relations are concerned, to refrain from any initiative or act likely to throw discredit on the other.
8. The two parties have agreed to study the practice of States and the international rules on the subject, with a view to eliciting such principles and practical criteria as might be of use in the case of the delimitation of the continental shelf between the two countries.
9. To that end, a mixed commission will be set up to be composed of national representatives.
10. The two parties agree to adopt a gradual rhythm in the negotiating process to be followed, after mutual consultation.

See; Türk – Yunan İlişkileri, "Bern Agreement between Türkiye and Greece (11 November 1976)", Date of Accession: 27.09.2022 from <http://www.turkishgreek.org/index.php/kuetuephane/item/50-bern-agreement-between-Türkiye-and-greece-11-november-1976>.

41 *BBC News Türkçe* (2022), "Ege sorunu: Yunanistan ve Türkiye hangi konularda anlaşamıyor?", 26.07.2022, Date of Accession: 27.09.2022 from <https://www.youtube.com/watch?v=mx6SNS3CUfU>.

42 Türkiye Cumhuriyeti Dışişleri Bakanlığı, "Başlıca Ege Denizi Sorunları", Date of Accession: 27.09.2022 from <https://www.mfa.gov.tr/baslica-ege-denizi-sorunlari.tr.mfa>.

43 It is available here; <https://www.un.org/depts/los/convention_agreements/texts/unclos/unclos_e.pdf>.

44 *Yeni Şafak* (2018), "Yunanistan'ın 12 mil kararı savaş sebebi sayılır", 27.10.2018, Date of Accession: 27.09.2022 from <https://www.yenisafak.com/gundem/yunanistanin-12-mil-karar-savas-sebebi-sayilir-3404929>.

45 Ibid.

46 Republic of Türkiye Ministry of Foreign Affairs, "Background Note on Aegean Dispute", Date of Accession: 27.09.2022 from <https://www.mfa.gov.tr/background-note-on-aegean-dispute.en.mfa>.

47 Republic of Türkiye Ministry of Foreign Affairs, "Background Note on Aegean Dispute", Date of Accession: 27.09.2022 from <https://www.mfa.gov.tr/background-note-on-aegean-dispute.en.mfa>.

48 See; Ozan Örmeci (2020), "Hagia Sophia Controversy: The Changing Status of the Historical Sanctuary", Uluslararası Politika Akademisi, 18.07.2020, Date of Accession: 27.09.2022 from <http://politikaakademisi.org/2020/07/18/hagia-sophia-controversy-the-changing-status-of-the-historical-sanctuary/>.

49 *CNNTürk* (2022), "Fatih Kaymakamlığı'ndan 'ekümeniklik' açıklaması", 15.08.2022, Date of Accession: 27.09.2022 from <https://www.cnnturk.com/turkiye/fatih-kaymakamligindan-ekumeniklik-aciklamasi>.

50 International Crisis Group (2021), "Türkiye-Greece: From Maritime Brinkmanship to Dialogue", Report no: 263, 31.05.2021, Date of Accession: 27.09.2022 from <https://www.crisisgroup.org/europe-central-asia/western-europemediterranean/263-Türkiye-greece-maritime-brinkmanship-dialogue>.

51 For an analysis on these moves, see; Alper Gülbay (2022), "2020 Yılı Özelinde Yunanistan-Güney Kıbrıs Rum Yönetimi İkilisinin Ege Denizi ve Doğu Akdeniz'de Gerginliği Artırıcı Faaliyetleri", *UPA Strategic Affairs*, Vol. 3, No: 1, pp. 168–199.

52 *Hürriyet Daily News* (2022), "'Greece violated Türkiye's airspace, waters 1,123 times this year'", 05.09.2022, Date of Accession: 26.09.2022 from <https://www.hurriyetdailynews.com/greece-violated-turkiyes-airspace-waters-1-123-times-this-year-176694>.

53 *Hürriyet Daily News* (2022), "Greece activates S-300s against Turkish F-16s over Aegean", 28.08.2022, Date of Accession: 26.09.2022 from <https://www.hurriyetdailynews.com/greece-activates-s-300s-against-turkish-f-16s-over-aegean-176479>.

54 *Hürriyet* (2022), "Son dakika: Türkiye S-300 tacizini NATO'ya taşıyor!", 31.08.2022, Date of Accession: 26.09.2022 from <https://www.hurriyet.com.tr/dunya/turkiye-s-300-tacizini-natoya-tasiyor-42129098>.

55 *Hürriyet* (2022), "ABD eski büyükelçisi Bryza'dan 'Yunanistan' yorumu: 'Türkiye sağduyulu davrandı ve NATO'ya gitti'", 21.09.2022, Date of Accession: 26.09.2022 from <https://www.hurriyet.com.tr/dunya/abd-eski-buyukelcisi-bryzadan-yunanistan-yorumu-turkiye-sagduyulu-davrandi-ve-natoya-gitti-42141042>.

56 *Hürriyet Daily News* (2022), "Ankara to send radar traces of S-300 harassment of Turkish jets to NATO", 31.08.2022, Date of Accession: 26.09.2022 from <https://www.hurriyetdailynews.com/ankara-to-send-radar-traces-of-s-300-harassment-of-turkish-jets-to-nato-176558>.

57 *Hürriyet Daily News* (2022), “Greek harassment of Turkish jets by S-300s not acceptable: Akar”, 29.09.2022, Date of Accession: 26.09.2022 from <https://www.hurriyetdailynews.com/greek-harassment-of-turkish-jets-by-s-300s-not-acceptable-akar-176515>.

58 *Hürriyet Daily News* (2022), “Defense Minister urges Greece to refrain from hostile acts”, 02.09.2022, Date of Accession: 26.09.2022 from <https://www.hurriyetdailynews.com/defense-minister-urges-greece-to-refrain-from-hostile-acts-176612>.

59 *Hürriyet Daily News* (2022), “Erdoğan warns Greece over Aegean airspace violations”, 04.09.2022, Date of Accession: 26.09.2022 from <https://www.hurriyetdailynews.com/erdogan-warns-greece-over-aegean-airspace-violations-176637>.

60 *Hürriyet Daily News* (2022), “Greek PM says he is open to meeting Erdoğan”, 12.09.2022, Date of Accession: 27.09.2022 from <https://www.hurriyetdailynews.com/greek-pm-says-he-is-open-to-meeting-erdogan-176876>.

61 This speech can be seen from here; <https://www.youtube.com/watch?v=YmXV9HRZR-E>.

62 *Cumhuriyet* (2022), “Erdoğan: Artık benim için Miçotakis diye birisi yok”, 23.05.2022, Date of Accession: 27.09.2022 from <https://www.cumhuriyet.com.tr/siyaset/erdogan-artik-benim-icin-micotakis-diye-birisi-yok-1939068>.

63 Tasos Kokkinidis (2022), “Erdogan Threatens Greece: “We May Come Suddenly One Night””, *Greek Reporter*, 03.09.2022, Date of Accession: 27.09.2022 from <https://greekreporter.com/2022/09/03/erdogan-threatens-greece-we-may-come-suddenly-one-night/>.

64 Sedat Ergin (2022), “President Erdoğan’s new rhetoric towards Greece”, *Hürriyet Daily News*, 08.09.2022, Date of Accession: 27.09.2022 from <https://www.hurriyetdailynews.com/opinion/sedat-ergin/president-erdogans-new-rhetoric-towards-greece-176756>.

65 *Hürriyet Daily News* (2022), “Turkish FM warns Greece against provocation”, 12.09.2022, Date of Accession: 27.09.2022 from <https://www.hurriyetdailynews.com/turkish-fm-warns-greece-against-provocation-176887>.

66 *Ekathimerini* (2022), “Dendias: Greece ‘deconstructs Türkiye’s unfounded claims’ with arguments”, 18.06.2022, Date of Accession: 27.09.2022 from <https://www.ekathimerini.com/news/1187082/dendias-greece-deconstructs-Türkiyes-unfounded-claims-with-arguments/>.

67 Ahmet Gençtürk (2022), “Growing US military presence in Greece can lead to undesired scenarios in Aegean, experts warn”, *Anadolu Ajansı*, 25.05.2022, Date of Accession: 26.09.2022 from <https://www.aa.com.tr/en/politics/growing-us-military-presence-in-greece-can-lead-to-undesired-scenarios-in-aegean-experts-warn/2596928>.

68 Yaşar Anter (2022), “Yunanistan tahrikte sınır tanımıyor! Sözde ‘soykırım anıtı’ dikecekler”, *Sözcü*, 25.08.2022, Date of Accession: 26.09.2022 from <https://www.sozcu.com.tr/2022/dunya/yunanistan-tahrikte-sinir-tanimiyor-sozde-soykirim-aniti-dikecekler-7328777/>.

69 *Hürriyet Daily News* (2022), “Greek coast guard boats leave area after Turkish retaliation”, 11.09.2022, Date of Accession: 26.09.2022 from <https://www.hurriyetdailynews.com/greek-coast-guard-boats-leave-area-after-turkish-retaliation-176831>.

70 Yorgo Kırbaki (2022), "'Greek forces fired more than 30 times at Turkish boat'", *Hürriyet Daily News*, 13.09.2022, Date of Accession: 26.09.2022 from <https://www.hurriyetdailynews.com/greek-forces-fired-more-than-30-times-at-turkish-boat-176886>.

71 *Al-Monitor* (2022), Türkiye protests US, Greece over 'violating non-military status' of Aegean Greek islands", 26.09.2022, Date of Accession 27.09.2022 from <https://www.al-monitor.com/originals/2022/09/Türkiye-protests-us-greece-over-violating-non-military-status-aegean-greek-islands#ixzz7g40JIiBl>.

72 *Hürriyet Daily News* (2022), "Türkiye dismisses EU's criticism of Erdoğan's Greece remarks", 06.09.2022, Date of Accession: 27.09.2022 from <https://www.hurriyetdailynews.com/urkiye-dismisses-eus-criticism-of-erdogans-greece-remarks-176710>.

73 Derya Gulnaz Ozcan (2022), "US military gains access to more bases in Greece", *Anadolu Ajansı*, 13.05.2022, Date of Accession: 27.09.2022 from <https://www.aa.com.tr/en/americas/us-military-gains-access-to-more-bases-in-greece/2587479>.

74 Yorgo Kırbaki (2022), "Alexandroupoli to become US naval base: Greek media", *Hürriyet Daily News*, 20.09.2022, Date of Accession: 26.09.2022 from <https://www.hurriyetdailynews.com/alexandroupoli-to-become-us-naval-base-greek-media-177061>.

75 *TeleSUR* (2022), "Türkiye: US Military Bases in Greece Don't Target Russia", 08.06.2022, Date of Accession: 27.09.2022 from <https://www.telesurenglish.net/news/Turkiye-US-Military-Bases-in-Greece-Dont-Target-Russia-20220608-0015.html>.

76 Ahmet Gençtürk (2022), "Growing US military presence in Greece can lead to undesired scenarios in Aegean, experts warn", *Anadolu Ajansı*, 25.05.2022, Date of Accession: 26.09.2022 from <https://www.aa.com.tr/en/politics/growing-us-military-presence-in-greece-can-lead-to-undesired-scenarios-in-aegean-experts-warn/2596928>.

77 *Ensonhaber* (2021), "Yunanistan'daki Amerikan üslerini gösteren harita", 03.04.2021, Date of Accession: 26.09.2022 from <https://www.ensonhaber.com/dunya/yunanistandaki-amerikan-uslerini-gosteren-harita>.

78 Anna Wichman (202), "The Entire France-Greece Defense and Security Agreement", *Greek Reporter*, 28.09.2021, Date of Accession: 27.09.2022 from <https://greekreporter.com/2021/09/28/the-entire-france-greece-defense-and-security-agreement/>.

79 Ibid.

80 Alexandros Fotiadis (2021), "Greece, Israel sign historic $1.65 billion defense agreement", *Euractive*, 19.04.2021, Date of Accession: 27.09.2022 from <https://www.euractiv.com/section/politics/short_news/greece-israel-sign-historic-1-65-billion-defense-agreement/>.

81 Rıfat Öncel (2022), "Greece's game plan: 'The Athenian Trap'", SETA, September 2022, Date of Accession: 27.09.2022 from <https://www.setav.org/en/greeces-game-plan-the-athenian-trap/>.

82 Ibid.

83 *Son Dakika Haber* (2022), "Cihat Yaycı: Türkiye'yi Nato'dan atıp Güney Kıbrıs ve İsrail'i dahil edecekler | yunan medyası", 13.09.2022, Date of Accession: 27.09.2022 from <https://www.youtube.com/watch?v=GKIX0sE1duE>.

84 *CNNTürk* (2022), "Türkiye ile Yunanistan arasındaki kriz savaşa döner mi? M. Hakkı Caşın'dan çok sert açıklamalar", 10.09.2022, Date of Accession: 27.09.2022 from <https://www.youtube.com/watch?v=1DimIDC2IZk>.

85 Özdem Sanberk (2022), "Türk-Yunan ilişkileri neden bir türlü rayına oturmuyor?", *T24*, 19.09.2022, Date of Accession: 27.09.2022 from <https://t24.com.tr/yazarlar/ozdem-sanberk/turk-yunan-iliskileri-neden-bir-turlu-rayina-oturmuyor,36770>.

86 Hasan Ünal (2022), "Yeni bir Yunanistan politikasına ihtiyaç var", *Milliyet*, Düşünenlerin Düşüncesi, 25.09.2022, Date of Accession: 27.09.2022 from <https://www.milliyet.com.tr/yazarlar/dusunenlerin-dusuncesi/yeni-bir-yunanistan-politikasina-ihtiyac-var-6830329>.

Current Situation in Türkiye-EU Relations: What Should Be Done for the Future?[1]

Introduction

Today, I will talk about Türkiye-EU relations, a subject that has been frequently discussed in universities, conference halls, televisions, and diplomatic circles for years. However, since there are experts much more knowledgeable and technically literate than me on this subject, and since such talks have been made thousands of times before and have become boring for the audience, I will put myself in the place of an impartial third country representative and even a creature that has come to Earth from space, and I will share with you some of the observations I have made by looking at Türkiye-EU relations from the outside and trying to be impartial. However, of course, in order for the presentation to be in line with the academic format and the spirit of the university, I will first repeat some historical and political information for those who do not know or want to remember. I thank you in advance for your patience.

What is the European Union?

The European Union, or the EU for short, is a political and economic union with exactly 27 members today. Although the EU is not one of the largest international organisations in the world, it is a very important project that largely preserves its supranational feature, the first and only one in the world. This project is often referred to as a 'civilisation project' due to the comprehensive principles, standards, rules, practices and regulations it has developed. The EU is also described as a 'peace project'. Because the EU, which was established to revive Europe that was destroyed after World War II and to integrate European countries that had previously fought against each other many times, stands out as the most successful international political and economic structure in human history that serves peace. At this point, I think it would be appropriate to ask the following question; Do you think it is a coincidence that despite the many wars that the United States, Russia and countries outside the EU were involved in after World War II and the many terrorist incidents they experienced in their countries, Europe has always managed to be a relatively more peaceful and secure continent? This is certainly not coincidental and is a natural result of neighbouring and nearby countries sharing a continent reaching a vision of sharing their wealth and developing/developing together instead of fighting and competing with each other.

The history of the EU and European integration begins with the establishment of the European Coal and Steel Community (ECSC) with the Paris Treaty of 1951. Thanks to this treaty, the 'founding six' countries, namely France, Germany, Italy, Belgium, the Netherlands, and Luxembourg, came together on the subject of coal and steel production, which had previously been the triggering causes of the First and Second World Wars, and agreed on a higher management beyond national logic on this issue. Another important step in the history of the EU was taken with the Treaty of Rome in 1957, and the European Economic Community (EEC) and the European Atomic Energy Community (EAEC) were established with the participation of the same six countries. In this way, the six states that were the forerunners of the EU agreed on the establishment of a common economic market among themselves and that the co-operation that had begun in the coal and steel industry would also cover the field of atomic energy and nuclear studies. With the Fusion Treaty signed in 1965 and entered into force in 1967, the primary organs of the ECSC, EEC and EAEC were merged to form a structure called the European Community or European Communities, or EC, which would provide a common administration. Important steps were taken towards the formation of the EC in the 1950s and 1960s.

In the 1970s, these steps accelerated, and new members were also accepted. In 1973, with the first enlargement, the United Kingdom (Britain), Denmark and Ireland became members of the EU, increasing the number of members to nine. The European Regional Development Fund was established in 1975. In 1979, elections were held for the first time by direct popular vote in the nine member states for the European Parliament deputies. In 1981, Greece became the 10th member of the EC. In 1985, the Schengen Agreement was signed with the participation of France, Germany, Belgium, Luxembourg, and the Netherlands, which included 5 EC members, and the first step was taken for people living in European states to travel to other countries without a visa. With the Iberian expansion in 1986, the number of EC members increased to twelve with Spain and Portugal. Also in 1986, the necessary steps were taken towards the formation of a single European market with the Single European Act. In 1990, a new agreement was signed for the implementation of the Schengen Agreement. Today, the Schengen area has twenty-six members, 22 of which are EU members.

With the Maastricht Treaty signed in 1992 and entered into force in 1993, the EC became known as the European Union (EU) and the common market between member states began to operate. The Maastricht Treaty is a historic treaty and a critical turning point that truly gave birth to the EU as a political and economic union. With the accession of Austria, Finland, and Sweden in 1995, the number of EU members reached 15. At the end of the process that began in 1999, the euro or euro was adopted as the EU's common currency in 2002. Today, 19 EU member states use the euro or euro as their official currency. However, this number will increase further in the coming years. In 2004, the EU carried out the largest expansion process in its history and gained exactly 10 new members. These ten member countries are: Czechia, Estonia, Republic of Cyprus (Greek Cypriot Administration of Southern Cyprus), Latvia, Lithuania, Hungary, Malta, Poland, Slovakia, and Slovenia. Thus, the number of EU members became twenty-five. With the accession of Romania and Bulgaria in 2007, the EU became a giant Union with twenty-seven members. Today, the reason for many of the difficulties experienced by the EU is shown as the fact that the rapid expansion processes in 2004 and 2007 have not yet been fully digested and the new member states have not been brought to the level of the old states. With the 2009 Lisbon Treaty, final regulations were made regarding the functioning and powers of EU institutions and the disruptions in the functioning of the EU were largely resolved. In 2013, Croatia became the 28th member of the EU. With the departure of the United Kingdom in 2020, the number of EU members will drop to twenty-seven. The EU has managed to reach consensus on many issues during the pandemic and has shown the entire file that it is not a collapsing structure. In addition, in the last few years, the EU's initiatives towards a defence union have begun to form and develop.

Brief History of Türkiye-EU Relations

The history of Türkiye-EU relations and Türkiye's participation in European integration begins with the Ankara Agreement, signed on 12 September 1963 and entered into force on 1 December 1964. The Ankara Agreement, signed with the aim of Türkiye's full membership in the EC, foresaw three different periods as 'preparation', 'transition', and 'the final stage of the Customs Union'. The preparation phase was relatively smooth, and Türkiye's transition process began with the 'Additional Protocol' accepted by the Association Council in July 1970 after Türkiye's application to the EC in May 1967. But, Türkiye, which experienced great economic difficulties and political instability during the transition process in the 1970s and thought that it was not yet ready for a common market and free competition, requested an additional period of 5 years from the EC in 1978. However, due to the military coup in Türkiye in 1980, the obstructive attitudes of Greece, which became a member of the Union in 1981, and the regression in Türkiye's democracy, Türkiye's membership application in 1987 was rejected in 1989 and it was recommended to focus on the Customs Union process. Following this, as a result of Türkiye's efforts, Türkiye was included in the EU's Customs Union as of 1996. With the Helsinki Summit in 1999, Ankara became a candidate country for full EU membership. Membership negotiations began on 3 October 2005, and on 12 June 2006, the first chapter, Science and Research, was opened and temporarily closed. To date, a total of sixteen chapters have been opened in Türkiye-EU relations. However, in 2006, the EU Council decided to suspend negotiations on eight chapters and not to close other chapters because Türkiye did not fulfil some of its commitments in the Additional Protocol to the EU-Türkiye Association Agreement, which expanded the Customs Union to include ten member states, including the Republic of Cyprus. In addition, the Republic of Cyprus, which we refer to as the Greek Cypriot Administration of Southern Cyprus, declared at the General Affairs Council meeting on 8 December 2009 that it unilaterally blocked progress on six chapters and made it conditional on normalisation of relations. In addition, during the Nicolas Sarkozy era, France also blocked the opening of five chapters in order to prevent Türkiye's membership; with the openings made during the François Hollande era, today only two chapters remain under French obstruction.

Identifying the Problems: Where Did We Go Wrong?

When I approach Türkiye-EU relations from an outside, realistic, and impartial perspective, I can identify the following problems. First of all, I find it right to divide the problems into two as problems originating from Türkiye and those originating from the EU.

1. Problems Originating from Türkiye

A-) The Security Bureaucracy's reluctant support for the EU: Although the goal of EU membership is always referenced in the decisions of the National Security Council (MGK) and political party programmes in Türkiye, when approached from an objective and sincere perspective, it can easily be concluded that the state, especially the security bureaucracy, does not believe in EU membership and does not wholeheartedly support it. The ideas I will express here are observation-based information obtained as a result of conversations I have had with my friends, students and relatives who have been members of the Turkish security bureaucracy for about 20 years. In this sense, even if they are not fully evaluated in the scientific category, they are definitely realistic and accurate observations.

As a basic observation, the following can be said first; of course, the Turkish security bureaucracy's concern is definitely not opposition to the EU. When we look at the basic sources of anxiety and fear of these groups and individuals; 1-) If Türkiye becomes a member of the EU, terrorism may decrease in Türkiye, 2-) Our Kurdish citizens, who constitute the majority of the population in the Southeastern Anatolia region of Türkiye, may want autonomy and even independence during this process and may obtain it, 3-) Institutions such as the Turkish Armed Forces (TSK), the Turkish Police Organisation, and the National Intelligence Organisation (MİT) may lose their effective positions in politics and state functioning, 4-) Turkish Cypriots may be subjected to massacres by Greek Cypriots again as in the 1960s and 1970s, 5-) Turkish youth may break away from values such as Islam and

Turkishness, and 6-) Türkiye may be forced to recognise the genocide allegations regarding the 1915 Events.

Therefore, these concerns and fears stem from patriotic motives rather than individual interests. However, I believe that these concerns and fears are unfounded; because there is not a single country that has lost its national identity, divided, experienced civil war or even experienced frequent terrorist attacks after becoming a member of the EU. In addition, in an EU member country, the salaries and living standards of soldiers, police officers, and intelligence officers, like all professional groups, will be much better and will increase. Values such as Turkishness and Islam will not decrease, but rather increase, since they will live together with Christian European societies and come into contact more frequently; however, since these will be within the framework of certain rules and laws under the EU roof, they will not cause any problems in political and social life. The Armenian Genocide claims are based entirely on political decisions taken by parliaments and have no legal basis. In any case, European law is a developed legal system based on universal legal norms and there should be no concern about this.

B-) Surrendering to nationalism in foreign policy: Even the most pro-EU circles in Türkiye, due to factors such as 1-) Turkishness and Muslim consciousness, 2-) patriotic instincts stemming from the Kemalist tradition, and 3-) pressure from the media and society, can immediately be carried away by the nationalist spirit, so to speak, when two agitations are experienced. Many people in Türkiye (even those who have reached the level of Rector and Professor among them) can express that we should fight Greece, which is a member of NATO, and that we should take control of all of Cyprus, etc. However, in my opinion, these are not realistic and reasonable approaches. Türkiye will of course demonstrate its hard power from time to time in foreign policy disputes and show that it is not an easy target. The TSK is still the most valuable and important power element of Türkiye and this national institution should never be allowed to be worn down. However, thoughts such as Türkiye going to war with the EU, which we are trying to become a member of, and the members of NATO, which we are a member of, are unrealistic. Even if very extreme governments come to power, they will never make imaginary attempts in this direction due to the warnings and interventions of state bodies (Ministry of Foreign Affairs of the Republic of Türkiye, MİT, etc.). In the twenty-first century, we must get used to solving our problems with our Western allies through diplomacy and over time.

C-) Not being able to break the mould in the Cyprus Conflict: The Cyprus Conflict constitutes the biggest obstacle on Türkiye's path to EU membership. Of course, it is natural and necessary for Türkiye to act emotionally on this issue due to the great sympathy that the Turkish people feel for the Turkish Cypriots, who have suffered great injustices in the past. However, if Türkiye is serious about EU membership, it must overcome the Cyprus Conflict and also improve its relations with the Greek Cypriots and Greece. Of course, there will be provocations from the other side; what is important is that the EU sees these and rewards Türkiye's good-willed efforts. Indeed, if Türkiye were to seriously consider the solution of the Cyprus Conflict, the blockades of the Greek Cypriot Administration of Southern Cyprus and Greece on the issues of Türkiye's EU membership and the solution of the Cyprus Conflict would mean nothing, and the major European powers would easily keep them in line.

D-) The decline in democracy standards since 2013: Türkiye must re-strengthen its democracy. A Türkiye that has withdrawn from the İstanbul Convention and lags behind African countries in world democracy indices cannot of course become an EU member. However, if the reformist Türkiye of the 1999–2013 period can be re-created, the EU's view of Türkiye will undoubtedly change.

2. Problems Originating from the EU

A-) Surrender to far-right arguments: Starting with the 2004 Annan Plan referendum and the Angela Merkel-Nicolas Sarkozy duo that came to power in the two central countries of the EU, the EU has taken on a structure that can easily be swayed by far-right arguments, whether in its approach to Türkiye or in its migration policy. This course of events is also in conflict with the founding values of the EU and is a very dangerous signal for the future of the EU. The EU was able to become a centre of attraction and prosperity in the 1990s and 2000s because it is a multicultural, democratic structure that respects different identities. Otherwise, the future of the EU, which adopts opposes Türkiye's membership on the grounds of Islam, will definitely not be bright and relations with Türkiye will deteriorate.

B-) Failure to convince the Greek-Greek duo: EU institutions and European states unconditionally abide by the attitudes of Greece and the Greek Cypriot Administration of Southern Cyprus, which is a member of the Union under the name of the Republic of Cyprus and represents the entire island, and do not take into account the problems they cause or the fact that the problems cannot be solved because of them. However, the Greek-Cyprus duo is the one most responsible for Türkiye departure from the EU and the regression of Turkish democracy. Indeed, the failure of the EU to keep the promises made during the 2004 Annan Plan referendum in Cyprus caused great anger and distrust towards Brussels in Turkish Cyprus and Türkiye and revived nationalist tendencies. In order to prevent this from happening again, the EU must duly fulfil its promises of assistance regarding Syrian migrants and take a balanced position regarding Turkish-Greek relations and the Cyprus Conflict.

C-) Turning to maximalist demands during the democratisation process: Türkiye is not a continental European country. It is a state established in a difficult geography, surrounded by countries such as Russia, Syria, Iran, Iraq, and Armenia, which are quite problematic, have civil wars, intense terrorist attacks, political instability on their lands, or whose ambitions towards Türkiye are not very friendly in every respect. In other words, Türkiye's neighbours are not the Netherlands, Switzerland, Belgium, etc. Therefore, the EU should be more realistic, not maximalist, in its criticisms of Turkish democracy and its demands from Ankara. If the EU immediately forces Türkiye to implement its own standards on many issues, especially the fight against terrorism, there could be major security risks in Türkiye, and this could cause serious doubts in the country and the world in terms of the EU's success. Therefore, the EU should approach Türkiye more reasonably and from a strategic point of view. Another important problem concerns the mistakes made while trying to establish the superiority of civilian democracy in Türkiye. Indeed, as the Ergenekon and Balyoz processes proved, the EU must understand that it cannot achieve civilian democracy by wearing down the security bureaucracy in Türkiye. This should be our biggest lesson from the 2000s.

D-) Elite Europe perception: The EU is perceived as an elite project in Türkiye and around the world. While this may have some advantages, it also has serious disadvantages in terms of reaching the public and gaining public support. Especially a state like Türkiye, which has recently adopted the motto of 'The World is Bigger than 5' in its foreign policy and has led and inspired 'oppressed nations' in the past, can undoubtedly choose to focus on the oppressed/needy rather than the elite/elite, which receives intense support from the public. The EU's migration policy etc. also reinforces this perception and creates the perception that human values have not developed in Europe. The recent events when Türkiye opened its borders to Syrian migrants as a reaction to the EU have undoubtedly reinforced this perception.

Conclusion

When the declaration of the EU Summit held in March 2021 is examined; The EU has started to approach Türkiye as a partner based on co-operation and mutual benefit rather than a potential member (this approach was first developed by French President Emmanuel Macron in January 2018, during Turkish President Recep Tayyip Erdoğan's visit to Paris, in front of the cameras and to his face); Türkiye is expected to act harmoniously regarding its areas of authority in the Eastern Mediterranean, the Cyprus Conflict, and relations with Greece; Türkiye is targeted for co-operation on critical issues such as the updating of the Customs Union, public health, climate change, the fight against terrorism, and regional issues; Türkiye and the EU are asked to develop ties in terms of people-to-people relations and mobility (the Erasmus+ programme and the visa-free Europe issue); Türkiye is asked to avoid unilateral steps in foreign policy; Türkiye's care of 4 million Syrian migrants is respected and more support is planned for Ankara; Türkiye is asked to continue its co-operation with the EU in the fight against illegal migration; a solution is targeted for the Cyprus Conflict; positive developments are expected from Türkiye on issues such as democracy, human rights, women's rights, and the rule of law; co-operation with Türkiye is desired in regional crises in the Caucasus and the Eastern Mediterranean, and that developments in Türkiye will continue to be followed closely.

Endnote

1 Speech given at the online conference organised by Aydın Adnan Menderes University on 27 April 2021.

Bibliography

Bozkır, Volkan (2002), "Türkiye ve Avrupa Birliği'ne Tam Üyelik Süreci", Türkiye Cumhuriyeti Dışişleri Bakanlığı, <https://www.mfa.gov.tr/turkiye-ve-avrupa-birligi_ne-tam-uyelik-sureci.tr.mfa>.

European Commission, "From 6 to 27 members", <https://ec.europa.eu/neighbourhood-enlargement/policy/from-6-to-27-members_en>.

European Council, "Statement of the Members of the European Council Brussels, 25 March 2021 SN 18/21, <https://www.consilium.europa.eu/media/48976/250321-vtc-euco-statement-en.pdf>.

Karaca, Kayhan (2010), *Birleşik Avrupa'nın Türk Öncüleri*, İstanbul: NTV Yayınları.

Karluk, S. Rıdvan & Dural, Betül Yücel (ed.), *Avrupa Birliği*, Eskişehir: Anadolu Üniversitesi Yayınları.

La Fontaine, Pascal (2007), *AB Nedir?*, Avrupa Komisyonu Basın ve İletişim Genel Müdürlüğü Yayınlar.

Örmeci, Ozan, Blog – Ozan Örmeci Articles, <https://ydemokrat.blogspot.com/>.

Örmeci, Ozan & Işıksal, Hüseyin (2016), *Mavi Elma: Türkiye-Avrupa İlişkileri*, Ankara: Gazi Kitabevi.

Sandalcılar, Ali Rıza & Erdoğan, Seven (2017), *Ekonomik Entegrasyonlar: Avrupa Birliği ve Türkiye*, Bursa: Ekin Basın Yayın Dağıtım.

Türkiye Cumhuriyeti Dışişleri Bakanlığı, "Türkiye-AB İlişkileri", <https://www.mfa.gov.tr/turkiye-ab-iliskileri.tr.mfa>.

Türkiye Cumhuriyeti Dışişleri Bakanlığı, "Türkiye-AB İlişkileri: Türkiye-AB ilişkilerinde temel tarihler", <https://www.mfa.gov.tr/turkiye-ab-iliskilerine-genel-bakis.tr.mfa>.

Türkiye Cumhuriyeti Dışişleri Bakanlığı Avrupa Birliği Başkanlığı, <https://www.ab.gov.tr/>.

A Recipe for Normalisation in Turkish Foreign Policy

The Republic of Türkiye recently celebrated its 100th anniversary. However, the country has problematic relations with many countries in the world. Here is a list of tips for both the government and the opposition bloc to get back to normal in Türkiye's democratisation process as well as classical Western-oriented Turkish Foreign Policy.

Solve the S-400 crisis: Türkiye is a member of NATO and a traditional US ally. However, Türkiye's strange choice of buying its air missile defence system from Russia recently created serious disturbance and harsh reactions in the United States as well as in other NATO allies. Türkiye was even removed from the F-35 programme due to its S-400 purchase. It is true that in the past the United States acted very reluctantly to sell its Patriot system to Ankara. Even the 45th President of the US Donald Trump confessed this reality. However, at the same time, this problem creates further problems and complications in Turkish-American relations. Thus, it is better for Ankara to sell the S-400 system to a third country or to convince Washington in implementing a formula (Turkish National Defence Minister Hulusi Akar already offered the '*Crete model*') to prevent additional problems to arise between two countries.

Get back to EU reforms: Türkiye's golden years in terms of economic growth and democratisation took place between 1999 and 2013. It was not a coincidence; Türkiye's aim to become a full member to the European Union and its reformist governments were the main reasons of the country's gradual success. Thus, it is very essential to revitalise Türkiye's EU membership process although it might take long years for Ankara to become a full member of the Union. Since the new US President Joe Biden and his Secretary of State

Antony Blinken are also known as pro-EU statesmen who care much more about Transatlantic ties compared to Trump administration, Turkish-EU normalisation could be realised at the same time with the Turkish-American normalisation. Providing French support to Türkiye's EU process would be crucial in doing this.

Support diplomacy instead of military moves: Türkiye has been recently criticised in the Western press and academia as a country whose foreign policy is largely militarised. Thus, Ankara might begin to prefer diplomatic methods over warfare and militaristic methods in Cyprus and the Eastern Mediterranean dispute, in Libya, and in Syria from now on. In addition, instead of two states solution, Ankara could prefer a thesis based on confederation or federation in Cyprus in order not to destroy UN Secretary-General António Guterres' sincere efforts. This will be welcomed by all sides including the United States, the EU, and the Russian Federation.

Normalisation with Armenia: Since Türkiye's number one ally Azerbaijan got back its territories in Nagorno-Karabakh with the recent war, Türkiye could try to normalise its relations with Armenia as well. Azerbaijan and Georgia could also join these two countries to establish a regional framework of co-operation. Of course, Armenian contribution to peace is also expected in this scenario.

More freedoms for the press and the academia: Although Türkiye is not living its best days as a democracy, it is also a fact that Türkiye is still much more developed and democratic compared to other Muslim countries (with the exception of Tunisian democracy). In order to develop Turkish democracy further, the government might allow more freedoms for the press and the academia in the following months. This will change the mood in the country and reduce Western criticism against the Turkish regime.

Political solution to Syrian crisis: In order to establish a normal democratic regime in Türkiye, the war in Syria must end. Türkiye, together with Russia, Iran, and the United States, should work on how to arrange the transition period in Syria and to create a unified country once again. This should be followed by Türkiye-Syria normalisation process which would help Türkiye to get normalised within its borders as well.

Normalisation with the Arab world and Israel: Türkiye should also normalise its relations with Arab countries and Israel. Türkiye does not have an ambassador now in Syria, Egypt, and Israel. Türkiye's relations with the

Gulf States – with the exception of Qatar – have also become very problematic in recent years. Thus, Ankara should try to improve its diplomatic relations in the Middle East in the new term to have a better political positioning.

These tips could be used as a basic recipe for Turkish government to improve Turkish Foreign Policy. Türkiye deserves a good reputation and image in its 100th anniversary since Turkish people are very friendly towards other nations.

Crisis of Football Diplomacy: the Turkish Super Cup Final Match in Riyadh Is Cancelled

Sports can be used in a way to enhance diplomatic relations and can help hostile nations to develop friendlier relations. In the past, during the Cold War, the Sino-American rapprochement began with the ping-pong diplomacy effort in 1971. It later led to President Richard Nixon's historic visit to China and the official initiation of diplomatic relations between Washington and Beijing in the coming years. Similarly, in the 2000s, Türkiye and Armenia tried to normalise their relations through forging football diplomacy. However, due to the illegal Armenian occupation of Azerbaijan lands, in those years, normalisation did not take place. The 2022 Qatar World Cup on the other hand helped this small Islamic country to embrace more modern and open ideas to satisfy international visitors and create a better image in the world. In that sense, what could be described as '*the unique power of sport to bring people, nations, and communities closer together via a shared love of physical pursuits*'[1], sports diplomacy has become a crucially important part of modern diplomacy. However, recently, the cancellation of a planned Super Cup match between Türkiye's two historic football clubs, Galatasaray and Fenerbahçe, in Saudi Arabia's capital Riyadh, on the grounds of political reasons, exemplified a terrible case of sports (football) diplomacy. The event led to a diplomatic crisis between the two countries, although there is still hope that relations could be improved and a re-match could be organised in the coming weeks/months.

Turkish Football Federation (TFF), with the idea of increasing its revenues as well as helping football clubs under heavy debt to recover their economy and increase their international reputation, recently initiated a new practice and started to promote Turkish Super Cup final matches to be played in foreign countries. Following this plan, TFF made a pre-agreement with the Kingdom of Saudi Arabia to organise Super Cup finals in this country for 5 years in exchange for millions of dollars[2]. Turkish football clubs Galatasaray and Fenerbahçe accepted the plan, a contract was signed between TFF and Saudi Arabia, and the teams went to the Saudi capital on 29 December, to make the first final match. Millions of Turkish football fans were ready to watch the final match between Türkiye's most popular football clubs having millions of fans. However, the match at Awal Park was cancelled at the last minute. Turkish press reported that the Saudi Arabian Football Federation did not approve the request of Galatasaray players to warm up on the field wearing Atatürk shirts. Similarly, according to news in the Turkish press, the Saudi Football Federation did not allow Fenerbahçe club's request to enter the field with a banner featuring Atatürk's famous quote '*Peace at home, peace in the world*'.[3] TFF later announced that the organisation was postponed with joint decision of clubs due to some problems in the organisation.[4]

Figure 11: Atatürk's image was perceived as a political symbol by Saudi authorities

The problem is caused by the lack of detailed technical arrangements between the two sides and misunderstanding. The Saudi press wrote that the Riyadh regime interpreted two football clubs' decision to wear Atatürk t-shirts as a political message or protest and insisted that there should not be any politics involved in sports games.[5] Saudi organisers also claimed that they allowed the playing of the Turkish national anthem and the displaying of Turkish flags in the stadium, but two Turkish clubs did not act per the agreement and insisted on wearing Atatürk t-shirts.[6]

Analysing the situation, the first thing to be said is that the TFF should have made a more detailed agreement by foreseeing a potential crisis. Next time, all details of the organisation should be specified in the contract leaving no place for misunderstanding or abuse. Turkish football authorities now fiercely criticise TFF President Mehmet Büyükekşi, accusing him of incompetence. Secondly, Saudi perception of Atatürk as a political symbol or message seems exaggerated for an average Turkish citizen. Of course, politics should not be involved extensively in politics. However, Mustafa Kemal Atatürk was Türkiye's first President (1923–1938) and heroic wartime leader during the National Resistance (1919–1922). In that sense, we should not conceive of Atatürk only as the founder and first chair of the pro-secular and pro-Western Republican People's Party (CHP), but as a great man who built modern Türkiye, a political figure above petty politics. Atatürk, in that sense, is not a political symbol representing some particular groups, but rather a symbol of the whole country. However, as an Islamic regime based on absolute monarchy rule, Saudi authorities' approach to Atatürk was overwhelmingly negative. Thirdly, Saudi authorities seem to forget the fact that 2023 was Türkiye's 100th anniversary, and it was very understandable that Turkish football clubs wanted to show their respect for the founder of the country. Thus, football diplomacy turned into a diplomatic crisis between the two countries.

However, despite both sides' mistakes, the match could be played in the coming weeks/months with a more detailed plan. Moreover, this could turn into an opportunity for the two states to improve their relations. It is a fact that the Saudi regime has some deficiencies in adapting itself to the secular, republican, militarist, and nationalist rhetoric of the Turkish state. However, Saudi Arabia's recent efforts to modernise itself and open the country to the world should not undermined and on the contrary, should be supported. In line with Saudi Crown Prince Mohammad bin Salman's 2030 Vision, the Saudi regime has been trying to curb Islamic radicalism/extremism in recent years.[7] Saudi regime recently allowed the opening of cinema theatres, allowing women to participate in (local) elections, drive their cars freely as well as go to stadiums to watch football matches. These reforms were supported by the Saudi Arabian Football league – Saudi Pro League's efforts to bring world stars such as Cristiano Ronaldo and Karim Benzema to rich Saudi football clubs including Al-Nassr and Al-Ittihad. Saudi

Arabia was also awarded as the host nation to organise the 2034 FIFA World Cup. Trying to make his holy country more secular, MBS also abolished the Commission for the Promotion of Virtue, replaced it with the Entertainment Authority, and allowed the holding of parties, promiscuous entertainment festivals, and socialising.[8] Although these reforms are often underrated, this is clear progress for Saudi citizens and especially for Saudi women. Reforms were so impressive for Christine Diwan of the Arab Gulf States Institute in Washington, who believes that '*it is not an exaggeration to say that Saudi Arabia has entered the post-Wahhabi era, although the precise religious lines of the state are still constantly changing.*'[9] According to Diwan, '*religion no longer has veto power over the economy, social life, and foreign policy*' in Saudi Arabia.[10] British journalist Richard Quest also wrote a report about his experience in Saudi Arabia after his last visit there and claimed that '*profound*' changes that are occurring at '*extreme*' speed in the Islamic country. He added in the article that the stereotype about Saudi Arabia, where women must be completely covered and there is no mixing between the sexes, and where there is an intolerant religious police force, has changed. These are clear proofs of a real programme of social change already initiated by the Saudi regime.

As a Muslim-dominated secular country, Türkiye can become a good role model for Saudi Arabia during this reform period. Riyadh's regime can do much more to increase the satisfaction of its citizens and to fix its distorted image by providing more rights to women and political freedoms to its citizens by establishing a parliament similar to Atatürk's Türkiye or contemporary Jordan. Saudi Arabian and Turkish regimes could be very different for the moment, but we should not forget the fact that, just a century ago, until the First World War, Saudi Arabia was part of the Turkish Empire known as the Ottomans. So, the shared history and some similar cultural values could help these two nations to follow a similar modernisation path. In that sense, Saudi authorities should be informed that Atatürk is not a divisive political figure, but rather Türkiye's only unifying political symbol, and the displaying of Atatürk's name, images, and quotes are by no means any disrespect to the Saudi regime or current more Islamic government/President in Türkiye. In fact, Turkish President Recep Tayyip Erdoğan always exalts Atatürk by calling him 'Gazi Mustafa Kemal' as a great founding leader. So, Saudi authorities should not act techy or shy on that matter.

To conclude, the crisis could turn into a deeper co-operation between the two countries and could lead to a better cause. Türkiye needs Saudi and other Arab countries' investments and tourists to recover its economy. Moreover, for Turkish artists, sports players, academics, and other professionals, Arab countries could be a good destination to increase their popularity, audience, and incomes. For all these reasons, I hope this Super Cup final match could be played in the coming weeks/months without any problem in Riyadh.

Endnotes

1 <https://www.sportanddev.org/thematic-areas/democracy/what-sports-diplomacy>.

2 <https://www.dunya.com/spor/super-kupa-bes-yil-boyunca-suudi-arabistan-da-oynanabilir-haberi-710746>.

3 <https://bianet.org/haber/super-cup-final-in-riyadh-canceled-galatasaray-and-fener-bahce-teams-have-left-stadium-289982>.

4 <https://www.aa.com.tr/en/middle-east/turkish-super-cup-final-in-saudi-arabia-post-poned/3095823>.

5 https://www.khalijisport.com/2023/12/29/%D8%B3%D8%A8%D8%A8-%D8%A7%D9%84%D8%BA%D8%A7%D8%A1-%D8%A7%D9%84%D8%B3%D9%88%D8%A8%D8%B1-%D8%A7%D9%84%D8%AA%D8%B1%D9%83%D9%8A-%D8%AA%D8%B9%D8%B1%D9%81-%D9%84%D9%85%D8%A7%D8%B0%D8%A7-%D9%84%D9%85/#google_vignette.

6 <https://m.elbotola.com/article/2023-12-30-20-40-133.html>.

7 https://alarab.news/%D8%AA%D8%B1%D8%B3%D9%8A%D8%AE-%D8%A7%D9%84%D8%A7%D9%86%D9%81%D8%AA%D8%A7%D8%AD-%D9%81%D9%8A-%D8%A7%D9%84%D8%B3%D8%B9%D9%88%D8%AF%D9%8A%D8%A9-%D9%8A%D8%B3%D8%AA%D9%88%D8%AC%D8%A8-%D9%85%D8%B1%D8%A7%D8%AC%D8%B9%D8%A9-%D8%A7%D9%84%D9%85%D9%88%D8%B1%D9%88%D8%AB-%D8%A8%D8%AC%D8%B1%D8%A3%D8%A9.

8 https://26sep.net/index.php/local/46249-2022-10-30-08-07-54.

9 https://www.watanserb.com/2021/06/21/%D8%A7%D9%84%D8%B3%D8%B9%D9%88%D8%AF%D9%8A%D8%A9-%D9%85%D8%A7-%D8%A8%D8%B9%D8%AF-%D8%A7%D9%84%D9%88%D9%87%D8%A7%D8%A8%D9%8A%D8%A9-%D8%AA%D9%82%D8%B1%D9%8A%D8%B1-%D9%8A%D9%83%D8%B4%D9%81/#google_vignette.

10 *Ibid.*

Turkish-American Relations: Past and Current Situation[1]

Introduction

Turkish-American relations, which have been on the agenda mostly with crises and polemics between the leaders of the two countries since the 2003 Iraq War, are actually in a harmonious structure that can be cited as an example in the literature of International Relations as a model of relations established between a great power and its regional ally during the Cold War. Indeed, although various problems were experienced in bilateral relations in the 1960s and 1970s, Turkish-American relations managed to recover each time and stronger than the previous one. However, traumatic events such as the rejection of the 1 March Memorandum and the 'sack incident' during the 2003 Iraq War, political relations that deteriorated as religious and national identities began to come to the fore in both countries, mutual foreign policy initiatives that began to overshadow alliance relations and, most importantly, the not-so-positive views of the people of the two countries towards each other have brought Turkish-American relations to a negative point today. This is certainly not an impossible situation to correct. However, it is also clear that Turkish-American relations will go through a difficult period in the coming period.

Some basic findings that will be emphasised in this speech are as follows:

- There has almost never been a war or conflict in the history of Turkish-American relations. This provided both states with a great advantage in terms of the transformation of bilateral relations into alliance relations after World War II. This situation is also a positive situation in terms of Turkish-American relations today.

- During the Cold War, Turkish-American relations, except for some periodic deviations, were generally shaped in accordance with the concept of alliance relations between a large state and a medium-sized state in its orbit. The driving force in the relations was military co-operation and security issues (Türkiye's NATO membership and the threat of Soviet Russia and communism). Although this situation provided a serious political advantage to the United States at the time, the fact that Washington was mostly associated with military coups in Türkiye and that it developed close relations with ultra-nationalist and Islamist circles caused great damage to the image and reliability of this country in the eyes of the public in the following years.
- Throughout the Cold War, an 'asymmetric' relationship was established between Washington and Ankara; Türkiye's capacity to influence the United States was much lower than the US capacity to influence Türkiye. Türkiye's political, diplomatic, and economic efforts to distance itself from the United States in the 1960s and 1970s each resulted in the two countries establishing closer relations.
- When the Cold War ended, different approaches began to develop on how Turkish-American relations would be shaped in the new period. Indeed, with the rejection of the 1 March Memorandum and the difficult process that followed, the United States began to approach its classical alliance relations focused on security with Türkiye, where the Turkish Armed Forces (TSK) had been at the centre until then, differently. While some circles in the United States wanted the classical Cold War paradigm to continue by adapting to new conditions, other circles that emphasised soft power elements in the new world order began to evaluate Türkiye as a 'model country' as a state with a large Muslim population located in a strategic region and trying to integrate with the Western world, and to present it as an example to other Muslim societies and newly established Turkic Republics. However, today, both the classical approach that emphasised military co-operation between the two countries, similar to the Cold War period, and the 'model country' approach seem to have failed.
- The foreign policy orientations and preferences of the two countries in recent years have begun to differ significantly due to the effects of their

economic connections and needs. This is a negative development for the future of relations. To give concrete examples; While Türkiye's energy needs bring Ankara closer to Russia and Iran, these countries are perceived as 'enemies' in Washington's perspective. States such as Israel and Saudi Arabia, with which the United States has very close relations in the Middle East region, are states that have had problematic relations with Türkiye in recent years.

- Turkish-American relations have not been developed to the desired extent in economic, cultural and social terms to date. In fact, in both countries, people have very negative feelings and prejudices towards each other. This situation is easily revealed in scientific research and surveys. Although this is not an irreparable situation, it is a very effective and negative factor in terms of creating a lack of trust in relations. In addition, although there is a reaction to some of the US policies in the Turkish people, the Turkish people, who love American movies, music and American culture in general, also admire the United States.
- The most important problems between the two countries today can be listed as follows: (1) Differing perspectives on Syria, (2) Incompatible policies on the future of the Kurds, (3) Disagreements on the Iran strategy, (4) Türkiye-Russia relations reaching the level of economic alliance and Ankara's natural gas dependency on Moscow, (5) Increasing Islamophobia in the United States, (6) Fethullah Gülen crisis, and (7) Türkiye's regime moving away from democracy in recent years.

The Past of Turkish-American Relations[2]

A) Establishment of trade relations

The history of Turkish-American relations is generally started from the 1770s when the United States began to establish trade relations with small states affiliated with the Ottoman Empire in the North African region. Before this period, no relations could be established between the two states and societies due to geographical distance. While the United States was rapidly advancing in the process of establishing itself in the 1770s, it signed various diplomatic agreements with small states in the process of becoming states such as Tripoli (Libya), Algeria, Tunisia, and Morocco, which were still North African lands affiliated with the Ottoman Empire on paper. It is striking that these agreements resemble agreements made with independent states. The United States even appointed Consuls to important Maghreb port cities in this region. The reason for this is that the Mediterranean played an important role in American foreign trade. In fact, one-sixth of the wheat and one-quarter of the salted fish exported by the United States at that time went to the Mediterranean countries, while the United States imported rice and corn from this region. American ships were trading in Ottoman territory under the British flag during this period, and therefore they did not encounter any obstacles. While the Ottoman Empire, which was in a period of decline and collapse, could not show any reaction in the face of these developments, even the armed conflicts between the United States and the administrations under its control in Libya, Algeria, and Tunisia at the beginning of the nineteenth century did not have any repercussions in the Ottoman Empire. The administrations in these regions, which were attacked by American warships after their piracy activities, did not ask for any help from the Ottomans at that time, and the Ottoman central government did not consider sending help to these states from İstanbul. These states, which were still loyal to the Ottomans on paper but were actually governed by the Western Corps, formed by Janissaries assigned to the region, took advantage of the fact that American ships did not fly the British flag after the declaration of independence and opened fire on American warships as part of their piracy activities to collect tribute, thus beginning the US's first diplomatic contacts in the region.

Following the declaration of independence by the United States, the Mediterranean became even more important in Washington's eyes during this period due to the fact that it had severed its trade relations with Britain and had customs problems with France and Spain. A group led by the US Ambassador to Paris, Thomas Jefferson, was particularly insistent on this issue and argued that the United States should trade with every region in the world that provided profit. When the harassment and attacks on American ships in the North African region intensified in 1784–1785, two different approaches emerged in Washington, put forward by the US Ambassador to Paris, Thomas Jefferson, and the Ambassador to London, John Adams. While Jefferson advocated establishing a strong navy in a short time and destroying pirates, Adams advocated signing treaties with the countries of the Maghreb and placing American ships under the protection of these states, just like the ships of Britain and France. Over time, Adams' view was accepted and the United States signed the first treaty in this region with the efforts of Thomas Barclay on 23 June 1786, with Morocco. The agreement with Morocco was relatively easy, because there was little piracy in the country and Morocco was already a sultanate that had gained its independence from the Ottomans. In Algeria, where the most intense attacks on American merchant ships had taken place until 1795, peace was only possible through force. When American warships set off for the Mediterranean in 1794 in the face of increasing attacks, the US-Algeria Peace and Friendship Treaty was signed on 5 September 1795. With this treaty, the United States also gained the right to have a consul in the port of Algiers. The United States signed its third treaty in the region with Tripoli (Libya) on 4 November 1796. The fourth and final treaty with Tunisia was dated 28 August 1797.

Despite these agreements, there were many small-scale conflicts between US ships and pirates in the region between 1801–1815, and these conflicts were called the 'Barbary Wars'. While the United States emerged victorious from these wars, according to Prof. Çağrı Erhan, this had five main results:

1. The success of the new state, the United States, in these wars ensured the unity of the American people and strengthened nationalist sentiments in this country.
2. The American State, which had been quite ignorant outside the American continent until that day, began to learn Eastern languages (especially Arabic) for the first time and to get to know the Islamic world thanks to the diplomats it assigned to the region.
3. The opening of consulates by the United States in the Maghreb region provided Washington with the opportunity to closely observe Mediterranean and Middle Eastern politics.
4. With these wars, the United States realised that it had to protect its commercial interests with military force and made this one of the basic principles of its foreign policy.
5. After American warships took control, American merchants' interest in Mediterranean ports increased.

During this period, North Africa was not the only region where American merchant ships began to engage in commercial activities within Ottoman territory. Indeed, the activities of American ships in the Port of İzmir were also quite important. The commercial relations that began with the T. H. Perkins Company were crowned with the appointment of William Steaward (also spelled William Stewart) as the Consul General of İzmir by Thomas Jefferson, who became the President of the United States in the following years, on 4 May 1802. However, Steaward was forced to leave İzmir in 1803, and after the rejection of Mr Sloane, who was appointed as Consul in İzmir in 1808, by the Sublime Porte, efforts in this direction were suspended. Despite this, commercial relations continued to increase, and in 1811, the Americans established the American Trade House as an unofficial organisation in İzmir to discuss problems that would arise between them and Ottoman bureaucrats and merchants from other foreign countries. Founded by David Offley, one of the partners of the American company Woodmans and Offley (Woodmans & Offley), this institution quickly became a place of call for American merchants in İzmir. At that time, this institution operated like a 'Consulate without a signboard'. During these years (1819), the publication of the book *A Memoir on the Commerce and Navigation of the Black Sea and the Trade and Maritime Geography of Turkey and Egypt in Boston* by American sailor Henry D. S. Dearborn, in which he devoted many pages to İzmir, played an important role in the Americans learning about İzmir and its surroundings and realising the trade opportunities. Following this book, other American companies based in İzmir, such as Langdon & Co. and Styth & Co., were also established and there was a noticeable increase in the number of American ships visiting the Port of İzmir. In addition, the Port of İzmir gained even greater importance during this period when Joseph Yasagi, an Armenian from İzmir, and Nicholas Reggio, of Genoese origin, settled in Boston in 1830 and began importing raisins and dried figs to the United States.

Apart from the Port of İzmir, the Straits and the Black Sea region were also among the regions visited by American merchant ships during this period. Although a ship flying the US flag arrived at the Port of İstanbul in 1786, this visit was not followed up since it was not a suitable port for opium, which was a basic import for American ships. Another important reason was that it was difficult to pass through the Dardanelles due to the lack of any trade agreement between the United States and the Ottoman Empire. Moreover, Britain was trying every way to prevent its former colony, the United States, which was now a commercial rival, from opening up to the Black Sea through the Straits. In addition, the customs duty called 'customs duty' that the Ottoman Empire levied on foreign merchants was also a discouraging factor for American merchants. Similar to Britain, American merchants were initially required to pay a 3 % customs duty. However, after independence, this duty was increased to 6 %. For this reason, Americans began to trade under the auspices of an organisation called the 'Levant Company' and began to pay a tax of 3 % again. However, when Britain later revoked this permission, Americans were again forced to pay a customs duty of 6 % as of February 1811. During this period, the Ottoman administration was unwilling to offend a great empire like Britain in order to gain an advantage over the newly established United States. Thereupon, David Offley, an influential American businessman in İzmir, stepped in and used his personal influence (his friendship with the Admiral Hüsrev Mehmed Pasha) to have the Ottomans accept the 2 % tax tariff applied to Austria for America as well. From 1816 onwards, with Offley's approval, the 3 % customs duty rate applied to France was also accepted for Americans. Businessman David Offley, who played the leading role in these negotiations, served as the 'unofficial American Consul' according to many during this period. In 1830, the first official trade agreement was signed between the United States and the Ottomans.

Thanks to the 1830 Treaty, American merchants gained the status of 'most favoured nation' in the Ottoman Empire. Thanks to this, American merchants who gained access to the Black Sea had equal rights with merchants from the largest countries of the period, such as Britain and France. Again, thanks to this treaty, it was decided that the United States could open consulates in any Ottoman port it wanted. Despite this, no significant development was observed in the bilateral trade volume after the treaty. The main reason for this was the geographical distance between the two countries and the increase in costs. In addition, the harsh climate of the Black Sea and the adverse currents in the Bosphorus caused American merchant ships not to be able to fully benefit from the Black Sea ports. Another reason was that American merchants began to prefer ports in other countries due to the high customs tariffs imposed by the United States on goods such as wool and opium that

American ships loaded from Ottoman ports. A fourth reason could be that the Ottoman Empire took opium, the product most popular with American merchants, under state monopoly, and this had a negative impact on trade. The fifth and final reason is that the Ottoman Empire preferred British companies for transportation between its commercial ports, and American merchants who earned money in this way turned to other ports. During this period, the main products exported from the Ottoman Empire to the United States were; opium, raisins, dried figs, tobacco, licorice, carpets, rugs, wool, and leather products. The main products exported by the United States were; cotton, mineral oils, processed leather, refined sugar, iron and steel products, alcoholic beverages, and of course firearms and their ammunition. In addition, interesting trade agreements could be made between the two countries from time to time. For example, it is an interesting historical event that the US government applied to the Sublime Porte in 1855 to import camels from the Ottoman Empire. Following the 1830 Trade Agreement, the volume of bilateral trade increased continuously. The trade volume, which was $560,101 in 1831, exceeded $2 million for the first time in 1868 and reached $2,153,661. After this date, it even exceeded $5 million in the following years. When we look at the trade during this period, it is interesting to see that the Ottoman Empire generally had a trade surplus with the United States. In addition, the participation of the Ottoman delegation in the World Fair held in New York in 1853 to develop trade is another interesting historical event.

The second trade agreement between the Ottoman Empire and the United States was signed in 1862. Initiatives that began with the efforts of Edward Joy Morris, the Resident Minister appointed to İstanbul at the end of 1860, took the Britain-Ottoman Trade Agreement as an example. As a result of these efforts and long-term negotiations, the US-Ottoman Friendship and Trade Agreement was signed on 13 February 1862. This agreement, consisting of twenty-three articles, contained extremely detailed provisions on trade. The provisions of the 1830 Treaty would continue in terms of nationality and jurisdiction. In addition, the second article of the agreement granted Americans the right to trade anywhere in the Ottoman Empire and the monopoly (*yed-i vahid*) practice was abolished. It was decided in articles 4 and 5 that no arbitrary bans could be imposed on trade other than prohibited products and that the customs duty, which was accepted as 8 %, would be reduced by 1 % each year. The agreement also included some commodities within the scope of the trade ban. Within the scope of this ban, regulated by Article 14, the import of American salt and tobacco into Ottoman territory was prohibited, while Article 15 declared that cannons, gunpowder, weapons and similar ammunition could not be brought into the country. However, this article would be terminated in the following years due to the Ottoman need for weapons and upon the request of the İstanbul government. The Sublime Porte also had a reciprocity article added to the treaty. Apart from these, the parties were given the right to terminate unilaterally at the end of the 14th or 21st year in the treaty, which was concluded for a period of 28 years. The treaty, which was approved by the Senate on 9 April 1862, was also approved by US President Abraham Lincoln without delay on 18 April. With Sultan Abdulaziz's approval of the treaty on 14 May 1862, a new trade regime between the two countries began on 5 June 1862. Following the entry into force of the treaty, various gifts were presented to Ottoman bureaucrats by the Americans in accordance with customs. The most striking among these are the 50 kg silver vase given to the Minister of Foreign Affairs Ali Pasha and the watches worth 5,000 francs each presented to Ali Pasha's assistant Said Pasha and the Customs Officer Kani Pasha.

One of the most important issues in Ottoman-US trade in the nineteenth century was arms trade. Especially after 1865, there was a great interest in American arms technology in the Ottoman Empire. This was closely related to the Ottoman military modernisation efforts. While arms were initially imported mostly from countries such as Britain (England) and France, over time the market share of the United States and Germany in the Ottoman Empire began to increase. In terms of naval arms trade, first, Kaptan-ı Derya Ahmet Pasha applied to the US Chargé d'Affaires David Porter at the end of 1836, requesting that four American naval officers be sent to serve in the Ottoman Navy. After this request was repeated on various occasions, an American sailor named Captain T. B. Tlyden joined the Ottoman Navy. Tylden was assigned as the commander of the frigate built by American engineer Foster Rhodes at the Ayvalık Shipyard. The Ottoman interest in American seafaring revived again in the 1850s. The report written by Major Emin Bey after visiting important shipyards and naval bases in America in 1851 was quite effective in this context. In fact, the Ottoman government decided to have a three-barrel warship built by the United States in 1857. Mehmed Pasha and Major Süleyman Efendi even visited the United States in this regard. However, as a result of intense pressure from the British, it was later decided that the ship would be built by Britain. Although this issue came up again in 1867 and 1882, each time due to a setback, it was not possible for the Ottomans to have a warship built by the United States. In 1900, the Ottoman Empire reached an agreement with the Cramps company (full name William Cramp & Sons) in Philadelphia and finally received the American-made warship, which was delivered in 1904. In fact, Sultan Abdulhamid II, who was very fond of this ship named 'Mecidiye', personally sent a telegram of thanks to the US President. The most important reason why not much progress was made in the naval arms trade during this period was Britain's attitude towards this issue.

In terms of land weapons, Ottoman-US trade was much more productive. First, upon the invitation of Serasker Pasha, who was very fond of the cannon invented by American inventor John Webster Cochran in the early 1830s, Cochran was assigned to Tophane in March 1835. After Cochran, some American military inventors were assigned to Ottoman lands from time to time until the 1860s. From the 1860s onwards, a period of direct land weapon purchases began. When the American Civil War ended in 1865, the United States made a rapid entry into the world arms market. The weapons of the 4 million soldiers who served in the war began to be sold to other countries. Moreover, the arms factories that had been continuously producing during the war now began to produce for export. Indeed, there was a noticeable movement in this regard from 1865 onwards. The first significant purchase was the purchase of approximately 40,000 Enfield infantry rifles. By the end of 1869, 239,000 Enfield and Springfield infantry rifles and their bayonets and cartridges had been imported by the Ottomans. A total of $1,331,000 had been paid for these. Although some restrictions were imposed by the 1862 US-Ottoman Friendship and Trade Treaty, arms trade increased even more in the 1870s when the Sublime Porte abolished this clause. In 1870, the volume exceeded $2 million for the first time. From 1872 onwards, arms production directly for the Ottoman Army was also adopted. In fact, a military delegation headed by Colonel Tevfik Bey visited the United States in 1872. In 1873, 400,000 new infantry rifles were purchased from the United States. During the 1877–1878 Ottoman-Russian War (93 War), arms purchased from the United States reached record levels. A total of $5,335,308 was paid to US companies for Martini-Henry, Peabody-Martini, and Winchester rifles and their ammunition. The United States was very pleased with the arms trade network it established with the Ottomans during this period. This was because the Ottomans did not cause any problems with payments despite the economic crisis and also relieved the American economy by making cash payments instead of instalments. However, as the Ottoman economy deteriorated from the 1880s onwards, arms sales made with promissory notes caused some problems and commercial disputes began to occur between the two countries. For example, an interesting event is that in 1882, when Winchester and Union Metallic companies could not receive their overdue payments from the Ottoman government, they contacted Sultan Abdulhamid II through the US Ambassador. Furthermore, with the involvement of Germany in the 1880s, the US share in the arms trade began to decline. Although arms trade continued until 1914, it was never again at the level of the 1870–1880 period.

B) Missionary activities

Another factor that was effective in the establishment of Ottoman-US relations was the activities of American missionaries. In fact, the two countries where American missionary activities were most intense at that time were China and the Ottoman Empire. The missionary organisation of American Protestants, the American Board of Commissioners for Foreign Missions (ABCFM), decided to start missionary activities towards the Ottoman Empire in 1818. For this purpose, two American missionaries, Pliny Fisk and Levi Parsons, were assigned. However, when Parsons, who came to İzmir in 1820 and started learning Greek, fell ill and died during a visit to Jerusalem in 1821, Fisk continued his work alone. Fisk, who made many trips to the region and especially collected information about Christian communities, convinced three Armenian priests in Beirut to convert to Protestantism, and wrote a letter to the ABCFM headquarters requesting the establishment of an Armenian mission in the region. Additionally, Fisk, who went to Malta in 1822, established a printing house with Daniel Temple to print religious publications. After travelling throughout the Levant region, Fisk decided that Beirut was the most suitable place for missionary activities and was instrumental in making it a missionary centre. The main reasons for Fisk's decision were the large number of Druze and Maronites in the region, the easy delivery of books from the Malta printing house since Beirut was located on the coast, and the lack of a suitable political climate for missionary activities in Jerusalem, the most important religious centre in the region. Indeed, following this decision, missionary schools rapidly increased in Beirut, and information about the region also began to increase. H. G. O. Dwight and Eli Smith's 700-page and 2-volume *Researches of the Rev. E. Smith And Rev. H. G. O. Dwight's Armenia* is the first important work written about the people and lives of the region. The first observation missionaries made about the Ottomans during this period was that it was almost impossible for Muslims to convert. This was because converts were generally punished with death. Also, conversions of Jews were very rare. For this reason, the groups that the missionaries welcomed most warmly were Christian Arabs and Armenians. The first converts to Protestantism came from these groups.

In 1829, the ABCFM decided to establish an Armenian mission in İstanbul. The reason for this was that İstanbul was the capital of the Empire, where all Christian denominations and the highest-level religious organisations of the Jews were located. In the years 1831–1832, missionaries such as Goodell, H. G. O. Dwight, and Gottlieb Schauffler came to İstanbul, visited the Armenian Patriarch and began missionary activities. Dwight grouped missionary activities under four headings: language studies, book studies, education-training studies, and contact with the public. The primary goal was for the missionaries to learn Turkish and Armenian well, to print religious books in these two languages, to spread English with schooling and to establish good relations with the public and to spread the American lifestyle. Establishing good relations with the Armenians, the largest Christian community in the Empire, was also a critical factor at this point. As a result of these studies, the first Turkish Protestant service was held for the Armenians of İstanbul in 1834. During this period, although the Ottomans followed these developments closely, they did not interfere with missionary activities within the framework of religious freedoms. However, if there were complaints from Christian communities, the state was forced to intervene at that point. For example, in 1841, the Patriarch, the religious leader of the Maronites, applied to the Governor of Syria, Zekeriya Pasha, and complained about the activities of American missionaries. For this reason, the Sublime Porte gave a note to the US Ambassador David Porter in May 1841, stating that the lives of the missionaries were in danger. From this incident onwards, the local Maronite and Armenian clergy began to react to the American missionaries because they were losing members of their communities who converted to Protestantism. In fact, during the term of Matteos, who was elected Patriarch of the Gregorian Armenian Church in 1844, the Patriarchate began to threaten to expel members of the community who met with Americans from the Church. Indeed, Matteos expelled the Protestants from the Gregorian Church in 1846. The Protestant Armenians, whose numbers began to increase, asked for help from the United States and Britain in order to gain a separate nation status in the Ottoman Empire. As a result of these efforts, on 15 November 1847, Sultan Abdulmecid recognised the Protestants as a separate nation. Thereupon, the Protestant community in İstanbul immediately elected a representative. Although this brought relief in terms of religious and political tensions, the discomfort that the activities of the American missionaries caused in the Armenian clergy continued for a while. In addition, in time, Muslim subjects also began to react to the missionary activities. In response to the Ottoman Empire informing them of these reactions, American diplomats stated that they did not organise the missionary activities themselves and that they should be evaluated within the scope of religious freedom and emphasised that no one was forced to convert.

Establishment of Diplomatic Relations

American diplomatic and consular structure in the Ottoman Empire

The first steps towards the establishment of Ottoman-US relations were taken by the United States The reasons for this were Washington's consideration of its commercial interests (there was no guarantee for the continuation of the agreement made with Offley's efforts) and the protection of American citizens who came to Ottoman lands due to the increasing missionary work in the region. In spite of this, there were some problems in the establishment of diplomatic relations. These were; the limited means of communication and transportation due to geographical distance (at that time, a letter written from the Ottoman Empire could only reach the United States in two months), the inability to establish healthy dialogue due to the Americans' lack of Turkish (Ottoman), the newly established United States being more concerned with its internal problems, and the Americans, who knew the Ottoman Empire from European books, not being very warm towards this country and its people at first. Although it was not possible to overcome the first problem immediately, the second problem was solved and significant progress was made in diplomatic relations with the appointment of two translators who knew Turkish well, William B. Hodgson and John Porter Brown. The third problem was overcome with the rapid transformation of the United States into an institutional state and the continuation of its economic development. The fourth problem was solved over time with the publication of books containing the observations of Americans who came to the Ottoman Empire. For example, the book *Sketches of Turkey in 1831 and 1832* by the American traveller James De Kay described the Ottoman Turks as cheerful, sincere, and polite people, contrary to what the Europeans wrote.

The Ottoman Empire, on the other hand, was hesitant to develop its relations with the United States during this period. The reasons for this were geographical distance, the fact that the United States was almost unknown to the İstanbul government, the lack of intense commercial and political interests between the two countries, Britain's various obstacles to the rapprochement of its former colony, the United States, and the fact that the Ottomans reacted because of the Americans' positive approach to Greek independence. Apart from these, there were also various reasons that pushed Ottoman statesmen to establish close relations with the United States. These reasons can be listed as follows; Russia's positive view of the US-Ottoman rapprochement – in order to weaken the power of Britain – the idea that the activities of American merchants could benefit the Ottomans in some circles in İstanbul, and the Ottomans' need for the United States in the construction of warships. Thanks to this, the first diplomatic relations began to be established with the emergence of positive thoughts on both sides. Following long years of efforts, the first Ottoman-US Trade Treaty was signed on 7 May 1830, following negotiations that began in İstanbul on 8 February 1830. With this treaty, the United States was granted the status of 'most favoured nation', and provisions such as establishing consular relations and guarantees for American merchants were also included in the treaty. Although there were difficulties during the acceptance of the treaty, this problem was overcome with the efforts of Commodore David Porter, who was assigned to the US Mediterranean Fleet by US President Andrew Jackson, and the treaty was ratified. In fact, following the treaty, a cutter was quickly built for Sultan Mahmud II through the efforts of Henry Eckford (1775–1832), one of New York's most famous naval engineers. After Eckford's early death from typhoid, another American, Foster Rhodes, continued shipbuilding work for the Ottoman Navy. As a matter of fact, Rhodes contributed to the construction of many frigates in İstanbul, where he stayed until 1840.

Following the economic agreement, it was time to establish diplomatic relations. In fact, the United States had opened a diplomatic representative office in İstanbul in 1831 and notified the Ottomans to open an Ottoman representative office in Washington. However, the Ottoman Empire waited until 1867 to open a representative office in the United States, a distant state that it did not attach much importance to. The US side, on the other hand, appointed David Porter as the Chargé d'Affaires in İstanbul in 1831. In contrast, Porter, who did not yet have the status of an ambassador, was treated coldly by the Sublime Porte officials and was not even allowed to present the President's letter to the Sultan. However, through his personal efforts, Porter established close relations with Sultan Mahmud II during a hunting party and obtained special permission to visit the mosques and palaces in İstanbul. During this period, Porter, who coordinated the construction of Eckford and Rhodes' warships, was also requesting that his rank be raised to the level of ambassador from the US Department of State. According to Porter, only in this way could the United States reach a level where it could better defend its interests. Following Porter's contacts in 1838 by going to the United States, he was appointed as the Resident Minister in İstanbul on 3 March 1839. In this way, Porter's and therefore the US's reputation in the Sublime Porte and his position within the diplomatic corps rose. All US diplomatic representatives appointed to İstanbul between 1840 and 1881 held the title of Resident Minister. During this period, the US Embassy in İstanbul employed a clerk, one or two translators, and guards called 'banners' established by the Sublime Porte. In addition, as the number of Americans committing crimes in Ottoman territory increased from the mid-1860s onwards, an Embassy Prison was opened, and officers were assigned there. American ambassadors, from the 1850s onwards, wanted the representation to be raised to the level of Ministerial or Ambassadorial, and stated that only in this way could they make advances in diplomacy. For example, in a letter dated 1858, Resident Ambassador James Williams wrote to Secretary of State Lewis Cass that the Turks acted according to titles, and therefore their status should be raised.

In 1882, the US representation in the Ottoman Empire was raised to the level of Ministerial Ambassador, and Lewis Wallace (Lew Wallace), who had previously served as Resident Minister, was appointed Ministerial Minister. Nine American Ministerial Ministers served in İstanbul between 1882 and 1906. During this period, Ministerial Ministers sent reports to Washington stating that they should be permanent ambassadors. Finally, in 1906, Ministerial Minister John G. A. Leishman was appointed as the first American Ambassador to İstanbul. During World War I, five American ambassadors served in İstanbul until diplomatic relations between the two countries were severed. These were John G. A. Leishman (1906–1909), Oscar S. Straus (1909–1910), William Woodville Rockhill (1911–1913), Henry Morgenthau (1911–1916), and Abram I. Elkus (1916–1917).

Consuls also played important roles in the development of US-Ottoman relations. For example, American Consul David Offley, who officially served in İzmir from 1830, was a very important person in terms of bilateral relations. With David Porter, who was appointed as the Chargé d'Affaires in İstanbul in 1831, Washington's efforts to open new consulates also began. Indeed, Porter, who carried out a very active diplomacy, managed to open 8 new consulates in Thessaloniki, İstankoy, Bozcaada, Alexandria, Beirut, Jerusalem, Bursa, and Çanakkale within a year. Either consuls were appointed to these places according to their importance, or consular officers or acting consuls were appointed. Although these consulates created economic costs for the United States, they also helped this new state to hold its own against the established European states. However, when the costs became too high, in 1840 President Martin Van Buren ordered the closure of all consulates except those in İstanbul, İzmir, and Thessaloniki. However, due to the reactions from the American people in the region, Van Buren later reversed this decision. By 1853, the United States had consulates in İstanbul, İzmir, Beirut, Aleppo, Damascus, Jaffa, and Bursa. By 1888, there were consulates general in İstanbul and Alexandria, and consulates in İzmir, Candia, Beirut, Jerusalem, Chios, Jaffa, Trabzon, Samsun, Adana, Ayntab, Rhodes, İstankoy, Midilli, Sivas, Sayda, Kale-i Sultaniye, Suez, Port Said, Latakia, Plovdiv, Thessaloniki, Candia, Chania, İskenderun, Bursa, Damascus, and Rethymno. This increase in the number of consulates indicates the importance the United States gave to the Eastern Question, also known as the Eastern Question. The fact that American Consulates granted 'protégé' status to some Armenians in these years was met with a reaction by the Sublime Porte. The interference of some American Consuls in the internal affairs of the Ottoman Empire (such as the Candia Consul Stillman, who supported the Cretan uprising, and the Tripoli Consul Vidal, who had a personal conflict with the Pasha of Tripoli in the early 1870s and wanted the US Navy to come to the region) and the appointment of non-Muslims who had not renounced Ottoman citizenship but had become American citizens as US Consuls or officials in Ottoman cities (such as the Armenian-born Ayıntab Deputy Consul named Nazaryan) were other important crisis issues in this period.

When American diplomacy during this period is examined, it is seen that American diplomats were received more positively by the Ottoman Empire compared to Europeans due to their policy of non-interference in the internal affairs of European states, including the Ottoman Empire, in line with the 1823 Monroe Doctrine. The fact that there had been no previous war between the two states also gave the United States a more respected position in İstanbul compared to European states. However, American influence over the Ottoman Empire was extremely limited during this period, and İstanbul was under intense European influence. American diplomats generally established good relations with the Ottoman Sultans during this period. David Porter's closeness to Sultan Mahmud II and Lewis Wallace's personal friendship with Sultan Abdulhamid II can be given as examples of this. However, some American diplomats, such as Wayne MacVeagh and David Thompson, who saw the Ottoman Empire as a place of exile, served in İstanbul for only short periods. The American diplomat Oscar S. Straus, who organised the Jewish migration to Palestine, was appointed to İstanbul at his own request and three different times (1887–1889, 1898–1900, 1909–1911). It was noteworthy that the American ambassadors serving in İstanbul during this period did not learn Turkish; they used English through an interpreter or spoke French. However, there were always officials who knew Turkish well at the Embassy. Among these people, John Porter Brown (1814–1872), David Porter's nephew, who served for 38 years (1834–1872), was a very important person. Brown, who was awarded the Medjidie Order three times, developed Ottoman-American relations and was a person loved by the Sublime Porte. Brown, who published articles praising the Ottomans in American newspapers during the Hungarian Revolution and the Crimean War, became a very influential person who knew many Eastern languages and had connections with missionary groups in the Ottoman Empire, İstanbul merchants and the Ottoman bureaucracy. An interesting incident from this period was the argument between Cyrus Hamlin, the President of Robert College and a prominent missionary, and the American Ambassador Alexander W. Terrell during the Armenian events in 1894–1895. Hamlin, who accused the ambassador of not helping them, sent letters of complaint to the US President at the time and sought the help of the British ambassador. In addition, two of the American diplomats serving in İstanbul, Samuel S. Cox and Oscar S. Straus, wrote detailed works describing the period they served in the Ottoman Empire, while many other American diplomats wrote various articles and books on political developments in the Ottoman Empire.

Ottoman diplomatic and consular structure in the United States

The first Ottoman diplomatic move towards the United States was the assignment of Tibgeoğlu Abraham to Boston in 1845 to regulate the trade of Ottoman ships and to protect Ottoman subjects in the United States. Another Ottoman policy during this period was the occasional visits of certain individuals to the United States as 'special representatives of the Sultan' in order to develop bilateral relations. The contacts of Major Emin Bey (1850–1851), who visited the United States for 6 months, and the visits of two naval officers named Mehmed Pasha and Major Süleyman Efendi to America in 1857 (1858) can be evaluated within this scope. With the opening of the Ottoman Embassy in Washington in 1867 – at the level of the Ministerial Council – some progress was made in diplomatic relations. The Ottoman diplomatic and consular structure in the United States, which began with Eduard Black Bey (1824–1895) who served in Washington between 1867–1873, expanded in a short time. Indeed, by 1881, there were Ottoman Consulates in cities such as New York, Baltimore, Chicago, Boston, Philadelphia, and New Orleans. In addition, Honorary Consuls were appointed to cities such as Washington, San Francisco, and Norfolk from time to time as needed. Eduard Black Bey, also known as Bulak Bey, the first Ottoman ambassador to the United States, was the son-in-law of Matt, an American doctor, and his wife was American. Although this family connection was effective in his selection for this position, another important reason was that he was one of the few people who spoke good English in Turkish diplomacy, where French was dominant. In addition, unlike many Ottoman diplomats of the period, Black Bey ventured to the unknown and distant United States.

Ottoman diplomats serving in America were unable to make major diplomatic breakthroughs during these years due to the geographical distance between the two countries, and because relations were not very intense. Considering that the Ottoman Foreign Service gave Tevfik Pasha, who was appointed to the US Ambassadorship, an annual salary of 240,000 liras, and that this salary was half of the salaries received by the Berlin, London and Paris Ambassadors, it can be assumed that the Empire did not attach much importance to relations. The low rank and salary, and the humid climate of Washington also contributed to Ottoman diplomats' negative attitude towards US missions. During the reign of Abdulhamid II, even the closure of the Washington Ambassadorship in order to save money was on the agenda. However, with the efforts of US Ambassador Lewis Wallace, this decision was later abandoned.

The Eastern Question and the United States

The Eastern Question is the issue of sharing the collapsing Ottoman Empire. This issue, which mostly concerned the European great powers of the period such as Britain, France, and Russia, began to concern the United States, which emerged as a new superpower candidate, in time, as its relations with the Ottoman Empire increased. However, unlike the European states, the United States, which never considered occupying Ottoman lands, never made this issue one of the priority agenda items of its foreign policy. With the Greek Revolt that began in 1821, the Eastern Question began to become a serious political agenda. There are two main factors in the US's perspective on this issue. The first is the indifference shown to this issue in line with the classical approach of not interfering in internal affairs. However, the second factor, also influenced by the negative views of American missionaries, who were influenced by Armenian propaganda, about the Ottoman Empire, brought the United States face to face with the Ottoman Empire. Realising this, the Ottoman Ambassador Eduard Black Bey sent a letter to *The New York Times* in 1869 and tried to explain that the Eastern Question was not a religious issue but a political one. Despite the efforts of the missionaries, the United States never directly took sides in the Eastern Question. American diplomats also warned Washington not to take sides in this matter. For example, in a letter he wrote to Foreign Minister Hamilton Fish in 1874, George H. Boker, who served as the ambassador to İstanbul, criticised the attitude of the European states. However, as signs of the collapse of the Ottoman Empire became widespread, the attitudes of American diplomats began to change. In fact, in a report he wrote to Foreign Minister Richard Olney in 1896, Ambassador Alexander W. Terrell even suggested that the US Navy send a powerful fleet to the area around Rhodes or Crete and intervene militarily against the Ottomans if the compensation requested for the American buildings damaged during the Armenian incidents was not paid. Therefore, it can be said that the US's view of the Eastern Question gradually came to be similar to that of European states after the Cretan Rebellion. The problems that the Ottoman State, an Islamic state, had with its Christian subjects and the negative view of the Armenian and Greek minorities towards the Sublime Porte in the following years were also effective in the perception of this issue as a religious conflict in the United States. In addition, the fact that the United States, which gained its independence by fighting a war against Britain, was governed by a republican regime based on democratic principles was also an effective psychological factor in its negative view of the Ottoman Empire, which ruled many Christian nations.

The Second Constitutional Revolution, carried out by the Committee of Union and Progress (CUP) in the Ottoman Empire in 1908–1909, was generally welcomed by the United States. The Young Turks' advocacy of values such as constitutional constitutionalism, modernism, women's rights, and development greatly pleased American intellectuals during these years. This period corresponds to the period when the United States, under the presidency of William Howard Taft (1909–1913), attempted to enter the Middle East through 'dollar diplomacy'. For this reason, American businessmen wanted to obtain various projects from the Ottoman government and increase their economic and political influence. Even with the initiatives of retired Admiral Colby M. Chester, serious efforts were made to build a railway called the 'Chester Project' that would extend from Sivas to Sulaymaniyah. This project, which granted the privilege of constructing a railway in Eastern Anatolia and operating the surrounding mines to the Ottoman-American Development Company, a US-Canadian partnership group, was accepted during the Republican era after long negotiations, but was later suspended due to the Mosul Problem, and a major investment move by the Americans was thus thwarted. In addition, diplomatic relations between the two countries had to be suspended during World War I due to the United States declaring war on Germany, an ally of the Ottoman Empire, in 1917. However, even during this period, despite being in different camps, the two states did not declare war on each other. In contrast, the events that took place during the Armenian deportation in 1915 played a very effective role in the negative view of the United States and Western countries in general towards the Ottoman Empire. For this reason, the sympathy that the Unionists had created in the Western world soon disappeared, and in its place, the image of the 'Barbarian Turk' began to emerge once again.

Relations With the United States in the Republican Period

Following the success of the National Struggle and the victory of the Turkish Army under the command of Mustafa Kemal (Atatürk), the first agreement between the United States and the newly established Republic of Türkiye was signed in August 1923. Although the parties recognised each other with this agreement, which was signed shortly after the Treaty of Lausanne on 6 August 1923, diplomatic relations could only be established in 1927. Although this agreement was rejected in the US Congress due to the propaganda of the Armenians during this period, the United States side initiated diplomatic relations in February 1927 with the 'modus vivendi' method. Thus, Joseph Grew (1927–1932) began his duty as the first US Ambassador to Türkiye, and the Turkish side appointed Ahmet Muhtar (1927–1934) as the Ambassador to Washington. During this period, Mustafa Kemal Atatürk's efforts to transform the Republic of Türkiye into a modern Western country attracted great interest and admiration in the United States as well as in Europe. The first US Ambassador, Joseph Grew, also earned the respect of the Great Leader Mustafa Kemal Atatürk and the young Republic of Türkiye with his work during this period. In fact, in 1927, Grew and Atatürk came together to record a video announcing the friendship of the two countries to the entire world. In this video, the two statesmen are seen complimenting each other's nations and states and exalting their interlocutors.

The efforts of the first Turkish Ambassador to Washington, Ahmet Muhtar (1927–1934), and the Turkish Ambassador Mehmet Münir Ertegün (1934–1944) who later took up this post, attempted to eliminate the negative 'Turkish' image in the United States, which had been damaged by Armenian propaganda. In addition, on 1 October 1929, the Trade and Navigation Agreement was signed between Türkiye and the United States. Thanks to this agreement, despite the Great Depression of 1929, bilateral trade relations began to develop. So much so that, in the period 1933–1939, the United States became Türkiye's largest customer after Germany, and Türkiye's exports to the United States reached 19 million liras. During the same period, the US's exports to Türkiye were also around 17 million liras. During these years, American businessmen were welcomed positively in Türkiye, and the United States was not considered a politically negative state. However, this positive approach was definitely not displayed towards every foreign state in those years. Because the Turkish state elite, who remembered very well that the economy of the Ottoman Empire was in the hands of foreigners during its collapse, thought in a very nationalist manner regarding foreign investments and the economy. Moreover, Ankara continued to pay off the debts inherited from the Ottoman period during these years. In addition, in addition to the close relations that began to be developed with the United States, very good relations were also established especially with the Soviet Union. Mustafa Kemal Atatürk, who turned to regional organisations (Sadabat Pact and Balkan Pact) rather than relying on one of the great powers in terms of security policy, managed to create a dynamic nation-state that rose from a collapsed Empire in a short time. Another interesting event regarding Atatürk's relations with the Americans is the meeting he had with American General Douglas MacArthur in 1932. During this meeting, it is claimed that Atatürk made accurate predictions that the Second World War was approaching. Standard Oil, American Tobacco and Ford were the first important American companies to enter the Turkish market during this period. In addition, the American ambassadors who served in Türkiye during this period (1927–1945) after Joseph Grew (1927–1932) were: Charles Hitchcock Sherrill (1932–1933), Robert Peet Skinner (1933–1936), John Van Antwerp MacMurray (1936–1941), and Laurence A. Steinhardt (1942–1945). The Turkish ambassadors who served in Washington during the same period were Mehmet Münir Ertegün (1934–1944) and Orhan Halit Erol (1944–1945).

Türkiye, which implemented a 'neutrality policy' during World War II and continued to trade with Nazi Germany, did not want to enter the war, despite the intense efforts of Britain and Prime Minister Winston Churchill's visit to Türkiye to meet with President İsmet İnönü. At the Allied Conference in Cairo on 4–6 December 1943, Prime Minister İsmet İnönü held a historic meeting with Churchill and US President Franklin Delano Roosevelt. However, all Turkish statesmen, starting with the 'National Chief' İsmet Pasha, were against their country, which had been founded only a few years earlier, had a small population, underdeveloped military technology and newly reconstructed cities, entering the war. For this reason, Ankara did not pay attention to the pressures and continued its policy of neutrality. During these years, Germany also realised Türkiye's importance and made various moves through its Ambassador Franz Von Papen to prevent Ankara from siding with the British. The trade network developed with Germany during this period, and especially the chrome trade, was an important factor in Germany's positive view of Türkiye and saved Ankara from a possible Nazi invasion. The Germans made some generous offers to Türkiye during these years to attract Ankara to their side. It is even known that Von Papen offered Türkiye land in the regions where the Muslim Turkish population lived in the Caucasus. Apart from this, a pro-German Pan-Turkist group – consisting of Enver Pasha's brother Nuri Pasha (Nuri Killigil) and a famous Pan-Turkist Professor Zeki Doğan – made an unofficial visit to Berlin during these years and met with Nazi officials. Such initiatives and the pro-German articles in the Turkish press were actually parts of İnönü's grand plan and his sole purpose was to prevent Türkiye from being subjected to Nazi invasion. According to William Hale, İnönü's understanding of foreign policy was based on a single principle: 'precaution'. Furthermore, İnönü was a true master of stalling and was always very good at stalling his opponents in diplomacy. However, when it was clear that the Allies would win World War II, towards the end of the war, diplomatic relations with Germany were first cut off, and then a mock war was declared on this country. In this way, it was aimed to sit at the same table with the victorious states in the new order to be established after the war. According to William Hale, the policy Türkiye followed in World War II is a great example of success. Because Türkiye, which got through this period without firing a single weapon and without being targeted by a single bullet, rapidly grew stronger during this period while all other states experienced great destruction and lost their populations. Moreover, Ankara did not suffer any loss of territory and increased its effectiveness in diplomacy. According to Hale, Türkiye actually became closer to the Allies (Britain, France, and the

United States) throughout the war. All other moves made due to the desire not to enter the war were strategic and tactical. During this period, İnönü and his friends used one power against the other, taking maximum advantage of Türkiye's strategic position, and were ultimately successful. However, some racist policies implemented domestically, such as the Wealth Tax, and the economic difficulties experienced during these years prevented the emergence of a picture of total success. Türkiye's neutrality policy during these years was also correct according to William Hale; because if Türkiye entered the war against the Germans, it would be invaded by the Nazis like Greece and could later be subject to Soviet occupation, and if it entered the war on the side of the Germans, it would again face Soviet occupation.

Cold War and the Alliance Period (1945–1991)

A) The beginning of allied relations in the 1945–1960 period

The event that initiated the process of Turkish-American relations rising to the level of alliance was the threats made by Soviet Union leader Joseph Stalin against Türkiye after World War II and the rude demands conveyed to Moscow Ambassador Selim Sarper. From this period onwards, Turkish-American relations began to be constructed within the framework of an alliance relationship. According to many, due to Stalin's threats, this was an inevitable situation rather than a choice. Indeed, the United States, which initially acted more moderately towards Soviet Russia and even suggested holding an international conference on the passage of warships of states bordering the Black Sea through the Straits, eventually began to believe that Russia wanted to occupy the Straits and chose to provide more intensive support to Türkiye, as Secretary of State James F. Byrnes stated in an unsent letter. The event that symbolised the alliance between the two countries was the anchoring of the American battleship Missouri, carrying the body of the deceased Turkish Ambassador to Washington Mehmet Münir Ertegün, in İstanbul on 5 April 1946. This event was a threat to the Soviet Union and an indication that Türkiye would soon be accepted into NATO, the Western security alliance, as an American ally. From this date onwards, Türkiye rejected the Soviets' demands for new talks on the Straits – with the assurance of the United States. During this process, the United States also turned to the strategy of containing

Russia and communism in the Cold War with the article 'The Sources of Soviet Conduct' written by George Kennan under the pseudonym 'X' in *Foreign Affairs* magazine (July 1947). The situation became even clearer with the Truman Doctrine and the Marshall Plan; because the United States began to provide military, economic and political support to Allied countries against the Soviet threat. Türkiye, along with Greece, would also partially benefit from this support. In parallel with these developments, Türkiye became a member of the Organisation for European Economic Co-operation (OEEC, later OECD) during this period. In addition, with the efforts of the CHP (Republican People's Party), many economic and military agreements were signed between the United States and Türkiye during the 1945–1950 period, and the principles of alliance relations emerged. However, this alliance became official in the 1950s when Türkiye became a member of NATO.

The 1950s were the beginning and golden years of the Turkish-American alliance. Türkiye, which attracted Washington's attention by sending troops to the Korean War, became a NATO member in 1952, and the İncirlik Base in Adana, which symbolised the military alliance of the two countries – the construction of which began in 1951 by a team called the US Engineering Group – was opened in 1954. In addition, President Celal Bayar's visit to the United States in 1954 was a very important and historic visit. Prime Minister Adnan Menderes also visited the United States twice, in 1954 and 1959. In the 1950s, during the rapprochement process with the United States, important changes were experienced in domestic politics, and after the single-party system, the liberal and Western Democrat Party (DP), led by the Adnan Menderes-Celal Bayar duo, came to power in the multi-party system. The DP ensured Türkiye's inclusion in NATO by sending troops to the Korean War. These developments were experienced with the support and approval of İsmet İnönü, who had moved from the presidency to the leadership of the opposition party. From that date on, Türkiye became a neighbouring Russia and an 'aircraft carrier' that never sank for Western powers and gained great military and strategic importance. Although relations with Russia softened for a while during the Nikita Khrushchev era after Stalin passed away in 1953, no change was seen in Türkiye's strategic preferences. In fact, the image of the Americans in Türkiye in those years was so positive that the following is stated in the work of 'Tango King' Celal İnce, 'The Song of Friendship':

'America, America, Turks, as long as the world stands, Are together with you in the war of freedom'.

During this period, Türkiye also rapidly developed its economic and political relations with Israel, which it recognised in 1949 and was one of the most important American allies in the region. The Baghdad Pact, or CENTO as it was called in later years, was another important issue of Turkish Foreign Policy during this period. This pact, established between Türkiye, Iran, Iraq, Pakistan, and the United Kingdom to prevent the Soviet Union from establishing influence in the Middle East, emerged with the support of the United States. In 1958, Türkiye even allowed the use of Incirlik Air Base to support the United States in its intervention in Lebanon. Also, during this period, Israeli Prime Minister David Ben-Gurion visited Türkiye and a secret 'Peripheral Pact' or 'Peripheral Pact' was established between Israel, Türkiye, Iran, and Abyssinia (Ethiopia). Furthermore, in 1959, the United States and Türkiye shook hands on the deployment of a total of fifteen Jupiter missiles in facilities around the Çiğli Air Base in İzmir. The Cyprus Conflict, which began during this period, would become an issue that would seriously damage Turkish-American relations from the 1960s onwards. The American ambassadors who served in Ankara during this period (1945–1960) were: Edwin C. Wilson (1945–1948), George Wadsworth (1948–1952), George C. McGhee (1952–1953), Avra M. Warren (1953–1956), and Fletcher Warren (1956–1960). The Turkish ambassadors who served in Washington during the same period were: Hüseyin Ragıp Baydur (1945–1948), Feridun Cemal Erkin (1948–1955), Ali Haydar Görk (1955–1957), Suat Hayri Ürgüplü (1957–1960), and Melih Esenbel (1960–1960).

B) The alliance model that began in the 1950s

When the alliance model established between Türkiye and the United States in the 1950s is examined, it is understood that this is certainly not a form of equal relationship established between two states of equal power. The United States, which emerged from World War II as a superpower, undoubtedly represents the strong side in this 'asymmetrical' relationship. However, as Nasuh Uslu states, unlike many alliance relationships established in the bipolar world order that emerged during the Cold War, a patron state-satellite state type relationship has not been established between Türkiye and the United States. If the reasons for this are examined; the increasing power of the Republic of

Türkiye, which was established as the heir of a great empire and far above a classic satellite state, and the great importance attributed to national honour by the Turks are the most prominent issues. Indeed, from the very first years of the alliance, Ankara saw itself as having the right and power to object to Washington on certain issues. Nasuh Uslu also justifies the Turkish-American alliance established in those years with several basic articles. These are; The security support that Türkiye needs against the expansionist threat of Soviet Russia is due to American economic aid, strategic reasons (the need to rely on a major power in a bipolar political world order, according to the 'Aron Paradigm' view developed by Raymond Aron), the two states developing common reflexes along the lines of anti-communism and their official ideologies being close to each other, domestic political reasons and the fact that a 'non-aligned' foreign policy is very risky for Türkiye.

When the Turkish-American alliance relations established in the 1950s are examined, it is seen that this is essentially a military-security alliance. Indeed, the main reason for Türkiye's alliance with the United States is the need for security against Soviet Russia, which is a communist and expansionist state and, moreover, has advanced nuclear weapons in its arsenal. Washington, on the other hand, has gained a very important ally in many different geographies such as the Middle East, the Caucasus, the Balkans, the Eastern Mediterranean, and North Africa thanks to Türkiye, which is a country close to Russia and is located at a place where three continents meet. Türkiye is also the 'southern flank' of NATO, protecting Europe from the threat of Russia and communism. Therefore, the driving force of the alliance between the two countries is the military organisations in both countries and the NATO organisation, of which the two countries are members. Although political and economic relations between the two countries developed over time – in parallel with security-oriented policies – this military-centred alliance relationship would struggle against the peaceful leftist winds of the 1970s and would enter a serious crisis after the Cold War. The main reasons for this were the strengthening of civilian politics in Türkiye and the reaction of the Turkish people and intellectuals to the US's contribution to military coups and its close relations with Islamists and ultranationalists.

According to Oral Sander, the alliance relations between the two countries established during the Cold War were built on extremely strong and solid foundations and were based on mutual interests. These foundations, which can be summarised as opposing Soviet expansionism and international communism, supporting peace and stability, and having similar strategic approaches towards the Middle East, have been challenged from time to time due to the differences in the strategies of the two countries due to the fact that the United States is a global actor and Türkiye is a regional player, but they have never collapsed. In fact, Sander thinks that the Turkish-American alliance will be permanent in the twenty-first century for two reasons when viewed from a realistic perspective. These are (1) Türkiye's geographical location and proximity to Russia, and (2) American military aid and alliance will always be important for Ankara – due to threats from Russia and security risks in the Middle East. On the other hand, the fact that the US's global and regional strategies and Türkiye's national and regional interests do not always match (for example, the Cyprus Conflict in the 1960s and 1970s, and today's Kurdish policy and Iran strategy) has strained relations from time to time and even brought them into crisis since the early years of the alliance. When the fact that the two countries come from different civilisational families (the United States has a large Christian population, while Türkiye is almost entirely a Muslim country) is added to this, maintaining alliance relations within democratic regimes where popular views are important has become a very difficult task that requires serious skill.

C) Frequent crises in the 1960s and 1970s

In the 1960s and 1960s, the Turkish-American alliance experienced many crises, and these crises resulted in a serious decrease in mutual trust. Among these crises; (1) the 1963 Cuban Missile Crisis, which led Türkiye to realise that it could be a nuclear target for Soviet Russia, (2) the 1964 'Johnson Letter' incident, which led Türkiye to realise that it could be deprived of US and NATO support for its national causes (such as the Cyprus Conflict), (3) the 'poppy problem', which led Türkiye to realise that its national economic interests could be ignored by the United States, and (4) the arms embargo imposed on Ankara by Washington in the 1975–78 period following the Cyprus intervention (Cyprus Peace Operation-1974) stand out. Indeed, this period, when relations with the United States became unstable, had a negative impact on Türkiye's domestic politics, and in the 1960–1980 period, Türkiye experienced two comprehensive military coups (27 May 1960 and 12 September 1980), a memorandum (12 March 1971) and many military coup attempts (the Talat Aydemir incidents and the 9 March incident). Despite these crises and Türkiye's efforts to distance itself from the United States, which it was angry with for various reasons, in foreign policy, the United States, which was a major partner, returned stronger than ever and increased its influence over Türkiye during this period (1960–1980). However, since this situation generally occurred through military coups where civilian politics were shelved, it also caused the United States to have a negative reputation in Türkiye in the following years.

Following the 1960 military coup, during the coalition governments between 1961 and 1965, Prime Minister İsmet İnönü went through two major crises with the United States. The first of these was the 1963 Cuban Missile Crisis, which occurred after an American satellite discovered that the Soviet Union had placed nuclear warheads in Cuba. Although this incident did not directly concern Türkiye, the Soviet Union's (Khrushchev's) request that the United States withdraw the Jupiter missiles from Türkiye in order to withdraw the missiles from Cuba led Ankara to realise that it could easily become the target of Moscow, a nuclear power, in a possible US-Russia war. Although US President John F. Kennedy, who successfully resolved the Cuban Missile Crisis, gained great sympathy worldwide with his charisma and his stance on the incident, the silent withdrawal of the Jupiter missiles in İzmir, which were agreed upon with Türkiye in 1959 and activated in 1962, caused Türkiye to have serious doubts about the extent to which it could trust Washington regarding its security, and shook its trust in the United States for the first time. After this move, Ankara was left completely defenceless against a nuclear attack by Moscow.

The second major problem of this period was Washington's negative attitude towards the Cyprus incidents after İsmet Pasha started to bring up the option of military intervention. Indeed, the 'Johnson Letter' sent by Lyndon Johnson, who became President after Kennedy was assassinated, to Turkish Prime Minister İsmet İnönü on 5 June 1964 is a historical document written to prevent Türkiye from intervening in Cyprus. In the letter, President Johnson informed Türkiye that it would not be able to use NATO weapons in Cyprus and that it would be deprived of NATO support against Soviet Russia in a possible war. This was the second major shock for Türkiye after the Cuban Missile Crisis and deepened the view that Ankara could not trust Washington regarding its security. Because the understanding in this letter also contradicted NATO's Article 5. Prime Minister İsmet İnönü gave his famous response after this incident: '*If necessary, a new world will be established and Türkiye will take its place in this world.*' Following this incident, a group of left-wing circles led by the Turkish Workers' Party (TİP) began to propagate the idea of Türkiye withdrawing from NATO and became extremely influential in national politics. Under the influence of this left-wing opposition, politicians such as Süleyman Demirel (1965–1969, 1969–1971, 1975–1977, 1979–1980) and Bülent Ecevit (1974–1974, 1977–1977, 1978–1979) who later became Prime Ministers and their Foreign Ministers (İhsan Sabri Çağlayangil, Turan Güneş, and Gündüz Ökçün) always gave importance to multi-dimensional foreign policy and never fully trusted the United States again. Some of Ecevit's advisers, such as Prof. Haluk Ülman, even took things a step further and began to advocate withdrawing from NATO as a rational policy. Starting from this period, the Soviet aid and investments in Türkiye towards industrialisation (for example, the iron and steel facilities in İskenderun) were also influential in this attitude. The balanced attitude of the Soviets between the Greeks and the Turks on the Cyprus issue was also pleasing to Ankara at that time. Therefore, Moscow was able to establish seriously warm relations with Ankara, although not on a par with Washington in these years, and Turkish-American relations also entered a crisis. This situation was definitely not due to Prime Minister Demirel and Ecevit being anti-American; due to structural problems and conflicting national interests, Ankara was acting closer to Moscow and trying to distance itself from Washington.

The third major crisis of this period occurred in 1974 when Prime Minister Bülent Ecevit allowed poppy cultivation and raw opium production in seven provinces (Afyon, Burdur, Isparta, Denizli, Kütahya, Uşak, and Konya) in order to improve the living conditions of farmers dependent on poppy production. Türkiye, which implemented a poppy ban domestically in the 1971–1974 period upon the suggestions of the United States, realised that despite this ban, drug trafficking in the United States and Europe was accelerating, understood that this ban made no sense and took a step considering its own citizens (farmers) despite the criticisms coming from Washington. However, this step was not welcomed by Washington and criticisms of Prime Minister Ecevit increased.

The fourth and most serious crisis between Türkiye and the United States occurred due to the Cyprus Peace Operation, which Türkiye carried out after the EOKA-B coup in Cyprus, which supported enosis (unifying Cyprus with Greece). In 1974, Türkiye, using its guarantor right, carried out a military intervention on the island with the Cyprus Peace Operation. This took place during the interesting coalition government of Atatürk's CHP, which had shifted to a socialist line under the leadership of Ecevit, and the Islamist Nationalist Salvation Party (MSP), led by Prof. Necmettin Erbakan. This situation was made possible when the junta in Greece organised a coup in Cyprus and overthrew the President of the Republic of Cyprus, Makarios, and replaced him with EOKA members. The EOKA members, who put the Akritas Plan into action to destroy the Turks, practically forced Türkiye to intervene on the island. The United States, on the other hand, was busy with the Arab-Israeli negotiations and the Watergate Scandal, during this period, when Henry Kissinger was involved. Although the United States and Britain opposed the intervention, they did not make much effort to prevent it. This intervention prevented a possible major massacre in Cyprus and led to the collapse of the junta government in Greece. Turkish-Greek relations had become quite tense during these years not only due to Cyprus but also due to the Aegean Question. An invasion of Cyprus would cause Greece to have great concerns about the Aegean Islands and to rapidly arm itself. The 1974 Cyprus crisis would also negatively affect Turkish-American relations. Under the influence of the Greek lobby, the United States made a decision to block military aid and sales to Türkiye during this period (1975–1978) and unintentionally triggered a breakthrough in the Turkish defence industry. Although this embargo was lifted within a few years, the conflict with the United States was reflected in Türkiye as economic difficulties. Under the influence of this embargo, Ecevit adopted a more Third Worldist rhetoric in the second half of the 1970s and even began to advocate leaving NATO. However, it did not make any active efforts in this direction and kept the issue on the table as a bargaining chip. For this reason, the process of breaking away from the West in the 1970s remained partial, temporary, and hesitant and never turned into a serious and official anti-Western policy.

During this difficult period (1960–1980), the American ambassadors who served in Türkiye were: Raymond A. Hare (1961–1965), Parker T. Hart (1965–1968), Robert Komer (1968–1969), William J. Handley (1969–1973), William B. Macomber Jr (1973–1977), and Ronald I. Spiers (1977–1980).

During this eventful period, due to rising student activism and leftist movements, there were also various attacks on American diplomats. For example, on 6 January 1969, the car of Robert Komer, the then US Ambassador and former CIA officer, who was coming to METU – which was built according to a gun plan established by the Americans themselves a few years earlier and aimed at Soviet Russia from a bird's eye view – was set on fire by leftist students. The Turkish ambassadors who served in Washington during the same period were the following valuable diplomats: Bülend Uşaklıgil (1960–1962), Turgut Menemencioğlu (1962–1967), Melih Esenbel (1967–1974, for the second time), Aydın Yeğen (1974–1975), Melih Esenbel (1975–1979, for the third time), and Şükrü Elekdağ (1979–1989).

D) 1980–1991

After the 12 September 1980 coup, Türkiye was quickly brought back into the American orbit by the Turkish Armed Forces (TSK). According to many, the coup was also carried out thanks to American support. This incident also showed that, under the conditions of the Cold War, Türkiye's efforts to distance itself from its major partner, the United States, backfired and Washington's influence on Ankara increased each time. Washington did not pay much attention to the human rights violations that occurred after the 12 September coup and its aftermath. The main reason for this was that Washington, which had lost one of its most important allies, Iran, in 1979 – due to the Iranian Islamic Revolution – could not tolerate losing another ally. For this reason, Washington generally preferred to remain silent in the face of the excesses of the 12 September regime. Regarding the embargoes initiated due to the Cyprus Conflict, the US's stance changed from 1978, before the coup, and no military, political or economic embargo was ever imposed on Türkiye again. Probably encouraged by this situation, the leader of the coup and the 7th President of Türkiye, Kenan Evren, supported the declaration of the Turkish Republic of Northern Cyprus (TRNC) in 1983, but this state has only been recognised by Türkiye to date. During this period, Türkiye recalled the Soviet threat as a result of the Soviet intervention in Afghanistan, and the pro-Russian atmosphere of the 1970s quickly dissipated. During this period, Türkiye's permission for Greece to return to NATO also increased the legitimacy of the 12 September junta in Washington and increased American support for Ankara.

During the post-coup period, during the civilian Turgut Özal government (1983–1989), Turkish-American relations began to experience a 'second spring' – after the 1950s. Özal, who was a great American ally and admirer, acted even more aggressively than the Celal Bayar-Adnan Menderes duo to make Türkiye a 'Little America' and transformed the Turkish economy from a closed statist system to an open free market economy. The Özal era, similar to the Ronald Reagan and Margaret Thatcher governments of the same period, was identified with privatisations, integration into the world economy and liberal conservatism. Özal was also the first Turkish leader to establish a personal friendship with a US President. So much so that Özal addressed US President George Bush as 'George'. However, from these years onwards, the 1915 Armenian deportation began to become a problem in US-Türkiye relations after many years, and the actions of the Armenian terrorist organisation ASALA targeting Turkish diplomats caused this issue to become a security issue. When we look at Türkiye's Middle East policy during this period, we see that Türkiye, understanding the importance of the Jewish lobby in the United States, tried to re-establish close relations with Israel after the troubled 1970s. In addition, under pressure from Türkiye, the Palestine Liberation Organisation (PLO) began to accept Israel's existence and the two-state solution during this period. However, problems with Syria continued, and good relations with Damascus, which was a Russian ally, were never established. Issues such as the Hatay problem, the support given to the PKK by the Hafez al-Assad regime in Syria, and control of the Euphrates and Tigris Rivers continued to be the fundamental difficulties in Turkish-Syrian relations. During the Iran-Iraq War in these years, Türkiye began to recall its tightrope-walking stance in World War II and continued trade with both countries. Another important domestic and foreign issue was the PKK terrorism and Kurdish separatism that began with the Eruh raid in 1983. Indeed, during these years, Türkiye became an unstable country where very bloody terrorist incidents began to occur. In contrast, the country's economic development continued rapidly.

During this period, which lasted until the end of the Cold War in 1991, the American ambassadors who served in Türkiye were: James W. Spain (1980–1981), Robert Strausz-Hupé (1981–1989), and Morton I. Abramowitz (1989–1991). Among these individuals, James W. Spain attracted attention with his 1984 book *American Diplomacy in Turkey: Memoirs of an Ambassador*

Extraordinary and Plenipotentiary. Spain also provided important information about the 12 September coup in his book. The Turkish diplomats who served in Washington during the same period were: Şükrü Elekdağ (1979–1989) and Nüzhet Kandemir (1989–1998). It is noteworthy that the diplomats Türkiye appointed to Washington during this period served for long periods. This shows that Ankara provides its ambassadors with the opportunity to establish a good political and diplomatic 'network' and attaches great importance to the United States. Indeed, Şükrü Elekdağ, who served in Washington for more than 10 years, is a very effective and popular Turkish diplomat in the Foreign Ministry.

Turkish-American Relations After the Cold War (1991–2019)

A) Chronological process and analysis

The end of the Cold War brought about a very serious transformation in terms of Türkiye and Turkish-American relations. Because Ankara's most important feature for the Western world during the Cold War was that it was a neighbour of Russia and a pro-Western country. The collapse of the Soviets and the emergence of new states, many of which were of Turkish and Muslim origin, created an uncertain situation similar to the 1920s. However, this time, Türkiye, which was very weak in the 1920s, was now much stronger and larger. Its rivals, as in the case of Greece, no longer posed as much of a threat to it as before. Only the newly established Russian Federation was a state stronger than Türkiye with its great military power and political influence. According to William Hale, Türkiye could consider leaving NATO and the Western alliance in such an environment. But this did not happen; because, as İsmet İnönü stated years ago, Türkiye believed that the Western alliance benefited its political and economic development. Indeed, NATO and the United States were quick to find new tasks suitable for Türkiye in this new period. In addition, after the Cold War, it would become possible for Türkiye to join the Customs Union of the EEC, which had transformed into the European Union, and to start negotiations for membership with the EU. However, the 1990s would also be even more difficult than the 1980s in terms of PKK terrorism and the Kurdish Question.

With the end of the Cold War, many experts initially thought that Türkiye's importance and role had diminished. There was even talk that NATO could be dissolved; because the Soviet Union, which was the reason for NATO's existence, had collapsed and the danger of communism, which had lost its prestige, spreading to Western democracies had automatically disappeared. In fact, some important thinkers such as Francis Fukuyama had even claimed that the 'End of History' had come in the West's triumphant excitement. It seemed that Türkiye's importance for the West had indeed diminished on paper, because it was no longer a buffer protecting the West against Russia. Moreover, it was not a member of the EU and had serious problems with EU member countries such as Greece and the Republic of Cyprus. Worst of all, it did not have very high marks on its report card in human rights issues, especially the Kurdish Question. However, it was soon understood that Türkiye was an important country in the fight against terrorism, regional stability in the Balkans, the Caucasus, and the Middle East, and the preservation of global peace. The emergence of radical Islamist terrorist organisations such as Al-Qaeda, which were supported by the United States against the Soviet occupation and emerged from the Taliban movement, and the destabilising policies implemented by Russia under the leadership of Vladimir Putin, also ensured that Türkiye maintained its importance in the Western world in the following years. In addition, in Özal's last years, with the collapse of the Soviets, Turkist and Islamist dreams began to revive. Demirel and Özal's talk of 'a great Turkic world from the Adriatic to the Great Wall of China' created great excitement, especially in right-wing circles, in those years, but not much progress was made in this regard. Türkiye's role in the US's Middle East policies also began to rise again during this period. Indeed, Türkiye's stance in the Gulf War and the Iraq War directly affected the US's success. In those years, it did not seem that Türkiye's importance would decrease in terms of Israel's security and stability. During this period, Turkish academics and intellectuals were trying to develop the appropriate strategy to establish relations with both the West and the East. For example, Ziya Öniş was one of the first people to make important observations on this issue and thought that this situation was in line with Türkiye's cultural heritage. In fact, Paul Henze, an important American security bureaucrat who was the head of the CIA's Ankara Office, saw Türkiye's Eastern and Islamic identities not as a disadvantage but as an advantage and claimed that the Western alliance could be more effective in the Islamic and Turkish worlds – with Türkiye's contributions. It was also clear as daylight that Islamist right-wing politics was on the rise in Türkiye and would soon come to power. Therefore, all conditions had emerged for the security-centred alliance relations from the Cold War to evolve into a new type of alliance.

However, the collapse of communism and the rise of Islamism also had some negative repercussions on Türkiye's domestic politics. The disappearance of the Soviets and communism as a balancing element made the Islamist and ultra-nationalist right-wing mentality very strong in Türkiye and disrupted the balance of the state's secular practices. The left, which Ecevit had carried to over 40 per cent of the vote in the 1970s, gradually diminished from those years onwards, while the collapse of the centre-right and the rise of the Islamist far-right began on the right. The failure of the centre-left and centre-right coalition governments established in these years (DYP-SHP and DYP-CHP coalition governments in the 1991–1995 period) to find solutions to economic problems and terrorism paved the way for Islamist politics, which had been considered 'far-right' in Türkiye until then, and brought the Islamists to power for the first time in the mid-1990s (Necmettin Erbakan's Welfare Party came first in the 1994 municipal elections and the 1995 general elections).

In the 2000s, the Islamists came to almost completely dominate Turkish politics with the Justice and Development Party (AK Parti) and its charismatic leader Recep Tayyip Erdoğan. Young centre-right leaders, who had high hopes for such as Tansu Çiller and Mesut Yılmaz, were unable to fill the shoes of strong centre-right politicians such as Özal and Demirel in these years, and they virtually gave way to the Islamists. The failure of Tansu Çiller, who had high hopes and was supported by the United States, caused great disappointment in Türkiye and the world during this period. The fact that the centre parties (Demirel's DYP and Özal's ANAP), which were greatly supported by the public during these years, became synonymous with corruption was also a major problem and increased the public support of the Islamists who talked about a 'just order' and 'clean politics'. Beyond these, the biggest problem was undoubtedly the economic crises (for example, the 1994 economic crisis). In addition, unemployment and inflation were breaking the back of the centre pole starting from the Özal period and increasing support for radical movements. The 28 February Process (1997) that took place during these years and when the actual coup was avoided is also an important event that went down in history. This event is important in terms of showing that the political enthusiasm of the army has not yet ended; however, it has also become clear during this process that a coup like the one on 12 September cannot be easily carried out in Türkiye anymore. In fact, the TSK tried to achieve results during this period by means of street demonstrations by the media and secular segments and by pressuring Prime Minister Necmettin Erbakan at the National Security Council (MGK) meeting. The merger of the SHP and the CHP, Devlet Bahçeli replacing the deceased Alparslan Türkeş in the MHP, and the Kurds forming a party and starting a civil political struggle are also the most important innovations of this period. Unsolved murders thought to be committed in connection with the PKK, Hezbollah, the mafia and other criminal groups are also among the most widely discussed political issues of this period. The repercussions of the military struggle with the PKK, which almost turned into a small civil war, were economic burden, political instability, and social unrest, and led to the collapse of central politics.

However, legendary politician Bülent Ecevit, nicknamed 'Karaoğlan', did the unthinkable once again in the late 1990s and established the last left-wing government in Türkiye (DSP-MHP-ANAP coalition) through a triple coalition. The capture of PKK leader Abdullah Öcalan during the minority government and his return to Türkiye brought Ecevit, who had been steadily rising since the 1980s with his newly founded Democratic Left Party (DSP), to power through a coalition with a great leap forward. During this period, Ecevit, with the efforts of Foreign Minister İsmail Cem, made Türkiye a candidate country for EU membership and made progress on some issues (Turkish-Greek relations and democratisation reforms within the scope of EU membership). However, after the disastrous 2001 economic crisis, which occurred at a time when health problems increased and power was weakened, the uninterrupted rule of Islamists together with the AK Parti began in Türkiye and this process continues today.

The 1990s were a period in which the multi-dimensional process that began in the 1960s in Turkish Foreign Policy continued. The experience of Süleyman Demirel, who became President after Özal's death, from his time as Prime Minister was also effective in this. In addition, business circles and civil society organisations became more powerful in these years and began to influence politics and foreign policy. For example, TÜSİAD, a representative of big capital and a pro-secular pressure group that was founded in 1971 and grew in strength in the 1980s and 1990s, began to make effective propaganda on the subject of integration with the West and especially EU membership. Smaller but broader Islamist civil society organisations and capital groups (such as MÜSİAD) also began to create public opinion for closer relations between Türkiye and the Islamic and Turkish Worlds. Therefore, foreign policy ceased to be a technical issue from this period onwards and became one of the main issues of domestic politics. Apart from these, the anti-Israeli sentiment originating from the Palestinian Question and nourished by Islamist sensitivities began to find serious support on the right wing from this period onwards. However, the deterioration of alliance relations with this country eventually led to a negative perception of Türkiye in Washington. In addition, economic rationality also began to play a more important role in Turkish Foreign Policy from these years onwards, and security policies lost their priority. With motives such as expanding trade volume and opening up to the world, many new steps were taken in foreign policy in these years, and the number of regions in which it was active was increased. In addition, energy policies and Türkiye's need for natural gas and oil would also become important foreign policy elements from this period onwards, making Türkiye dependent on Russia and other Eurasian countries. Indeed, the Baku-Tbilisi-Ceyhan Pipeline project was one of the most important initiatives of this period. İsmail Cem, who served as Minister of Foreign Affairs for a long time between 1997–2002, was one of the influential figures at the state level who, in addition to his pro-Western stance, also guided the multi-dimensional foreign policy process together with President Demirel. Kemal Derviş, who was brought to Türkiye as a special authority and almost as a 'Super Minister' after the 2001 economic crisis, was also a very important person who directed the economy during this period and drew Türkiye's economic route in the 2000s. Derviş was a figure who was also given great political support by the United States, but could not be politically influential.

During the AK Parti government, which lasted for a very long time (2002-), there were many different interim periods in Turkish Foreign Policy. The first years of the AK Parti were marked by the close alliance relationship developed with the EU against the risk of a 'secular' coup domestically and the rapid reforms made for full EU membership; the AK Parti even took a surprising and bold position during this period and supported the Annan Plan referendum (2004) held for a solution in Cyprus. However, due to the Greek Cypriots' rejection of the plan and the EU's ambivalent attitude on this issue, the positive atmosphere of this period quickly dissipated. In addition to the close relations developed with the EU during this period, leaders from Islamism such as Abdullah Gül and Recep Tayyip Erdoğan, who established close co-operation with Russia on energy projects, managed to show an incredibly successful performance in the economy in their first years. The Erdoğan-Gül duo also gained the favour of the Turkish people and strengthened their position by opposing the declaration published by the Turkish Armed Forces (known as the 'e-memorandum' in the Turkish media) and defending civil democracy during the 2007 presidential election process, which also turned into a crisis at home. However, in the following years, the AK Parti's Western orientation weakened due to mutual problems and mistakes, the government's Islamist discourse and practices caused some reactions at home and abroad, Türkiye's EU membership became difficult due to the Cyprus Conflict and the rising Islamophobia, populism and far-right in Europe, and many problems began to occur with the United States. Türkiye's rhetoric towards Israel reached a very harsh level of opposition, which cast a shadow over relations between Washington and Ankara starting from this period. In such an environment, the 'zero problems with neighbours' approach developed by Foreign Minister Ahmet Davutoğlu, which aimed to make Türkiye a 'regional power', was initially implemented quite successfully, but it had to collapse – during the Arab Spring. Following the 15 July 2016 coup attempt, Türkiye began to show an increasingly anti-Western and anti-democratic orientation, and its relations with both its neighbours and allies deteriorated. Türkiye being drawn into a major trap in the Syrian civil war was also effective in this process.

During this eventful period, the American ambassadors who served in Türkiye from 1991 to the present are: Richard Clark Barkley (1991–1994), Marc Grossman (1995–1997), Mark Robert Parris (1997–2000), W. Robert Pearson (2000–2003), Eric S. Edelman (2003–2005), Ross Wilson (2005–2008), James Franklin Jeffrey (2008–2010), Francis J. Ricciardone (2011–2014), John R. Bass (2014–2017), David M. Satterfield (2019–2022), and Jeff Flake (2022–2024). Tom Barrack, who was chosen by US President Donald Trump as ambassador to Ankara, recently received Congressional approval and started his duty a few months ago. Again, of these diplomats who served during a very difficult period, Francis J. Ricciardone is especially remembered for his good Turkish and cheerful demeanour. James Jeffrey, who was also the US special representative for Syria, has also distinguished himself as a respected ambassador. Although American ambassadors serving in Türkiye have always been very polite in public, they have not been able to perform miracles due to frequent political crises and polemics between governments. In fact, when Turkish-American relations became tense, harsh news articles were published against the ambassadors in the Turkish press and American diplomats were targeted in public. A relatively recent example is the very harsh criticism directed at Ankara Ambassador John R. Bass in the Turkish press after the 15 July coup attempt. The Turkish ambassadors serving in the United States during the same period are: Nüzhet Kandemir (1989–1998), Baki İlkin (1998–2001), Faruk Loğoğlu (2001–2005), Nabi Şensoy (2006–2010), Namık Tan (2010–2014), Serdar Kılıç (2014–2021), Hasan Murat Mercan (2021–2024), and Sedat Önal (2024-). All Turkish ambassadors tried to achieve successful results as much as they could in line with the authorities and duties given by the government, but due to the influence of Turkish-American relations, which were tense and on the verge of deterioration from time to time, they could not create miracles either.

Theoretical Framework of the Turkish-American Alliance Established After the Cold War

The Turkish-American alliance, which was almost reconstructed after the Cold War, has not yet been placed in a final framework. Two basic approaches have emerged in Washington regarding Türkiye after the Cold War. Military and security circles in the United States, generally close to the Republican Party, want the classical Cold War paradigm to continue with some changes and transformations, and in this direction, they highlight – in addition to a classical enemy such as Russia – dictators who disregard human rights such as Saddam Hussein and radical Islamist terrorist organisations such as Al-Qaeda and ISIS as common targets and enemies of Türkiye and the United States. For these circles, Ankara is still a very important military ally and the TSK is a reliable Western institution. Other circles close to the Democratic Party in the United States, who draw attention to the importance of soft power elements in the new world order, have begun to evaluate Türkiye as a 'model country' as a state with a large Muslim population located in a strategic region and trying to integrate with the Western world (European Union) and have begun to present it as an example to other Muslim societies and newly established Turkic Republics. In this approach, Türkiye's central position in terms of energy transmission lines is also highlighted. However, today, both the classical approach that prioritises military co-operation as a continuation of the Cold War period and the 'model country' approach have failed and collapsed. Therefore, it is essential to develop a new logical framework in Turkish-American relations or to revive one of these frameworks.

When we look at the initial period after the Cold War (George Bush period 1989–1993), we see that the classical Cold War approach focused on security was still at the forefront in US-Türkiye relations. Indeed, in the frequent discussions held in Washington during this period on 'What are we going to do with Türkiye?', Türkiye's military power and commitment to the Western alliance were generally emphasised and praised. During the George Bush-Turgut Özal duo period, when the ambitious Özal, who wanted to enter Mosul and annex it to Türkiye, was prevented by the General Staff from participating in the Gulf War with the United States, Ankara was content with only opening the Incirlik Air Base to the United States during this process, while the security-oriented co-operation approach continued in harmony. The reason for this was that, despite Özal's personal initiatives, no strategic commitment was made to the United States regarding entering the war together. The main concern of the Turkish Armed Forces (TSK) since this period has been that the United States, while trying to overthrow bloodthirsty dictators, would disrupt the delicate balances in the Middle East and cause a 'Kurdish awakening' that could cause trouble for Türkiye. Indeed, since the Gulf War, the Kurds have been a nation that has been constantly growing stronger and entering the process of becoming a nation, and they have felt a great deal of American support. The Turkish General Staff has also been reluctant to fight neighbouring countries with large Muslim populations (such as Iraq) – for fear of public reactions. Consequently, it has become more difficult to continue the classical Cold War paradigm between Washington and Ankara in these years, and Türkiye, feeling that its national security sensitivities are not being given sufficient importance by the United States, has begun to develop more active policies and projects in its foreign policy towards other blocs such as the European Union, Russia-Eurasia, the South Caucasus, Islamic countries, and the Turkish World.

During the term of Bill Clinton (1993–2001), who was a very popular President in Türkiye, Turkish-American relations continued well at the military level, and the theme of Türkiye as a 'model country' to become an EU member and to guide the Islamic world began to come to the fore. Indeed, Clinton, who paved the way for Ankara's EU membership, also constantly praised the secular and democratic system that Türkiye, a country with a large Muslim population, was trying to implement. During this period, the military interventions carried out by the United States in Bosnia and Kosovo also ensured that it had a very good image in the Muslim world and brought Turkish-American relations back to a good level (the level of 'strategic partnership' in the popular expression of the period). Furthermore, from this period onwards, Washington realised Türkiye's geopolitical advantage in terms of energy transmission lines, which were becoming increasingly important in the new world order and encouraged Ankara to take a role in Nabucco and similar projects (TANAP can be given as an example in this regard today) as a balancing actor against Russia. From this period onwards, the concept of a 'model country' began to come to the fore, but military co-operation also continued intensively. Clinton's visit to Türkiye, which witnessed a very successful 'public diplomacy', is also remembered during this period.

During the George W. Bush era (2001–2009), Turkish-American relations experienced major and serious crises following the 11 September (9/11) disaster. The signals given by Prime Minister Erdoğan – while he was not yet Prime Minister and as the Chairman of the AK Parti – that Türkiye would support the United States in the Iraq War or the Second Gulf War, greatly angered Washington, whose war plans were disrupted after the 1 March Memorandum was rejected in the Turkish Grand National Assembly due to the large mass demonstrations in favour of peace. This situation both led the United States to change its war plans and caused the United States financial losses. The United States, which already harboured a great grudge against Islamists due to the trauma of 11 September, made some scandalous statements (President Bush's 'Crusade' speech) and actions (the 'sack incident' staged against allied Turkish soldiers in Suleymaniye) that put the Turkish government and the Turkish Armed Forces in a very difficult position during this period. However, the United States has also taken the Turkish people against it with these policies and has come to the point of losing a good ally completely. Therefore, after 11 September, the possibility of reviving the classical perspective focused on military co-operation emerged; however, due to the peace-loving attitude of the Turkish public and the erroneous actions of the United States, this opportunity could not be evaluated well. From this period onwards, the United States began to question the power of the Turkish Armed Forces in the system in the new period and, according to many analysts, found the blame for the rejection of the memorandum not on the AK Parti and Erdoğan but on the TSK and the Chief of General Staff, General Hilmi Özkök. This situation can be easily understood from the statements of the US Deputy Secretary of Defence at the time, Paul Wolfowitz. As a result, after the great tensions experienced, in order to prevent a complete breakdown of relations between the two allies, a mysterious plan known as the 'Greater Middle East Project' (BOP) was agreed upon between the Foreign Ministers of the two countries, Abdullah Gül and Condoleezza Rice, and Türkiye's 'moderate Islam' identity was accelerated to be presented to other Islamic countries as a 'model country'. In addition, starting from this period, the United States made efforts to develop relations between Türkiye and the Iraqi Kurds and encouraged negotiations with the terrorist organisation PKK to solve the Kurdish Question domestically. However, despite all these efforts, the United States became an object of hatred in Türkiye during this period and Ankara's shift towards Russia and the Islamic world accelerated.

During the Barack Obama era (2009–2017), the relations between Türkiye and the United States, which had been very strained during the Bush era, were reheated. In line with the relationship type called 'model partnership', the 'model country' approach that had been developed for years was thoroughly concretised and during the Arab Spring process, Türkiye's Islamist leaders (especially Erdoğan) became very popular in the Arab world. However, the 'model partnership' ended when the Arab Spring process turned into a military coup in Egypt and civil wars in Libya and Syria, and the successful democratisation drive in Tunisia remained a singular and exceptional example. In addition, the Syrian civil war that started during this period brought the United States and Türkiye face to face over time. While both states initially opposed the Bashar Assad regime, the United States, which did not take action regarding the chemical massacres allegedly carried out by the Assad regime, eventually began to support Kurdish groups such as the

PYD and YPG against the Assad regime, while Türkiye continued to provide active and intensive support to Sunni opposition groups (the Free Syrian Army). While it was gradually understood that the regime in Syria would not be overthrown by Russia's military intervention, the two allies eventually fell into disagreement over the future of the Kurds. Indeed, Obama and Erdoğan's sincere friendship evolved into a tense relationship that continued with harsh statements from each other. As a result, President Erdoğan, who was very disturbed by the US's stance following the Gezi Park Incidents and especially the 15 July 2016 coup attempt, hardened his stance on relations with the United States and, turning a deaf ear to criticism from Washington, turned to a kind of regional co-operation with Russia and Iran on Syria. The United States also quickly pushed its relations with Ankara into the background due to the Turkish government's administration abandoning its 'model partnership' approach and moving away from democracy. The situation of Islamic thinker and community leader Fethullah Gülen, who provided the government with the greatest support until 2012, following the 15 July coup attempt and the Reza Zarrab case are also issues that damaged bilateral relations during the Obama era. During this period, anti-American sentiment in Türkiye decreased rapidly, especially with Obama's speeches and sympathy, but it rose rapidly again after 15 July.

Recommendations

The suggestions I can make as of today regarding the restoration of Turkish-American relations to a good position can be listed as follows:

- The two allies should make more efforts to align their foreign policies with each other. The most fundamental issues at this point are the agreement to be reached on the future of Syria, similar approaches to be developed on the future of the Kurds, especially in Iraq and Syria, and the common strategy to be followed regarding Iran. Considering that a good agreement cannot satisfy both parties one hundred percent, the parties should make some concessions to each other on these issues and try not to lose each other. Considering that the United States is still the world's only superpower and Türkiye is a regional power, it is a reasonable approach for the continuation of relations for Turkish statesmen and the Turkish people to be more flexible on these issues. Because although it is certain that losing Türkiye will be a very negative development for the United States, the consequences of losing the United States for Türkiye may be even more dangerous. At this point, Washington should respect Türkiye's security concerns and Ankara should understand that it has to act in harmony with its partner as an ally of the United States. If a common approach cannot be developed on these issues, bilateral relations may enter a period of serious difficulties.

- Türkiye's increasing energy dependency on Russia and Iran is a strategic issue that Washington should also consider and plan for. If this continues, Ankara may soon enter Moscow's orbit, and Russia may begin to regulate Türkiye's domestic politics. At this point, Washington needs to support alternative energy projects such as TANAP and help Türkiye diversify its energy policy. In the event of a rapprochement between the United States and Russia, this issue will cease to be a problem on its own.
- The two governments should show their reactions towards each other in a way that will not reflect on social relations and the people. For example, the US government's suspension of visa procedures in response to the Turkish government a while ago caused a justified reaction from the Turkish people. In my opinion, it is necessary to be more careful about these issues and not to reflect the negativity on the people by showing the reactions to the governments. Otherwise, the mutual social trust and sympathy, which are already at a low level, may decrease even further and drag the relations to a point where they cannot be fixed. In this context, it is also obvious that the United States should make more efforts regarding its image in Türkiye and Türkiye's lobbying power in Washington.
- In addition to their military and political relations, the two countries should definitely develop their economic and cultural relations rapidly. It is difficult for an alliance that only has a security dimension to survive in today's world. For this reason, the two countries should develop joint projects and intensify their relations in many areas, especially in education.
- The two populist leaders (Erdoğan and Trump) should be careful about their tones and not offend each other and the societies. Because harsh rhetoric used for daily successes in domestic politics can later turn into social hostility.

- American and Turkish intellectuals and bureaucrats should be more respectful of the leaders elected by the people of their friendly and allied countries. In this context, just as Turks do not have to like and approve of Donald Trump, Americans do not have to like and approve of Recep Tayyip Erdoğan. What is important is that the people of these countries continue to democratically elect the leaders most suitable for them.
- Washington should pave the way for Ankara's EU membership and presence in Western institutions.
- Türkiye should definitely start making democratisation reforms to alleviate concerns in the United States. This is certainly not an obstacle to the fight against terrorism or military operations. Providing good rights and opportunities to its citizens and taking tough action against terrorists are compatible policies for a democratic state.
- Türkiye should support the United States in its relations with the Middle East and the Turkic world by preserving its secular system that respects the Islamic religion and its social practices (covering, prayers and other religious practices) and should stay away from propaganda that will strengthen negative prejudices about the United States.
- Many new channels and platforms for dialogue should be established between the two countries, and despite political disagreements, it should be ensured that diplomatic and economic relations continue intensively.
- Populist politicians in the US Congress should abandon their negative attitudes towards the Republic of Türkiye and its citizens today due to the tragic events that took place in the Ottoman Empire 110 years ago in order to gain the support of the Armenian diaspora. Historical hostilities can only be resolved by softening them, not by fanning the flames. Moreover, the United States is not a theocratic state like the Vatican, which is only concerned with the problems of the Christian world and nations. Therefore, American foreign policy should be pursued in line with what President Trump calls 'Principled Realism' and based on mutual interests, and religious fanaticism should be avoided.
- US President Donald Trump should pay an official visit to Türkiye soon and try to find solutions to important issues by sincerely meeting with his counterpart Recep Tayyip Erdoğan. Trump, who is a businessman, and Erdoğan, who can take a very conciliatory and flexible position when

necessary according to the balance of power, can easily reach an agreement when the right conditions arise and develop common solutions to their countries' problems.

- The development of Turkish-Israeli relations can also contribute to the improvement of Turkish-American relations. If Israel, which has a strong lobbying power and influence in the United States, can establish a friendly relationship with Türkiye as it has done before, it can benefit Ankara in various areas.
- Türkiye should continue its co-operation with the United States in the field of defence industry. At this point, Washington should not cause any problems for Türkiye regarding the Patriot air defence system or the F-35s, of which it is a joint manufacturer. Otherwise, the process of Türkiye turning to Russia and other alternatives in the defence industry, which is the area where bilateral relations are strongest, may begin.

Endnotes

1 This is the updated text of the speech given at the 2nd School of Politics and Diplomacy organised at Marmara University, with the co-operation of Marmara University Career Center (MARKAM) and Marmara University Continuing Education Center (MÜSEM), on 12 March 2019.

2 This section is mostly summarised from Prof. Dr Çağrı Erhan's work, *Türk – Amerikan İlişkilerinin Tarihsel Kökenleri* and Murat Önsoy's chapter "Early Encounters Between the New World and the Middle East: Ottoman Empire-United States Relations in the 19th and the Early 20th Century".

Bibliography

Amerika'nın Sesi, <https://www.amerikaninsesi.com/>.

Baba, Gürol (2016), "Türkiye-Avrupa Birliği İlişkilerinde Amerika Birleşik Devletleri Faktörü: Arka Plan, Diskurlar, Etkileşimler", in *Mavi Elma: Türkiye-Avrupa İlişkileri* (eds. by Hüseyin Işıksal & Ozan Örmeci), Ankara: Gazi Kitabevi, pp. 177–203.

BBC News, <https://www.bbc.com/news>.

BBC Türkçe, <https://www.bbc.com/turkce>.

Çakır, Armağan Emre (2016), *The United States and Turkey's Path to Europe: Hands Across the Table*, New York: Routledge.

Çınar, Ali (2015), "Turkey-USA Relations", in *Turkish Foreign Policy in the New Millennium* (eds. by Hüseyin Işıksal & Ozan Örmeci), Frankfurt am Main: Peter Lang, pp. 505–513.

DW Türkçe, <https://www.dw.com/tr/g%C3%BCndem/s-10201>.

Erhan, Çağrı (2015), *Türk – Amerikan İlişkilerinin Tarihsel Kökenleri*, 2. Baskı, Ankara: İmge Kitabevi Yayınları.

Erhan, Çağrı & Sıvış, Efe (2017), "Determinants of Turkish-American Relations and Prospects for the Future", *Insight Turkey*, Vol. 19, no: 1, pp. 89–115.

Hale, William (2013), *Turkish Foreign Policy Since 1774*, 3rd edition, Routledge.

Hale, William (2003), *Türk Dış Politikası 1774–2000*, Mozaik Kitap.

Kurtbağ, Ömer (2015), "The Recent State of Affairs in Turkish-American Relations: Before and After the 'Model Partnership'", in *Turkish Foreign Policy in the New Millennium* (eds. by Hüseyin Işıksal & Ozan Örmeci), Frankfurt am Main: Peter Lang, pp. 515–543.

"List of ambassadors of the United States to Turkey", *Wikipedia*, <https://en.wikipedia.org/wiki/List_of_ambassadors_of_the_United_States_to_Turkey>.

NATO, <https://www.nato.int/>.

Okur, Mehmet Akif (2015), "The American Geopolitical Interests and Turkey on the Eve of the September 12, 1980 Coup", *CTAD*, Year: 11, No: 21 (Spring 2015), pp. 199–222.

Önsoy, Murat (2020), "Early Encounters Between the New World and the Middle East: Ottoman Empire-United States Relations in the 19th and the Early 20th Century", in (eds. by Ozan Örmeci & Hüseyin Işıksal), *Historical Examinations and Current Issues in Turkish-American Relations*, Berlin: Peter Lang, pp. 23–40.

Örmeci, Ozan, Blog – Ozan Örmeci Articles, <https://ydemokrat.blogspot.com/>.

Örmeci, Ozan (2015), "Anti-American Reflections of the Arab Spring in Turkey", in *Turkish Foreign Policy in the New Millennium* (eds. by Hüseyin Işıksal & Ozan Örmeci), Frankfurt am Main: Peter Lang, pp. 545–558.

Örmeci, Ozan (2017), *Amerikan İç ve Dış Politikası*, İstanbul: Cinius Yayınları.

Örmeci, Ozan & Reginbogin, Herbert (2024), *Turkish-American Relations in the 21st Century*, New York: Lexington Books.

Sander, Oral (2006), *Türkiye'nin Dış Politikası*, Editör: Dr Melek Fırat, Ankara: İmge Kitabevi Yayınları.

Türkiye Cumhuriyeti Vaşington Büyükelçiliği, <http://washington.emb.mfa.gov.tr/Mission/MissionChiefHistory>.

"Türkiye Sosyal-Siyasal Eğilimler Araştırması (TSSEA) 2018 Sonuçları Açıklandı", <http://www.khas.edu.tr/news/2074>.

Uslu, Nasuh (2000), *Türk-Amerikan İlişkileri*, Bilim Araştırma serisi 3, Ankara: 21. Yüzyıl Yayınları.

Yılmaz, Şuhnaz (2015), *Turkish-American Relations, 1800–1952: Between the Stars, Stripes, and the Crescent*, New York: Routledge.

Possible Developments in Turkish-American Relations in the Second Trump Era

The 60th United States (US) Presidential election was won by the Republican Party candidate and the 45th President of the United States, businessman Donald Trump, who has the honour and success of serving as the 47th President of the United States for the period 2025–2029 – starting in January. Trump's election, which was actually quite predictable, was also largely favoured by the Turkish government and state structures. Turkish President Recep Tayyip Erdoğan had already made his reaction to the 46th US President Joe Biden and the Democratic administration, who did not even speak to him on the phone for months after his election and then did not invite him to the White House for the Democracy Summit. Erdoğan, last year even declined an official invitation from American officials at last minute and played all his cards for Trump's election. In this sense, Ankara will undoubtedly be much more willing and determined to overcome some problems with Trump in the new era. Let us now comment on possible developments based on these issues.

Unlike Democratic administrations, Republican President-elect Donald Trump, who prefers to interfere less in the domestic affairs of allied states, may be less critical of Ankara on Türkiye's domestic issues in the new term, except for issues that are important to him, such as the security of Americans and not fuelling anti-Americanism, not allowing threats to Israel's security, protecting the non-Muslim population and not putting obstacles to the religious freedoms of Christians, etc., and this may lead to some warming in relations. The fact that both leaders like the kind of leader diplomacy with weaker institutional foundations and try to present a strong presidential profile may also cause them to have chemistry with each other, which can be traced in Trump's first term as President (2017–2021).

Another important issue concerns arms sales. While the sale of F-16s, which Türkiye has been trying to secure by delaying Finland and Sweden's membership in NATO, has not still materialised despite promises given to Ankara, the Trump administration may act much faster and more willingly in this regard and finalise the sale of fighter jets to Türkiye. The Trump administration may also give the green light for Türkiye's readmission to the F-35 programme if the S-400 issue, which is seen as objectionable for NATO security, is somehow resolved. For Trump, who came to power with the goal of revitalising the American economy, arms sales are an important issue that will improve the economy.

As for the PKK-affiliated PYD/YPG groups in Syria, which the United States has been supporting for years against the Assad regime and ISIS (Islamic State), Trump may not allow policies to be implemented that would completely eliminate the terrorist-linked Kurdish presence in the region to the extent imagined by Türkiye, but he may prefer Ankara's continued military presence in the region and a certain degree of reconciliation between the two American allies against ISIS through dialogue. For Trump, the presence of the Turkish Armed Forces (TSK), a NATO member, on the ground would be an advantageous situation if they act in concert with the United States. This can also be said for the Turkish Armed Forces' de facto presence in Northern (North) Cyprus. However, I should add that unlike 2017–2021 period, now US foreign policy is much closer to Greek Cypriots as proven by the recent defence agreement between Washington and Nicosia.

Another factor that makes Trump attractive for Türkiye is his desire to end the Russia-Ukraine War. Given that Türkiye has not cut its economic ties with Russia throughout the war, despite all the pressure from the Western world, a US-Russia reconciliation could be a relief for Ankara, which has intensive commercial, energy, and political relations with Moscow. Since this would also allow the Erdoğan administration to improve its economy, which is suffering from high inflation and the rapid depreciation of the Turkish lira, facilitating trade with Russia could make Trump a good President for the current Turkish government. What economists are reluctant to say is that international markets still respond to signals from the United States when it comes to investment.

Another factor that makes Trump attractive for Türkiye may be the fact that the US President's foreign policy rhetoric and actions mostly target countries such as Iran and China. Ankara, which, despite its close relations with Iran, can also be positioned as a rival in regional politics, may welcome Trump's escalation of tensions with Iran, knowing that it will gain importance in geopolitical projections and strategic moves in the region. While the Erdoğan administration will not want to jeopardise the recently good political and economic relations with China, it may not be unhappy with the escalation of tensions between the United States and China and the raising of the Uyghur Turks or East Turkestan issue by American officials. In fact, Ankara's official policy is to protect the cultural autonomy and religious freedoms of the Uyghur Turks, although this issue has not been brought up much in recent years in order not to disturb China.

The choice of Trump's Secretary of State is also an important issue, with Florida Senator Marco Rubio's name being frequently mentioned in the American press. Rubio is a foreign policy hawk and is not known to be pro-Türkiye. This suggests that it would be unrealistic to expect a '*spring*' in relations in the new term.

In any case, it is not yet realistic to expect a rapid improvement and a new spring in Turkish-American relations. The problems are structural, and relations are frayed. Nevertheless, a new administration always means a new chance, and we hope that the two states will not miss this opportunity. The Israeli-Palestinian issue will be the most difficult challenge for the two states. In the event of continued US support for Israel's brutal policies, Erdoğan should not be expected to remain silent, given the rise of alternative Islamist parties in Türkiye (the New Welfare Party/YRP). However, if Trump comes with a reasonable peace plan (e.g. a revised version of the Deal of the Century) and Israel halts its military operations, there may be no crisis.

Development Road Project

Introduction

While the trend to facilitate trade and human mobility and to contribute to global peace and prosperity by increasing economic, political and social/cultural interactions between states is gaining strength all over the world (China's Belt and Road Initiative, the European Union's Global Gateway Project and the US-backed India-Middle East-Europe Economic Corridor/IMEC are the most well-known ones), Türkiye is not left out of this trend and is developing regional projects that will work in harmony with global economic projects in its own region. In this context, the Development Road Project, which was officially announced with the signatures signed during President Recep Tayyip Erdoğan's visit to Iraq (Baghdad) in April 2024, is extremely important in terms of understanding Ankara's strategic goals. This article will analyse the Development Road Project.

What is the Development Road Project?

The Development Road Project, which was announced to the public during President Erdoğan's recent visit to Iraq, is a new transportation and development project implemented with a quadripartite memorandum of understanding between Iraq, Türkiye, Qatar and the United Arab Emirates (UAE). The English name of the project was announced as 'Development Road' or 'Iraq Development Road'.[1] President Erdoğan and Turkish Foreign Minister Hakan Fidan first shared the project with the public at the G20 meeting held in New Delhi in September 2023.[2]

Figure 12: The Development Road Project's railway and road routes[3]

The project, which covers a 1,200-kilometre highway and railway line in the Türkiye-Iraq direction[4], is a comprehensive development-transportation-trade line project that will start from the Great Faw Port, which is located at the entrance of the Persian Gulf at the Khor Abdullah Cape in the city of Basra in Iraq, at the mouth of the Shatt al-Arab and is built to be the new largest port in the Middle East[5], and will reach Türkiye by passing through places such as Nasiriyah, Qadisiyah, Najaf, Karbala, Samarra, Tikrit, Mosul, and will continue in both Europe and the Caucasus (Asia) directions through the existing lines in Türkiye.[6] The project will connect to centres such as Mersin Port and İstanbul through Türkiye, thus accelerating trade and human mobility.[7]

The Development Road Project will connect the Middle East to Europe[8]. The project, which is supported greatly by the Iraqi government as well as Türkiye, will be a great gain for Iraq in terms of connecting it to Europe and will also accelerate and facilitate trade in the region in terms of creating an alternative route to the Suez Canal.[9] The project, which is also called the 'New Silk Road' due to its use of the historical land trade route and was initially thought to be called the 'Dry Canal', is a very rational and important geopolitical move in terms of bringing Iraq, which was neglected in China's Belt and Road Initiative and IMEC routes, into global trade.[10] Indeed, regarding

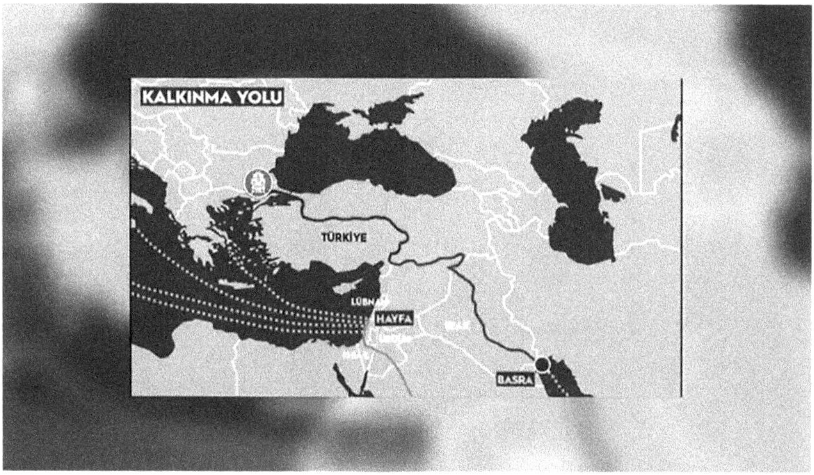

Figure 13: Kalkınma Yolu map

the project, which is fully supported by the Iraqi government and its local components, Baghdad Chamber of Commerce President Firas al-Hamdani said the following regarding the Development Road, which is expected to cost 17 billion dollars – some sources say 20 billion dollars[11]: '*Our most important strategic partner in the Development Road Project is our neighboring country, Türkiye. Türkiye is also an important strategic partner in the development of Iraq.*'[12] While Iraqi Prime Minister Mohammed Shia al-Sudani openly supported the project, other important supporters/partners of the project are Gulf countries such as the UAE and Qatar, which have coasts on the Persian Gulf. While Turkish President Recep Tayyip Erdoğan also stands out as one of the most enthusiastic political leaders regarding the project, Erdoğan, who visited Iraq after 13 years in April[13], said during his visit that this project would bring Turkish-Iraqi relations to a new stage and that this would be a 'turning point'.[14] While Türkiye allocated 5 billion dollars for the development of Iraq and the implementation of the project[15], the key role in the concretisation of the project and the signing of the contract was played by Turkish Foreign Minister and former MİT President Hakan Fidan.[16] Fidan convinced the parties by talking less and doing more using the shuttle diplomacy method and accelerated the signing of the contract.

Figure 14: Foreign Minister Hakan Fidan's first concrete action was the formalisation of the Development Path Project[17]

Evaluating the project, which is expected to be fully implemented in 2029 and is expected to accelerate trade between China and Europe[18], Dr Enes Bayraklı from the Turkish-German University believes that the implementation of this project will strengthen Iraq-Türkiye relations and create a new alternative trade route regionally and globally at a time when global and regional conflicts are increasing.[19] BICC expert Osman Bahadır Dinçer emphasises that the project faces the risk of being destabilised due to passing through a difficult geography.[20] Another risk element will be the attitude of Iran and the PUK led by Bafel Talabani, who is closer to Iran, towards the project.

Türkiye's Geopolitical Goals with the Development Path: Trade Instead of Terrorism and War, Iraq's Territorial Integrity, Cheap Energy and Regional Power Vision

It can be said that Ankara is trying to achieve several basic geopolitical goals with the Development Path Project, which it greatly supports. The first of these is undoubtedly that Türkiye, which has been forced to confront the PKK-PYD-YPG terrorist organisations and their political separatist demands for years, originating from Northern Iraq and Syria, wants to solve the problem on the Iraq-Northern Iraq line with the economic integration method and provide support against terrorism by creating good relations and win-win situations with both the Iraqi central government and the Kurdistan Regional Government. Indeed, the Prime Minister of the Iraqi Kurdistan Regional Government, Masrour Barzani, also supports the project, but he puts forward the 'east of the Tigris' option, which would be less costly and more economically beneficial in terms of the route.[21] Foreign Minister Fidan, Defence Minister Yaşar Güler and MİT Director İbrahim Kalın, who went to Baghdad before President Erdoğan's visit, reached an agreement with the Iraqi government and signed a new agreement/understanding text on the fight against the PKK.[22] In this sense, although Ankara has not yet been able to resolve its problems in Syria in the fight against terrorism, it has achieved significant success in Iraq.

Secondly, by helping the development of Iraq and the Kurdistan region with this project, Türkiye wants federal Iraq to become a stable and territorially unified actor and thus wants to secure itself in the fight against terrorism and the independent Kurdish state. Indeed, President Erdoğan, in his official speeches regarding the project, always emphasises Iraq's territorial integrity and acts as a spokesperson/interpreter for the state's sensitivity in Ankara on this issue.[23]

The third factor that makes the project important for Ankara is that Türkiye wants to work closely with Iraq on energy (oil and natural gas) expenses, which constitute a very important item in its annual budget, and to reduce energy costs in an environment of economic uncertainty. Ankara, which had rights to Iraq's oil revenues due to the Mosul issue in the past, was unsuccessful in the diplomatic struggle with Britain at that time and was forced to give up its rights in Mosul. However, today, Türkiye wants to reduce energy costs and gain a share of energy revenues as a transit country by working closely with the Iraqi central government and the Kurdistan Regional Government through peaceful methods and friendly relations.[24] This is an approach similar to the vision that Ankara has developed with countries such as Russia, Azerbaijan and Iran, and that Türkiye should be a natural gas transfer centre, especially emphasised by Russian President Vladimir Putin.

Finally, Ankara wants to become the main trade route in the region and increase its importance in world trade and politics by connecting the Development Road Project to major global projects (for example, the Middle Corridor leg of the Belt and Road Project). This is an appropriate approach that is compatible with the peaceful, anti-terror and anti-war regional power vision that Türkiye wants to realise in the twenty-first century. Indeed, on other issues such as the Ukraine-Russia and Hamas-Israel conflicts, Türkiye is appreciated by the world public opinion with its always peaceful approaches that invite the parties to compromise and international law.

Conclusion

As a result, Türkiye's efforts to become a regional power and to ensure political and economic stability in the region continue unabated. Ankara focuses on humanitarian policies and hopes to transform its region into a region of peace and prosperity. In this context, Türkiye, which emphasises hard power in the fight against terrorist groups and soft power in its relations with other states and peaceful groups, also needs a third element to be successful in this strategy. This last critical element is the democratic rights to be provided to the peoples of the region. The critical element here may be to ensure the support of the Kurdish people. In this context, rights such as education in the mother tongue and humane living conditions may be steps that Ankara can easily take and that will make the region more stable and integrated. However, of course, in order to be able to speak definitively on these issues, it is essential to conduct serious preliminary research and cooperate with actors who reject terrorism and violence.

Endnotes

1 Ylenia Gostoli (2024), "What's behind Türkiye and Iraq's 'Development Road' project?", *The New Arab*, 30.04.2024, Date of Accession: 27.05.2024, From <https://www.newarab.com/analysis/whats-behind-Türkiye-and-iraqs-development-road-project>.

2 Mehmet Alaca & Haydar Karaalp (2023), "Türkiye-Iraq Development Road Project: Enhancing regional connectivity, trade", 17.09.2023, Date of Accession: 27.05.2024, From <https://www.aa.com.tr/en/middle-east/turkiye-iraq-development-road-project-enhancing-regional-connectivity-trade/2993555>.

3 *TRT Haber* (2024), "Kalkınma Yolu'nu kim, nasıl gördü?", 26.04.2024, Date of Accession: 27.05.2024, From <https://www.trthaber.com/haber/dunya/kalkinma-yolunu-kim-nasil-gordu-853665.html>.

4 Mehmet Alaca & Haydar Karaalp (2023), "Türkiye-Iraq Development Road Project: Enhancing regional connectivity, trade", 17.09.2023, Date of Accession: 27.05.2024, From <https://www.aa.com.tr/en/middle-east/turkiye-iraq-development-road-project-enhancing-regional-connectivity-trade/2993555>.

5 Mehmet Alaca (2022), "Orta Doğu'nun en büyük limanlarından Irak'taki Büyük Faw'ın inşası hız kesmeden sürüyor", *AA*, 09.12.2022, Date of Accession: 27.05.2024, From <https://www.aa.com.tr/tr/dunya/orta-dogunun-en-buyuk-limanlarindan-iraktaki-buyuk-fawin-insasi-hiz-kesmeden-suruyor/2759271>.

6 John Calabrese (2024), "Iraq's "Development Road": Rough Terrain Ahead", *Modern Diplomacy*, 04.05.2024, Date of Accession: 27.05.2024, From <https://moderndiplomacy.eu/2024/05/04/iraqs-development-road-rough-terrain-ahead/>.

7 *TRT World* (2024), "Türkiye, Iraq, Qatar, UAE sign deal to advance Development Road Project", Date of Accession: 27.05.2024, From <https://www.trtworld.com/turkiye/turkiye-iraq-qatar-uae-sign-deal-to-advance-development-road-project-17876699>.

8 *CNNTürk* (2024), "Kalkınma Yolu Projesi neden önemli? Bölgenin kaderi değişecek…", *AA*, 24.04.2024, Date of Accession: 27.05.2024, From <https://www.cnnturk.com/turkiye/kalkinma-yolu-projesi-neden-onemli-2108537>.

9 Mehmet Alaca & Haydar Karaalp (2023), "Türkiye-Iraq Development Road Project: Enhancing regional connectivity, trade", 17.09.2023, Date of Accession: 27.05.2024, From <https://www.aa.com.tr/en/middle-east/turkiye-iraq-development-road-project-enhancing-regional-connectivity-trade/2993555>.

10 Ylenia Gostoli (2024), "What's behind Türkiye and Iraq's 'Development Road' project?", *The New Arab*, 30.04.2024, Date of Accession: 27.05.2024, From <https://www.newarab.com/analysis/whats-behind-Türkiye-and-iraqs-development-road-project>.

11 Sabena Siddiqui (2024), "Can $20B Iraq Development Road project rival India-Middle East corridor?", *Al-Monitor*, 27.04.2024, Date of Accession: 27.05.2024, From <https://www.al-monitor.com/originals/2024/04/can-20b-iraq-development-road-project-rival-india-middle-east-corridor#ixzz8bQVbol8V>.

12 Mehmet Alaca & Haydar Karaalp (2023), "Iraklılar Türkiye'nin liderlik ettiği Kalkınma Yolu Projesi'ni bekliyor", *AA*, 15.09.2023, Date of Accession: 27.05.2024, From <https://www.aa.com.tr/tr/dunya/iraklilar-turkiyenin-liderlik-ettigi-kalkinma-yolu-projesini-bekliyor/2992494>.

13 *Daily Sabah* (2024), "Türkiye, Iraq, Qatar, UAE sign deal on Development Road project", 22.04.2024, Date of Accession: 27.05.2024, From <https://www.dailysabah.com/business/economy/turkiye-iraq-qatar-uae-sign-deal-on-development-road-project>.

14 *TRT World* (2024), "Türkiye, Iraq, Qatar, UAE sign deal to advance Development Road Project", Date of Accession: 27.05.2024, From <https://www.trtworld.com/turkiye/turkiye-iraq-qatar-uae-sign-deal-to-advance-development-road-project-17876699>.

[15] Mehmet Alaca & Haydar Karaalp (2023), "Türkiye-Iraq Development Road Project: Enhancing regional connectivity, trade", 17.09.2023, Date of Accession: 27.05.2024, From <https://www.aa.com.tr/en/middle-east/turkiye-iraq-development-road-project-enhancing-regional-connectivity-trade/2993555>.

[16] Mehmet Alaca (2024), "Turkish president's Iraq visit to boost momentum for Development Road Project", *AA*, 22.04.2024, Date of Accession: 27.05.2024, From <https://www.aa.com.tr/en/middle-east/turkish-presidents-iraq-visit-to-boost-momentum-for-development-road-project/3199087>.

[17] Senem Görür Yücel (2023), "5 soruda Hakan Fidan'ın Irak ziyareti", *Medyascope*, 22.08.2023, Date of Accession: 27.05.2024, From <https://medyascope.tv/2023/08/22/5-soruda-hakan-fidanin-irak-ziyareti/>.

[18] Feyzullah Tuna Aygün (2023), "Development Road: Iraq's Future Vision", ORSAM, 27.09.2023, Date of Accession: 27.05.2024, From <https://www.orsam.org.tr/en/development-road-iraqs-future-vision/>.

[19] Yusuf Kamadan (2024), "Türkiye-Iraq Development Road Project forges new trade path", TRT World, Date of Accession: 27.05.2024, From <https://www.trtworld.com/turkiye/turkiye-iraq-development-road-project-forges-new-trade-path-17929034>.

[20] Ylenia Gostoli (2024), "What's behind Türkiye and Iraq's 'Development Road' project?", *The New Arab*, 30.04.2024, Date of Accession: 27.05.2024, From <https://www.newarab.com/analysis/whats-behind-Türkiye-and-iraqs-development-road-project>.

[21] *K24* (2024), "Başbakan Barzani: Kalkınma Yolu güzergahının Dicle'nin doğusundan geçmesini önerdik", 12.05.2024, Date of Accession: 27.05.2024, From <https://www.kurdistan24.net/tr/story/97579-Ba%C5%9Fbakan-%E2%80%8B%E2%80%8BBarzani:-Kalk%C4%B1nma-Yolu-g%C3%BCzergah%C4%B1n%C4%B1n-Dicle%27nin-do%C4%9Fusundan-ge%C3%A7mesini-%C3%B6nerdik>.

[22] Ezgi Akın (2024), "Iraq bans PKK as security ties with Türkiye gain momentum", *Al-Monitor*, 14.03.2024, Date of Accession: 27.05.2024, From <https://www.al-monitor.com/originals/2024/03/iraq-bans-pkk-security-ties-Türkiye-gain-momentum#ixzz8bQWO0zrz>.

[23] Presidency of the Republic of Türkiye (2023), "We will turn the Development Road project into the new 'Silk Road' of our region", 21.03.2023, Date of Accession: 27.05.2024, From <https://www.tccb.gov.tr/en/news/542/144355/-we-will-turn-the-development-road-project-into-the-new-silk-road-of-our-region->.

[24] Feyzullah Tuna Aygün (2023), "The Development Road: Connecting Iraq and Türkiye", ORSAM, 12.05.2023, Date of Accession: 27.05.2024, From <https://www.orsam.org.tr/en/the-development-road-connecting-iraq-and-turkiye/>.

The End of the Civil War in Syria?

The civil war that has been going on for over 13 years in our neighbouring Syria ended in a period of about a week to ten days without anyone understanding what was going on, when the Syrian opposition, led by Hayat Tahrir al-Sham (HTŞ), which Türkiye also considers a terrorist organisation, took over the capital Damascus. So much so that Syrian President Bashar Assad, who had resisted the opposition for years and had attended the Extraordinary Summit of the Organisation of Islamic Cooperation and the Arab League just a month ago, fled to Moscow, where he had obtained asylum with his family, leaving the country under the control of the opposition. Assad, who persistently ignored Türkiye's calls for talks and compromise, was forced to bid his country a humiliating farewell, at least for now.

While the rapid end of the Syrian civil war came as a shock to journalists and experts in Türkiye and around the world, HTŞ leader Muhammed Colani or Abu Muhammed al-Jawlani (Ahmed al-Sharaa) stood out as the charismatic leader who led the opposition during this process. Although Turkish President Recep Tayyip Erdoğan paused his policy of changing the regime in Syria after 2016 due to ISIS terrorism, he generally drew attention with his moderate statements supporting the opposition during this process. By emphasising Assad's uncompromising personality and implying that these events might not have happened if they had met, Erdoğan wanted to emphasise Türkiye's power over Syria. While a cautious optimism prevailed in the general public in Türkiye during this process, especially the visit of National Intelligence Organisation (MİT) President İbrahim Kalın to Damascus with HTŞ leader Colani on 12 December 2024 and his subsequent prayers at the Umayyad

Mosque created a great impact in the national public opinion. However, it should also be noted that the group Türkiye supports in Syria is not HTŞ, but a more moderate opposition group called the Syrian National Army (formerly known as the Free Syrian Army-FSA).

Figure 15: MIT President İbrahim Kalın went to the Umayyad Mosque, which gained symbolic significance during the civil war, and demonstrated Türkiye's determination regarding the transition process

While Russia and Iran have received harsh reactions to the events in Syria, especially the threatening statements of influential Russian thinker Aleksandr Dugin towards Ankara have caused great reactions in the public. In this way, Dugin and Russia, who were appreciated in our country for their support for the civilian government in Türkiye during the failed coup attempt in 2016, suffered a serious loss of image and prestige during this process. The United

States, Israel, and Western states – despite their reservations about radical Islam – have generally given unexpectedly positive reactions to the developments in Syria. The United States has announced its support for the transition process by emphasising Syria's territorial integrity. However, Washington has also announced some preconditions such as respect for minority rights, facilitating humanitarian aid, preventing terrorist activities and destroying chemical and biological weapons stockpiles. Israel, on the other hand, took advantage of the overthrow of the regime in Syria and sent its military units into the country and began to create a large buffer zone for Israel's security, going beyond the Golan Heights. Although Israeli officials stated that this was a temporary measure, it should always be kept in mind that for Israel, a geopolitical state that attaches great importance to territorial gains, the idea

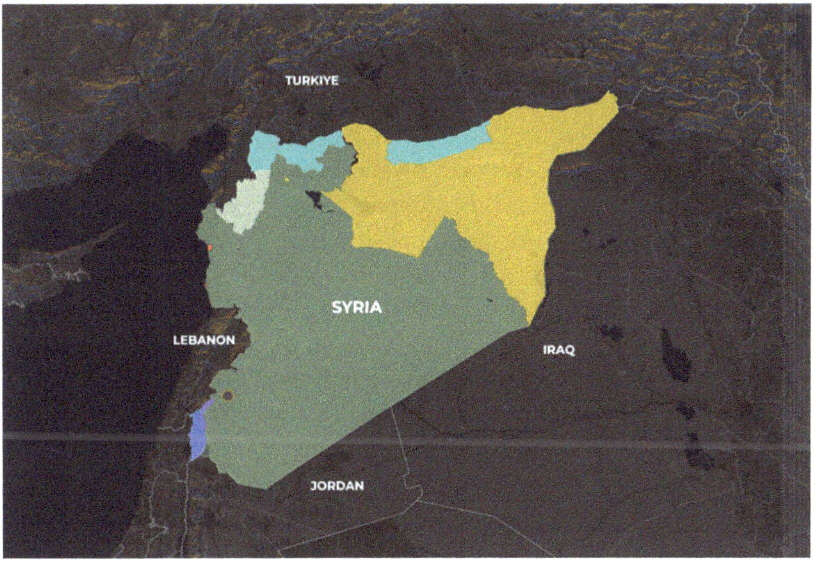

Figure 16: Current map of Syria

Green: HTŞ and its allies (current government)

Blue: TSK presence

Yellow: Kurdish region

Dark Blue: Israeli forces

of gaining new territory in the event of Syria being divided could become a very attractive alternative in the coming months. A similar situation is actually the case for Türkiye, which currently has a military presence in two separate large pockets in the north-west and north of Syria, extending thirty kilometres into the north of Syria. In the face of geopolitical risks posed by widespread PYD/YPG terrorist elements in the north-east of the country, Türkiye may want to strengthen its military presence in the region and expand further into the Kurdish region in the coming months. Because the autonomy or independence of the Kurdish region, which is under the control of US-backed PKK affiliates (the umbrella organisation is the Syrian Democratic Forces-SDF), which is considered a 'terrorist state' by Türkiye, is still not well-received by the public or the upper echelons of the state.

I think it is possible to learn some lessons from the 13-year-long Syrian civil war in terms of Political Science and International Relations. I can list them as follows:

1. **A regime that cannot feed its people and army cannot survive:** Despite the army, intelligence and bureaucracy that are numerically minority in Syria and rely on a significant belief base (Nusayrîs), the fact that the state forces defending President Bashar Assad have disintegrated like a paper tiger in the past few days shows the negative stage that the economic difficulties in Syria have reached. This shows us that the first and most important element for a regime, regardless of its ideological softness/strictness or legitimacy-power, is its ability to feed its people and state forces. Indeed, the fact that Syrian soldiers, who have not been paid for months, are refraining from fighting as HTŞ advances shows the economic impasse the country has fallen into due to the civil war.
2. **A stable government can only be shaped in accordance with the people's tendencies:** The second important lesson that can be learned from the Syrian civil war is that a strong and legitimate regime must be shaped in accordance with the people's ethnic-religious-social-cultural identity and tendencies. Indeed, despite the fact that the vast majority of its population consists of Sunni Muslims, the Syrian regime has been unable to integrate this identity into the country's mainstream ideology symbolised by the Baath Party and the Assad family, and as a result of negative influences from outside, it has first dragged the country into a

bloody civil war and then into a revolutionary process in which radical forces took control. Ankara, which predicted that the regime in Syria would not survive, has proven this to everyone, albeit belatedly.

3. **Türkiye is a game-changing actor in the region:** Despite defending democracy and popular sovereignty during the Arab Spring process that has been going on since 2011, Türkiye has been constantly criticised mercilessly due to the West's double standards and the Eastern Bloc countries' opposition to democracy, and has thus shown the entire world that a regime that it does not approve of cannot survive. In this sense, the necessity of the new administration to be established in Syria – similar to the central government in Iraq – to get along with Ankara will be understood even better in the future. If Türkiye can help the approximately 4 million Syrian refugees who have been Turkified by staying in Türkiye for years to return to their country and gain political power, it can become the main actor in the new period in Syria.
4. **The weakening of Russia and Iran brought about the end of Assad:** The unexpectedly easy collapse of the Assad regime in Syria also proved that the regime can survive with the support of foreign states such as Russia and Iran rather than local elements. In fact, as a result of Russia's failure to support Syria, which was very busy with Iran, which has recently lost a lot of blood due to Israel's attacks on Iranian militias (Hezbollah, etc.) in Lebanon and Syria, and the ongoing bloody war in Ukraine, and which had the risk of entering a major war with all NATO countries that it had no chance of winning, the Assad regime collapsed easily.
5. **The Kurdish State project may become geopolitical a reality**: The most negative aspect of this process for Türkiye is that the Kurdish presence in Syria will cause Ankara trouble in the future with its demands for autonomy and independence, as a result of the organisation of the PYD-YPG forces, an extension of the PKK, under the roof of the SDF and the serious power they have received for years as a result of the training and massive arms support they have received from the United States. Because for Ankara, due to the pressure from the West and the international community, a bloody and comprehensive intervention option does not seem to be a realistic possibility. Moreover, the Syrian Kurds, who have gained serious prestige by fighting against ISIS, are

romanticised in the Western public opinion and can find serious support thanks to their modernist ideology. When Ankara, which is struggling with its chronic economic problems, is added to this, it can be said that we do not have any serious evidence that Türkiye is preparing for a major land war that could last for years. However, it is certain that Türkiye will continue to oppose a Kurdish State with an extension of the PKK with diplomatic and economic pressures and pinpoint operations on the ground. The ideal scenario for Türkiye would be to build a Syria that maintains its territorial integrity and becomes economically dependent on Türkiye in the new period.

6. **Syria may be divided:** Although every regional actor and major state official currently uses the term 'territorial integrity' for Syria, I believe that Syria's territorial integrity is now under serious threat for various reasons. For example, if we consider the hypotheses that Israel, which generally manages to shape US and Western public opinion, can easily turn to the idea of territorial gains, that Syrian Kurds almost completely defend the idea of independence, and that the idea of a Kurdish state for Türkiye can only be accepted in domestic public opinion if there are certain territorial gains in Syria that are reminiscent of the first Republic period (Hatay joining the homeland), it can even be claimed that the possibility of Syria being divided is now a stronger scenario.
7. **Russia's stance is important:** Despite suffering a serious loss of prestige in this process, it should always be kept in mind that Russia will not want to give up its military gains in Syria and that it has the capacity to overthrow a possible new regime in Syria. In fact, the idea that there may be a tacit consensus between Russia-US-Israel-Türkiye-opposition in the process of overthrowing the Assad regime does not seem unreasonable to me. Because Moscow, which can gather soldiers from all over the world for the Ukraine War or the Wagner Group, has not been supporting the Assad regime at all in this recent period, which raises questions in minds. In this sense, it can be thought that Russia is either in a very bad situation due to the struggle to the death in Ukraine that risks evolving into war with NATO, or that it is preparing for the new period by getting rid of the Assad regime that has become a burden to it. I think that Moscow, which is in a situation that is in the combination of these possibilities, may approach the idea of solving the Ukraine

Problem with US President Donald Trump in the new period and a ceasefire that preserves its military gains in Syria.

8. **When things get tough, Israel wins in every way:** Another fact we have seen recently regarding Middle East politics is that Israel, which always makes preparations in this direction in cases of civil war, terror and conflict and is unconditionally supported by the United States, always ends up winning more. Indeed, when we look at what happened after the major Hamas attack on 7 October, it can be said that Hezbollah and Iran were pushed back a lot in the region, the anti-Israeli Syrian regime was destroyed, the Hamas leadership was completely destroyed, Gaza was taken under control, and despite the loss of image in the international public opinion and the ongoing judicial process at the International Court of Justice, Israel benefited from this process.
9. **If you can make a revolution and establish a well-functioning state, you are not considered a terrorist:** The fact that Islamist groups, which are considered terrorist organisations all over the world, took over the administration and made a revolution in Syria has once again brought the debate between terrorists and revolutionaries to the agenda. In fact, it has become clear that groups called terrorists by the old regime during the civil war can easily advance from terrorists to statesmen if they make a revolution and establish a regime that is recognised by other states and can survive in their own countries.

As a result, the Syrian civil war, which has been ongoing since the beginning of 2011, will continue to be examined/researched as a major case that will go down in political history and diplomacy books. The process is not yet complete, and our wish is for Türkiye and humanity to win in this process.

Türkiye's New Multi-Dimensional Foreign Policy

Introduction

There are serious criticisms, especially in the Western world, about Türkiye's ambitious foreign policy, which has been implemented in recent years and aims to develop political/diplomatic, economic, social and cultural relations with different geographies and power blocks. So much so that Türkiye's loyalty and involvement in the Western block is being seriously questioned in the Western world and the perception of Ankara as an enemy is strengthening. To exemplify these; the critical articles of important American Türkiye experts such as Steven Cook, Amanda Sloat, Michael Rubin, and Doug Bandow and the resounding article of the famous magazine *The Economist* dated 2023 can be brought to the agenda. In this context, an interesting and very resounding assessment of Turkish Foreign Policy was recently made by the then Presidential Adviser and current President of the National Intelligence Organisation (MİT), İbrahim Kalın, under the title of 'precious loneliness' (*değerli yalnızlık*).

Likewise, Turkish President Recep Tayyip Erdoğan (2014-) frequently criticises Western political actors such as the United States (US) and the European Union (EU) for applying 'double standards'. This situation indicates the deep disagreements experienced by the two sides in perceiving the situation and that the problem stems from structural problems rather than the whims of individuals. Because these criticisms stem from perceiving this new policy, which is a reflection of Türkiye's deep-rooted foreign policy accumulation and strong state tradition, more at the level of the leader and as a result of personal preferences.

However, the multi-dimensional foreign policy implemented by Türkiye in the last few years is a natural result of a comprehensive transformation and structural requirements that also have deep philosophical and social extensions. In this study, the basic justifications and bases of Türkiye's new multi-dimensional or multi-vector foreign policy will be analysed and explained.

In this context, following the 'Introduction' section, the research will first briefly summarise Türkiye's foreign policy tradition and the transformations experienced over time. Secondly, some important elements of recent Turkish Foreign Policy will be analysed. Thirdly, the basic dynamics of multi-dimensional foreign policy will be explained. The research will end with the 'Conclusion' section.

Türkiye's Foreign Policy Tradition

The Republic of Türkiye has always been a 'unique' and 'different' Western ally since the period it was founded and joined the Western bloc. Türkiye, which had to fight a national War of Independence against Western states during its founding period, was already a sovereign and independent state that was trying to make its people adopt Western modern values, not Western ones. During this period, under the leadership of Great Atatürk and İsmet İnönü, Türkiye established close relations with the Soviet Union. After World War II, due to its policy of 'active neutrality' throughout the war and its continued trade with the Nazis, it incurred the wrath of Stalin, the harsh leader of Soviet Russia, which emerged victorious from the war. Due to Stalin's demands conveyed to the Turkish Ambassador Selim Sarper in Moscow, such as a base in the Straits, revisions in the Montreux Treaty, and the transfer of Kars and Ardahan to Russia, it turned to an alliance with the rising power of the Western world, the United States of America (US). In this sense, the 1946 battleship USS Missouri visit has a symbolic meaning in terms of political history and officially marks the beginning of the period in which Türkiye turned to a policy centred on the United States and the West.

In this context, during the Cold War (1947–1991), Türkiye was a loyal and good Western ally and NATO's 'flank country' or 'southern flank' and assumed the role of a wall against communism and Soviet expansionism. However, even during these harsh periods when relations between the blocs were constructed in a hostile manner, Ankara had different characteristics from other members of the Western world. With its population consisting almost entirely of Muslims, its strong state (centred on the military) tradition and its own political culture, Türkiye has always maintained this different position in the following years, despite becoming a member of the Council of Europe in 1950 and NATO in 1952, being declared a candidate country for the European Union in 1999 and officially starting membership negotiations in 2005.

Türkiye's high self-confidence and sense of grandeur, which is different from Western countries, stems from its deep-rooted imperial tradition; namely, its glorious Ottoman past and the sense of responsibility of the society and state elite in defending the just causes of Muslim peoples (Palestine Issue, etc.). As a result, Türkiye, which is the only Muslim-majority member of NATO, has had an important function in the context of values that the Western world also claims to be universal; however, due to civilisational differences and differing national interests, political crises have frequently occurred between Türkiye and its Western allies (United States, France, Germany, etc.). As a medium-sized state (OBD) trying to achieve its national goals, Türkiye's differing interests with the United States (US) and the Western bloc were felt even during the Cold War, and Ankara was able to use its guarantor rights in 1974 to launch a military intervention in Cyprus, despite Washington's warnings. In the late 1960s and 1970s, Türkiye also tried to develop economic relations with the USSR despite the United States and succeeded in this to a certain extent. Türkiye was even subject to US sanctions (arms embargo) for a while during this period (1975–1978) due to the effects of the Cyprus Conflict and the poppy issue. In this sense, according to Nasuh Uslu, even during the Cold War, the Turkish-American alliance was not suitable for the satellite state-patron state model and Ankara always had various moves and strategies to protect its own independence. While the rising anti-American wave within the country in the context of the problems experienced in relations with the United States during the Cold War period served more as a kind of leverage used in relations with the United States, academics/experts such as Nur Bilge Criss and Füsun Türkmen have reached the view that the wave of anti-Americanism seen during this period was a result of Türkiye's attitude towards protecting its national sovereignty. However, some thinkers such as Prof. Haluk Ülman and Prof. Türkkaya Ataöv, who were also advisers to then-Prime Minister

Bülent Ecevit, took this further and justified the withdrawal from NATO and tried to defend it in realpolitik. But the dominant paradigm of the period and the most powerful institution that shaped politics, the attitude of the Turkish Armed Forces, was always towards developing relations with the Western world and especially the United States.

Recent Turkish Foreign Policy

Following the end of the Cold War and the elimination of the threat of communism (USSR), starting in the 1990s, Türkiye's population and economy grew more self-confident, and Ankara's foreign policy goals determined in line with its own national interests increased. Starting in these years, Ankara increasingly sought to develop its relations with non-Western countries such as the Russian Federation (Russia) and the People's Republic of China (China). Ankara also sought to maintain and develop close relations with the newly established Turkish states, Arab/Islamic countries in its vicinity, the Islamic Republic of Iran (Iran) and distant Muslim states, as well as its traditional allies the United States (US) and the European Union (EU). Former Turkish Prime Minister and President Süleyman Demirel explained this with the phrase '*a country with influence from the Adriatic Sea to the Great Wall of China*'. This situation was based on the country's increasing energy demand as well as its search for new markets to grow its economy as an emerging market economy. Therefore, in addition to the classical Transatlantic (United States and EU) focused foreign policy approach, starting from these years:

- A new foreign policy perspective centred on the geography of Russia such as Eurasianism,
- The dream of uniting the Turkic world,
- The desire to lead the Islamic world that has become headless,
- The ability to represent the Islamic world in a civilisation-centred dialogue process with the West against the threat of the 'Clash of Civilizations' predicted by Samuel Huntington,
- Diversifying relations by investing in developing countries in the Balkans, the Middle East, Africa, Asia and Latin America, Turkish Foreign Policy was further developed and diversified with new views.

Although these perspectives were initially perceived as marginal tendencies, in the early 2000s, it was understood that even the highest level of the state showed interest in establishing a new axis with Russia and Iran against the policies implemented by the United States, with a shocking proposal made by the Secretary of the National Security Council (MGK) at the time, General Tuncer Kılınç. The rise of these alternative tendencies even among the senior members of the Turkish Armed Forces, the most Western-oriented institution in the country, was proof of the deep disagreements in relations with the West. With the rise of the Islamist-oriented Justice and Development Party (AK Parti) and its charismatic leader Recep Tayyip Erdoğan to power in the 2000s, Türkiye entered a rapid transformation process. Erdoğan, a strong leader, virtually reshaped the Turkish state and Turkish Foreign Policy in line with his own ideology and preferences, which he considered a remedy for structural problems, and he was largely successful in this.

First, Erdoğan and the AK Parti, who took bold steps in the process of full EU membership, eliminated the military tutelage regime in this process, strengthened the system based on civilian superiority and popular will in Türkiye, and tried to eliminate the threat of a military coup. During this process, Türkiye also developed rapidly economically and began to display the characteristics of a 'regional power'. In these years, Prof. Ahmet Davutoğlu tried to make Türkiye the most popular, rapidly developing and invested centre in the region with his 'zero problems with neighbours' policy. However, due to the failure to achieve full EU membership for various reasons and the increasing criticism from the West, Erdoğan implemented foreign policies in line with other new and alternative trends over time.

Türkiye, which sought to become a 'model country' or 'big brother state' to Sunni Islamic countries with US support during the Arab Spring in the 2010s, determined a new course and implemented different strategies after the failed coup attempt in 2016, when it saw that its relations with its neighbours Russia, Iran, and Syria were deteriorating, security risks were increasing and it was far from the goal of 'zero problems with neighbours'. These can be stated as:

- Very close political and economic relations and joint projects with neighbouring/brotherly states such as Azerbaijan, the Turkish Republic of Northern Cyprus (TRNC), Iraq, and Qatar,

- Economic and political relations with Russia based on mutual interest and respect, and a careful and alert policy against the influences of the West aimed at damaging relations with Russia,
- Investing in the 'Red Apple' ideal with the Organisation of Turkic States (TDT),
- Developing relations with the Islamic world in every way,
- Trying to spread diplomatic organisations and economic relations all over the world,
- More distant relations with the United States and the EU based on interests.

The Western world's support for the military coup process in 2016 and its bold use of the Kurdish card, which was the most sensitive issue for Ankara, especially in Syria, accelerated these trends. As a result, interestingly, Türkiye, one of the most Western-oriented states of the Cold War, has increasingly begun to turn to a multi-dimensional diplomatic line similar to the Non-Aligned Movement during the Cold War.

Fundamental Dynamics of Multi-dimensional Foreign Policy

Today, it is possible to conceptualise the fundamental foundations of Türkiye's multi-dimensional or multi-vector foreign policy as follows:

Meeting energy needs

For Türkiye, which attaches great importance to economic growth due to its increasing population, solving its energy needs in the cheapest and safest way and establishing permanent relations/projects in this area has been one of the strongest foreign policy motivations since the 2000s. This is one of the main reasons why Ankara does not want to participate in anti-Russian sanctions today.

As can be seen from the tables, the most critical ally for Ankara in this area is Russia. In recent years, Turkish-Russian co-operation, which has intensified particularly in the field of energy, began with the 1992 agreement, and for the first time in history, the two states began to define each other as 'friendly states'. Today, Moscow is not only the largest natural gas and oil

Table 1: Türkiye's natural gas purchases (2022)

Türkiye's natural gas purchases (2022) – EPDK	Country	Percentage
21,575	Russian Federation	40
9,405	Islamic Republic of Iran	17.2
8,705	Azerbaijan	16
5,642	United States of America	10
5,261	Algeria	9.6
2,231	Egypt	3.3

Table 2: Türkiye's oil purchases (2022)

Türkiye's oil purchases (2022) – EPDK	Country	Percentage
	Russian Federation	40.75
	Iraq	26.39
	Kazakhstan	9
	India	4.73
	Saudi Arabia	4.01
	Nigeria	2.51

provider for Ankara; it is also a reliable partner in critical energy projects such as the Mersin-Akkuyu Nuclear Power Plant and Turkish Stream. Other critical countries for Türkiye's energy security are Azerbaijan, Iraq and Iran. For this reason, Türkiye has not always been able to show similar reactions to its Western allies in the generally unsuccessful Western-oriented policies pursued against Russia in recent years (colour revolutions and attempts to bring countries such as Georgia and Ukraine into the Western axis).

Sustaining economic growth

In parallel with its growing population and strengthening private sector, Türkiye is an eager state that is constantly searching for new markets. Industrialising in the 1960s and 1970s and transitioning to a market economy under the leadership of Turgut Özal in the 1980s, Türkiye has gradually begun to transform into a significant trading state capable of producing in various qualities and levels in many different sectors. In this context, Türkiye, which does not want to lose the Western market (EU and United States), which is still the most critical element for it, also wants to enter newly developing giant markets; for this reason, it participates at different levels in organisations such as the Organisation of Islamic Cooperation, MIKTA, Shanghai Cooperation Organisation (SCO), Black Sea Economic Cooperation Organisation (BSEC), Organisation of Turkic States (TDT) and finally BRICS+. Particularly due to the recent prominence of the Asian market, Ankara has also implemented a new Asian initiative in 2019 under the name of 'Anew Asia Initiative'.

The New Asia Initiative, which was established under the leadership of the Presidency of the Republic of Türkiye and the Ministry of Foreign Affairs in line with the demands and suggestions from the private sector, aims to systematically and consistently strengthen Türkiye's relations with Asian countries on the basis of a holistic and comprehensive strategy, by developing regional, sub-regional and country-specific approaches. The primary goals of the New Asia Initiative include issues such as establishing a balanced structure in trade with Asia and increasing economic co-operation and mutual investments. High value-added, high-tech sectors, tourism, finance and defence industry sectors, infrastructure, transportation, logistics, green energy and sustainable development projects are the areas of co-operation planned to be implemented within the framework of the initiative.

Within the scope of the New Asia Initiative or 'Asia Anew' as it is officially known in English, Türkiye has been the term president of the Asian Parliamentary Assembly since 2017. The presidency of the Asia Cooperation Dialogue and Economic Cooperation Organisation, which has been in effect since 2019, and the presidency of the Organisation of Developing Eight Countries (D-8), which has been in effect since 2017, have been transferred as of 2021. In this way, Türkiye wants to be effective outside Western markets in the coming years and create alternative routes that can eliminate the West's economic blackmail due to political disagreements (Cyprus Conflict, Kurdish issue, criticism of the regime at home, etc.).

The MIKTA initiative, which was launched with Mexico, Indonesia, South Korea and Australia, is an initiative that has been ongoing since 2013, similar to the Asia Anew Initiative, and was launched with the aim of diversifying Türkiye's economic and political portfolio. The seven basic priorities of the MIKTA countries, as declared by the Ministry of Foreign Affairs of the Republic of Türkiye, are as follows:

- Energy,
- Fight Against Terrorism and Security,
- Trade and Economic Co-operation,
- Good Governance and Democracy,
- Sustainable Development,
- Gender Equality,
- Peacekeeping Operations.

Türkiye has recently applied for membership in the BRICS or BRICS+ organisations, which are rapidly rising platforms in world politics and have made a name for themselves, and obtained the status of a 'partner state' at the 2024 Kazan Summit. Türkiye's full membership in the BRICS+ organisation may also be realised in the coming years.

Türkiye, currently the 17th largest economy in the world with its \$1.3 trillion economy, aims to continue its economic growth in the coming years in a way that will challenge the top 10. The most critical bloc in terms of Türkiye's foreign trade is the EU, which currently accounts for half of its exports. For this reason, despite serious political and geopolitical disagreements, Ankara does not want to cut ties with the EU, which is both a critical bloc for it economically and which it believes will contribute to its progress as a civilisation project, and aims to develop relations through issues such as updating the Customs Union and visa exemptions. However, Ankara, which does not trust Brussels and Washington on political issues, is also taking determined strategic steps to reduce its economic dependence on Western countries and diversify its economic and political portfolio.

Elimination of security risks in the nearby geography

Türkiye, a unitary and secular state, suffers from terrorist organisations and separatist groups operating in its nearby geography. Ankara, which has lost tens of thousands of people due to terrorism, also suffers economic losses of billions of dollars. In this context, Türkiye is making great efforts to prevent terrorist and violent groups, which are concentrated on two political axes, from being effective in its nearby geography and is designing its military and security policies accordingly. This situation also plays an important role in Türkiye's failure to transition to a consolidated democracy and to reduce its military expenditures.

If we need to group the two sources of terrorism that Türkiye is facing, these are:

1. Kurdish separatist far-left terrorist organisations such as PKK/PYG/YPG/KCK, which threaten national integrity and unitary structure,
2. Far-right and radical religious terrorist organisations such as Al-Qaeda/ISIS/FETÖ, which target secular and modern life and economic development.

The main reason why Türkiye has not been able to establish good relations with its Western allies in recent times is that these states have been consciously or unconsciously supporting terrorist organisations, thus putting the security of the Turkish state and the Turkish people at risk. These policies implemented by Western countries in the form of supporting terrorist organisations are contrary to the spirit of NATO alliance, and of course, are not compatible with international law and human values. Unfortunately, due to strong intellectual and social tendencies such as anti-Türkiye and anti-Islamism, the Western world has embarked on such a wrong path years ago.

Revision of the international system

Under the leadership of President Recep Tayyip Erdoğan, Türkiye has been very consciously and resolutely advocating reform in the United Nations (UN) system in recent years with the discourse of 'The World is Bigger than Five' that will provide an environment for a more just and inclusive international system. This discourse and determination are not a personal decision of President Erdoğan, but an expression of the conclusion and judgement reached by the thousands of years of Turkish state tradition. In this context, Ankara advocates the reorganisation of the current UN system and the provision of more representation opportunities to rising powers and oppressed nations, also citing the ongoing human rights violations in Syria, Ukraine and Palestine. This situation also adds a third-world type anti-imperialist atmosphere to Türkiye's multi-dimensional foreign policy. In this way,

Türkiye also gains the favour of many victimised states and peoples who are uncomfortable with the international system and becomes a popular state in the international arena.

Multipolarity

In line with its energy policy, economic policy, security policy and attitude towards the UN, Ankara has recently been constructing the theoretical framework of its foreign policy on the basis of multipolarity. The most important power centres in this approach are the United States, China, Russia, the EU, and India. Türkiye also wants to be included in this equation with Turkish and Islamic geopolitics. Türkiye plans and takes all its strategic steps with the reflex and desire to be a great power. Recently, it has been observed that the Minister of Foreign Affairs of the Republic of Türkiye, Hakan Fidan, frequently includes the concept of 'multipolarity' in his speeches and tries to address this issue. President Erdoğan, while criticising the UN system through concepts such as 'fair international order' and 'Türkiye Century', is creating the intellectual and social infrastructure of multipolarity.

Turkish humanism based on Islamic values

The philosophical approach that holds the foundation of this new foreign policy perspective very firmly and is dominant in Anatolia is Turkish humanism based on Islamic values, reflecting the accumulation of tens of centuries of Turkish-Islamic culture. In line with this approach, Türkiye considers helping all victimised nations, especially Muslim peoples, as a humanitarian duty and never accepts the ruthless policies of states such as Israel, even in return for any benefit. Rising on the basis of humanist values, Türkiye also wants to be more effective in the international system and the UN in this way.

Conclusion

In conclusion, in recent years, 'multi-dimensional foreign policy' or 'multidimensionality' has increasingly become a permanent foreign policy trend in Türkiye. Despite its historical Western ties and turbulent economic structure, the main reasons for this new and strong trend for Ankara can be listed as; Türkiye's problems with the West on many strategic issues (Cyprus issue, Kurdish issue, relations with Russia and Israel, etc.), Türkiye's increasing dependence on Russia in the field of energy, interest in rising Asian markets, and Türkiye's increasing criticism of the international system and Western-centrism.

The most serious problems Ankara faces in terms of achieving success with multi-dimensional foreign policy can be listed as follows:

- Not yet being strong enough economically,
- The risk of Türkiye, a NATO member, being stuck in the middle and being subject to sanctions in cases where West-East conflict increases,
- Not yet reaching the desired level of diversity in economic markets,
- The secular-Islamist, Turkish-Kurdish, Sunni-Alevi, right-leftist, etc. polarisations such as these have not yet been completely resolved,
- The new political system has not yet been rooted and has not been sufficiently adopted by the people and elites.

If these problems are overcome, it is possible for Türkiye to make its multi-dimensional foreign policy a permanent diplomatic trend. However, the opposition parties in Türkiye are still more inclined to the old Western paradigm, and this raises questions about the permanence of the multi-dimensional foreign policy in the event of a change of government.

Bibliography

Anadolu Ajansı (2018), "Cumhurbaşkanı Erdoğan: Çifte standart karşısında sahada olmamız gerekiyor", 16.04.2018, <https://www.aa.com.tr/tr/gunun-basliklari/cumhurbaskani-erdogan-cifte-standart-karsisinda-sahada-olmamiz-gerekiyor/1119771>.

Bandow, Doug (2022), "Why Is Turkey Still in NATO?", CATO Institute, 14.07.2022, <https://www.cato.org/commentary/why-turkey-still-nato>.

Cook, Steven A. (2017), "Turkey: Friend or Frenemy? A Tangled Relationship Keeps Getting Worse", Council on Foreign Relations, 13.11.2017, <https://www.cfr.org/blog/turkey-friend-or-frenemy-tangled-relationship-keeps-getting-worse>.

Criss, Nur Bilge (2002), "A Short History of Anti-Americanism and Terrorism: The Turkish Case", *The Journal of American History*, Vol. 89, no: 2, pp. 472–484.

Duman, Melih (2022), "70. Yılında Türkiye-NATO İlişkilerinin Tarihsel Boyutu", *Akademik Hassasiyetler*, Vol 10, no: 21, pp. 400–429.

EPDK, <https://www.epdk.gov.tr/>.

Kalın, İbrahim (2013), <https://x.com/ikalin1/status/362746057513385984, 01.09.2013>.

Örmeci, Ozan, Blog – Ozan Örmeci Articles, <https://ydemokrat.blogspot.com/>.

Örmeci, Ozan (2019), "Turkish-Russian Relations during AK Parti Rule: Could Economic Partnership Transform into a Strategic Partnership? A Realistic Outlook", *International Journal of Economics, Administrative and Social Sciences (IJEASS)*, Vol. 2, no: 2, December 2019, pp. 126–145.

Örmeci, Ozan (2020), "Turkish-American Relations in the Post-Cold War Era", in *Historical Examinations and Current Issues in Turkish-American Relations* (eds. by Ozan Örmeci & Hüseyin Işıksal), Berlin: Peter Lang, pp. 61–115.

Örmeci, Ozan (2024), "Decoding anti-Americanism in Türkiye", in *Turkish-American Relations in the 21st Century* (eds. by Ozan Örmeci & Herbert Reginbogin), New York: Lexington Books, pp. 37–53.

Örmeci, Ozan (2024), *Türk Dış Politikası Yazıları*, İstanbul: Urzeni Yayıncılık.

Örmeci, Ozan (2024), "Türkiye's New Multi-Dimensional Foreign Policy", *Russian Law Journal*, Vol. 12, no: 2, pp. 86–99.

Rubin, Michael (2018), "It's time for Turkey and NATO to go their separate ways", *The Washington Post*, 16.08.2018, <https://www.washingtonpost.com/news/democracy-post/wp/2018/08/16/its-time-for-turkey-and-nato-to-go-their-separate-ways/>.

Sloat, Amanda (2018), "The West's Turkey conundrum", Brookings, February 2018, <https://www.brookings.edu/articles/the-wests-turkey-conundrum/>.

The Economist (2023), "Turkey has a newly confrontational foreign policy", 16.01.2023, <https://www.economist.com/special-report/2023/01/16/turkey-has-a-newly-confrontational-foreign-policy>.

Türkiye Cumhuriyeti Dışişleri Bakanlığı, <https://www.mfa.gov.tr/default.tr.mfa>.

Türkmen, Füsun (2010), "Anti-Americanism as a Default Ideology of Opposition: Turkey as a Case Study", *Turkish Studies*, Vol. 11, no: 3, pp. 329–345.

Uslu, Nasuh (2000), *Türk Amerikan İlişkileri*, Ankara: 21. Yüzyıl Yayınları.

The Pesco Initiative and the Risks of a Possible European Army for a Türkiye Outside the EU

Introduction

The Republic of Türkiye has systematically pursued the goal of Westernisation and integration with the Western world for more than 200 years starting from the nineteenth century, including the last century of its predecessor, the Ottoman Empire. In this context, following extensive reforms in the late Ottoman Empire and increasing political, economic, military and cultural interactions with Western countries, Türkiye institutionalised itself as a Western-type secular nation-state and joined the Council of Europe in 1950, NATO in 1952, and the Customs Union of the European Union (EU) in 1995, taking its place in Western strategic institutions. Since 2005, Türkiye has also been negotiating to become a full member of the EU. Türkiye, with one of NATO's most important and powerful armies, the Turkish Armed Forces (TSK), has a crucial role to play in the security of the Western world in terms of the migrant (refugee) crisis, Russia's military operations in its neighbourhood, such as in Georgia and Ukraine, the fight against radical Islamist and other terrorist organisations, the fight against human trafficking and narcotics, and the spread of Western values such as democracy, human rights, rule of law, and secularism to the Middle East and the Turkic world. Therefore, the Western world cannot afford to sacrifice Türkiye's security and allow it to move to another camp.

In this article, the issue of the institutionalisation of the European Army, which is an issue that may create problems between Türkiye and the EU and European countries in the near future – especially if the issues of sovereign jurisdiction and exclusive economic zone (EEZ) in the Eastern Mediterranean are not resolved – in these highly strategic and unbreakable relations will be evaluated. In this context, the paper will first briefly summarise the previous European Army initiatives and provide a historical background. Then, PESCO (Permanent Structured Cooperation) and the European Intervention Initiative (EI2) will be analysed. In the third and final part, some of the risks that Türkiye, as a full member of the EU and outside of these initiatives, may face in Cyprus and the Eastern Mediterranean will be speculated. The reasons why I say speculate is that there is not yet enough done on these issues and there are only possibilities to make interpretations based on future imaginations and predictions.

European Army Initiatives

In the aftermath of the Second World War, before the European Coal and Steel Community (ECSC), which laid the foundations of the EU, the Treaty of Brussels signed on 7 March 1948 established the Western European Union (WEU) as a new European security and defence organisation, and the first attempt at a European Army was made with the participation of Belgium, France, Luxembourg, the Netherlands, and the United Kingdom. Although the Western European Union (WEU), which was institutionalised in a structure that initially excluded Italy and Germany, later accepted these countries as members, the idea of a European Army (the project known as the Pleven Plan), which had been voiced by French statesmen André Philip and René Pleven in the early 1950s, was rejected with the influence of the United States, which played a critical role in the restructuring of Europe at the time. The United States, of course, at that time, wanted NATO forces to act together and in unison against the threat of communist expansionism emanating from the Soviet Union, rather than preventing a European Army. In 1952, the European Defence Community (EDF) was established as a step forward in this direction, but no serious progress could be made on the European Army, no doubt due to the overarching structure and enormous influence of the United States and NATO in an environment of Cold War dynamics.

In the following period, as the Cold War deepened, in 1966, France, under the leadership of Charles de Gaulle, withdrew from NATO's military wing in order to act more independently in its foreign policy due to its problems with the United States. Following this move, the institutionalisation of the

European Army through the institutionalisation of the EEU (European Economic Community) and the EDF under the leadership of France was attempted, but these initiatives did not yield the expected positive results. During these periods, the European Economic Community (EEC) and European Community (EC) initiatives, the predecessors of the EU, preferred to act in concert with the United States and NATO in the face of the Soviet threat, both because they could not allocate as large a share of their defence budgets as a huge economy like the United States, and because they were primarily focused on improving the welfare of their peoples.

After the formation of the European Union with the Maastricht Treaty (1992), even though Europe's integration goal deepened and began to include new members, the commitment to Washington and NATO in military-security policies continued and no concrete and successful progress was made on the European Army. However, in the 2000s, when the EU became an economic giant under the leadership of Germany and evolved into a power that could compete with the United States and Russia, especially with the economy and other soft power instruments, the idea of a European Army started to gain strength again, also due to diplomatic disagreements with the United States. In fact, in this new period, when the EU started to establish the Common Security and Defence Policy (CSDP), initiatives such as the European Defence Agency, the Petersberg Missions, the European Security Strategy, the Berlin Plus Treaty, and the European Union Battlegroups were established to take steps forward in European defence. The 2009 Lisbon Treaty's authorisation of joint EU military actions has also strengthened this trend. In 2007, high-profile leaders such as Angela Merkel, who called for the establishment of a common European Army among the EU members, have become increasingly prominent.

PESCO and the European Intervention Initiative

PESCO, or Permanent Structured Cooperation, is the most important initiative of the EU, which has been reduced to twenty-seven members after the United Kingdom's withdrawal from the Union, to create a European Army. Launched in 2017, PESCO included all EU members except Malta – whose constitution enshrines the principle of neutrality – bringing the number of members to 26. The objectives of PESCO are summarised as follows:

- Planned and harmonised independent projects and initiatives of member states to improve Europe's defence capacity,
- Ensuring capacity building in line with the CSDP objectives and initiatives,
- Consistent and aligned with the European Defence Fund (EDA) and the Coordinated Annual Defence Review (CARD).

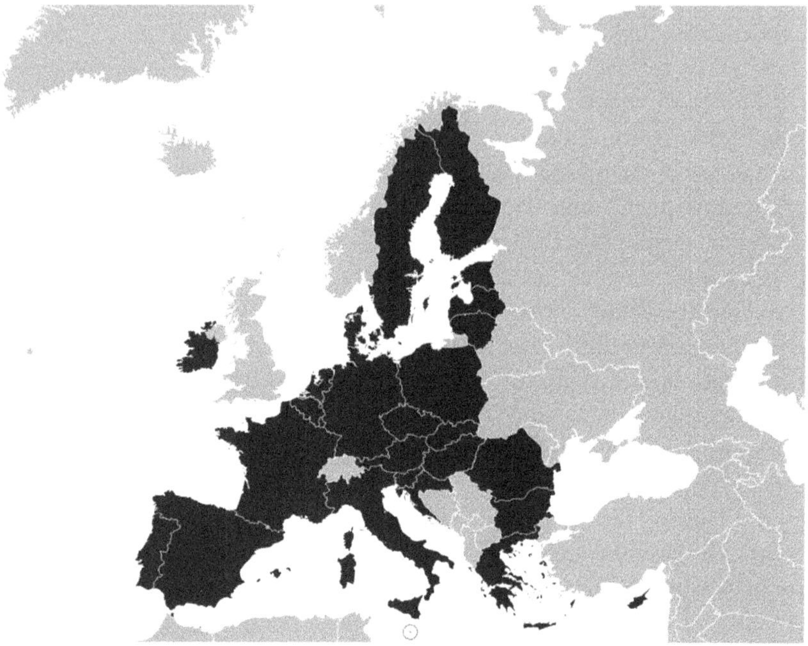

Figure 17: PESCO map

Based on the Lisbon Treaty, PESCO has emerged as an intergovernmental and international initiative linked to the supranational EU. The PESCO initiative is open to third countries and has so far attracted interest from the United States, Norway, Canada, the United Kingdom, Türkiye, and other countries. PESCO has not emerged as an alternative to NATO but rather aims to make the scattered and uncoordinated defence expenditures and initiatives of European states coherent and harmonised. In fact, Guy Verhofstadt, a prominent Belgian politician and one-time leader of the ALDE group in the European Parliament, emphasised that EU countries have 240 billion euros in defence resources, four times more than Russia, and made statements in the past year that one united army could be established instead of twenty-seven scattered armies, also with the impact of the Ukraine crisis.

Another European defence-security initiative is the European Intervention Mechanism or EI2 for short. Launched in 2018 on the initiative of French President Emmanuel Macron, the European Intervention Mechanism is a 13-member security initiative that includes 11 EU member states (Germany, Belgium, Denmark, Estonia, Finland, France, the Netherlands, Spain, Sweden, Italy, Italy, Portugal) as well as the United Kingdom and Norway.

Similar to PESCO, rather than being a competitor to NATO, EI2 aims to improve strategic culture and coordination between member states and aims to enhance co-operation between member states on issues such as scenario planning, intelligence sharing, military doctrine and co-operation. Considering Macron's remarks criticising NATO, it can be argued that although these initiatives are not an alternative to NATO, European leaders have always had the idea of a European Army in mind.

Potential Risks for Türkiye Outside the EU

In a future, where Türkiye, which became a member of European institutions decades ago and is expected to be included in European institutions in the future, remains outside the EU due to various political (Cyprus issue, Eastern Mediterranean, etc.) and structural problems (democracy and the rule of law cannot be developed due to the difficult conditions in the geography and the political culture is not inclined to democracy), there is no doubt that the tensions between Türkiye and the countries included in the European defence initiatives PESCO and EI2 carry the risk of gaining a military character. These countries are, naturally, Greece, with whom we have problems regarding maritime jurisdiction areas, territorial waters and EEZ areas in the Aegean and Eastern Mediterranean, and the Greek Cypriot Administration of Southern Cyprus (officially known as the Republic of Cyprus registered with the UN) with whom political relations have not been normalised due to the unresolved Cyprus Conflict. These countries, undoubtedly, are trying to include the European institutions, which Türkiye is also trying to include, due to their own national interests and because they do not have the capacity to solve their problems with Türkiye politically and militarily. In fact, in the 2020–2022 period, France had to engage in very harsh polemics and even some de facto situations (the Courbet incident) with Türkiye on this issue, and relations between the two countries have been seriously strained. While France stated that it had to protect the member states included in the EU and PESCO initiatives of which it is a member, Türkiye emphasised its NATO alliance and defended itself in this way. Similarly, the stopping of a Turkish ship off the coast of Libya in 2020 within the scope of the EU's Operation Irini gives us an idea of the tensions that may arise in the near future.

At this point, when a realistic future is imagined, I think it is possible that initiatives such as PESCO and EI2, which are gradually becoming a European Army, or a European Army structure that can develop independently of these, will become actors in the problems between Türkiye, Greece, and Cyprus, and that serious problems and perhaps military conflicts will occur between Türkiye and its European allies. The main reason for this is that there is no agreement between the parties on this issue and the problems are constantly postponed, creating a suitable ground for a possible major crisis in the future. In other words, unless an agreement is reached on territorial waters, maritime jurisdictions, EEZs and of course Cyprus in the Eastern Mediterranean, the tensions between the EU, which is gradually beginning to exhibit an image of unity, and Ankara may also reach a crisis level. The way to prevent this should be to make Türkiye an EU member or to reach an agreement on these issues.

In addition, Türkiye will of course have important trump cards in its hands against these problems. First of all, the security and threat perceptions of EU member states are not yet monolithic. For example, while the primary threat for Eastern European and Baltic countries is Russia, and in this context NATO and US support is essential, for Western European countries the Russian threat was not such a significant issue until the invasion of Ukraine, and US-NATO support was less sought after. Of course, this situation changed with the Russian invasion of Ukraine and although a kind of unity has now been achieved in Europe, it is still difficult to say that the positions of countries such as Hungary and Poland, which have close relations with Türkiye, and Greece and the Greek Cypriot Administration of Cyprus, are homogeneous. More importantly, a Türkiye that is a NATO member and has improved its relations with the United States undoubtedly has a greater chance of receiving support from NATO and Washington compared to its less effective Western allies in military, political, and economic terms, such as Greece and the Greek Cypriot Administration of Cyprus. Ankara, which has not severed its relations with Russia, is trying to position itself as an important power in the region in this context. Thanks to its great potential, Ankara could have already achieved this if it were not for its economic problems. Another issue is undoubtedly the heavy responsibilities that Türkiye has undertaken in combating irregular migration originating from the Middle East and North Africa. Ankara, which makes a major contribution to European security in this way, is therefore not an ordinary partner that can be discarded by Brussels in line with the demands of Athens or Nicosia. However, of course, a Türkiye that has problems with countries such as France and Germany and cannot improve its relations with the United States will likely experience more serious problems in the Eastern Mediterranean and Cyprus.

Conclusion

In conclusion, as the second century of the Republic begins, uncertainties about Türkiye's future are disappointing. If Türkiye truly wants the EU membership goal, it should act accordingly. If Ankara does not want this, alternative strategic plans should be made. To make the situation more concrete; if a solution in Cyprus and EU membership is not seen as a serious alternative, then in order to avoid economic problems, foreign trade should be directed to different countries (Asia, Middle East, etc.) from now on. Because as long as the EU is the largest market and foreign trade partner economically, Türkiye may have to make concessions on political issues. If it is serious about its EU membership goal, then Ankara should seek democracy, rule of law, human rights, freedom of press-publication-idea, and solving problems in the Eastern Mediterranean in accordance with EU standards.

Minister of Foreign Affairs Hakan Fidan's Visit to China

Introduction

Hakan Fidan (1968–), an experienced Turkish bureaucrat whose appointment to a highly media-oriented and popular position such as the Ministry of Foreign Affairs was initially considered strange due to his secretive and media-free intelligence (MİT) career, continues to make a name for himself with his appearances and visits since taking office. This article will analyse Hakan Fidan's actions in the first months of his term as the Minister of Foreign Affairs, and especially his visit to China this week.

Hakan Fidan Era: Ankara's Quest to Become a Regional Power

Hakan Fidan, who was appointed to a new and important position as the Minister of Foreign Affairs on 4 June 2023, is an experienced security bureaucrat who served as the President/Undersecretary of the MİT for over 8 years (2015–2023), and is a person who knows all of Türkiye's internal and external problems very well and has a clear roadmap in his mind about what needs to be done. Fidan has also clearly stated these views in the article titled 'Turkish Foreign Policy at the Turn of the "Century of Türkiye": Challenges, Vision, Objectives, and Transformation' published in the Summer 2023 issue of *Insight Turkey* magazine.[1]

In this work, Fidan criticised the failure of major powers to comply with international law and multilateral diplomacy and the discrediting of the United Nations in line with his vision of a regional power called the 'Turkish

Century' (*Türkiye Yüzyılı*) and drew attention to various current problems such as armed conflicts, terrorism, mass irregular migration, xenophobia, Islamophobia (anti-Islamism), climate crisis, food shortages, and cyberattacks. Fidan wrote that 9.2 per cent of the world's population is at risk of starvation and 2.4 billion people face threats to food security and called for global breakthroughs and inter-state co-operation in services such as economy, security, development, transportation, and health. Describing Türkiye as a 'regional system-transforming actor' in the new period, Fidan focused on issues such as new co-operation models, institutionalised foreign policy, approaches that will develop a welfare environment and global goals, and signalled that Türkiye will continue to act as a responsible actor by establishing a kind of balance between the global system and its national interests.

After taking office, Fidan criticised the weapons, ammunition, and diplomatic support provided by the United States to groups such as the PYD-YPG, an extension of the terrorist organisation PKK in Syria, under the pretext of ISIS, and said, '*I recommend that third parties stay away from PKK/YPG facilities and individuals*.'[2] Following these words, which were perceived as a warning from Türkiye to the United States, the United States shot down a Turkish drone near Hasakah in northwestern Syria in early October 2023, opening the door to a new diplomatic crisis.[3] Although the issue fell off the agenda due to the Hamas-Israel War that began after this incident, the negative course of Turkish-American relations was once again confirmed with this incident, and Fidan created the perception that he would act in accordance with a more multi-dimensional foreign policy instead of a purely pro-US one.

The second important development during the Hakan Fidan period was the rapid completion of the Development Path Project, which President Recep Tayyip Erdoğan and Türkiye had been working on for years and which included Qatar and the United Arab Emirates (UAE) along with Iraq, and the rapid development of the process through shuttle diplomacy between the parties, taking it to the next stage.[4] The project is a very important geopolitical move that will serve as a beneficial development, transportation and connectivity function for Iraq, Türkiye, and the entire region, and the completion of the project that was dragged on for years has been an important data showing Fidan's practical side. So much so that, as a result of these contacts, Iraq declared the PKK a 'banned organisation' and banned its activities.[5]

A third issue during Fidan's term was Türkiye's proposal to be a guarantor in the face of the humanitarian tragedy in Gaza. The proposal, which diplomatic sources found 'vague'[6] and was not perceived as very realistic due to the tensions with Israel, nevertheless went down in our history of foreign relations as a creative and new idea.

Thus, Fidan, who made a rapid entrance into the Ministry of Foreign Affairs, created the agenda again with his 3-day China visit in June 2024 and delivered very important messages during this visit.

Hakan Fidan in China: Are the Foundations of a Multipolar World Order Being Laid?

Minister Fidan, upon the invitation of Chinese Foreign Minister Wang Yi, carried out a 3-day China trip covering Beijing, Urumqi and Kashgar on 3–4–5 June 2024. Fidan, who was accepted by Wang Yi as well as Chinese State Security Minister Chen Wenqingq in the capital Beijing and gave a speech titled 'Turkey-China Relations in the Changing World Order' at a leading think-tank, conveyed the message that they were against the exploitation of the Uyghur Turks issue by Western countries with their emphasis on the countries' interference in each other's internal affairs, but also showed their sensitivity on this issue by defining Urumqi and Kashgar as 'ancient Turkish-Islamic cities'.[7] The fact that Fidan is the first high-level Turkish official to be allowed to visit the Xinjiang Uyghur Autonomous Region since 2012 is also an important indication of the Chinese side's trust in Fidan.

In his speeches in China, Minister Fidan emphasised that the trade volume between the two countries has approached 50 billion dollars and that China has become one of Türkiye's largest trade partners (second only to Russia) in recent years, and suggested that a more balanced picture be presented in trade and that co-operation in the fields of tourism, technology, civil aviation, energy and research and development be increased.[8] He also emphasised that the Development Road Project is an initiative that complies with the Chinese Belt and Road Initiative and will accelerate global trade, and he made an effort to fulfil the 'Middle Corridor' (*Orta Koridor*) vision.

Evaluating Fidan's visit to China, Hasan Ünal, a well-known Turkish Professor of International Relations and a faculty member at Başkent University, interpreted the co-operation between the two countries as a natural reflection of the newly formed multipolar world order, while stating that Fidan's statements were the result of a well-studied China policy and that Türkiye's participation in BRICS was possible.[9] Ünal also criticised NATO's recent perception of threat towards China, adding that Türkiye stood against this policy.

Prof. Çağdaş Üngör from Marmara University, on the other hand, opposed the interpretation of this visit as a new era, but emphasised that there has been a real rapprochement between China and Türkiye in recent years, and that the main reason for this is the problems Türkiye has with Western countries.[10]

Indeed, it can be claimed that due to Türkiye losing its enthusiasm and hope on the path to full membership in the European Union and the serious problems experienced with the United States through the PYD-YPG, a serious rapprochement has been experienced in foreign policy with countries such as Russia and China in recent years and the foundations of a new multi-dimensional foreign policy based on becoming a regional power have been laid. However, since Türkiye, as a medium-sized state (OBD) member of NATO, does not have the power to make and implement completely autonomous and free decisions in terms of either military or economic terms, these policies will always pose a risk due to the restriction/blocking decisions to be taken by the United States and the EU (for example, CAATSA sanctions regarding relations with Russia). In order to overcome these restrictions, Ankara needs to diversify its economy and get rid of its export dependency on Europe.

In this sense, although Asian markets are a very good alternative for Türkiye, BRICS membership cannot of course be considered on a par with EU membership. The main reason for this is that the EU is a comprehensive and consistent civilisation project with its political, economic, and legal dimensions, while BRICS is an alternative to the West and operates as a loose platform in economic and political terms. However, of course, as the balances in the global economy are shifting towards Asia every passing day, it is an extremely correct and rational strategy for Türkiye to try to be effective in this continent with the Organisation of Turkic States (TDT) and BRICS. The Shanghai Cooperation Organisation (SCO), on the other hand, may not create the right perspective for Türkiye, a NATO member, due to its military dimensions. The Asia Anew Initiative, on the other hand, should not be forgotten and should be examined well as an initiative focused on export-economy and reflecting Türkiye's peaceful and win-win economic perspective.

Conclusion

In conclusion, Minister Fidan's visit to China can be interpreted as an important development that shows the multi-dimensional foreign policy line that Türkiye, which has been experiencing various problems with the Western world in recent times, is trying to institutionalise. China's enormous investment potential and the tourist sending power provided by its huge population, and Türkiye's rapprochement with Ankara at a time when it is going through a difficult economic period, could increase the sympathy and respect felt for this country in Türkiye and could lead to a more neutral and multi-dimensional foreign policy for a traditional American ally. In this respect, it is necessary to evaluate Minister Fidan's visit well and look at the big picture. That is, Ankara wants trade and regional integration and relations with its neighbours, especially Iraq.

Endnotes

1 See; <https://www.insightturkey.com/commentary/turkish-foreign-at-the-turn-of-the-century-of-turkiye-challenges-vision-objectives-and-transformation>; <https://politikaakademisi.org/2023/10/10/turkiye-cumhuriyeti-disisleri-bakani-dr-hakan-fidandan-yeni-donemde-turk-dis-politikasinin-rotasini-isaret-eden-bir-makale/>.

2 See; <https://www.yeniakit.com.tr/haber/hakan-fidan-ucuncu-taraflarin-pkkypg-gli-tesislerden-ve-sahislardan-uzak-durmasini-tavsiye-ediyorum-demisti-amerikadan-yanit-geldi-1793032.html>.

3 See; <https://politikaakademisi.org/2023/10/07/turk-amerikan-iliskilerinde-yeni-bir-kriz-mi-abd-turk-sihasini-dusurdu/>.

4 See; <https://politikaakademisi.org/2024/05/27/kalkinma-yolu-projesi/>.

5 <https://www.bbc.com/turkce/articles/cmjml1lpdveo#:~:text=Ortak%20a%C3%A7%C4%B1klamada%2C%20bu%20konuda%20at%C4%B1lan,Irak%20makamlar%C4%B1%20taraf%C4%B1ndan%20kamuoyuna%20duyurulmam%C4%B1%C5%9Ft%C4%B1>.

6 <https://www.bbc.com/turkce/articles/cd1dp7gjjjro>.

7 <https://www.bbc.com/turkce/articles/cn006g2ve87o>.

8 <https://www.bbc.com/turkce/articles/cn006g2ve87o>.

9 <https://www.youtube.com/watch?v=cMVfvPBWnp0>.

10 <https://www.youtube.com/watch?v=fYBzTvLrqkQ>.

Türkiye's Most Important Foreign Trade Partners in Recent Years

Introduction

The economy and its basic components, foreign trade between countries, have become one of the most important parameters determining how politics and diplomacy will manifest themselves today. While states seek secure and stable foreign markets in various sectors and commodities where they have production advantages, they also seek reliable and stable sellers in sectors and commodities where they do not have them or where production conditions are disadvantageous for market actors and the state. In this way, both states and their peoples can have quality goods cheaply, while at the same time, processes can be experienced in which historical hostilities between states and peoples can soften or even disappear over time. The best-known and most successful example of this is the close economic and political relations established by Germany and France, who competed with each other for centuries and then tried to destroy each other during the First and Second World Wars, starting with the European Coal and Steel Community (ECSC) process. These relations brought the two states and their peoples closer together and also gave rise to a very successful and one-of-a-kind supranational structure such as the European Union (EU).

In this context, in this article, believing in the virtue and benefits of foreign trade, I will try to reveal Türkiye's foreign trade picture in recent years to determine our most important partners and to explain to what extent the foreign trade balance is in our favour or against us in our relations with these partners. The statistical data used in the article was obtained from the official website of the Turkish Statistical Institute (TÜİK).

Türkiye's Most Important Foreign Trade Partners in Recent Years

This section will list the countries with which Türkiye has had the most intensive foreign trade in the last 7 years (2018, 2019, 2020, 2021, 2022, 2023, and 2024), starting from 2018. The foreign trade balance figures indicated in red indicate the countries with which Türkiye has a foreign trade deficit and the rate of this deficit. It should also be noted that there have been extensive changes in international trade due to the COVID-19 (coronavirus) pandemic, especially in 2020 and 2021, and the figures have been turned upside down. In this sense, the data for 2018, 2019, 2022, and 2023 may be more reliable in terms of reflecting general trends. In the data for 2024, statistics from the first 11 months were used. The data is taken from https://biruni.tuik.gov.tr/.

Table 3: The ten countries with which Türkiye had the most intensive foreign trade in 2018 and the total import-export levels made with these countries

Rank	Country	Türkiye's Export ($)	Türkiye's Import ($)	Total Trade ($)	Trade Balance ($)
1	Germany	16,136,904,904	20,407,264,000	36,554,168,904	-4,270,359,096
2	Russia	3,399,662,315	21,989,573,934	25,389,236,249	-18,589,911,619
3	China	2,912,538,278	20,719,046,410	23,631,584,688	-17,806,508,132
4	US	8,304,648,518	12,377,680,691	20,682,329,209	-4,073,032,173
5	Italy	9,560,164,290	10,154,156,347	19,714,320,637	-593,992,057
6	UK	11,106,981,096	7,446,107,100	18,553,088,196	3,660,873,996
7	France	7,287,092,957	7,413,025,177	14,700,118,134	-125,932,220
8	Spain	7,708,391,366	5,492,455,981	13,200,847,347	2,215,935,385
9	Iraq	8,346,025,862	1,420,433,371	9,766,459,233	6,925,592,491
10	Iran	2,392,778,213	6,931,257,943	9,324,036,156	-4,538,479,730

Table 4: The ten countries with which Türkiye had the most intensive foreign trade in 2019 and the total import-export levels with these countries

Rank	Country	Türkiye's Export ($)	Türkiye's Import ($)	Total Trade ($)	Trade Balance ($)
1	Germany	15,425,718,615	17,977,666,396	33,403,385,011	-2,551,947,781
2	Russia	3,852,993,806	22,453,026,441	26,306,020,247	-18,600,032,635
3	China	2,586,637,371	18,496,580,460	21,083,217,831	-15,909,943,089
4	US	8,056,583,541	11,186,782,986	19,243,366,527	-3,130,199,445
5	Italy	9,299,208,053	8,612,017,979	17,911,226,032	687,190,074
6	UK	10,866,184,086	5,426,647,002	16,292,831,088	5,439,537,084
7	France	7,637,927,461	6,353,527,372	13,991,454,833	1,284,400,089
8	Spain	7,661,440,029	4,227,382,797	11,888,822,826	3,434,057,232
9	Iraq	8,997,643,075	2,517,521,666	11,515,164,741	6,480,121,409
10	Netherlands	5,443,805,843	3,071,256,794	8,515,062,637	2,372,549,049

Table 5: The ten countries with which Türkiye had the most intensive foreign trade in 2020 and the total import-export levels with these countries

Rank	Country	Türkiye's Export ($)	Türkiye's Import ($)	Total Trade ($)	Trade Balance ($)
1	Germany	14,850,485,794	20,641,798,425	35,492,284,219	-5,791,312,631
2	China	2,657,019,713	22,044,440,572	24,701,460,285	-19,387,420,859
3	Russia	4,164,184,889	17,086,212,040	21,250,396,929	-12,922,027,151
4	US	9,238,007,655	10,840,947,748	20,078,955,403	-1,602,940,093
5	UK	10,887,810,590	5,402,071,875	16,289,882,465	5,485,738,715
6	Iraq	8,077,167,546	8,103,501,701	16,180,669,247	-26,334,155
7	Italy	7,635,329,931	8,371,029,850	16,006,359,781	-735,699,919
8	France	6,856,857,067	6,722,953,874	13,579,810,941	133,903,193
9	Spain	6,355,179,522	4,893,440,589	11,248,620,381	1,461,738,663
10	Netherlands	4,930,426,318	3,420,648,450	8,351,074,768	1,509,777,868

Table 6: The ten countries with which Türkiye had the most intensive foreign trade in 2021 and the total import-export levels with these countries

Rank	Country	Türkiye's Export ($)	Türkiye's Import ($)	Total Trade ($)	Trade Balance ($)
1	Germany	17,985,230,280	20,514,682,292	38,499,912,572	-2,529,452,012
2	China	3,366,110,271	30,952,738,332	34,318,848,603	-27,586,628,061
3	Russia	5,289,612,607	27,598,784,620	32,888,397,227	-22,309,172,013
4	US	13,693,672,112	12,392,673,887	26,086,345,999	1,300,998,225
5	Italy	10,752,189,720	10,671,921,452	21,424,111,172	80,268,268
6	UK	13,298,673,094	5,377,167,123	18,675,840,217	7,921,505,971
7	France	8,719,235,150	7,611,082,675	16,330,317,825	1,108,152,475
8	Spain	9,236,749,802	6,015,975,626	15,252,725,428	3,220,774,176
9	Iraq	10,003,529,869	1,442,064,080	11,445,593,949	8,561,465,789
10	Netherlands	6,384,277,640	4,385,165,583	10,769,443,223	1,999,112,057

Table 7: The ten countries with which Türkiye had the most intensive foreign trade in 2022 and the total import-export levels with these countries

Rank	Country	Türkiye's Export ($)	Türkiye's Import ($)	Total Trade ($)	Trade Balance ($)
1	Russia	7,666,749,642	57,362,105,078	65,028,854,720	-49,695,355,436
2	China	3,017,842,583	38,682,077,743	41,699,920,326	-35,664,235,160
3	Germany	19,208,120,332	22,247,395,028	41,455,515,360	-3,039,274,696
4	US	15,485,677,360	14,102,336,436	29,588,013,796	1,383,340,924
5	Italy	11,444,925,212	12,899,396,555	24,344,321,767	-1,454,471,343
6	France	9,111,235,078	8,883,783,023	17,995,018,101	227,452,055
7	UK	12,534,275,266	5,444,960,869	17,979,236,135	7,089,314,397
8	Spain	9,121,471,793	6,698,192,760	15,819,664,553	2,423,279,033
9	Iraq	11,766,911,690	854,912,871	12,621,824,561	10,911,998,819
10	Netherlands	7,492,166,585	4,238,855,848	11,731,022,433	3,253,310,737

Table 8: The ten countries with which Türkiye had the most intensive foreign trade in 2023 and the total import-export levels with these countries

Rank	Country	Türkiye's Export ($)	Türkiye's Import ($)	Total Trade ($)	Trade Balance ($)
1	Russia	9,445,031,536	43,925,939,546	53,370,971,082	-34,480,908,010
2	China	3,072,885,417	43,008,215,046	46,081,100,463	-39,935,329,629
3	Germany	18,817,298,108	26,428,406,694	45,245,704,802	-7,611,108,586
4	US	13,289,478,414	14,500,196,583	27,789,674,997	-1.210.718.169
5	Italy	11,186,844,128	13,340,840,080	24,527,684,208	-2,153,995,952
6	France	9,826,239,627	10,891,979,441	20,718,219,068	-1.065.739.814
7	UAE	7,976,608,988	11,429,505,781	19,406,114,769	-3,452,896,793
8	Spain	9,176,339,648	9,005,123,386	18,181,463,034	171,216,262
9	UK	11,867,014,976	5,987,903,157	17,854,918,133	5,879,111,819
10	Iraq	11,020,077,090	694,319,954	11,714,397,044	10,325,757,136

Table 9: The ten countries with which Türkiye had the most intensive foreign trade in 2024 and the total import-export levels with these countries

Rank	Country	Türkiye's Export ($)	Türkiye's Import ($)	Total Trade ($)	Trade Balance ($)
1	Russia	8,563,000,594	44,018,616,356	52,581,616,950	-35,455,615,762
2	China	3,388,442,297	44,930,562,744	48,319,005,041	-41,542,120,447
3	Germany	20,432,312,176	27,084,550,815	47,516,862,991	-6,652,238,639
4	US	16,351,880,115	16,227,486,674	32,579,366,789	124,393,441
5	Italy	12,953,700,964	19,311,974,984	32,265,675,948	-6,358,274,020
6	France	10,038,621,300	12,499,806,084	22,538,427,384	-2,461,184,784
7	UK	15,289,516,746	6,845,524,027	22,135,040,773	8,443,992,719
8	Spain	9,782,569,120	9,362,741,506	19,145,310,626	419,827,614
9	UAE	8,294,360,827	7,363,387,810	15,657,748,637	930,973,017
10	Iraq	13,006,477,324	1,827,058,437	14,833,535,761	11,179,418,887

Comments

If we need to interpret these official and correct data politically, the most important points I would like to emphasise are as follows:

- Despite the pandemic and other negative conditions, Türkiye's foreign trade is constantly improving.
- Türkiye-Russia economic relations have made revolutionary progress in the last two years and exceeded a trade volume of $65 billion in 2022. This volume, which is the highest foreign trade rate of all time, shows that Russia, which was sanctioned by Western countries due to the Ukraine War, is turning to Türkiye. In 2023 and 2024, bilateral economic relations – although slowing down slightly – continue at a high-level.
- Germany, which was Türkiye's largest foreign trade partner for years, has now fallen to third place (in the last two years) behind Russia and China. Although it is possible for Germany to surpass China and Russia in the coming years, this points to the major change-transformation experienced recently in Türkiye's economic policy as well as its political relations.
- Türkiye is a net importer against countries such as Russia and China and has a very high foreign trade deficit. While this is due to its heavy natural gas and oil purchases against Russia, Türkiye is a good buyer of manufactured products against China.
- Türkiye's foreign trade with Western countries is largely balanced. Türkiye, which has always had a trade surplus against the United Kingdom, Spain, and Netherlands, also has a quite balanced picture in its foreign trade with countries such as Germany, the United States, France, and Italy.
- Other than listed countries, Romania and Poland are also important trade partners for Türkiye.
- Türkiye's most of the exports go to Europe, which shows the crucial importance of Customs Union and EU accession process for Turkish economy.
- Iraq and the UAE are two most important Muslim trade partners for Ankara.

Trade Restriction From Türkiye to Israel

Introduction

In response to Israel's disproportionate violence against Palestinian civilians living in Gaza, which has so far resulted in the deaths of over 45,000 people[2] following the surprise Hamas attack on 7 October 2023, dubbed the 'Aqsa Flood'[1] which killed over 1,000 Israelis, Türkiye imposed restrictions on exports to Israel in fifty-four product items. In this article, I will summarise Türkiye's recent decision to impose trade restrictions on Israel and recent important developments in Türkiye-Israel economic relations.

Export Restriction Decision

Announced on Tuesday, 9 April 2024, by the Ministry of Trade, Türkiye's export restrictions on Israel will apply to the following fifty-four products/sectors:[3]

1. Aluminium Profiles
2. Aluminium Wires
3. Paints
4. Copper Profiles, Rods and Wires
5. Concrete Mixers
6. Steel Pipes and Fittings
7. Steel Wire Rod
8. Steel Containers and Tanks
9. Steel Bridge Components

10. Steel Towers
11. Steel Profiles
12. Cement
13. Blocks and Slabs for Construction from Cement, Concrete or Artificial Stone
14. All Construction Materials made of Iron and Steel
15. All Iron and Steel Wires
16. Excavators
17. Electric Cables
18. Electric Panels
19. Tiles
20. Fiberoptic Cables and Electrical Conductors
21. Forklifts
22. Granite
23. Rope and Cables
24. Hardware Products
25. Hydraulic Oils
26. Construction Iron
27. Construction Machinery
28. Construction Insulation Materials
29. Glass Used in Construction
30. Chemical Compounds
31. Chemical Fertilisers
32. Clinker
33. Buckets, Grabs, Shovels, Grapples and Hooks
34. Sulphur
35. Lubricants
36. Roller Chains
37. Marble
38. Metal Processing Machines
39. Chemicals Used in the Processing of Metals
40. Mineral Fertilisers
41. Engine Oils
42. Pallets
43. Plastic Pipes
44. Sandwich Panels

45. Ceramics
46. Solvent Dyes
47. Wire Drawing Machines
48. Saw Machines
49. Bricks
50. Aircraft Gasoline and Jet Fuel
51. Varnishes
52. Cranes
53. Adhesives and Glues
54. Flat Steel Products

The statement also condemned Israel's military operation in Gaza, which targeted civilians, and emphasised Türkiye's active efforts to stop the bloodshed and meet the needs of the people of Gaza, and denied the allegation that some media outlets in Türkiye had sold military equipment to Israel.[4] The statement also referred to the resolutions of the United Nations Security Council (resolutions 2728, 2720, and 2712), the General Assembly (resolutions ES-10/21 and ES-10/22), the Human Rights Council (resolution A/HRC55/L.30) and the International Court of Justice in The Hague (injunction resolutions of 26 January and 28 March 2024) and the decisions of the International Court of Justice in The Hague (interim injunctions dated 26 January and 28 March 2024),[5] underlining that the decision was taken from an international law and universal perspective, and that it was certainly not intended to cause any special animosity towards Israel or the Jewish people.

Following this decision, which hit the agenda of Türkiye and the international community like a bombshell, Turkish President Recep Tayyip Erdoğan announced that trade restrictions would continue until uninterrupted, unimpeded, and sufficient humanitarian aid was delivered to Gaza, and emphasised that news reports on trade with Israel were 'manipulation and distortion'.[6] In this way, Ankara made the export restriction to Tel Aviv conditional on allowing uninterrupted and sufficient humanitarian aid to Gaza. Speaking after President Erdoğan, Turkish Minister of Trade Ömer Bolat congratulated Palestine's new Minister of Economy, Muhammed al-Amur, on the phone, and stated that his Palestinian counterpart expressed his satisfaction with this decision.[7]

Israeli Foreign Minister and Likud Party member Yisrael Katz, who immediately reacted to the decision, claimed that President Erdoğan had 'sacrificed the economic interests of the Turkish people' for the sake of supporting Hamas and said that Israel would also take countermeasures that would harm the Turkish economy.[8] Katz stated that they would impose restrictions on products exported from Israel to Türkiye and that they would also contact the Jewish lobby in the United States to prevent investments in Türkiye and impose sanctions on Ankara.[9] Katz also drew attention with interesting statements he made on his Twitter (X) account after the local elections in Türkiye on 31 March 2024, saying, 'The local elections in Türkiye resulted in defeat for Erdoğan's candidates. Congratulations to @ekrem_imamoglu in İstanbul and @mansuryavas06 in Ankara. This is a clear message to @RTErdogan: Attacking Israel is no longer working; he needs to find new materials.'[10]

Were Military Equipment Sold to Israel?

The claim that military equipment was sold to Israel, which some opposition groups in Türkiye insisted on and in a sense forced the Turkish government to impose restrictions, was denied in separate statements made by the Ministry of National Defence, the Ministry of Trade and the Presidency of Defence Industries in late March.[11] Minister of Trade Ömer Bolat emphasised that these claims were spread by the Israeli intelligence service MOSSAD and the Islamist-American terrorist organisation FETÖ, which organised the 15 July 2016 coup attempt, and emphasised that the sales of gel fuel, lighter fluid, smoothbore hunting rifle spare parts, and accessories and fishing equipment (harpoons, etc.) to Israel were presented as military equipment sales.[12] The Ministry of National Defence also insisted that they did not engage in any joint activities with Israel, including military training, exercises and defence industry co-operation.[13]

The opposition journalist Metin Cihan, who was one of the first people to make the claims, emphasised that he obtained the data he used from official state institutions and that he did not share any false information.[14] Cihan also specifically stated that these claims did not belong to him and were obtained from open sources of state institutions and claimed that state officials could not deny their views.[15] At this point, it should be emphasised that the fundamental issue that the Turkish public wants to understand is not whether there is trade with Israel or whether Turkish businessmen send merchant ships there, but whether military materials and equipment are sold to this country. The extent to which products such as boron, aviation gasoline, jet fuel, construction materials, and steel profiles, which are included in the trade with Israel, are used militarily is undoubtedly a subject that needs to be carefully investigated. In this sense, waiting for detailed examinations by experts on the subject and not being prejudiced seems to be the most correct approach for now.

Türkiye-Israel Trade Figures

According to the official website of the Turkish Statistical Institute (TÜİK) at <https://biruni.tuik.gov.tr/>, the bilateral trade figures between Türkiye and Israel in recent years are as follows:

Table 10: Türkiye-Israel foreign trade (2010–2023)[16]

Year	Import (dollar)	Export (dollar)
2010	1,359,638,700	2,080,147,766
2011	2,057,313,741	2,391,148,260
2012	1,710,401,175	2,329,530,503
2013	2,417,954,924	2,649,663,186
2014	2,881,261,733	2,950,902,396
2015	1.672.500.782	2.698.138.811
2016	1,385,605,217	2,955,544,978
2017	1,505,113,435	3,407,436,059
2018	1,714,355,242	3,894,499,070
2019	1,742,927,163	4,356,291,938
2020	1,420,509,601	4,553,257,888
2021	1,942,371,620	6,141,675,931
2022	2,169,558,582	6,742,760,503
2023	1,621,988,416	5,173,906,234

When these figures are examined, the following determinations can be made:

- Türkiye is a country that has a serious foreign trade surplus with Israel and is more profitable from this relationship. Roughly speaking, in recent years, if Türkiye buys one unit of goods from Israel, it sells 3–3.5 times more goods.
- The bilateral trade volume reached a record level in 2022, approaching 9 billion dollars. However, the fact that 10 billion dollars has not yet been reached shows that Israel is not one of the most important countries in Türkiye's foreign trade. In fact, according to *BBC* research, Israel is only Türkiye's 13th most important export market (after Germany, the United States/US, Iraq, Britain/UK, Italy, Russia, France, Spain, the United Arab Emirates/UAE, the Netherlands, Romania, and Poland).[17]
- Despite the decline in 2023, Türkiye's exports to Israel have been increasing steadily and at a significant pace since 2016. This shows that the trade relations between the two countries have improved after 15 July. Türkiye's imports from Israel sometimes increase and sometimes decrease. The fact that imports have not yet exceeded $2 billion shows that Türkiye is not a key trade partner for Israel.

The Impact and Evaluation of the Decision

The decision to restrict exports to Israel, which the government in Türkiye was forced to take due to public pressure, was of course a decision that would be generally welcomed by the people in the country in this pessimistic environment where innocent civilians were being massacred in Gaza. The failure of the AK Parti (Justice and Development Party) government to achieve the expected success in the 2024 local elections and the successful opposition led by the Islamist New Welfare Party (YRP) under the leadership of Fatih Erbakan, who advocated suspending trade and even all political relations with Israel during these elections, can also be cited as an influence on this decision.

However, if the humanitarian situation in Gaza is excluded and an economic logic is used, trade with Israel is quite valuable and beneficial, if not vital, for Türkiye and Turkish businessmen. For this very reason, the Turkish government has emphasised that the decision is temporary and that trade with Israel will continue after the humanitarian conditions in Gaza are improved. Because Türkiye, whose economic situation has not been very bright in recent years, cuts off economic relations with Israel, which is in its close geography, and this will undoubtedly have a positive impact on the Turkish economy. However, the government, which has recently had to do something against the unscrupulous attitude displayed by the extremist government in Israel, has expressed the anger of the people by implementing such a restriction and has felt the need to remind Israel and the United States that they must remain within international law.

In this sense, the AK Parti government, which comes from Islamist roots but advocates free trade and liberalisation, is, in my opinion, a rational government that wants to maintain a balance between extremist groups that advocate unconditional support for Israel and want to cut off all relations with Israel under Turkish conditions and tries to act reasonably. Therefore, it should be said that the restriction decision is correct due to humanitarian reasons, and that even harsher decisions could have been made if similar conditions were valid in other countries, and that this decision was not made for political reasons. Because if this decision was made before the elections, the AK Parti and President Erdoğan, who could easily increase their votes, did not want to act populist and this time, they did not act with ideological motives as in the '*Nas-Faiz*' (interest rate) issue. The fact that the decision is measured and temporary also reflects this rational approach. The people and the state in Türkiye have no special hostility towards Israel and the Jews, and if Israel acts in accordance with international law and human values, Türkiye-Israel relations can easily be improved. The most concrete example of this is that President Erdoğan shook hands with Israeli Prime Minister Benjamin Netanyahu as early as September 2023. In this context, I think the 7 October 2023, Hamas attack should also be carefully investigated as an operation targeting Türkiye-Israel normalisation.

Conclusion

In conclusion, although it is more correct in developing countries like Türkiye not to always evaluate economy and politics, and even diplomacy and politics, on a single level and in a strictly ideological manner, in extreme situations that hurt the conscience of the public, I think it is right and appropriate to take such moderate measures. In this sense, I think President Erdoğan's rational and moderate attitude should be praised, not criticised as in the leftist and Islamist opposition press. Because the fundamental duty of a state administrator in a democratic country is to think about the well-being of his own people and economy and to act responsibly. However, at the same time, considering the other nations we share the world with, a state administrator may also want to draw attention to and react to grave humanitarian/ethical situations, which is a very responsible attitude. Therefore, in my opinion, the balanced attitude of the government in Türkiye is the most rational policy set/preference possible. On the other hand, excessively harsh measures to be implemented in relations with Israel will undoubtedly return to Türkiye as more negative economic and political conditions due to the influence of the Jewish lobby and the United States. The absence of military supplies in trade with Israel will undoubtedly ease the conscience of the people in Türkiye.

In addition, it should be noted as a final note that when Türkiye's current military, political, economic, soft power, and the state of the Islamic world are evaluated, the impact of Türkiye's harsh policies on Israel may be very limited. In this sense, the country that needs to take action to correct Israel's policies is – without a doubt – the superpower United States. When it is also considered that the fundamental dynamic that brought the Islamist movement to its peak in Türkiye after the 28 February process was democratic politics and a non-Western Islamist foreign policy, the AK Parti and Erdoğan should not take criticism from both the right and the left as a problem and should persevere on their own path.

Note: Later the government extended this decision to all trade with Israel due to Israeli government's continuation of aggressive policies in Gaza, Lebanon, and Syria.

Endnotes

1. Ozan Örmeci (2023), "A Major Shock to Israel: Hamas's Al-Aqsa Flood Attack and Its Possible Consequences", Uluslararası Politika Akademisi, 09.10.2023, Accessed 12.04.2024 from https://politikaakademisi.org/2023/10/09/israile-buyuk-sok-hamasin-aksa-tufani-saldirisi-ve-olasi-sonuclari/.
2. *TRTNews* (2024), "Death toll in Gaza rises to 32,333", 25.03.2024, Accessed 04.12.2024 from https://www.trthaber.com/haber/dunya/gazzede-olu-sayisi-32-bin-333e-yukseldi-846709.

html#:~:text=israeli%20army%20enters%20Gaza%20Strip, s%C3%BCrd%C3%BCrd%C3%BC%C4%9F%C3%BC%20sald%C4%B1r%C4%B1lara%20ili%C5%9Fkin%20bilgi%20verildi.

3 Ministry of Trade of the Republic of Türkiye (2024), "Export Restrictions on Israel", 09.04.2024, Accessed 12.04.2024 from https://ticaret.gov.tr/haberler/israile-ihracat-kisitlamasi.

4 *Ibid.*

5 *NTV* (2024), "Turkey imposes restrictions on trade with Israel: Export limits on 54 product groups", 09.04.2024, Accessed 12.04.2024 from https://www.ntv.com.tr/dunya/turkiye-israille-ticarete-kisitlama-getirdi,mmDjCAuU1kSjs-_-7Vo1XA.

6 *BBC Türkçe* (2024), "President Erdoğan announces trade restrictions with Israel: 'They will continue until sufficient aid arrives'", 09.04.2024, Accessed 12.04.2024 from https://www.bbc.com/turkce/articles/crgyrvn1j88o.

7 *NTV* (2024), "Turkey imposes restrictions on trade with Israel: Export limits on 54 product groups", 09.04.2024, Accessed 12.04.2024 from https://www.ntv.com.tr/dunya/turkiye-israille-ticarete-kisitlama-getirdi,mmDjCAuU1kSjs-_-7Vo1XA.

8 *BBC Türkçe* (2024), "President Erdoğan announces trade restrictions with Israel: 'They will continue until sufficient aid arrives'", 09.04.2024, Accessed 12.04.2024 from https://www.bbc.com/turkce/articles/crgyrvn1j88o.

9 *Ibid.*

10 See; https://twitter.com/Israel_katz/status/1774525368503771248.

11 *Aydınlık* (2024), "Ministries respond to allegations of arms sales to Israel", 28.03.2024, Accessed 04.12.2024 from https://www.aydinlik.com.tr/haber/israile-silah-iddialarina-bakanliklardan-yanit-463277.

12 *Ibid.*

13 *Ibid.*

14 *Halk Tv* (2024), "Journalist Metin Cihan Reveals Trade with Israel!", 09.04.2024, Accessed 12.04.2024 from https://www.youtube.com/watch?v=sitfU42GXbI.

15 *Ibid.*

16 Biruni.tuik.gov.tr, Accessed 12.04.2024 from https://biruni.tuik.gov.tr/disticaretapp/disticaret.zul?param1=4&param2=0&sitcrev=0&isicrev=0&sayac=5808.

17 *BBC Türkçe* (2024), "President Erdoğan announces trade restrictions with Israel: 'They will continue until sufficient aid arrives'", 09.04.2024, Accessed 12.04.2024 from https://www.bbc.com/turkce/articles/crgyrvn1j88o.

The Alliance of Civilizations and Dynamics of Türkiye-Spain Relations[1]

1. Short History of Contemporary Turkish-Spanish Relations

Türkiye/Ottoman Empire-Spain relations were formalised in history first through the signing of the Treaty of Peace, Friendship, and Commerce in 1782. The date of 25 April 1783, when the ratification documents of this Treaty were ceremoniously presented to the Ottoman Sultan Abdulhamid I by the Spanish Ambassador Juan de Bouligny, can be considered the beginning of modern-day Turkish-Spanish relations. The Spanish Embassy in Istanbul started its activities on the same date. The Turkish Embassy in Madrid on the other hand began its activities in 1857.

Türkiye made a historic regime change in 1923, embracing a Republican system and gradually transforming into a modern secular nation-state under the leadership of Mustafa Kemal Atatürk. During the Spanish Civil War (1936–1939), Türkiye was able to overcome the regime change in Madrid without any problems by maintaining official relations with the Republican Government while also establishing a channel of communication with the General Franco administration (the Spanish Embassy in Ankara was under the Republic, while the Consulate General in Istanbul was under Franco).

Diplomatic relations between Türkiye and Spain were elevated to the level of Embassy as of 1 January 1951. Although Türkiye's relations with Spain under the rule of General Franco (1936–1975) have not been vibrant, a mutual and measured understanding of friendship and co-operation has been maintained. In fact, a Treaty of Friendship was signed between the two countries on 16 April 1959. It must be added that the two countries were both US allies during the Cold War against the USSR and communist expansionism.

Bilateral relations have taken on a new dimension by the mid-1980s, as a result of Spanish accession to NATO (1982) and the EU (1986), as well as through the implementation by both countries of similar economic policies which give priority to liberalisation and access to new markets. Bilateral political dialogue and economic relations have been strengthened with reciprocal high-level visits realised since the 1980s. In addition, a new Treaty of Friendship was signed between the two countries on 16 April 1989.

In 1989, Turkish Prime Minister Turgut Özal's visit to Spain gave impetus to the revival of relations and since then relations have intensified in political, military, and economic fields. As a result, King Juan Carlos of Spain paid a state visit to Türkiye in 1993. In the following period, Turkish President Süleyman Demirel visited Spain in March 1998 and during Prime Minister José María Aznar's visit to Türkiye in July 1998, a '*Joint Action Plan for the Development of Relations*' was signed, which envisaged regular consultations between the two countries, particularly in the fields of foreign policy and security.

Moreover, with the Helsinki Summit, Türkiye became a candidate country for the EU in 1999. Accession talks began in 2005, intensifying Türkiye's political, economic, and social/cultural relations with all European countries including Spain. Spain has always supported Turkish accession to the EU. Turkish President Recep Tayyip Erdoğan and then-Spanish Prime Minister José Luis Rodríguez Zapatero initiated the Alliance of Civilizations initiative in 2005 with the common understanding that only a broad coalition defending the mutual respect among different cultures could tackle the growing tendencies of alienation and polarisation.

On the other hand, Türkiye-Spain Intergovernmental Summit (*Reunión de Alto Nivel*) meetings, the first of which was organised in Istanbul in 2009 and held eight times so far, have carried the bilateral relations to the highest level. The last Intergovernmental Summit was held in Madrid on 13 June 2024. Spanish support for Türkiye's EU membership further strengthened the co-operation between the two countries. Spain's humanitarian stance concerning the Palestinian Problem and its peaceful stance against all political disputes increased the prestige of this state in Türkiye and in the Islamic world.

Morever, in the last two decades, the Spanish football league *'La Liga'* became very popular in Türkiye due to the Barcelona-Real Madrid competition (*El Clásico*) and Turkish footballers playing for Spanish teams such as Nihat Kahveci, Hamit Altıntop, Arda Turan, and most recently Arda Güler.

Despite government changes in Spain and Türkiye's recent transformation into a more statist and hyperpresidential system, the two countries have kept their friendly relations, developed their volume of trade, and never engaged in serious political confrontations. However, Spain is still not publicly very well-known country and identified in Türkiye as an ally or hostile state. Rather, the country remains largely unknown to ordinary people. This means a brighter future could be established since the two countries do not have a historical enmity or a vital competition in politics and economics.

According to İlke Toygür, since there is no historical baggage or public opinion to please, the bilateral relationship between Türkiye and Spain is based on fruitful co-operation in various spheres.[2] Turkish-Spanish relations are especially intense in terms of trade and security co-operation through NATO. Lately, Spanish investments in Türkiye have intensified and reached out to important sectors of the Turkish economy, like the banking sector. For this reason, the modernisation of the Customs Union (CU) with Türkiye could also be seen as a contribution to the Spanish economy.

Military co-operation between the two countries has been further strengthened in recent decades with some purchases made by Ankara. For example, Türkiye had previously purchased the licence rights to the CASA CN-235 light military transport aircraft from Spain and started to produce it itself in the 1980s. Moreover, Türkiye purchased A400-M transport aircrafts manufactured at Airbus' facilities in Spain. Named *'Atlas'*, Türkiye has also become a production partner of this transport aircraft and has deployed the aircraft in Kayseri.

In addition, TCG Anadolu, the Turkish Navy's unmanned aerial vehicle-carrying amphibious assault ship, is modelled on the Spanish Navy's Juan Carlos I amphibious landing ship, named after the former King of Spain. In recent years, the procurement of Turkish HÜRJETs as part of Spain's procurement plan to retire its ageing F-5 jet trainers and renew its inventory has also been on the agenda between the officials of the two countries, and positive messages have been received from Spanish officials in this direction.

In terms of military co-operation, the last important issue is the potential Eurofighter Typhoon fifth-generation jet fighter aircraft procurement of Ankara in the coming months. Produced by Airbus Defence and Space (46 per cent), BAE Systems (33 per cent), and Leonardo (21 per cent), this new European made jet fighter is considered more advantageous by many military experts in Türkiye compared to F-35s.

Spain has an Embassy in Ankara and a Consulate General in Istanbul. Türkiye has an Embassy in Madrid and a Consulate General in Barcelona. The Turkish ambassador in Spain is Her Excellency Nüket Küçükel Ezberci, the Spanish ambassador in Ankara is Her Excellency Cristina Latorre Sancho. We are trusting in the skills of two extraordinary female diplomats to further improve Turkish-Spanish relations.

2. Türkiye vs Spain in Comparison

If we have to compare Türkiye and Spain in terms of their power bases, a table such this can be drawn:

Table 11: Türkiye vs Spain in numbers

	TÜRKIYE	SPAIN
Population (million)	85.7 (18)	49 (31)
Area Size (km^2)	783,562 (36)	505,370 (50)
GDP (U.S. dollars)	1,458,000,000,000 (17)	1,828,000,000,000 (14)
GDP Per Capita (U.S. dollars)	\$12,814 (65)	\$33,814 (29)
Military Power (GFP)	9th	17th
Democratic Quality (Freedom House)	Not Free (33/100)	Free (90/100)
Human Development Index (UNDP)	45th (0.855)	27th (0.911)
Global Diplomacy Index (Lowy Institute)	3rd	12th
Universities in the Top 1000 (Times Higher Education)	11	35

Table 12: Türkiye vs Spain in international organisations

	TÜRKIYE	SPAIN
United Nations (UN)	✓ (1945)	✓ (1955)
Council of Europe	✓ (1950)	✓ (1977)
World Bank	✓ (1947)	✓ (1958)
IMF	✓ (1947)	✓ (1958)
World Trade Organization (WTO)	✓ (1995)	✓ (1995)
World Health Organization (WHO)	✓ (1948)	✓ (1951)
European Union	×	✓ (1986)
NATO	✓ (1952)	✓ (1982)
OECD	✓ (1961)	✓ (1961)
OSCE	✓ (1973)	✓ (1973)
UfM	✓ (2008)	✓ (2008)
Organization of Turkic States	✓ (2009)	×
Organization of Islamic Cooperation	✓ (1972)	×
Other Platforms	ADB, AfDB, BSEC, IAEA, IEA, MIKTA, SCO (dialogue partner), BRICS (partner country), EBRD, ILO, IMO, Interpol	ADB, AfDB, Arctic Council (observer), EBRD, IAEA, ICC, IEA, ILO, IMO, Interpol, LAIA (observer), Union Latina

3. Recent Developments

During the Catalonian independence referendum process in 2017, Türkiye openly defended Spanish territorial integrity and objected to the unilateral declaration of independence. Spain also supports Türkiye's territorial integrity and defends peaceful and legal resolution methods for the solution of ethnic and political problems in Türkiye. Both countries suffered from ethnic secessionism and terrorism in the past and they understand each other's sensitivities.

According to retired Turkish diplomat Akın Özçer, Spain is a true friend of Türkiye in Europe. Özçer also underlines that both the PSOE on the left and the PP on the right support developing relations with Ankara. Moreover, Özçer claims that Spain considers Türkiye's inclusion into the EU or its co-operation with Brussels as a strategic asset. He further thinks that the Turkish-Spanish strategic partnership is not only a further tightening of bilateral relations in all areas but also an opening for Türkiye to Latin American countries and for Spain to the countries in Türkiye's immediate neighbourhood and the newly established Organisation of Turkic States region.

However, after Türkiye's military activism in Syria in 2019, Spain – together with France, Germany, and many other European states – began to implement an arms embargo on Türkiye despite being traditionally an important arms supplier to Ankara. This embargo was never really put into practice and friendly relations between the two countries continued despite severe criticisms coming from the European political circles towards the Turkish government for its preferred political methods in recent years.

Spanish Prime Minister Pedro Sánchez defines Türkiye as '*a key economic partner for Spain and an important player in its region*'. Sánchez also said that '*Türkiye and Spain have a common past, a dynamic and ambitious present, and a promising future.*' According to Turkish President Recep Tayyip Erdoğan, '*Spain is one of our friends who best understands Türkiye's contribution to the European Union and has given the strongest support to our accession process from the very beginning.*' President Erdoğan visited Spain in 2022 as part of the NATO Summit and in 2024 for the 8th Türkiye-Spain Intergovernmental Summit.

Another new dynamic in bilateral relations is the success of Turkish TV series in Spain in recent years. Jose Antonio Anton from Atresmedia Group underlines that Turkish TV series are very successful in Spain and Spanish people liked them better compared to other countries' productions due to the diversity of themes and similar cultural traits. Anton also thinks that these productions show the modern features of Türkiye as well and establish new bridges between the two nations. Most successful Turkish series in Spain in recent years are: Kızım (2018–2019), Kadın/Women (2017–2020), Sadakatsiz/ Unfaithful (2020–2022), Bir Zamanlar Çukurova/Bitter Lands (2018–2022), Sen Çal Kapımı/Love Is in the Air (2020–2021), and Fatmagül'ün Suçu Ne?/ What Is Fatmagul's Fault? (2010–2012).

4. Economic Relations

Economic relations between Türkiye and Spain are quite developed. Spain constantly ranks at number 8 in Türkiye's total foreign trade behind China, Russia, Germany, the United States, Italy, France, and the UK. Türkiye has always been in Spain's top 10 trade partners as well in recent years after France, Germany, Italy, the UK, the United States, Portugal, China, and the Netherlands. Moreover, Türkiye is a net exporter and always gives a trade surplus against Spain even though the margin is small and looking at the overall picture, the bilateral trade is very well balanced.

According to the Turkish Foreign Ministry, the main Turkish exports to Spain are automobiles, textiles, flat-rolled products of iron or non-alloy steel, petroleum oils and oils derived from bituminous minerals, components and parts for road vehicles, motor vehicles for the transportation of goods (Türkiye ranks second after China in Spain's textile and apparel imports). Main imports from Spain, on the other hand, are automobiles, components and parts for road vehicles, unprocessed zinc, cyclic hydrocarbons, polymers of propylene and other olefins, helicopters, airplanes, spacecraft (including satellites), motor vehicles for the transport of goods, refined copper and copper alloys, petroleum oils and oils derived from bituminous minerals, live cattle (except horses, donkeys, mules and bardos), iron or non-alloy steel profiles, new rubber outer tyres.

Table 13: Turkish-Spanish trade in recent years

Türkiye-Spain Trade (TÜIK)	Export (U.S. dollars)	Imports (U.S. dollars)	Total (U.S. dollars)	Difference (U.S. dollars)
2017	6,584,920,544	6,531,630,970	13,116,551,514	53,289,574
2018	8,121,096,071	5,682,749,878	13,803,845,949	2,438,346,193
2019	8,138,744,012	4,446,112,934	12,584,856,946	**3,692,631,078**
2020	6,683,488,350	5,039,427,792	11,722,916,142	1,644,060,558
2021	9,619,641,951	6,311,610,815	15,931,252,766	3,308,031,136
2022	9,654,317,928	7,004,013,122	16,658,331,050	2,650,304,806
2023	**9,783,655,162**	**9,507,243,383**	**19,290,898,545**	276,411,779
2024	9,782,569,120	9,362,741,506	19,145,310,626	419,827,614

Table 14: Türkiye's most intensive trade partners in recent years

Year	Türkiye's Most Intensive Trade Partners
2021	Germany, China, Russia, the U.S., Italy, the UK, France, **Spain**, Iraq, Netherlands
2022	Russia, China, Germany, the U.S., Italy, France, the UK, **Spain**, Iraq, Netherlands
2023	Russia, China, Germany, the U.S., Italy, France, UAE, **Spain**, the UK, Iraq
2024	Russia, China, Germany, the U.S., Italy, France, the UK, **Spain**, UAE, Iraq

The total amount of direct investments from Spain to Türkiye in the period of 2002–2023 March is around 11 billion 277 million US dollars, while the figure is 334 million dollars for investments from Türkiye to Spain in the same period. President Erdoğan recently announced his intention to reach 25 billion euros in 5 years in our bilateral trade volume of 20 billion dollars. This is a plausible expectation that could be realised in a few years with some efforts on both sides.

Furthermore, Spain is the fifth largest investor in Türkiye. Around 775 Spanish firms have direct investments in Türkiye amounting to 11.277 billion euros. The number of Turkish companies currently investing in Spain is approximately 125. In 2023, 324,690 Spanish tourists visited Türkiye. Tourism potential has not been efficiently used so far.

The most famous Spanish brands known in Türkiye are:

- SEAT
- Mango
- Zara Home
- Oysho
- Pull and Bear
- DIA
- Ormazabal
- Roca
- Barcelo
- Teka

In the 8th Intergovernmental meeting in Madrid last year, as part of the Spain-Türkiye Business Meeting, five key targets were agreed between the two parties.

1. To initiate the revision of the Reciprocal Protection and Promotion of Investments Agreement (APPRI).
2. ICEX and the Turkish Presidency Investment Office will sign a memorandum of understanding to exchange information, promote investment, and systematise collaboration for the benefit of both companies, considering new investments and those already in the pipeline.
3. The Spanish development finance company COFIDES and the Turkish sovereign wealth fund will strengthen their collaboration to mobilise finance for joint investments not only in Spain and Türkiye but also in third countries.
4. The two export credit insurance agencies, CESCE and Eximbank, will sign an agreement that will result in increased coverage and security for trade and investment, both bilaterally and in third countries.
5. The Directorate-General of Insurance and Pension Funds and its Turkish counterpart (SEDDK) will sign a memorandum of understanding for the promotion of co-operation and exchange of information.

5. Cultural Relations

Türkiye and Spain have a Cultural Agreement signed on 28 March 1956, a Cultural Co-operation Programme dated 9 March 2006, a Scientific and Technological Co-operation Agreement which entered into force on 7 August 2009, and a Co-operation Agreement in the Field of Education signed on 3 October 2013.

In Türkiye, there are departments of '*Spanish Language and Literature*' at Ankara University, Istanbul University, Burdur Mehmet Akif University, and Istanbul Medeniyet University (all state universities and for 4 years of education) and an '*Applied Spanish and Translation*' associate degree programme (2 years education) at Istanbul Aydın University.

Named after Miguel de Cervantes (1547–1616), author of *Don Quixote*, *Instituto Cervantes* (Cervantes Institute) is a non-profit organisation founded by the Spanish government in 1991. It is the largest institution in the world dedicated to teaching the Spanish language and culture. The organisation has fifty-four branches in twenty different countries, teaching Spanish and Hispanic American culture and the Spanish language. More than 20,000 students have attended the Spanish courses of the Cervantes Institute in Istanbul since its establishment in 2001.

There is also a growing interest in Spanish music and cinema in Türkiye in recent years. Some popular songs and projects in recent years are as follows:

1. La Casa De Papel (2017–21)
2. Shakira songs
3. Enrique Iglesias songs
4. Celda 211 (2009)
5. Nino-Amor (1999)
6. El laberinto del fauno (2006)
7. El Secreto de Sus Ojos (2009)
8. La Habitación De Fermat (2008)
9. Las Ketchup-Asereje (2002)

In addition, some popular Spanish celebrities in Türkiye are:

1. Alvaro Morata
2. Penelope Cruz
3. Rafael Nadal
4. Antonio Banderas
5. Julio/Enrique Iglesias
6. Pablo Picasso
7. Javier Bardem
8. Pep Guardiola
9. Salvador Dali
10. Fernando Alonso
11. Guti Hernández
12. Pau Gasol

Within the framework of the 'Cooperation Protocol' signed in 2002 between the Presidency of the Council of Higher Education (YÖK) and the Spanish Ministry of Education, Culture and Sports, contacts are established between the rectors and academics of major Spanish universities and their counterparts in Turkish universities. On the other hand, the Erasmus programme is important for the development of our cultural relations and inter-university co-operation. In this framework, Spanish universities are among the most preferred universities in Europe by Turkish university students participating in the Erasmus programme.

Based on observations and informal talks, Turkish students prefer Spain for education and especially for Erasmus visits because they think life in Spain is less costly, people are warmer, more friendly, and more tolerant, the climate is much better compared to other European countries, and the education level is very good.

There are no separate chairs for Turkish language and Turkish studies in Spanish universities. Currently, Turkish language education is offered as an elective course at the Departments of Arabic and Islamic Studies at Complutense and Autonoma Universities in Madrid and the Department of Translation and Interpreting at Granada University. Moreover, private Turkish courses are offered at the language course affiliated with Complutense University and at the IPOA language school affiliated with the University of Barcelona. In addition, the Department of Arab and Islamic Studies at Autonoma University offers undergraduate and graduate courses on the Ottoman Empire and Türkiye-EU relations.

The number of Turkish citizens living in Spain increased significantly in the mid-2000s. While in 2001, according to Turkish records, the number of Turkish citizens residing in Spain was around 1,000, this number started to increase with the introduction of a law adopted by the Spanish Parliament in 2005 that facilitated the process of obtaining residence and work permits for foreigners residing and working illegally in Spain. As of May 2017, the total number of registered Turkish citizens is 5,357, including 3,078 registered at the Consular Section of the Embassy in Madrid and 2,279 registered at the Consulate General in Barcelona. Most of the Turkish citizens in Spain work as wage earners. In addition, some Turkish citizens have jobs in fields such as tourism and textiles. A significant portion of the Turks in Spain reside in Madrid and Catalonia Autonomous Administration. Apart from these regions, it is seen that Turkish citizens prefer coastal cities. Andalusia, Basque Country, Valencia, Canary, and Balearic Islands are the leading regions.

6. Alliance of Civilizations

The Alliance of Civilizations was initiated in 2005 by then-Turkish Prime Minister Recep Tayyip Erdoğan and then-Spanish PM José Luis Rodríguez Zapatero. It was subsequently endorsed by the Secretary-General of the United Nations (UN) and became a UN initiative named UNAOC – United Nations Alliance of Civilizations.

Figure 18: UNAOC logo

Faced with the exploitation by various extremist elements of the climate of mutual suspicion, fear, and polarisation between Muslim countries and Western societies, the Alliance was initially motivated by the understanding that only a comprehensive coalition could prevent the worsening of this situation, which was approaching a level that could threaten international stability and aimed to counter this trend through mutual respect between cultures.

'In my capacity as representative of a country created and enriched by diverse cultures, before this Assembly I want to propose an Alliance of Civilizations between the Western and the Arab and Muslim worlds.' – José Luis Rodríguez Zapatero (Former Spanish PM)

On 14 July 2005, then-UN Secretary-General Kofi Annan formally announced the launch of the Alliance of Civilizations to member states in a statement at the United Nations Headquarters in New York. On that occasion, he referred to the new initiative as a response to the need for a

Figure 19: Recep Tayyip Erdoğan and José Luis Rodríguez Zapatero: Two visionary leaders who initiated the Alliance of Civilizations initiative

joint effort on the part of the international community to build bridges, overcome prejudices, and avoid polarisation. He also stated that the Alliance of Civilizations should be collaboration against extremist forces and a movement to strengthen mutual respect for traditions and religious beliefs. The Alliance of Civilizations henceforth became a special initiative of the UN Secretary-General with the co-sponsorship of the governments of Spain and Türkiye.

A High-Level Group of experts was formed by Mr Annan to explore the roots of polarisation between societies and cultures today and to recommend a practical programme of action to address this issue. The report of the High-Level Group provided analysis and put forward practical recommendations that form the basis for the implementation plan of the United Nations Alliance of Civilizations. In its 2006 report, the High-Level Group identified five priority areas for action: Education, Youth, Migration, Media, and Women as peace mediators. UNAOC project activities are fashioned around these areas, which can play a critical role in helping to reduce cross-cultural tensions and build bridges between communities.

> *In these troubled times, the Alliance is a unique and inclusive platform for Member States, the private sector, youth, civil society and the media to exchange views and commit to dialogue and new partnerships. It is closely aligned with my own priorities and the vision that I have outlined in my prevention agenda.* – António Guterres (UN Secretary-General)

The United Nations Alliance of Civilizations High Representative and Secretariat are based and operating from New York. The Alliance maintains a global network of partners including states, international and regional organisations, civil society groups, foundations, and the private sector to improve cross-cultural relations between diverse nations and communities.

The initiative is based on the premise that all societies are interdependent on each other for development, security, environment, and prosperity, and primarily aims to build a common political will to tackle prejudice, misperception, and polarisation. Having gained increasing visibility since its launch, the initiative has become a prominent initiative that is recognised in different geographies of the world. The Group of Friends of the Alliance of Civilizations, which was established under the UN umbrella in the context of the initiative, has 158 members consisting of countries and international organisations.

In the framework of the appointments made by the UN Secretary-General, the High Representative for the initiative was Jorge Sampaio, former President of Portugal, from 2007 to 2013, and Nassir Abdulaziz Al-Nasser (Qatar), who also served as President of the 66th UN General Assembly from 2013 to 2019. As of 7 January 2019, Miguel Moratinos, former Minister of Foreign Affairs of Spain, assumed the post of High Representative.

The most high-level and political activity of the Alliance of Civilizations initiative is the periodic Global Forums. Previously held in Madrid (2008), Istanbul (2009), Rio (2010), Doha (2011), Vienna (2013), Bali (2014), Baku (2016), New York (2018), Fes, Morocco (2022), and Cascais, Portugal (2024), the Global Forums are attended by representatives of governments and international organisations, civil society and private sector representatives from the Alliance of Civilizations Friends Group. In the last Forum, which was held in Portugal in November 2024, Türkiye was represented by Foreign Minister Hakan Fidan.

A secretariat operates in New York to coordinate the initiative and handle the administrative affairs of the Alliance. The secretariat promotes the Alliance internationally and carries out projects on media, youth, migration, and education, which are the priority areas of the initiative. The Geneva Office of the initiative was opened on 8 November 2021 as a result of the initiative spearheaded by Türkiye and is headed by Ambassador Namık Güner Erpul.

According to the initiative's Geneva Office Head Namık Güner Erpul, Türkiye and Spain are the largest donors of the initiative. Erpul underlines that from 2005 to 2019, Türkiye tops the list of countries that have contributed to UNAOC with USD 11.4 million. In second place is Spain, with a contribution of 8.1 million dollars. These contributions are meaningful in terms of financially demonstrating both Ankara and Madrid's sincere efforts to create a single humanity.

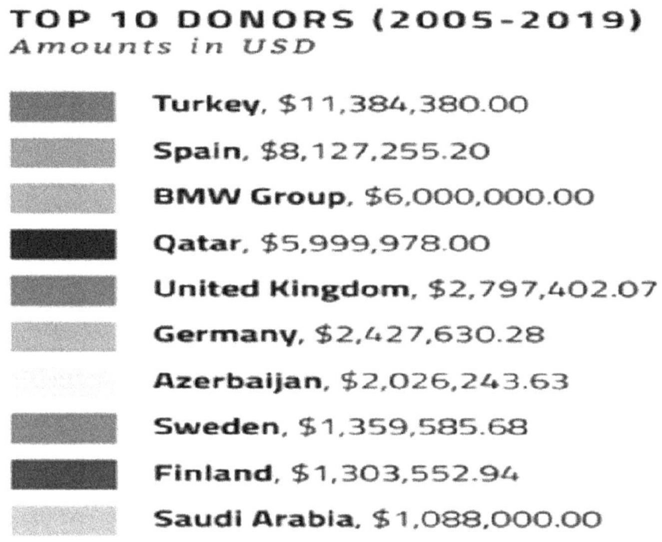

Figure 20: Top ten donors of UNAOC (2005–2019)

The Alliance of Civilizations was a timely initiative at a period when there were growing reactions in the Islamic world against Western countries due to the American invasion of Iraq which followed the 9/11 incident and growing Islamophobia in the West. The initiative is still crucial for preventing the spread of hatred feelings and prejudices towards different civilisations, states, societies, people, and ethnic/religious/sectarian groups including Muslims, Christians, Jews, and other groups.

The Alliance of Civilizations continues its active work in combating challenges that threaten international peace and security as well as social tranquillity, such as racism, discrimination, xenophobia, and Islamophobia. It is a functional and very vital institution to prevent the '*Clash of Civilizations*' in the twenty-first century, which was foreseen by American Political Scientist Samuel P. Huntington.

However, according to Özcan Öğüt, two critical problems prevented the Alliance of Civilizations to be more successful:[3]

1. Türkiye's transformation into a more Islamist and authoritarian state simultaneously with the initiative,
2. The failure of the '*Arab Spring*' process and the lack of efficiency of the initiative in global politics.

7. Conclusion

To end my paper, I can come up with some key ideas derived from the information and data I provided throughout this talk:

1. Türkiye and Spain can be two close allies since their interests are not conflicting and there are no oceans separating these two countries.
2. Economic relations are benefiting both sides and could be further developed with joint efforts and the update (revision) of the Customs Union (CU) to include the services sector as well.
3. The Alliance of Civilizations provide Türkiye and Spain key leadership positions in representing Sunni Islam and Catholic Christian faiths. The Alliance could be much more successful if Türkiye becomes a real democracy.
4. NATO membership and Türkiye's EU membership goal create similar approaches to global problems among both countries' political elites.
5. In order to prevent Türkiye's slip into the BRICS-SCO bloc, Spain acts more responsibly compared to other major EU countries, which makes Madrid a trusted ally for Ankara.

6. With partnership agreement between Yunus Emre Institute and Cervantes Institute, the two countries could further develop their cultural co-operation.

Endnotes

1 This paper was presented by Professor Ozan Örmeci at UCAM Catholic University of Murcia on 14.05.2025 as a conference presentation. For details, see; Ozan Örmeci (2025), "The Alliance of Civilizations and Dynamics of Türkiye-Spain Relations", Presentation made at the public lecture organised by UCAM Catholic University of Murcia, 14.05.2025, UCAM Catholic University of Murcia, Murcia, Spain, Date of Accession: 01.07.2025 from <https://www.academia.edu/129286388/_%C3%96rmeci_Ozan_2025_The_Alliance_of_Civilizations_and_Dynamics_of_T%C3%BCrkiye_Spain_Relations_Presentation_made_at_the_public_lecture_organized_by_UCAM_Catholic_University_of_Murcia_14_05_2025_UCAM_Catholic_University_of_Murcia_Murcia_Spain>.

2 İlke Toygür (2020), "Turkey and Spain: bilateral relations and the road ahead for Customs Union modernisation", Real Instituto elcano Royal Institute, 29.09.2020, Date of Accession: 05.04.2025 from <<https://www.realinstitutoelcano.org/en/analyses/turkey-and-spain-bilateral-relations-and-the-road-ahead-for-customs-union-modernisation/>.

3 Özcan Öğüt (2017), *Yakın Dönem Türkiye-İspanya İlişkileri ve İspanya Siyaseti*, İstanbul: Cinius Yayınları, pp. 40–44.

Bibliography

Anadolu Ajansı (2022), «Büyükelçi Erpul, BM Medeniyetler İttifakına en büyük katkıyı Türkiye'nin sağladığını belirtti», 09.10.2022, Date of Accession: 10.04.2025 from <https://www.aa.com.tr/tr/dunya/buyukelci-erpul-bm-medeniyetler-ittifakina-en-buyuk-katkiyi-turkiyenin-sagladigini-belirtti/2706546>.

Anadolu Ajansı (2024), "İspanya Başbakanı Sanchez: Türkiye, İspanya için anahtar bir ekonomik ortak ve bölgesinde önemli bir oyuncu", 13.06.2024, Date of Accession: 04.04.2025 from <https://www.aa.com.tr/tr/dunya/ispanya-basbakani-sanchez-turkiye-ispanya-icin-anahtar-bir-ekonomik-ortak-ve-bolgesinde-onemli-bir-oyuncu/3248713>.

Anadolu Ajansı (2024), "Dışişleri Bakanı Fidan, BM Medeniyetler İttifakı 10'uncu Küresel Forumu'na katılacak", 24.11.2024, Date of Accession: 04.04.2025 from <https://www.aa.com.tr/tr/gundem/

disisleri-bakani-fidan-bm-medeniyetler-ittifaki-10uncu-kuresel-forumuna-katilacak/3402806>.

Bolelli, Şenhan (2021), "Türk dizileri, İspanyol ve Türk toplumlarını birbirlerine daha da yakınlaştırdı", *AA*, 26.11.2021, Date of Accession: 14.04.2025 from <https://www.aa.com.tr/tr/kultur-sanat/turk-dizileri-ispanyol-ve-turk-toplumlarini-birbirlerine-daha-da-yakinlastirdi/2431230>.

Daily Sabah (2024), "Türkiye, Spain tout 'immense' potential, ambition to further ties", 13.06.2024, Date of Accession: 04.04.2025 from <https://www.dailysabah.com/business/economy/turkiye-spain-tout-immense-potential-ambition-to-further-ties>.

Defence Turk.net (2024), «İspanya'ya HÜRJET tedarikinde ilk adım!», 20.12.2024, Date of Accession: 10.04.2025 from <https://www.defenceturk.net/ispanyaya-hurjet-tedarikinde-ilk-adim>.

DEİK, "TÜRKİYE – İSPANYA İŞ KONSEYİ", Date of Accession: 04.04.2025 from <https://www.deik.org.tr/turkiye-avrupa-is-konseyleri-turkiye-ispanya-is-konseyi>.

La Moncloa (2024), "Pedro Sánchez: 'Turkey and Spain have a common past, a dynamic and ambitious present and a promising future'", 13.06.2024, Date of Accession: 04.04.2025 from <https://www.lamoncloa.gob.es/lang/en/presidente/news/paginas/2024/20240613-spain-turkey-intergovernmental-summit.aspx>.

La Moncloa (2024), "Pedro Sánchez announces agreements in five key areas to intensify economic and trade cooperation with Turkey", 13.06.2024, Date of Accession: 04.04.2025 from <https://www.lamoncloa.gob.es/lang/en/presidente/news/paginas/2024/20240613-spain-turkey-business-meeting.aspx>.

Oftex International (2023), «The international trade situation in Spain», Date of Accession: 10.04.2025 from <https://www.oftex.es/en/the-international-trade-situation-in-spain/>.

Onedio.com (2021), "Siestaya Dizi Arası! İspanya'da En Çok Hangi Türk Dizileri İzleniyor?", Date of Accession: 14.04.2025 from <https://onedio.com/haber/siestaya-dizi-arasi-ispanya-da-en-cok-hangi-turk-dizileri-izleniyor-1013728>.

Öğüt, Özcan (2017), *Yakın Dönem Türkiye-İspanya İlişkileri ve İspanya Siyaseti*, İstanbul: Cinius Yayınları.

Örmeci, Ozan, Blog – Ozan Örmeci Articles, <https://ydemokrat.blogspot.com/>.

Örmeci, Ozan (2025), "The Alliance of Civilizations and Dynamics of Türkiye-Spain Relations", Presentation made at the public lecture organised by UCAM Catholic University of Murcia, 14.05.2025, UCAM Catholic University of Murcia, Murcia, Spain, Date of Accession: 01.07.2025 from <https://www.academia.edu/129286388/_%C3%96rmeci_Ozan_2025_The_Alliance_of_Civilizations_and_Dynamics_of_T%C3%BCrkiye_Spain_Relations_Presentation_made_at_the_public_lecture_organized_by_UCAM_Catholic_University_of_Murcia_14_05_2025_UCAM_Catholic_University_of_Murcia_Murcia_Spain>.

Özçer, Akın (2021), "GÖRÜŞ – Türkiye'nin Batı Avrupa'daki gerçek müttefiki: İspanya", *Anadolu Ajansı*, 17.11.2021, Date of Accession: 04.04.2025 from <https://www.aa.com.tr/tr/analiz/gorus-turkiyenin-bati-avrupadaki-gercek-muttefiki-ispanya/2423065>.

Recep Tayyip Erdoğan (2024), <https://x.com/RTErdogan/status/1801283402865287394>, 13.06.2024.

Republic of Türkiye Ministry of Foreign Affairs, "Relations between Türkiye and Spain", Date of Accession: 05.04.2025 from <https://www.mfa.gov.tr/relations-between-turkiye-and-spain.en.mfa>.

Republic of Türkiye Ministry of Foreign Affairs, "Commercial and Economic Relations between Türkiye and Spain", Date of Accession: 05.04.2025 from <https://www.mfa.gov.tr/commercial-and-economic-relations-between-turkiye-and-spain.en.mfa>.

SETA, "Türkiye-İspanya İlişkileri", Date of Accession: 04.04.2025 from <https://www.setav.org/tag/turkiye-ispanya-iliskileri>.

T.C. Dışişleri Bakanlığı Avrupa Birliği Başkanlığı (2017), "AB Bakanı ve Başmüzakereci Ömer Çelik'in Katalonya'nın Bağımsızlık Kararına İlişkin Değerlendirmeleri", 11.12.2017, Date of Accession: 07.04.2025 from <https://www.ab.gov.tr/ab-bakani-omer-celikin-katalonyanin-bagimsizlik-kararina-iliskin-degerlendirmeleri_50970.html>.

Toygür, İlke (2020), "Turkey and Spain: bilateral relations and the road ahead for Customs Union modernisation", Real Instituto elcano Royal Institute, 29.09.2020, Date of Accession: 05.04.2025 from <https://www.realinstitutoelcano.org/en/analyses/

turkey-and-spain-bilateral-relations-and-the-road-ahead-for-customs-union-modernisation/>.

TÜİK Portal, Date of Accession: 04.04.2025 from <https://iz.tuik.gov.tr/>.

Türkiye Cumhuriyeti Dışişleri Bakanlığı, “Medeniyetler İttifakı Girişimi”, Date of Accession: 05.04.2025 from <https://www.mfa.gov.tr/medeniyetler-ittifaki-girisimi.tr.mfa>.

Türkiye Cumhuriyeti Dışişleri Bakanlığı, “Türkiye-İspanya İlişkileri”, Date of Accession: 05.04.2025 from <https://www.mfa.gov.tr/turkiye-ispanya-siyasi-iliskileri.tr.mfa>.

Türkiye Cumhuriyeti Madrid Büyükelçiliği, “Türkiye-İspanya İkili İlişkileri, 7.06.2017”, Date of Accession: 04.04.2025 from <https://madrid-be.mfa.gov.tr/Mission/ShowInfoNote/121361>.

UNAOC, Date of Accession: 10.04.2025 from <https://www.unaoc.org/>.

Conclusion

In this last part, I would like to share with you some of my ideas and views on the future of Turkish Foreign Policy.

Having successfully celebrated its 100th anniversary in 2023 and managed to hold largely democratic elections despite some problems, Türkiye is currently facing some serious problems. These problems can be listed as follows; rapid erosion of democracy and human rights in recent years; the increasing population, ultra-liberal immigration policy, and intense economic problems that have increased based on hyperinflation and the depreciation of the Turkish lira, which also pose a risk to Türkiye's political stability; the aggressive policies implemented from time to time by some states in Türkiye's region and the high military expenditures made out of necessity due to terrorist organisations; the constitutional order and democratic regime that have still not been established and established in a century; the polarisation environment based on ethnic/religious/ideological differences (Turkish-Kurdish, Sunni-Alevi, and Islamist-secular) within the country; the country's high energy dependence on some countries; the increasing possibility of being excluded from Western institutions with the institutionalisation of multi-dimensional foreign policy; policies that are not always compatible with the international system, and the inability to find a reliable partner in foreign policy.

In this context, I think we should first ask ourselves the following question: What kind of a country do we want Türkiye to be in the future where our children can live in security and peace? If this can be answered with a clear answer and future vision that at least 60 per cent of the society would approve (for example, a Türkiye that is a regional power or a democratic and developed Türkiye that is a member of the EU), then it will be possible to draw a political and diplomatic route accordingly. However, due to the fragmented structure of the society, the political polarisation environment and the influence of intellectual competition, these issues cannot be discussed openly in Türkiye and an environment of consensus cannot be created. Since making definite decisions, making sharp choices and entering irreversible paths in foreign policy in a globalising world can be wrong, a foreign policy line that keeps Türkiye's options open for a long time and forms the foundations of multi-dimensionality will be the most correct direction. In this context, Türkiye should first create a stable, democratic, law-abiding, and publicly legitimised governance model. Neither the current presidential system, where civilians are at the forefront, nor the parliamentary system implemented in the previous period and maintained by the military in the background – in which the President had additional powers after 12 September – have been able to achieve this. Finding the most ideal form of government that is suitable for society, and our political culture should be the duty of all of us in this new period. The responsible attitude showed by the Republican People's Party (CHP) under its new leader Özgür Özel after its outstanding success in the local elections in this year and its warm approach to state institutions (including the Presidency) were increasing hopes in this direction. This was definitely not giving up on the goal of power but acting responsibly for the normalisation of Türkiye. In my opinion, this attitude will definitely be an approach that the voters will also reward and adopt. However, due to most recent judicial operations against opposition municipal leaders, including CHP's Istanbul Mayor Ekrem İmamoğlu, Özel's responsible attitude became awkward for the moment. But I am hoping that Özel and CHP could still contribute more to Türkiye's normalisation with the drafting of a new civilian constitution and a new Kurdish opening process to end the four-decade-old era of PKK terrorism. To achieve this, the government should also embrace the opposition and to provide the rule of law in the country.

In the new period, a more balanced presidential or semi-presidential system that is in line with the leader-oriented structure of our people but also observes the principles of a democratic state of law can be created, and the necessary arrangements can be made to make this system permanent. This system should of course be created on a basis where the powers of the

TBMM will be increased, and the Assembly will be made functional again. In this new system, Recep Tayyip Erdoğan can continue in active politics and seeks re-election for another time, choose another AK Parti member as his successor (there are potential candidates such as Foreign Minister Hakan Fidan, Erdoğan's son Bilal Erdoğan, Erdoğan's son-in-law '*king of drone*' Selçuk Bayraktar, the chief of Turkish intelligence service-MİT İbrahim Kalın, and TBMM Speaker Numan Kurtulmuş) or someone from the main opposition party CHP (e.g. party chair Özgür Özel, detained Istanbul Mayor Ekrem İmamoğlu or Ankara Mayor Mansur Yavaş) can be elected as the President and take over the country to get the Türkiye back on track. At this point, of course, comprehensive policies aimed at increasing the sense of belonging of our Kurdish citizens to the state will also be extremely necessary and beneficial. In my opinion, providing more cultural rights (the right to education in the mother tongue in addition to education in the official language) to our Kurdish citizens within the unitary state structure and democratising the system in general will largely solve our problems. In this context, I think we can take the ELCO system in France and the EU local government reforms as examples. Because Türkiye's medium-sized structure and population level make us more similar to European countries such as Britain, France, and Germany rather than the United States, China, and Russia.

Secondly, Türkiye should try to solve its structural problems in order to ensure its economic stability. These can be listed as; reducing/diversifying external dependency in critical sectors (defence industry, energy, high technology, etc.), paving the way for foreign investment to come to the country by establishing better relations with the United States and European countries and reopening the path to EU membership, organising this strategic area in line with the labour market by integrating the education system with industry, determining some concrete goals/ideals that will motivate and unite the society (such as EU membership, becoming one of the ten largest economies, ensuring the recognition of the TRNC, establishing a Turkic world Army, etc.) and making progress on this path. If all stakeholders act in harmony while establishing these goals, it will be easier to act more decisively in policies.

Thirdly, after Türkiye determines its strategic goals in consensus with the society and the opposition, it should be operational and determined to achieve them. In other words, once a concrete plan is put forward for Türkiye's national interests, its implementation should be carried out successfully with the integrated joint efforts of all state institutions. Frequent decision changes on certain issues and insufficient perseverance will overshadow stability and success in foreign policy. In this context, it may be considered to establish a mechanism that will provide coordination between state institutions and especially security bureaucracy elements in the coming years. Because our political history is full of military coups and recent events such as the Ergenekon and Balyoz cases show that there are serious disagreements and divisions in the security bureaucracy, which is not befitting of Türkiye's respected state status.

Fourthly, priority areas of influence should be selected, and comprehensive strategies should be developed accordingly in order to guarantee Türkiye's future. In this context, the Eastern Mediterranean, the South Caucasus, and the Balkans are the most important areas in Türkiye's immediate neighbourhood. A power projection for these areas, the development and implementation of an integrated strategy based on political/diplomatic, economic and soft power, is, in my opinion, a matter that should be started without delay. In this context, the TRNC in the Eastern Mediterranean, Azerbaijan in the South Caucasus and Bosnia-Herzegovina and Kosovo in the Balkans should be selected as pivot countries for Türkiye and major political, diplomatic, economic, cultural, and social investments should be made in these countries. In addition, the rapidly developing continent of Africa is another geography that Türkiye should learn, invest, and discover more.

Fifthly and finally, in my opinion, the most critical issue for the establishment of political stability and national psychology will be the establishment of a Turkish philosophy suitable for the new age. A new national consciousness and philosophy that includes other ethnic identities/cultures that have an impact on Turkishness and Anatolian culture, is based on love for Atatürk, includes Islamic characteristics, and is open to democracy and market economy will make our people more self-confident, integrated, and powerful. Due to the Jacobean nature of some cultural revolutions that alienated society in some areas, the greatest favour that can be done to our people, who still live in disjointed masses in our country even after a century, will be to create a philosophy and consciousness that will turn them into a common nation. However, at this point, religious institutions (Presidency of Religious Affairs), educational institutions (universities), and political-social institutions (political parties and civil society organisations) have not made enough efforts, and a successful model has not yet been created. However, we have many reasons to be more hopeful in the new period. Because there are now developing higher education institutions and young and successful academics everywhere in Türkiye.

In conclusion, Türkiye will always be an important state in world politics and the global economy. Our country's structural problems (earthquake risk, being located in a difficult geography, economic problems, etc.) do not constitute a major obstacle to our success in these matters as long as the determination and desire of 85 million people to work can be channelled in the right direction and in line with common goals ... achieving this is now our common responsibility in the new era ... everyone should understand that, Türkiye, despite its problems, is a major stabilising actor in the global system and often acts responsibly to keep the balance between the West and the East.

Finally, as stated by Great Atatürk, Türkiye's founder, Türkiye aims to reach '*peace at home and peace in the world*'. Accordingly, Ankara is the friend of all peaceful countries ...

Ozan ÖRMECİ, 10.07.2025, Kartal/İstanbul

www.ingramcontent.com/pod-product-compliance
Ingram Content Group UK Ltd.
Pitfield, Milton Keynes, MK11 3LW, UK
UKHW021921120926
8556IPUK00042BA/1091

9 783631 936870